D1388534

Hitler's
'National Community'

Hitler's
'National Community'

Society and Culture in
Nazi Germany

LISA PINE

For Gaim,
Thank you for your
support.
With very best wishes,
Lisa.

Hodder Arnold

A MEMBER OF THE HODDER HEADLINE GROUP

First published in Great Britain in 2007 by
Hodder Education, a member of the Hodder Headline Group,
338 Euston Road, London NW1 3BH

www.hoddereducation.com

© 2007 Lisa Pine

All rights reserved. No part of this publication may be reproduced or
transmitted in any form or by any means, electronically or mechanically,
including photocopying, recording or any information storage or
retrieval system, without either prior permission in writing from the
publisher or a licence permitting restricted copying. In the United
Kingdom such licences are issued by the Copyright licensing Agency:
Saffron House, 6–10 Kirby Street, London EC1N 8TS.

The advice and information in this book are believed to be true and
accurate at the date of going to press, but neither the authors nor the
publisher can accept any legal responsibility or liability for any errors or
omissions.

British Library Cataloguing in Publication Data
A catalogue record for this book is available from the British Library

Library of Congress Cataloging-in-Publication Data
A catalog record for this book is available from the Library of Congress

ISBN 978 0 340 888 46 9

1 2 3 4 5 6 7 8 9 10

Cover photo © Hulton-Deutch Collection/CORBIS

Typeset by Phoenix Photosetting, Chatham, Kent
Printed in Malta

What do you think about this book? Or any other Hodder
Education title? Please send your comments to the feedback
section on www.hoddereducation.com

For Andy, Gaby
and Sasha

CONTENTS

PREFACE

This book is intended to help readers grappling with the vast literature on Nazi Germany to understand the complexities of society and culture under the Hitler regime. This important area of investigation illuminates the nature of a dictatorship driven by war, conquest of *Lebensraum* and the desire for 'racial purity', by exploring the social context within which its policies were executed. Research into different aspects of Nazi social and cultural history has moved fast, particularly since the 1990s. We now know a great deal more about everyday life in Nazi Germany – in particular, about the motivations for people's behaviour, the relationship between coercion and consent, and the functioning of the dictatorship. The literature continues to grow as new research pushes forward the boundaries of our historical knowledge and understanding. The impact of the Third Reich on the German population is a subject whose relevance has lasted to this day. A regime that lasted for 12 years – six of them as a peacetime dictatorship, six of them as a wartime dictatorship – left an enduring legacy, both for its victims who survived and their successors, and for the German nation which still feels the need to come to terms with its past.

It is a pleasure to acknowledge the help of those who have helped me in the process of writing this book. I should like to thank the staff at the various libraries I have worked in during the preparation of this book, and in particular the staff at the Wiener Library, London. I am especially grateful for the SPUR Fellowship I received from London South Bank University, which funded research leave between September 2005 and February 2006, allowing the lion's share of this book to be written. I should like to thank Jeffrey Weeks and Kate Hudson for their support, as well as several colleagues and friends who have read the text and been willing to discuss ideas, especially Laurence Marlow. I should also like to thank Magnus Brechtken and the other reviewers of the draft manuscript whose comments have helped me to improve the text and saved me from a number of errors. I should like to thank my editors Susan Millership and Liz Wilson at Hodder Arnold for all their help and enthusiasm. My thanks are also due to my previous editor Tiara Misquitta, to Michael Strang who commissioned this book in the first place, and to my copy editor, Vivienne Church. I am particularly grateful to Katrine Nielsen for her excellent help with looking after my children and thereby giving me the time to write. Finally, I am thankful for the forbearance of my family during the writing of this book. I should like to take this opportunity to thank my husband, Andrew Fields, for his unfailing encouragement, and my two daughters, Gaby and Sasha, for their patience. This book is dedicated to them.

Lisa Pine
London, September 2006

INTRODUCTION

Germans welcoming their leader Adolf Hitler at a harvest festival in 1935.
© The Wiener Library

An examination of the impact of National Socialism upon German society is one of the most significant aspects of historical enquiry into the Third Reich, shedding light on the nature and impact of the Nazi dictatorship as a whole and the social context in which its policies were executed. Yehuda Bauer has argued that 'National Socialist Germany was ruled by a criminal, murderous regime, and the day-to-day life of its citizens was coloured by this'.[1] Everyday life – even the most trivial parts of it – took place within this context. A significant part of the historical literature on the Third Reich has developed to explore this. The first major work on Nazi social history in English was Richard Grunberger's *A Social History of the Third Reich*.[2] Grunberger's book, which was first published in 1971, covers a wide range of subjects, from the Party and the civil service to Nazi speech and humour. While the book is still of interest, the historiography has grown so extensively in recent decades that it has become outdated. Contributions to Richard Bessel's *Life in the Third Reich* and David Crew's *Nazism and German Society* give a more detailed analysis of specific issues, such as women or workers, in the light of research carried out in the 1970s and 1980s.[3] Pierre Ayçoberry's *The Social History of the Third Reich, 1933–1945*, which divides the Nazi era into the pre-war years and the wartime period, is a useful study of many aspects of German society in the

Nazi era.[4] These works are all significant contributions to the historiography of Nazi Germany. However, a substantial amount of new research on particular aspects of Nazi social and cultural history has been published since the 1990s. There has not been a recent survey in English that encompasses the findings of the latest empirical research, nor a book that combines an examination of both social and cultural history. It is the intention of this book to fill these two significant gaps in the secondary literature on Nazi Germany.

The purpose of this book is to provide a clear and accessible history of society and culture in Nazi Germany in the light of new debates and developments in the historiography over recent years. It combines a synthesis of the existing literature with fresh insights and interpretations. It is distinctive in its approach to the subject and in its scope. The approach to the subject here is to blend 'top-down' history with 'history from below'. It is intended that by presenting both an examination of Nazi policy and a consideration of the experiences of the people, a rounded picture will emerge. This will allow readers to view the subject from a fuller perspective. This approach may enable us to comprehend more about the nature of the Nazi regime and about why people behaved in the ways that they did. This is the proper purpose of historical enquiry into the subject. Richard Evans has rightly criticised the recent tendency of historians of the Third Reich 'to abandon analysis, argument and interpretation in favour of the exercise of moral judgement'.[5] This book seeks to provide historical explanation of both society and culture in Nazi Germany and of the close relationship between them. It is an empirical study that will help readers to understand the complexities of society and cultural life in Nazi Germany.

The main theme of the book is the creation of identity in Nazi Germany, in terms of inclusion and exclusion from the *Volksgemeinschaft* ('national community'). The essence of the word *Volksgemeinschaft* is difficult to convey in translation. Scholars in the field have translated it variously as 'national community', 'People's Community' or 'people's ethnic community'. For the purpose of this book, the term is understood to mean 'national community', as this conveys the concept of national cohesion and homogeneity sought by the Nazi regime. The 'national community' is a pivotal theme of this book because it was so central to Nazi ideology. The Nazi regime sought to create a 'national community' made up of 'racially pure', 'hereditarily healthy', physically fit, politically reliable and socially responsible *Volksgenossen* ('national comrades'). The Nazis made it abundantly clear who belonged to the German nation and who did not. They labelled and categorised enemies and 'aliens' – both internal and external. Those groups that remained outside the 'national community' did not belong to the nation and were treated accordingly as outsiders. Furthermore, the impact of inclusive and exclusionary policies on cultural life during the Nazi era was highly significant and was reflective of such distinctions applied to society. The 'national community' was not only a construct comprising 'national comrades' but also a 'cultural community' encompassing 'pure' German culture. Societal and cultural life in Nazi Germany were intricately linked.

A brief survey of the historiography is useful at this point in order to locate this book within the context of historical writing on Nazi Germany. We shall begin with an overview of one of the major debates surrounding the impact of Nazism on German society, a subject that has created a fundamental historical controversy: did Nazism entail 'social reaction' or did it bring about 'social revolution'? We shall then move on to look at some of the major trends in the social history of the Third Reich. Further reference to the main developments in and contributions to the secondary literature relating to specific subjects or themes will be made throughout the book.

One of the major historiographical debates dealing with the impact of Nazism on German society has centred on the issue of whether Nazism was fundamentally reactionary or revolutionary in its nature. The subject is further complicated by the need to distinguish between the social objectives of the regime, on one hand, and its methods of achieving them, on the other, as Nazi aims and policies were often inconsistent with each other. Another level of complexity is added by the necessity of determining which outcomes were intentional (that is, the direct result of Nazi policies) and which were unintended by-products of the regime.

Marxist accounts have described the reactionary nature of the Nazi regime and have proposed that existing class structures in Germany were strengthened under National Socialism.[6] They argue that Nazism shattered the trade unions and strengthened the position of employers. They maintain that the Third Reich was a reactionary dictatorship that perpetuated existing class relationships and maintained the capitalist system. Furthermore, the historians of the former GDR (East German Republic) did not discuss the possibility of social change in the Third Reich; it was simply not relevant to them. The only true social revolution was a Marxist one. Hence, the GDR historiography disregarded the long-term effects of Nazism upon the development of German society.

In contrast, liberal scholars have argued that the changes in the structure of German society under Nazism were so fundamental that they could be described as a 'social revolution'. Ralf Dahrendorf suggested that the Nazi regime resulted in 'a strong push to modernity' by breaking with tradition and the German past as it was embodied in Imperial Germany.[7] Dahrendorf further stated that Nazism completed the 'social revolution' held up by the faults of the German Empire and the contradictions of the Weimar Republic. He spoke of the Nazis' unintentional modernisation of society, arguing that the Nazis' *Gleichschaltung* ('co-ordination') of German society destroyed German 'tribal loyalties', broke down traditional bonds and levelled society. Dahrendorf argued that by eliminating long-established loyalties and values, and by equalising everyone into 'national comrades', Nazism 'finally abolished the German past as it was embodied in Imperial Germany'. He went on to state: 'There could be no return from the revolution of National Socialist times.'[8] David Schoenbaum developed this argument in his influential work, *Hitler's Social Revolution*. Schoenbaum argued that in order to wage war against a bourgeois industrial society, the Nazis needed the tools of a bourgeois industrial society. This led to a distinction between Nazi rhetoric and reality or between what Schoenbaum called 'interpreted' and 'objective' social reality. According to Schoenbaum, Nazism resulted in the destruction of traditional class structures and led to social mobility on an unprecedented scale. He spoke of the 'classless reality of the Third Reich'.[9] Schoenbaum's view has been rejected by scholars who argue that class barriers remained quite rigid and that upward social mobility did not increase markedly. Hartmut Berghoff, for example, has suggested that the Nazi regime 'fundamentally altered neither the composition of elites nor the distribution of wealth'.[10]

A third line of interpretation concerns itself with the concept of modernisation. Henry Turner interpreted Nazism as 'a utopian form of anti-modernism', but argued that the Nazis used 'modernisation out of necessity in order to pursue their fundamentally anti-modern aims'.[11] Werner Abelshauser and Anselm Faust considered Nazism to be no more and no less than a 'catalyst of modernisation, in that it exploded with force the bonds of tradition, region, religion, and corporation which were so specially pronounced in Germany'.[12] There was indeed an ambivalent relationship between the traditional and the revolutionary, between the reactionary and the modern in the Third Reich. Jeffrey Herf's term 'reactionary modernism' is quite useful in terms of conceptualising this ambivalence.[13] Herf noted the paradoxical combination of irrationalism and political reaction with an acceptance of modernity and technological progress in Nazi policy-making. A more recent treatment of 'modernisation' by Rainer Zitelmann claims that the Nazi leadership not only brought about a modernising revolution in Germany but that it did so intentionally. Zitelmann argues that Hitler was not atavistic, looking back to the recreation of an agrarian idyll, but rather that he looked forward to the establishment of an advanced industrial and technological society. He argues that Hitler was a social revolutionary who intended and strove to transform German society.[14]

Within the 'modernisation' approach, it is also important to try to make a distinction between change that was an intentional and direct result of the Nazi regime and change that was an unintended or indirect result of it, particularly because the Second World War contained its own impetus for massive social change. Jeremy Noakes has argued that 'the Nazi revolution was the war – not simply because the war accelerated political, economic and social change to a degree which had not occurred in peacetime, but more profoundly because in war Nazism was in its element … Nazism was truly "a revolution of destruction", of itself and of others on an unparalleled scale'.[15] Detlev Peukert also emphasised the 'destructive forces' of National Socialism, paving the way for a more 'modern' society after 1945, without speaking of a 'social revolution'.[16] Michael Burleigh has argued more recently that 'given the secular drift from a class to a mass consumer society ... it is notoriously difficult to isolate the impact of any single factor on this process, whether twelve years of peace and wartime dictatorship, or the maelstrom of devastation and dispossession visited upon Germany from 1945'.[17]

More recently, the debate surrounding the impact of the Nazi regime upon German society has moved on. Richard Evans has urged historians to move beyond the idea that the Nazis were attempting to revolutionise society. He argues: 'The problem with arguing about whether or not the Third Reich modernised German society, how far it wanted to change the social order and in what ways it succeeded in doing so, is that society was not really a priority of Nazi policy anyway ... Above all, what Hitler and the Nazis wanted was a change in people's spirit, their way of thinking and their way of behaving ... Their revolution was first and foremost cultural rather than social.'[18] Whether or not one agrees that 'society was not really a priority', the second part of this argument is certainly very useful in pushing forward the way we think about the Nazi dictatorship. The concept of a 'cultural revolution' is very significant and has been understated in the literature. Its importance to the National Socialists is evident from their attempts to engender a spiritual mobilisation or awakening of the German population. The Nazi revolution was envisaged as a 'total' one. Josef Goebbels, Minister of Popular Enlightenment and Propaganda, talked of National Socialism as 'all-encompassing'. On 17 June 1935, he stated: 'We hope that the day will come when nobody needs to talk about National Socialism any more, since it has become the air that we breathe! Thus National Socialism cannot be content with mere lip-service – it must be acted upon with hand and heart. People must get used inwardly to this way of behaving, they must make it into their own set of attitudes – only then will it be recognised that a new will to culture has arisen from National Socialism and that this will to culture determines our national existence in an organic manner.'[19] Hence, cultural life played a significant role in the aims of National Socialism for the German population.

Let us now turn to the main developments in the social history of the Third Reich. Until the 1970s, the study of Nazi social history remained relatively unexplored. The field quickly opened up and expanded considerably with a new and growing interest in *Alltagsgeschichte* ('the history of everyday life') or *Geschichte von unten* ('history from below'). The emphasis moved away from studies of traditional political history to studies of the experiences of different social groups. Detlev Peukert convincingly argued the case for analysing the Third Reich from the perspective of everyday life and everyday experience. By concerning itself with 'the contradictory and complex experiences of "ordinary people"', Peukert asserted that this approach helps us to understand how Nazi racism and terror were possible, tolerated and indeed partially endorsed. Furthermore, it allows us to ascertain more about sources of resistance to and support for the regime.[20] The 'history of everyday life' or 'history from below' approach adds 'a different angle of vision' to our understanding of the Third Reich, by examining what life was like for the people who lived through it.[21] In 1984, Richard Bessel noted this new trend in the historiography, that 'historians of Nazi Germany at last have discovered the German people'.[22]

The themes and analytical tools for the study of National Socialism have changed over recent years. Class, and the working class in particular, was a very popular subject of study within the field in the 1970s and early 1980s. Tim Mason was the pioneer of the history of the working class under National Socialism. In particular, his book *Social Policy in the Third Reich: The Working Class and the 'National Community'* and a number of important articles collected in the edition *Nazism, Fascism and the Working Class: Essays by Tim Mason*, published posthumously, are important contributions to this field, subsequently developed by other scholars.[23] In the 1980s, gender replaced class as an analytical concept in the study of National Socialism. In this field of study, Mason contributed two very important articles and Jill Stephenson wrote two of the first major studies of women in Nazi Germany.[24] After that, many aspects of women's lives under National Socialism began to receive attention from historians. The focus of historical research moved even more specifically to Nazi racial and eugenics policies in the 1990s. Prominent in the shift of work in this direction was *The Racial State: Germany 1933–1945* by Michael Burleigh and Wolfgang Wippermann.[25] In *Social Outsiders in Nazi Germany*, Robert Gellately and Nathan Stoltzfus have built on this theme, arguing that the Nazis targeted individuals and groups long regarded as outsiders or nuisances, those that were already feared or hated by the German population.[26]

The history of the victims of racial and eugenics policies, history 'from below', revealed the impact of persecution as well as 'new levels of everyday complicity' in pushing along racial discrimination against the Jews and other minorities.[27] Hence, the social history of Nazi Germany has progressed from its early concerns with everyday opposition and dissent to concerns with the approval and complicity of ordinary people. In *Backing Hitler*, Robert Gellately shows the nature of the relationship between coercion and consensus in the Third Reich.[28] He argues that the patterns of and motives for denunciations reflected a social consensus and acceptance of the Nazi system of rule. This leads us to another very significant contribution of social history to our understanding of the Nazi era as a whole and the Holocaust in particular, namely the integration of 'normality' and 'barbarism'. In this regard, recent work on the social history of the Third Reich has shown that 'there can be a social context in "civilised society" in which genocide becomes acceptable'.[29] Ian Kershaw argues that 'under "extreme" conditions, "normal" daily and private concerns consume such energy and attention that indifference to inhumanity, and thereby indirect support of an inhumane political system, is significantly furthered'.[30]

It has taken careful consideration to decide upon what to include and how to structure a book on this subject. The structure and content are outlined below, but it is important to state at the outset that this book does not deal with the political or military history of Nazi Germany, nor does it treat the Nazi economy.[31] It explores the impact of the Nazi dictatorship upon German societal and cultural life. It examines the aim of the Nazi regime to break down traditional loyalties – to class, family, region or religion – and to replace them with allegiance to Hitler, the Nazi Party and the 'national community'. While the book covers the whole period from 1933 to 1945, it does not deal with the wartime period in a separate section but incorporates coverage of the war years in each of the chapters. This ensures that the main theme of the book is not jeopardised by a structural division of the book into the periods 1933–1939 and 1939–1945. Instead, the book is divided into three parts, which reflect the theme of inclusion and exclusion, and its application to society and culture during the Nazi era.

The first part of the book analyses the attempts of the Nazi government to forge a new self-identity and national awareness among the German population. The Nazis aimed to create a 'national community' that accorded with their ideals. Did they achieve their 'national community' or was it more of a propaganda construct than a reality? Did they succeed in transforming German society in line with their intentions? This section of the book is a consideration of policies directed at those sectors of the German population that belonged to the 'national community'. Chapter 1 analyses the way in which the Nazi regime endeavoured to manufacture consensus for its ideology and its policies. It explores the methods used by the regime to create conformity within the 'national community', including the *Gleichschaltung* ('streamlining' or 'co-ordination') of different groups and organisations, the use of propaganda aimed at raising national awareness and the propagation of the Hitler myth. Furthermore, it considers the issue of social class in Nazi Germany. Class has been an important analytical concept in the study of National Socialism and this chapter explores the impact of the Nazi regime upon the working class, the middle class and aristocracy in Germany. How genuine was the Nazi claim to have achieved a classless society?

Chapter 2 examines the use of coercion, terror and surveillance. This was the reverse side of consensus and conformity. Terror and coercion were employed to achieve the aims of the dictatorship when consensus failed. This chapter explores the function of the SA (stormtroopers), the SS-SD-police complex and the concentration camps in the Third Reich. Furthermore, it examines the role and function of the traditional legal and prison systems in Nazi Germany within this context. Chapter 3 analyses the role of education in the creation of the 'national community'. This examination of formal education in schools and through the curriculum is complemented by the next chapter, which focuses on socialisation in the Nazi youth groups, the Hitler Youth and the League of German Girls. This chapter demonstrates the nature of the roles assigned to both German boys and girls in the creation and maintenance of the 'national community' and in the ambitious expansionist aims of the National Socialist regime during the war.

Chapter 5 explores the subject of women and the family in the Third Reich.

It discusses the role of the Nazi women's organisations, as well as conceptions and realities about women's lives under National Socialism. It examines the impact of the Nazi regime upon the German family. Nazi ideology extolled the family as the 'germ cell of the nation', but what was the impact on the German family of Nazi policy in practice? Chapter 6 explores the institutions of the churches and the *Wehrmacht*. It considers their role in Nazi society and their relationship to the Nazi state, as these important institutions influenced the lives of millions of Germans during the Nazi era.

The second section of the book deals with those groups or sectors of society that were outside the 'national community'.[32] Exclusion from the 'national community' was applied to particular sections of society that were considered not to belong to it by the National Socialist regime. Individuals and groups that chose to live in ways that meant they could not belong also stood outside the 'national community'. The approach of the chapters in the second section of the book is to synthesise Nazi policy 'from above' with the everyday experience of the targets of this policy and the responses of the German population. This is an important approach, as it links events with people, analysing the social impact of Nazi policies. This is a perspective that has been largely overlooked in the secondary literature until very recently.

Chapter 7 examines the Nazi persecution of the Jews, who were excluded from the 'national community' on racial grounds. It should be noted that this chapter is not intended as a treatment of the Holocaust or the 'Final Solution', the Nazis' genocide of European Jewry, as a whole, which is covered in a highly complex historiography of its own, but as an analysis of the experiences of Germany's Jews in the Nazi era. Chapter 8 discusses the fate of Germany's Gypsies (Sinti and Roma) under National Socialism. The Sinti and Roma remained outside the 'national community' both on account of their 'racial inferiority' and their itinerant lifestyle. Chapter 9 deals with the persecution of the 'asocial' and the disabled. The term 'asocial' was applied to tramps, vagrants and the 'workshy' on account of their lack of productivity or use to society. The physically disabled and the mentally ill were regarded as 'ballast existences' and the Nazi 'euthanasia' campaigns directed against both children and adults were designed to eliminate them from society. Chapter 10 examines the treatment of sexual outsiders in Nazi Germany. Homosexuals were persecuted by the regime on the grounds of their 'deviant' sexual behaviour. This chapter examines Nazi policy towards lesbians and Nazi policies towards prostitutes as sexual outsiders.

Chapter 11 considers the fate of dissenters and resisters. This includes a discussion of Jehovah's Witnesses in the Third Reich. Their religious beliefs disallowed entry to the armed forces and thus as conscientious objectors, Jehovah's Witnesses remained outside the 'national community'. This chapter also treats the subject of resistance, as resisters to the regime, through their own actions and choices, stood outside the 'national community'.

The third part of the book examines cultural life and the 'national community'. Apart from being a racial community, the Nazis regarded the 'national community' as a cultural community. They sought to purge cultural life of 'unGerman' aspects and to cleanse it of 'Bolshevik' and 'Jewish' influences in particular. As Evans has argued compellingly, the Nazis wanted 'to create a new German culture that would reflect their values alone'.[33] Clearly, then, it was important to the Nazi regime to control the radio and the press, in order to influence the flow of information available to the German public. Chapter 12 examines the impact of Nazism upon the German radio and press. But the regime also sought control across all aspects of cultural life and artistic endeavour. It broadly applied the term 'degenerate' to any aspects of or influences upon artistic or cultural life of which it disapproved. The German population was made amply aware of what was acceptable and what was not. Chapter 13 explores the role of the cinema and the theatre in the building of the 'national community'.

Chapter 14 examines art and architecture. It considers what the Nazi dictatorship regarded as acceptable art, sculpture and architecture, that represented the true German culture, and what was regarded as unacceptable, 'degenerate' and therefore excluded. Chapter 15 examines music and literature in the Third Reich. It explores what was allowed and what was prohibited in the context of the presentation of these aspects of German culture to the 'national community'.

Before turning to the main subject of the book, the last part of this introduction briefly outlines the background to the Nazi era, in particular Hitler's rise to power, in order to place it in its historical context.[34] One of the principal debates surrounding the rise of Nazism is whether it arose as part of a continuation of German history – that is, that modern Germany developed a *Sonderweg* ('special path') of development whose logical outcome was Nazism – or whether it came about as the result of a particular set of crises and circumstances which created the conditions for it to take root and flourish. The *Sonderweg* approach asserts that the modern German state was 'peculiar', developing without the same democratic tradition as other European states, and that its 'national character' was authoritarian and nationalist. Wolfgang Mommsen asserted that Germany had disassociated itself 'from the common stream of Western political culture' from the end of the eighteenth century onwards, rejoining it only after 1945. Karl Bracher identified the emergence of 'a special German sense of destiny'. Volker Berghahn outlined the 'structural peculiarities' of modern German society, in which the most advanced industrial economy co-existed with backward agriculture and a similarly old-fashioned political system. This approach suggested that modern Germany somehow deviated from the path of 'normal' western development towards parliamentary democracy and that this development led ultimately to the rise of Nazism.[35] Geoff Eley, among others, has criticised the *Sonderweg* approach and emphasised instead a crisis of capitalism.[36] An alternative approach to the rise of Nazism, then, is to view it as a response to a particular set of crises and circumstances. Jill Stephenson has compared this situation to an 'industrial accident' and referred to it as 'dropping a spanner in the works'.[37] More recently, Michael Burleigh has conceptualised the advent and course of the Third Reich compellingly as the moral breakdown and transformation of an advanced industrial society, in which 'sections of the German elites and masses of ordinary people chose to abdicate their individual critical faculties in favour of a politics based on faith, hope, hatred and sentimental collective self-regard for their own race and nation'.[38]

The origins of Nazism, both as an ideology and as a political movement, partly dated back to the period before the First World War. A number of nationalist, radical right-wing groups sprang up in Germany at the end of the nineteenth century and the start of the twentieth century. However, the history of the radical right in Germany was deeply influenced by the First World War and the post-war circumstances of defeat and revolution out of which the Weimar Republic was born. The period of social and economic crisis between 1918 and 1923 fostered the rise of new radical right-wing organisations in Germany, including the Nazi Party. Such groups promoted the 'stab in the back' legend, maintaining that the army had not been defeated on the battlefield but had been betrayed by the 'November criminals'. They complained that the new Weimar Republic had brought defeat upon the country and signed the unpopular Treaty of Versailles, imposed upon Germany by the victorious allies. The Weimar Republic overcame its initial problems and under the direction of Gustav Stresemann, Germany's economy improved, as did her status in Europe. Indeed, the period between 1923 and 1929 were the 'golden years' of the Republic, yet it was during this time that the Nazi Party was organising itself, in some respects in the background, as the German population enjoyed the relative stability of these years.

In 1919, Anton Drexler and Karl Harrer set up the German Workers' Party (DAP). It was one of more than 70 radical right-wing organisations, completely unremarkable until the combination of Hitler's leadership and the economic crisis of 1929 pushed it into a more prominent political position. Hitler joined the party in 1919 and his early association with it was crucial to its success. In 1920, the party changed its name to the National Socialist German Workers' Party (NSDAP) or Nazi Party and formulated its 25-point programme. By the following year, Hitler had succeeded in establishing himself as party leader. The NSDAP set up its own newspaper, the *Völkischer Beobachter* (People's Observer), as well as its own paramilitary organisation, the SA (*Sturmabteilungen*) in 1921. These were significant developments because all the established political parties had their own newspapers and paramilitary groups. The NSDAP progressed in its early years with the help of individuals in political and military circles more powerful than itself. Hitler gained an entrée into Munich salon society through early converts to Nazism, such as the Bechstein and Bruckmann families.[39] This support and patronage enabled Hitler and the NSDAP to move to a position of prominence within the radical right.

Despite his failed attempt at a putsch in Munich in November 1923, the break up of his Party and his imprisonment at Landsberg Castle, Hitler managed to resurrect the fortunes of the Nazi movement in 1925 when he consolidated and reaffirmed his control over the refounded Party. Between 1925 and 1928, Hitler emerged as *Führer* (leader) within the Party. The Party worked hard on recruitment, fundraising and canvassing. In 1928, Gregor Strasser was placed in charge of party organisation. The Party was organised from the centre down into regions (*Gaue*), each headed by its own regional leader (*Gauleiter*). This vertical structure was complemented by a horizontal organisational structure in the form of associations for different social or occupational groups, such as doctors, teachers, lawyers, students and war veterans.

The Nazi Party exploited popular fears and prejudices, using modern technology to disseminate its message. It posed as the party that would protect Germany from the threat of communist revolution, capitalising on popular concerns about the rising numbers of votes for the German Communist Party (KPD). In particular, the SA openly and violently participated in street fights and brawls with communists. Richard Bessel has described this SA presence in itself as propaganda for the NSDAP, for while some people were alarmed by the violence, many were pleased that a stand was being taken against communism.[40] The Party used posters, leaflets, parades and rallies to publicise its cause, while Hitler used simple slogans and messages in his public appearances to win support for his party. He vehemently attacked the Treaty of Versailles and the corruption and decadence of the Weimar Republic, as well as scapegoating the Jews and blaming the communists for Germany's problems.

However, without the Depression and the subsequent disintegration of the mainstream liberal and conservative political parties, the Nazi Party would not have become a mass movement and would have remained on the fringes of German politics as it was in its infancy. Hence, the other significant development between 1925 and 1929 was the change in the party political landscape. During these years, voters began to drift away from the traditional political parties and became associated instead with other groups, including the NSDAP. By the late 1920s, support for the political centre had fallen away. The Nazi Party capitalised upon this trend and began to target the middle-class vote. In 1929, after the Wall Street Crash, when the middle classes' finances and status were left in ruins, the Nazi Party was able to attract increasing numbers of voters.[41] Peter Baldwin has noted that 'the Nazis were deliberately opportunistic, courting whatever groups could be won in their bid for power'.[42]

Widespread disillusionment with the parliamentary system allowed the NSDAP to attract millions of voters after 1929 and ensured that it became the decisive factor in German politics during the political, social and economic crises of the early 1930s. Burleigh has highlighted the 'climate of despair and hopelessness', explaining how the NSDAP was able to appeal to such a large percentage of the population. He argues that 'Nazism offered intense inclusivity in a society that had been scarred by deep divisions, dynamism ... a lofty sense of purpose, almost a national mission'.[43] In July 1932, the NSDAP attracted 13.75 million votes (37.3 per cent of the vote), making it the largest parliamentary party. Although it lost 2 million votes in the elections of November 1932, Hitler declined President Hindenburg's offer of the vice-chancellorship. Hitler's ability to take advantage of circumstances as they arose eventually tipped him into power, following a complex process of intrigues among the conservative and nationalist politicians surrounding Hindenburg. On 30 January 1933, Hindenburg invited Hitler to become Chancellor, albeit of a coalition government. The NSDAP hailed this moment as its *Machtergreifung* ('seizure of power').

Once Hitler became Chancellor, he and his party wasted no time in consolidating their power. Hitler seized the chance provided by the burning down of the Reichstag by a Dutch anarcho-syndicalist, Marinus van der Lubbe, on 28 February 1933, to create the pretext for an emergency decree to be signed by Hindenburg, allowing the cabinet the autonomy to take any steps it considered necessary to safeguard public order. This law was swiftly followed by the Enabling Act, which was passed by the Reichstag on 23 March 1933. This gave the cabinet the right to rule by decree. The socialist and communist movements in Germany were swiftly destroyed. In July 1933, Germany became a one-party state, as all other political parties other than the NSDAP were outlawed. By this time, the largest trade union movement in Europe had been smashed and the Nazi Party had begun its process of *Gleichschaltung* in order to bring as many organisations and people as possible into line with National Socialism. When Hindenburg died on 2 August 1934, Hitler transferred all executive power to himself, as 'Leader and Reich Chancellor'. On the same day, the army swore an unconditional oath of personal allegiance to Hitler. Hence, within a period of just 18 months, Hitler had consolidated his initial 'seizure of power'. During this time, the new National Socialist regime began to implement his aims for German society and cultural life with enthusiasm and alacrity.

NOTES

1 Y. Bauer, 'Overall Explanations, German Society and the Jews or: Some Thoughts about Context', in D. Bankier (ed.), *Probing the Depths of German Antisemitism: German Society and the Persecution of the Jews, 1933–1941* (New York, 2000), p. 16.

2 R. Grunberger, *A Social History of the Third Reich* (London, 1971).

3 R. Bessel (ed.), *Life in the Third Reich* (Oxford, 1987); D. Crew (ed.), *Nazism and German Society* (London, 1994).

4 P. Ayçoberry, *The Social History of the Third Reich, 1933–1945* (New York, 1999).

5 R. Evans, 'Introduction', *Journal of Contemporary History (Special Issue: Understanding Nazi Germany)*, Vol. 39, No. 2 (2004), p. 163.

6 For example, F. Neumann, *Behemoth. The Structure and Practice of National Socialism* (London, 1942), p. 298.

7 R. Dahrendorf, *Society and Democracy in Germany* (London, 1968), p. 403.

8 Ibid., p. 418.

9 D. Schoenbaum, *Hitler's Social Revolution* (New York, 1967), p. 283.

10 H. Berghoff, 'Did Hitler Create a New Society? Continuity and change in German social history before and after 1933', in P. Panayi (ed.), *Weimar and Nazi Germany: Continuities and Discontinuities* (London, 2001), p. 99.

11 H. Turner, 'Fascism and Modernisation', in H. Turner (ed.), *Reappraisals of Fascism* (New York, 1975), p. 121.

12 W. Abelshauser and A. Faust, *Wirtschafts- und Sozialpolitik. Eine nationalsozialistische Sozialrevolution?* (Tübingen, 1983), p. 16.

13 J. Herf, *Reactionary Modernism: Technology, Culture and Politics in Weimar and the Third Reich* (Cambridge, 1984).

14 R. Zitelmann, *Hitler. Selbstverständnis eines Revolutionärs* (Hamburg, 1987). See also M. Prinz and R. Zitelmann (eds), *Nationalsozialismus und Modernisierung* (Darmstadt, 1991). Zitelmann's thesis is examined in I. Kershaw, *The Nazi Dictatorship: Problems and Perspectives of Interpretation* (London, 2000), pp. 243–8. On the relationship between Nazism and modernism, see also P. Betts, 'The New Fascination with Fascism: The Case of Nazi Modernism', *Journal of Contemporary History*, Vol. 37, No. 4 (2002), pp. 541–58.

15 J. Noakes, 'Nazism and Revolution', in N. O'Sullivan (ed.), *Revolutionary Theory and Political Reality* (London, 1983), p. 96.

16 D. Peukert, *Inside Nazi Germany: Conformity, Opposition and Racism in Everyday Life* (London, 1987), p. 247.

17 M. Burleigh, *The Third Reich: A New History* (London, 2000), p. 251.

18 R. Evans, *The Third Reich in Power* (London, 2006), p. 503.

19 Cited in ibid., p. 211.

20 Peukert, *Inside Nazi Germany*, p. 22.

21 Ibid., p. 23.

22 R. Bessel, 'Living with the Nazis: Some Recent Writing on the Social History of the Third Reich', *European History Quarterly*, Vol. 14 (1984), p. 211.

23 T. Mason, *Social Policy in the Third Reich: The Working Class and the 'National Community'* (Oxford, 1993) and T. Mason, *Nazism, Fascism and the Working Class: Essays by Tim Mason* (Cambridge, 1995).

24 T. Mason, 'Women in Germany, 1925–1940: Family, Welfare and Work. Part I', *History Workshop Journal*, No. 1 (1976), pp. 74–113; T. Mason, 'Women in Germany, 1925–1940: Family, Welfare and Work. Part II (Conclusion)', *History Workshop Journal*, No. 2 (1976), pp. 5–32; J. Stephenson, *Women in Nazi Society* (London, 1975); J. Stephenson, *The Nazi Organisation of Women* (London, 1981).

25 M. Burleigh and W. Wippermann, *The Racial State: Germany 1933–1945* (Cambridge, 1991).

26 R. Gellately and N. Stoltzfus (eds), *Social Outsiders in Nazi Germany* (Princeton, 2001), pp. 4–5.

27 Kershaw, *The Nazi Dictatorship*, p. 266.

28 R. Gellately, *Backing Hitler: Consent and Coercion in Nazi Germany* (Oxford, 2001).

29 Kershaw, *The Nazi Dictatorship*, p. 236.

30 Ibid.

31 On the Nazi economy, see R. Overy, *War and Economy in the Third Reich* (Oxford, 1994). For a recent treatment of the subject, see A. Tooze, *The Wages of Destruction: The Making and Breaking of the Nazi Economy* (London, 2006).

32 Space constraints do not allow an investigation of all groups and individuals 'outside' the 'national community'. On the experiences of black people in Nazi Germany, see T. Campt, *Other Germans: Black Germans and the politics of race, gender and memory in the Third Reich* (Ann Arbor, 2004) and H. Massaquoi, *Destined to Witness: Growing up*

Black in Nazi Germany (London, 2001). On Freemasons, see H. Neuberger, *Freimaurerei und Nationalsozialismus: Die Verfolgung der deutschen Freimaurerei durch völkische Bewegung und Nationalsozialismus 1918–1945* (Hamburg, 1980); H. Neubach, *Winkelmass und Hakenkreuz. Der Freimaurer und das Dritte Reich* (Munich, 2001).

33 Evans, *The Third Reich in Power*, p. 118.

34 For a more detailed treatment of the rise of Nazism, see C. Fischer, *The Rise of the Nazis* (Manchester, 1995) and R. Evans, *The Coming of the Third Reich* (London, 2004).

35 An analysis of the *Sonderweg* argument is presented in J. Kocka, 'German History before Hitler: The Debate about the German *Sonderweg'*, *Journal of Contemporary History*, Vol. 23 (1988), pp. 3–16.

36 G. Eley, *From Unification to Nazism* (London, 1986).

37 J. Stephenson, 'The Rise of the Nazis: *Sonderweg* or spanner in the works?', in M. Fulbrook (ed.), *Twentieth Century Germany: Politics, Culture and Society 1918–1990* (London, 2001), p. 79.

38 Burleigh, *The Third Reich*, p. 1.

39 J. Noakes, 'Nazism and High Society', in M. Burleigh (ed.), *Confronting the Nazi Past: New Debates on Modern German History* (London, 1996), pp. 52–3.

40 R. Bessel, 'Violence as Propaganda: The Role of the Stormtroopers in the Rise of National Socialism', in T. Childers (ed.), *The Formation of the Nazi Constituency, 1919–1933* (London, 1986), pp. 131–46.

41 On Nazi voters, see T. Childers, *The Nazi Voter: The Social Foundations of Fascism in Germany, 1919–1933* (Chapel Hill, 1981); Childers (ed.), *The Formation of the Nazi Constituency*; J. Falter, *Hitlers Wähler* (Munich, 1991).

42 P. Baldwin, 'Social Interpretations of Nazism: Renewing a Tradition', *Journal of Contemporary History*, Vol. 25 (1990), p. 14.

43 Burleigh, *The Third Reich*, p. 12.

PART ONE

INSIDE THE 'NATIONAL COMMUNITY'

1

THE CREATION OF CONSENSUS AND CONFORMITY

'You have to save 5 marks a week, if you want to drive your own car!' A
poster advertising the KdF scheme. © The Wiener Library

Once Hitler came to power, the NSDAP began a concerted effort to
homogenise German society and to bring the population round to an acceptance of National Socialism. The Nazi movement had been driven by its beliefs
and convictions about the future of Germany and intended to convey the
sense of the urgency of its mission to any waverers or doubters. The National
Socialists endeavoured to create consensus for their regime and conformity to

its ideological aspirations. This chapter explores the principal ways in which the Nazis attempted to create consensus for their rule and to shape their 'national community'. It examines the process of *Gleichschaltung*, the attempts of the regime to break down class barriers, as well as the role of propaganda and the Hitler myth in the creation of the 'national community'.

THE PROCESS OF *GLEICHSCHALTUNG*

The process of *Gleichschaltung* (streamlining or 'co-ordination') was designed to bring all aspects of German life under National Socialist control and to homogenise German society.[1] Richard Evans has noted that 'almost every aspect of political, social and associational life was affected, at every level from the nation to the village'.[2] Within the space of a few weeks of the 'seizure of power', the Nazis took over the federated state governments in March 1933. They appointed Reich Commissioners to replace the existing administrations and the federal system ended in January 1934. By the end of July 1933, all political parties, with the exception of the NSDAP, had been banned or had dissolved themselves. The leadership of the SPD (German Social Democratic Party) had gone into exile. The new regime 'co-ordinated' the civil service by means of the Law for the Restoration of the Professional Civil Service of 7 April 1933. Other public and state institutions were treated similarly. Between 30 January and 1 May 1933, 1.6 million people joined the NSDAP in order to safeguard their employment.[3] The decisions they made were often prompted by intimidation or physical violence on the part of Nazi stormtroopers or SS (*Schutzstaffeln*) men. On 1 May 1933, the NSDAP banned further new memberships, so overwhelming had been the rush to join the Party in the previous three months.

'Co-ordination' of cultural life was achieved with the creation of the Reich Chamber of Culture (RKK). This institution was established in September 1933, enabling Goebbels to control all aspects of German arts and culture. It was subdivided into seven chambers: literature, theatre, music, radio, film, fine arts and press. Each chamber closely monitored and controlled work within its sphere. The chambers kept registers of members and issued permits. It was impossible to work within any of these areas without a permit. Jews and political opponents of the regime were excluded from the RKK and therefore deprived of their livelihood in these areas. The teaching profession was 'co-ordinated' into the National Socialist Teachers' League (NSLB). Jewish teachers, who were barred from entry into the NSLB, were excluded from their profession. Many business and professional associations and other organisations either voluntarily 'co-ordinated' themselves with the new regime or dissolved themselves. Forcible 'co-ordination' ensued in instances of reluctance or hesitation. 'Co-ordination' was designed both to remove the possibility of opposition and to organise society in such a way that people could be imbued with the spirit of National Socialism. Yet the process of 'co-ordination' – although it was carried out on such a large scale – was imperfect. Membership of the Party or one of its formations did not necessarily imply true ideological loyalty to National Socialism. Indeed, some people who joined the Nazi Party remained committed to ideologies of the political left. They were described as 'beefsteak Nazis' – 'brown' (Nazi) on the outside, 'red' (Communist) on the inside. Yet the process of *Gleichschaltung* did succeed in eliminating serious widespread opposition to the regime.

THE BREAKING DOWN OF CLASS BARRIERS

The Nazi regime was particularly concerned with the need to undermine traditional class loyalties and to replace them with a new national consciousness. The Nazi Party had started out its life as a workers' party, founded in 1919 as the DAP (German Workers' Party), changing its name in 1920 to the NSDAP (National Socialist German Workers' Party). Yet it succeeded in destroying the most powerful labour movement in Europe within five months of coming to power. The German trade union movement had comprised the Free Trade Unions (affiliated with the Social Democratic Party), the Christian Trade Unions (associated with the Catholic Centre Party) and the Hirsch-Düncker Unions (aligned with the Liberal parties). The Free Trade Unions and Hirsch-Düncker Unions were 'co-ordinated' during the first week of May, while the Christian Trade Unions held on until the end of June 1933, when they too were banned.[4] As well as smashing the trade unions, the National Socialists broke up the social environment of the workers, including sports and leisure facilities, in order to destroy the social identity of the workers. While the Nazis did not completely suppress worker solidarity, they did manage to largely depoliticise the workers. However, as Dick Geary has pointed out, 'the experience of mass and long-term unemployment in the Weimar Republic had already done a great deal to fracture, demobilise and demoralise large sections of the German working class before the Nazi seizure of power'.[5] Yet, because the regime was initially very fearful of the possibility of working-class resistance, it clamped down hard on workers' organisations and incarcerated prominent Socialists and Communists.

In the place of the trade unions, the German Labour Front (*Deutsche Arbeitsfront* or DAF) was set up on 6 May 1933 under Robert Ley, *Gauleiter* of Cologne.[6] The DAF, in addition, took over the earlier established and numerically much smaller Nazi Factory Cell Organisations (NSBO). The DAF had 20 million members by 1938.[7] It was not a trade union organisation and had no power to negotiate wage settlements. Its main purpose was to preserve industrial peace and to promote social welfare schemes, and thereby to raise the self-esteem and productivity of the workers. The title 'worker' was extended to include white-collar workers and employers, not just blue-collar workers as before. This was part of the regime's symbolic attempt to remove from the working class its sense of being separate or distinct from the rest of society. The DAF was intended to symbolise the nation, by diminishing the significance of class and raising the status of the 'worker'. Within the DAF, workers were to stand side by side with employers, 'no longer separated into groups which serve to maintain special economic or social distinctions or interests'.[8] The ultimate aim of the DAF was to educate all working Germans to support the National Socialist state.

The National Day of Labour, which replaced the traditional socialist May Day celebration, was also intended to underpin the 'national community', as employers and employees paraded together. The Law for the Ordering of National Labour, introduced in January 1934, reorganised industrial relations. It stated: 'The employer works in the factory as leader of the plant, together with employees and workers who constitute his retinue, to further the aims of the plant and for the common benefit of the nation and state.'[9] Hence, it envisaged harmony for the overall good of the workplace and the nation rather than disputes between employer and employees, as everyone was working towards the same goal.

In general, however, very little changed at first for the workers in terms of their economic circumstances. As the economy recovered in 1935–1936, many of the unemployed secured jobs again and some stability ensued, although this was not accompanied by any real improvement in their living conditions, wages or housing.[10] Indeed, real earnings did not recover their 1929 level until 1941. The workers did enjoy some tangible benefits, however, such as the introduction of a minimum of six days' annual holiday, although these were largely designed to create support among the workers for the regime or at least to politically neutralise them.

National Socialism, therefore, claimed to create a classless society in which class barriers were broken down and workers had new opportunities. On a superficial level, this appeared to be the case, with hitherto middle-class pursuits and opportunities now within the reach of the working class. For example, mass tourism and leisure were introduced under the aegis of the *Kraft durch Freude* (KdF or 'Strength through Joy') organisation.[11] It was a sign of the upward mobility of the working class, as such travel opportunities had previously been the privilege and preserve of the middle and upper classes. The KdF organised hikes and sporting activities. Furthermore, it arranged subsidised holidays to the Black Forest and other regions of Germany, which were partly designed to reverse German regional particularism by encouraging people to visit other parts of their homeland. This formed part of the process of building the 'national community'. The KdF arranged steamship tours on the Rhine and the Danube. By 1938, the KdF was organising cruises to Madeira and the Norwegian fjords, as well as trips to other destinations in Europe.[12]

Furthermore, there was greater accessibility to the theatre, cinema and other cultural activities. In addition, workers were encouraged to save for a KdF car or *Volkswagen* ('people's car'), potentially available to every German. This was symbolically significant, as previously car ownership had been reserved only for the upper echelons of society.[13] In the event, the outbreak of war precluded the production of the KdF cars. Yet the opportunities provided by the KdF were all designed to enhance workers' esteem, to raise their productivity and to give them a sense of their importance to the 'national community'. The KdF's organisation of leisure time served to keep workers occupied, to divert their attention from the loss of their trade unions, to persuade them that the government was concerned with their well-being and therefore to decrease the possibility of disaffection or political opposition.[14]

The *Schönheit der Arbeit* ('Beauty of Labour') was another organisation that played a significant role in this respect. Geraniums were placed at factory entrances to brighten them up, wholesome canteen food was provided and hygiene conditions in factories were improved. 'Beauty of Labour' instigated a number of campaigns designed to improve factory conditions, such as 'Good Light – Good Work' in 1935 and 'Hot Food in the Factory' in 1938. These measures were devised to create a sense of attachment to their workplace among workers and thereby to raise productivity. Furthermore, they were an attempt to at the very least politically neutralise the workers (to wean them away from Communism and Socialism) or ideally to convince them to positively accept Nazism.

Ulrich Herbert has argued that the attitude of the majority of workers towards National Socialism was 'generally one of distance', but that the economic recovery and foreign policy successes meant that they approved of some aspects of Nazi policy.[15] Hence, it was difficult to relate individual experiences to political outlook. Tim Mason called this a 'disassociation of consciousness'. Economic recovery between 1936 and 1939 had a significant impact on the attitude of the workers towards the regime. Once the war began, military successes further promoted the workers' acceptance of and even loyalty to the regime.[16] Michael Burleigh has noted that although working hours increased and the range of consumer goods decreased, 'there were enough compensations, including Nazi foreign policy, for working-class resistance ... to remain sufficiently chimerical'.[17]

In addition, the Nazis' use of enforced foreign labour removed some of the burdens of the war from German workers.[18] By 1944, foreign workers made up over 25 per cent of all those employed in the German economy and 50 per cent in sectors such as armaments, construction, mining and agriculture. By the autumn of 1944, there were 7.7 million foreign civilian workers and prisoners of war (POWs) employed in the German economy (the largest group from the USSR).[19] Towards the end of the war, 80–90 per cent of workers were foreign. This situation created upward social mobility for the German workers, who took on roles as supervisors and foremen. The other benefit of the extensive use of foreign workers was that there was less pressure for German women to work; the Nazi regime conscripted German women late and haphazardly.[20]

But the war did, of course have negative effects on the morale of the home front, with rationing, food shortages and the Allies' aerial bombing campaign all contributing to a breakdown of support and consensus for the regime.[21] The density of urban working-class districts meant that workers suffered most from the bombing of the large cities and industrial areas. The Allied aerial bombing campaign destroyed the conditions of widespread consensus for the Nazi regime.[22] The popular mood turned to one of apathy and disinterest, though still not to any broadly based political opposition on the part of the workers.

What was the impact of National Socialism on the middle classes?[23] During the last years of the Weimar era, the old middle class, such as farmers, artisans, shopkeepers, salaried employees and civil servants, believed that the Nazis would champion their interests and protect the 'little man' from competition from big business and the department stores. Indeed, the middle classes had formed the core of the Nazi vote in the years 1929–1933. However, once in power, the Nazi Party dissolved or 'co-ordinated' middle-class economic associations, such as the Combat League of Middle-Class Tradespeople, hence artisans and shopkeepers were brought under closer state control. The Law for the Protection of Retail Trades (12 May 1933) and the Law for the Provisional Construction of German Craft Trades (29 November 1933) protected artisans to some extent, by restricting access to artisan crafts and keeping down competition.[24] However, industrial concentration was accelerated and the banks and big businesses thrived at the expense of small businesses and shops. The small business sector became despondent but not openly hostile to the regime because it hoped to make gains from the exclusion of the German Jews from the economy. Yet it was the banks and big businesses that benefited most in this respect too – for example, the department stores owned by Jews, such as Tietz, Schocken and Wertheim, were taken over by banks and big businesses.

Similarly to artisans' and traders' associations, agrarian interest groups and associations were 'co-ordinated'. Walter Darré, the Minister of Agriculture, reorganised agriculture through the Reich Food Estate, a syndicate that was aimed at bringing this sector of the economy under state control. Agricultural policy was largely designed to serve the interests of the regime, not the farmers.[25] The Reich Food Estate kept files on each farm, imposed production targets and penalised farmers for illegal slaughtering or black market activities. Propaganda measures, such as the annual harvest festival at Bückeburg and the romantic idealisation of pastoral life, were designed to maintain the consensus of the middle classes and to compensate for the failure of Nazi policy to live up to their expectations and hopes. Indeed, Bernd Weisbrod has argued that Hitler ultimately destroyed the 'last defences' of the middle class by shattering the 'conventional morals of bourgeois society'.[26]

As for the upper class, between 1929 and 1933 a number of nobles had joined the higher ranks of the SA, including Prince August Wilhelm of Prussia and Prince Philipp of Hesse. The SS, however, was to become the real elite organisation of the Nazi movement.[27] Although Himmler, like Hitler, had no particular regard for the German aristocracy, he saw the need to win over the nobility as a way of gaining elite status for the SS. During the period after 1930, with its electoral successes, the Nazi Party had attracted more and more noblemen into its ranks. In addition, Hitler had gained an entrée into Berlin salon society. As had been the case a decade earlier in Munich, when society ladies had invited Hitler into their homes, individual hostesses in Berlin, such as Helen von Carnap, Viktoria von Dirksen and Manna von Winterfeld, welcomed Hitler to their gatherings.[28] In this way, the Nazi Party had gained social acceptability, which had proven very important for its political success, especially between 1930 and 1933, when political power was increasingly concentrated in the hands of a few key members of Berlin high society, who were close to President Hindenburg.

Apart from Hitler, Goering, Goebbels and Ribbentrop began to participate in the Berlin high society to which their official positions gave them access. In addition, members of the German aristocracy flooded to join the SS. Many were motivated by opportunism – determined to place themselves favourably for what the new regime might have to offer them, or to protect their positions – rather than by any true ideological empathy with the regime. Equally, Himmler and the SS were not concerned with nobility or inherited wealth. Himmler's elite was to be based on merit and achievement in service to the 'national community'. Hence, there was never any real sense of accommodation between the Nazis and the German aristocracy. Although many nobles joined the SA and subsequently the SS, others were not won over at all by the Nazi movement. By the late 1930s, they increasingly distanced themselves from the regime, and during the war the aristocracy withdrew into its traditional social milieu, into a space the Nazis could not penetrate. Jeremy Noakes argues that much of the German high aristocracy was 'more or less totally detached from the regime and regarded it with a mixture of contempt and disgust'.[29]

Hence, despite its aims and claims, the Nazi regime did not create a classless society. It disappointed the middle classes and ultimately repulsed the aristocracy. Although the lot of the average German worker appeared to have improved in some respects, the Nazi regime did not succeed either in removing class barriers or in drawing workers away from their traditional loyalties. Burleigh has commented that despite the Nazis' egalitarian rhetoric, 'working-class people persisted in a "them and us" mentality'.[30] The regime's claims to have created a classless society were inaccurate. Improvements in status and working conditions did not necessarily compensate for the loss of the trade unions or poor wage increases. A large gap remained between the myth of the classless 'national community' and social reality, and especially during the war perceptions of class divisions became stronger than ever because of the strains of wartime civilian life.[31]

THE ROLE OF PROPAGANDA AND THE HITLER MYTH IN THE CREATION OF THE 'NATIONAL COMMUNITY'

The Reich Ministry of Popular Enlightenment and Propaganda was established in March 1933. Josef Goebbels, its new Minister, stated at a press conference on 15 March 1933: 'It is not enough for people to be more or less reconciled to our regime, to be persuaded to adopt a neutral attitude towards us, rather we want to work on people until they have capitulated to us.' He added that 'the new Ministry has no other aim than to unite the nation behind the idea of the national revolution' (i.e. National Socialism). Rallies and parades, posters, feature films, newsreels, the press and the radio were all employed to generate consent for the regime and its aims. The creation of the 'national community' was, as David Welch has recently argued, 'a key element in the revolutionary aims of the Nazi regime'.[32]

Nazi propaganda addressed itself to large masses of people in order to create uniformity of opinion and action and a re-education of society based upon National Socialist principles. Welch has shown that Nazi propaganda was most successful when it reinforced pre-existing beliefs and popular opinion.[33] The building of the 'national community', the need for racial purity, the hatred of 'enemies' and the leadership cult were among the most consistent themes of the Nazi propaganda machinery, as well as its emphasis upon the regime's domestic and foreign policy successes. These were linked by the regime's overall aim to create its ideal society, a 'racially pure' 'national community', purged of the 'enemies' of Bolshevism, Judaism and Freemasonry, under the leadership of the *Führer*. Posters and slogans called for allegiance to the nation and its leader: 'One People! One Reich! One *Führer*!' Nazi propaganda appealed to national unity by calling for people to place the needs of the 'national community' ahead of their own selfish desires. This was encapsulated in the slogan 'The community before the individual'. The introduction of the *Eintopf* ('one-pot dish') was designed to encourage national unity and foster a sense of 'national community'. On one Sunday each month, German families were urged to make savings against their usual Sunday lunch by having a 'one-pot dish' and to give a donation for their needy 'national comrades'. This 'meal of sacrifice for the Reich' was an expression of the 'national community'.[34] The Winter Aid Programme, which encouraged wealthier Germans to give food, money and clothes to distressed and impoverished 'national comrades', was another illustration of this. The Party's involvement in these types of activities gave its members a role and purpose. Furthermore, it projected the image of the Party as the leader of the local community and as part of the wider 'national community'.[35]

However, Nazi propaganda was only partially successful. Peukert has shown that despite the Nazis' claims to have created an integrated 'national community', there were many expressions of non-conformist behaviour. This spanned from refusal to take part in the *Eintopf* Sundays to sheltering victims of persecution. Jokes, whisperings and rumours formed a significant manifestation of discontent among the population. These were documented in reports on popular opinion and morale compiled by the *Sicherheitsdienst* (SD or Security Service).[36] Peukert argued that the documentation of 'malicious offences' enables us 'to form a very precise picture of everyday popular feeling and opinion'.[37] Opposition found its best expression in informal activities. Peukert investigated whether this criticism was to be found among certain groups, whether it was directed against the regime as a whole or only against particular measures, and especially the relationship between relatively fre-

quent expressions of critical words and the less frequent occurrence of oppositional actions. Price increases, the regime's failure to keep its promises and
corruption among 'brownshirt bigwigs' were frequent themes of criticism.
The 'contradictions in the mood of the "little man"' were highlighted by critical comments about restrictions on the activities of the churches and the persecution of priests, yet silence on the issue of the use of terror against political
dissidents.[38] Criticisms and 'grumbling' existed alongside a passive acceptance of the regime and its authority.

The image of Hitler as an infallible leader was the principal rallying point
for the 'national community'. The focus for loyalty and national unity, Hitler
himself was the most important legitimising force within the regime. Ian
Kershaw has argued that 'the "Hitler myth" was consciously devised as an
integrating force by a regime acutely aware of the need to manufacture consensus'.[39] Hitler was portrayed as the leader of Germany's destiny. Yet this
heroic leadership was 'as much an image created by the masses as it was
imposed on them'.[40] Hitler's 'charismatic authority', based upon the popular
perception of his 'exceptional powers' or 'exemplary character', was
bestowed upon him by his followers.[41] Pierre Ayçoberry states that 'the construction of the Hitlerian myth resulted from a combination of autosugges-
tion, deliberate fabrication and a quasi-universal acceptance'.[42] After the
Night of the Long Knives (30 June 1934), Hitler's reputation was elevated,
despite the illegality of his actions. He was regarded as the defender of the
'little man' against the 'big shots' and as the upholder of public morality.
Curbing the excesses of the SA appealed to the pubic's desire for law and
order, while the murder of its openly homosexual leader, Ernst Röhm,
accorded to 'the healthy instincts of the people'.[43] In addition, the recovery
of the nation's economy, the massive public works schemes, such as motorway construction, and the elimination of mass employment in the mid-1930s
were regarded as the personal achievements of the *Führer*.

Standing above and beyond the day-to-day realities of the regime, Hitler
remained disassociated from unpopular decisions and from the avarice and
hypocrisy of the Party functionaries. Hitler was popular as a leader among all
social groups and was personally exempted from criticisms of the regime. Any
blame was always directed at other Nazi leaders or officials. The Hitler myth
enabled people to voice their quotidian grumbles and concerns, yet consent
to the Nazi regime as a whole.[44] This co-existence of complaint and compliance is significant to our understanding of the nature of popular opinion in
the Third Reich. Much of the appeal of the Hitler myth was the yearning for
security and leadership by a population in disarray and despair. While the
regime continued to make achievements and restore order (or at least appeared
to do so), with its visionary leader at its centre, popular consensus remained.

Additionally, the Nazi regime won people to the national cause by means of
its foreign policy successes. A nation brought to its knees by the punitive
Treaty of Versailles in 1919 could only rejoice in Hitler's wholesale revocation of its terms. The 'bringing home' of the Saarland in 1935 and the march

into the Rhineland on 7 March 1936 met with rapturous popular approval. These events signified success and recovery for the German nation under their great 'leader'. The *Anschluß*, with Austria in 1938 was another massive triumph for the 'national community' and its *Führer*. While Nazi foreign policy continued to succeed, the sense of 'national community' was enhanced. Even a nation hesitant to go to war again in September 1939 accepted Hitler's decision and reaped the benefits during the initial *Blitzkrieg* successes. Popular support reached its high point after the Nazi occupation of Paris in 1940. Hitler was regarded throughout this period as a great wartime leader. Kershaw argues that even on 'the eve of the invasion of the Soviet Union … Hitler's popular standing was undiminished, and confidence in his leadership among the great majority of the population unbroken'.[45] It was only after the tide of the war turned against Germany, and in particular after the Battle of Stalingrad in January 1943, that both Hitler's infallibility and the strength of the nation began to be called into question. Yet this disillusionment was not translated into any determined resistance or revolt. There were three main reasons for this, namely: the Nazis' apparatus of terror remained intact until the end of the war; the burdens and strains of the war led people to a reaction of resignation rather than rebellion; and Nazism had created an 'atomisation of social relations' which stood in the way of a communal resistance effort.[46]

Before Stalingrad, direct, personal criticism of Hitler was extremely rare, but 'in the case of Stalingrad, Hitler was directly implicated in the catastrophe' and the 'Hitler myth' began to falter.[47] The Allied bombing campaigns were another significant factor in the decline of the 'Hitler myth', particularly from 1943 onwards. The bombing caused considerable demoralisation and anger directed against the Nazi leadership for failing to prevent it, despite continued Nazi propaganda directed at the home front.[48] In the months following the 20 July 1944 bomb plot on Hitler's life, the *Führer* retreated from public life.[49] In the last phase of the war, the 'Hitler myth' collapsed entirely. Hence, the '*Führer* myth', significant as it was, is not sufficient on its own as an explanation for the continuing acceptance of the Nazi regime, particularly after the tide of the war turned against Germany.

Another part of the explanation is what Peukert termed 'a retreat from the public sphere into the private'.[50] As National Socialism penetrated traditional social milieux and institutions, partly by breaking them up and partly by taking them over, people were pushed into the private domain to express their opposition. While this behaviour contradicted Nazi mass mobilisation imperatives, paradoxically it also benefited the regime, for it stood in the way of effective mass resistance. In addition, many acts of non-conformist or dissident behaviour either remained private or did not call into question the regime as a whole.[51]

During the years 1933–1939, the Nazi government employed a combination of initiatives in order to form the society or 'national community' it desired and to manufacture consensus for that society among those who belonged to it. These included 'co-ordination' or the streamlining of society and the attempt to break down class barriers. Propaganda and the Hitler myth also played a significant role in the creation of the 'national community'. The mid-1930s were characterised by a large degree of loyalty to the regime and popular enthusiasm for the *Führer*. Many Germans were caught up in the sense of the 'national community' and the *Führer* myth. The population approved of Nazi social and economic policies, the hard line taken by the regime against its 'enemies' and the strict imposition of 'law and order' in German society. The population sought security, recovery and order, and the Hitler regime appeared to bring all these things. The hopes and needs of large sections of the German population were reflected in its ideology and policies, and this created consensus for its rule. However, image differed from reality under the Nazi dictatorship, which failed to fulfil many of its promises.

During these years of consensus, the expansion of Heinrich Himmler's SS complex went largely unnoticed, yet it was during this very period that many of the preconditions of later radicalisation and terror were created. Indeed, Kershaw has described the Hitler myth and terror as 'two indispensable sides of the same coin' and argued that it was no coincidence that 'terroristic repression escalated wildly in the final phase of the waning regime as the binding force of Hitler's popularity weakened and collapsed'.[52] While propaganda played a significant role in mobilising popular support for the regime, it was not sufficient on its own to sustain Nazism for the duration of the regime. It is also important to recognise the gap between the myth of the 'national community' and the reality of life in the Third Reich. For while 'national community' propaganda and policies had some impact upon popular conceptions of the Third Reich, the class structure in Germany was not essentially changed. Welch is therefore correct to emphasise that 'in real terms there can be no suggestion of a revolutionary transformation of society between 1933 and 1945'.[53] The Nazi regime was not entirely successful in achieving its aims to homogenise society and to create consensus for its rule. In the end, the 'national community' was an atomised society, not a homogenous one. The Nazi image of the 'national community' differed from social reality. In order to redress its failure to achieve consensus and conformity, the Nazi regime stepped up its use of coercion, terror and surveillance.

NOTES

1 On this, see N. Frei, *Der Führerstaat. Nationalsozialistische Herrschaft 1933 bis 1945* (Munich, 2001).

2 R. Evans, *The Coming of the Third Reich* (London, 2004), p. 381.

3 R. Evans, *The Third Reich in Power* (London, 2006), p. 14.

4 P. Brooker, *The Faces of Fraternalism. Nazi Germany, Fascist Italy, and Imperial Japan* (Oxford, 1991), p. 136.

5 D. Geary, 'Working-Class Identities in the Third Reich', in N. Gregor (ed.), *Nazism, War and Genocide* (Exeter, 2005), p. 51. On this, see also D. Geary, 'Unemployment and Working-Class Solidarity in Germany, 1929–1933', in R. Evans and D. Geary (eds*), The*

German Unemployed: Experiences and Consequences of Mass Unemployment from the Weimar Republic to the Third Reich (London, 1987), pp. 261–80.

6 On Ley, see R. Smelser, *Robert Ley: Hitler's Labour Front Leader* (Oxford, 1988).

7 M. Schneider, *Unterm Hakenkreuz. Arbeiter und Arbeiterbewegung 1933 bis 1939* (Bonn, 1999), p. 178. See also F. Carsten, *The German Workers and the Nazis* (Aldershot, 1995).

8 Cited in J. Noakes and G. Pridham (eds), *Nazism 1919–1945: State, Economy and Society* (Exeter, 1984), pp. 338–9.

9 D. Welch, 'Nazi Propaganda and the *Volksgemeinschaft*: Constructing a People's Community', *Journal of Contemporary History*, Vol. 39 (2004), p. 220.

10 On economic recovery, see R. Overy, *War and Economy in the Third Reich* (Oxford, 1994), pp. 37–89.

11 On this, see S. Baranowski, *Strength through Joy: Consumerism and Mass Tourism in the Third Reich* (New York, 2004). See also K. Semmens, *Seeing Hitler's Germany: Tourism in the Third Reich* (London, 2005).

12 M. Merritt, 'Strength through Joy: Regimented Leisure in Nazi Germany', in O. Mitchell (ed.), *Nazism and the Common Man: Essays in German History (1929–1939)* (Washington D. C., 1981), pp. 74–5.

13 Merritt, 'Strength through Joy', p. 86.

14 H. Weiss, 'Ideologie der Freizeit im Dritten Reich: Die NS-Gemeinschaft "Kraft durch Freude"', *Archiv für Sozialgeschichte*, Vol. 33 (1993), pp. 289–303.

15 U. Herbert, '"The Real Mystery in Germany". The German Working Class During the Nazi Dictatorship', in M. Burleigh (ed.), *Confronting the Nazi Past: New Debates on Modern German History* (London, 1996), p. 29.

16 See S. Salter, 'Structures of Consensus and Coercion: Workers' Morale and the Maintenance of Work Discipline, 1939–1945', in D. Welch (ed.), *Nazi Propaganda: The Power and the Limitations* (London, 1983), pp. 88–116.

17 M. Burleigh, *The Third Reich: A New History* (London, 2000), p. 251.

18 On this, see U. Herbert, *Hitler's Foreign Workers: Enforced Foreign Labour in Germany under the Third Reich* (Cambridge, 1997).

19 Herbert, '"The Real Mystery in Germany"', p. 31.

20 However, on female mobilisation, see also the view presented by Richard Overy in *War and Economy in the Third Reich*, pp. 303–11.

21 On the impact of food shortages and rationing on popular morale, see J. Noakes (ed.), *Nazism: A Documentary Reader*, Vol. 4, pp. 510–26.

22 On the impact of the air raids on popular opinion and morale, see ibid., pp. 552–71. See also I. Kershaw, *The 'Hitler Myth': Image and Reality in the Third Reich* (Oxford, 1987), pp. 206–7.

23 See especially A. von Saldern, *Mittelstand im 'Dritten Reich'. Handwerker – Einzelhändler – Bauern* (Frankfurt am Main, 1979) and M. Prinz, *Vom neuen Mittelstand zum Volksgenossen* (Munich, 1986).

24 M. Burleigh and W. Wippermann, *The Racial State: Germany 1933–1945* (Cambridge, 1991), pp. 276–7.

25 D. Münkel, *Nationalsozialistische Agrarpolitik und Bauernalltag* (Frankfurt am Main, 1996).

26 B. Weisbrod, 'The Crisis of Bourgeois Society in Interwar Germany', in R. Bessel (ed.), *Fascist Italy and Nazi Germany. Comparisons and Contrasts* (Cambridge, 1996), p. 38.

27 H. Ziegler, *Nazi Germany's New Aristocracy: The SS Leadership, 1925–1939* (Princeton, 1989).

28 J. Noakes, 'Nazism and High Society', in M. Burleigh (ed.), *Confronting the Nazi Past*, p. 56.

29 Ibid., p. 63. On the relationship of the aristocracy and National Socialism, see also G.

Kleine, 'Adelsgenossenschaft und Nationalsozialismus', *Vierteljahrshefte für Zeitgeschichte*, Vol. 26 (1978), pp. 100–41.

30 Burleigh, *The Third Reich*, p. 251.

31 L. Rupp, '"I Don't Call That *Volksgemeinschaft*": Women, Class and War in Nazi Germany', in C. Berkin and C. Lovett (eds), *Women, War and Revolution* (New York and London, 1980), pp. 37–9.

32 Welch, 'Nazi Propaganda and the *Volksgemeinschaft*', p. 213.

33 See D. Welch, 'Propaganda and Indoctrination in the Third Reich: Success or Failure?', *European History Quarterly*, Vol. 17 (1987), pp. 403–22. See also D. Welch, *The Third Reich. Politics and Propaganda* (London, 2002). Ian Kershaw has also shown the significance of this upon the popular acceptance of the 'Hitler myth'. See I. Kershaw, *The 'Hitler Myth': Image and Reality in the Third Reich* (Oxford, 1989), pp. 4–5.

34 Welch, 'Nazi Propaganda and the *Volksgemeinschaft*', pp. 228–9.

35 J. Noakes, 'Leaders of the People? The Nazi Party and German Society', *Journal of Contemporary History*, Vol. 39, No. 2 (2004), p. 205.

36 Edited selections of these reports can be found in H. Boberach (ed.), *Meldungen aus dem Reich 1938–1945: Die geheimen Lageberichte des Sicherheitsdienstes der SS* (Herrsching, 1984).

37 D. Peukert, *Inside Nazi Germany: Conformity, Opposition and Resistance in Everyday Life* (London, 1987), p. 52.

38 Ibid., p. 57.

39 Kershaw, *The 'Hitler Myth'*, p. 3.

40 J. Stern, *Hitler. The Führer and the People* (London, 1975), p. 111.

41 On 'charismatic authority', see Kershaw, *The 'Hitler Myth'*, pp. 8–9. The model of 'charismatic authority' was proposed by Max Weber. See M. Weber, *Economy and Society* (Berkeley, 1978), pp. 241–2.

42 P. Ayçoberry, *The Social History of the Third Reich, 1933–1945* (New York, 1999), p. 68.

43 Kershaw, *The 'Hitler Myth'*, pp. 91–2.

44 Peukert, *Inside Nazi Germany*, p. 73.

45 Kershaw, *The 'Hitler Myth'*, p. 160.

46 Peukert, *Inside Nazi Germany*, p. 63.

47 Kershaw, *The 'Hitler Myth'*, p. 193.

48 On this, see G. Kirwan, 'Allied Bombing and Nazi Domestic Propaganda', *European History Quarterly*, Vol. 15 (1985), pp. 341–62. See also G. Kirwan, 'Waiting for Retaliation – a Study in Nazi Propaganda Behaviour and German Civilian Morale', *Journal of Contemporary History*, Vol. 16, No. 3 (1981), pp. 565–83.

49 Kershaw, *The 'Hitler Myth'*, p. 219.

50 Peukert, *Inside Nazi Germany*, p. 77.

51 Ibid., p. 83.

52 Kershaw, *The 'Hitler Myth'*, p. 258.

53 Welch, 'Nazi Propaganda and the *Volksgemeinschaft*', p. 213.

2

COERCION, TERROR AND SURVEILLANCE

Detained communists in March 1933. © The Wiener Library

The Nazi regime underpinned its methods to create consensus for its rule with the threat or use of terror. This chapter examines the role of the Nazi system of terror, particularly highlighting the function of the SS, the Gestapo and the concentration camp network. It then examines the legal and prison systems which formed another important part of the Nazi terror apparatus. From the outset, the Nazi 'New Order' was made possible partly by the use of violence. This began with the activities of the SA, whose members engaged in street brawls with communists even before the Nazi 'seizure of power'.[1] Indeed, as Neil Gregor has argued, violence and coercion were 'absolutely central to the seizure and consolidation of power'.[2] Richard Evans has emphasised 'the near-universal violence' of the first six months of Nazi rule.[3] After the 'seizure of power', violence carried out by the SA and the SS, together with the establishment of 'wild' concentration camps, where enemies were imprisoned and tortured, served to create an atmosphere of terror. There was an official crackdown on the regime's enemies, particularly Communists and Social Democrats, but the SA and the SS also meted out a large amount of illegal terror. In June 1933, after a young Social Democrat resisted a stormtrooper raid in a Berlin suburb, killing three SA men, the SA responded by arresting and torturing more than 500 Social Democrats, killing 91 of them, in the 'Köpenick blood-week'.[4] Such violence was intended to have a 'demonstration effect' on the family, friends and neighbours of the victims, as well as society as a whole.[5] While the Nazi violence was centred upon communists and Social Democrats, it affected people 'from all walks of life and all shades of political opinion apart from the Nazis'.[6]

During the Weimar years, the police had had rather limited powers, for example in terms of the length of time they could detain a person who had been arrested. But in the aftermath of the Reichstag fire of 27 February 1933, with Hitler's support, police powers were drastically extended.[7] During the Nazi era, the police were able to detain individuals in custody indefinitely, without trial or any involvement of the legal authorities. The police made extensive use of these new powers and locked away tens of thousands of political opponents, criminals, deviants and 'asocials'. By the end of 1933, between 60,000 and 100,000 Communists were detained in prisons or concentration camps and by the mid-1930s, after several waves of arrests, the basis of Communist resistance in Germany had been almost entirely wiped out.

The establishment and development of the Nazi system of terror and surveillance were carried out during the mid to late 1930s while the German population was distracted by both the domestic and foreign policy successes of Hitler's government. The two most important agencies of the Nazi apparatus of terror, the Gestapo and the *Sicherheitsdienst* of the NSDAP, were housed at the Prinz-Albrecht-site in Berlin. This was where Nazi terror was both planned and administered. The Gestapo, led by Himmler, was headquartered at 8 Prinz-Albrechtstraße. This was also the location of its 'house prison', where political opponents, including prominent Communists and Social Democrats, were held and interrogated. The Gestapo used 'heightened interrogation', a euphemism for brutal torture, to extract information from inmates, many of whom were driven to suicide. The SD, led by Heydrich, was based at the Prinz-Albrecht-site from 1934. The SD became the Party's sole intelligence agency and reported on popular opinion in Germany.[8]

Between 1936 and 1939, Himmler laid the foundations of his system of control largely unnoticed by the public. Ayçoberry argues that 'at the time, public opinion for the most part did not perceive that this apparatus of repression constituted the very core of the system'.[9] From the start, Himmler's aim had been to institutionalise political surveillance and terror within the SS. In realising this ambition, Himmler was supported by Hitler, who appointed him as *Reichsführer-SS* and Chief of German Police on 17 June 1936. Himmler was thus given the institutional competence necessary for the SS to emerge as an independent nexus of power, with the police force now institutionally merged into it. The ambitious Himmler succeeded in making the SS a special force, separate from party and state.[10] Himmler was responsible to Hitler alone; no other person or institution had any power over him and he used his position to create a huge powerbase for the SS.

The main functions of the SS included the surveillance, suppression and elimination of all political opponents of the regime. Furthermore, the SS was responsible for the preservation of the 'Aryan' race and the creation of a 'racially pure' *Volksgemeinschaft*, to be achieved by the systematic persecution and eventual elimination of the Jews and other 'inferior' groups. Beyond these functions, the SS was charged with the task of expansion of the superior 'Aryan' race. This was to be achieved by the acquisition of *Lebensraum* ('living space') by means of territorial conquest and the racial restructuring of conquered lands, particularly in the East. The SS strove to achieve these essential goals of National Socialist policy. It played a decisive role in both the 'racial purification' of the German population and the planning and execution of subjugation and annihilation in Poland and the Soviet Union.

On 27 September 1939, the Reich Security Main Office (RSHA), which also had its headquarters at the Prinz-Albrecht-site, was established. This was the official merger of the Gestapo (Secret State Police), the Kripo (Criminal Police) and the Security Service (SD) into one institution under Heydrich. The RSHA was both a government agency and a part of the SS empire. The RSHA, under the aegis of Heydrich and Himmler, became the most significant agency of Nazi terror and repression. By 1943, the RSHA had expanded beyond its original headquarters to occupy more than 30 buildings in Berlin, from which it directed a vast network of agencies, including all the different branches of the police. The RSHA was pursuing increasingly extreme, unrestrained and radical policies by this time.[11]

Recent research by Robert Gellately has examined the public side of terror in Nazi Germany and investigated the relationship between consensus and coercion in the Third Reich.[12] The coercive side of the Nazi regime was widely publicised in the press, which provided coverage of the activities of the 'People's Court' and the concentration camps. The use of 'police justice' and special courts for dealing with specific 'enemies' throughout the 1930s was unconcealed. Indeed, there was a great deal of popular support for their use, particularly against political opponents, criminals and 'asocials'.[13] The relationship between the police and society was fostered by publicity events such as the 'Day of the German Police', held for the first time in 1934. The mission of the police in Nazi Germany to cleanse the nation of 'harmful' or 'degenerative elements' was carried out rigorously and publicly.[14] Coercive measures were conducted openly because the Nazis believed that they would win public approval in this way and their strategy was successful. The majority of law-abiding citizens were pleased that those regarded as 'outsiders', 'asocials', 'useless eaters' or 'criminals' were being detained and incarcerated. Many ordinary Germans not only passively accepted the use of terror but also actively aided it by making denunciations to the police. Gellately argues that the population became convinced of the positive side of the Nazi dictatorship and accepted a 'surveillance society' in exchange for crime-free streets, economic recovery and law and order. Nazi terror and repression were highly selective and did not affect the majority of Germans until the very last months of the war when 'German-on-German terror became the order of the day'.[15]

THE GESTAPO

Within Himmler's vast SS-SD-police complex, the Gestapo, headed by the ambitious Heinrich Müller, became the key link in the system of terror and surveillance in the Nazi state. The Gestapo was certainly an institution that inspired fear and terror among the German populace. Recent research has shown, however, that the popular image of the Gestapo as omniscient and omnipotent is a myth that was instigated by Gestapo leaders and perpetuated in the post-war period by historians who accepted the statements of Gestapo leaders at face value. Klaus-Michael Mallmann and Gerhard Paul have shown that the Gestapo simply did not have the necessary manpower resources to be 'omniscient and omnipotent'.[16] Its leaders carefully and deliberately adopted the propaganda image of the ubiquitous Gestapo both to intimidate German society and to conceal its own deficiencies. But in reality, the Gestapo was not a completely thoroughgoing mechanism of repression. Instead, it was an under-staffed and over-bureaucratised organisation, incapable of comprehensive surveillance. Nor was the Gestapo comprised of ardent believers in Nazi ideology. Many career policemen from the Weimar era who stayed on and adjusted to the new regime made up its ranks. In the Gestapo, as Gellately notes, they 'played the part of loyal enforcers of the dictatorship's will'.[17] Most joined the Party sooner or later, but in 1939 only 3000 of the Gestapo's approximately 20,000 employees held an SS rank.

In reality, there were remarkably few Gestapo agents on the ground and they relied on both amateur and professional helpers. For example, in 1937, the Dusseldorf Gestapo office manned by only 126 agents controlled a town of 500,000 inhabitants. The Essen Gestapo office comprised 43 agents for a town with 650,000 inhabitants.[18] Gellately has shown the largely reactive nature of the Gestapo and has described the method developed by the Gestapo as 'a kind of auto-policing, or at least an auto-surveillance system'.[19] With the co-operation of neighbours, friends, acquaintances and family members, the Gestapo could infiltrate even the private realm of the home, in order to monitor compliance with the dictates of the regime. Hence, recent studies have underlined the significance of denunciations to the work of the Gestapo. Without the help of informers, the Gestapo would have been virtually blind. Denunciations were the key link in the interactions between the police and the population. The Gestapo did not have adequate resources to generate its own cases, but relied heavily upon the supply of information from outside.[20] Following denunciations, the Gestapo relentlessly pursued and interrogated individuals – often using torture – in order to extort statements that led to arrests. But on its own – that is, without the help of informers – the Gestapo was not in the position to engage in comprehensive surveillance or perfect repression.

Recent research on denunciation has demonstrated clearly mixed motivations on the part of informers. There were affective motivations, such as anti-Semitism, but also a vast array of instrumental or selfish reasons that provided the impetus for denunciations.[21] Indeed, there was proportionally a higher rate of German-on-German denunciations than racially inspired ones. Informing was used as a way of gaining personal advantage. People used denunciations to settle scores with fellow workers or employers, or even family members, including spouses and siblings. For example, one girl lodged a complaint against her brother 'to show him he's not always right'.[22] Gellately argues that this demonstrated a growing social consensus and acceptance of the surveillance process. Many Gestapo cases reflected the development of a type of 'therapeutic system' in the Hitler dictatorship, in which the state or its organs were utilised by members of the public to regulate aspects of social life and to settle personal disputes. This denunciatory atmosphere was the result of citizen collaboration, but not always the product of racism or an ardent belief in Nazism. Regardless of the motives, however, denunciations were all 'system-supportive'.[23] A recent study by Vandana Joshi has shown how ordinary women articulated and resolved their conflicts through unsolicited denunciations. Joshi concludes that women, 'as denouncers, employed the mechanism of state control and self policing largely in their own interest'.[24] Such findings have greatly enhanced our understanding of the nature of Nazi society and of the complex relationship between the population and the state apparatus.

THE CONCENTRATION CAMPS

From a very early date, the Nazis set up various types of camps, for a number of reasons, which developed into a large system of concentration camps and death camps at the height of the regime's power. The concentration camps formed a significant segment of the Nazi camp system and lay at the heart of the Nazis' network of terror.[25] Eugen Kogon outlined the function of the Nazi concentration camps: 'Their main purpose was the elimination of every trace of actual or potential opposition to Nazi rule. Segregation, debasement, humiliation, extermination – these were the effective forms of terror. Any concept of justice was put aside.'[26] The concentration camp system was designed to either 're-educate' or eliminate opponents of the regime. Concentration camps were instruments of social terror, first established to isolate and terrorise Communists and Social Democrats. The camps also had a number of subsidiary functions. They were used to intimidate all potential enemies of the regime and to have a deterrent effect upon the rest of the population. They served as the training grounds where the SS Death's Head units were toughened up and inured to brutality. They were centres for 'the collection and exploitation of SS labour slaves' and for 'large-scale scientific experimentation'.[27]

The very first 'wild' concentration camps were set up in 1933. There were about 50 of these, mainly in and around Berlin, but also elsewhere in Germany. They were established and run by the SA. Dachau, established near Munich in March 1933, was the only one of these early camps to survive. Theodor Eicke, a high-ranking SS officer and Commandant of Dachau, was made Inspector of Concentration Camps on 1 July 1934.[28] He was assigned the task of reorganising and expanding the camp system. Dachau, with its clearly defined rules for camp behaviour, its classification of prisoners, its graduated system of punishments, its observation towers and barbed wire electrified fences, served as a model for the organisation and running of other concentration camps. At first, the concentration camps had been envisaged as a temporary measure, just to be used until the regime had consolidated its power, but as time passed they became a permanent feature of life in the Third Reich. After the abandonment of the early camps, the SS planned and constructed its new, major purpose-built concentration camps: Sachsenhausen (1936), Buchenwald (1937), Flossenbürg (1938), Mauthausen (1938) and Ravensbrück (1939). Once their main purpose of eliminating political enemies had been achieved, the concentration camps took in other opponents of the regime, including the 'workshy', Gypsies, Jews, homosexuals and Jehovah's Witnesses. Additionally, the concentration camp system took in the 'asocial' and 'undesirable' individuals considered by the Nazis to be unproductive and 'inferior'.

The concentration camp represented a closed universe, whose boundaries could not be crossed. On arrival, inmates were processed in a humiliating, brutal ritual that instantly devalued their past and removed their social identities. This process was designed to strip them of their personal and moral integrity.[29] The violence and terror that prisoners experienced on their arrival was not a temporary state of affairs but a signal of the continued threat to their lives. Prisoners were forced to undress and give up their belongings. All their head, face and body hair was closely shaven. They were given camp uniforms to wear. These were distributed randomly so that they inevitably did not fit. The uniforms were intended to efface any individuality from the prisoners: 'Differences in external appearance were completely levelled and erased. The prisoners were hardly able to recognise themselves. Yet because all looked the same, each became the image of everyone else.'[30] To remove the very last traces of individuality, the prisoners were then assigned a number. This signified the transformation from a personal society into a nameless one. This transition from the world outside to the world of the concentration camp was forced upon the prisoners abruptly, not gradually. It was designed to shock, humiliate and overwhelm them.

Notions of space and time took on completely different forms in the concentration camps. Social and power structures were unfamiliar. Inmates were trapped in a system of terror at the mercy of their captors and guards. Life in the concentration camps was characterised by the extreme and arbitrary violence of the SS guards, as well as desperately poor living conditions. Disease was rife and food rations were completely inadequate. The prisoners were forced to carry out hard labour. A decree of December 1937 designated the concentration camps as 'state correction and labour camps'. Thereafter, the SS systematically exploited the forced labour of camp prisoners for lucrative economic enterprises, setting up the German Excavation and Quarrying Company Limited to monitor production and distribution.[31] As well as for the coffers of the SS, concentration camp prisoners were exploited as labourers for private companies including Heinkel, IG Farben, Siemens, Volkswagen, Daimler-Benz and BMW.[32] Forced labour became one of the main features of concentration camp life. The workers were kept in line by means of harsh discipline and arbitrary punishments and torture. Punishments included being forced to stand for long periods of time in the roll-call areas, often after a day of exhausting labour, whippings and beatings, 'fatigue drill' and the death penalty. The SS enacted harsh reprisal measures against camp inmates for transgressions of the camp rules or attempted escapes. The culmination of the forced labour policy was 'annihilation through labour'. Many prisoners died from exhaustion, clearing the Dachau marshes or quarrying stone at Flossenbürg.

After the outbreak of the war, conditions in the camps deteriorated sharply and the population changed. Daily routines became more rigid, food rations more limited, detentions intensified and roll-call times extended. Epidemics and starvation caused mortality rates to rise. Death rates soared during the first winter of the war, to unprecedented levels. The percentage of German prisoners in the camps decreased as the camps filled with foreign prisoners from the Nazi-occupied lands. During the war, German prisoners constituted only 5–10 per cent of the total prisoner population. Flossenbürg, for example, which had been set up in 1938 as a camp for 'asocial' and other non-political German prisoners, had a pre-war camp population of approximately 1500 inmates. By 1945, it held 52,000 prisoners, of which the largest contingents were Poles and Soviets.[33] Flossenbürg grew so much during the war that by 1945 it had 92 sub-camps linked to the main camp.

As the war progressed, the camp system expanded into the territories occupied by the Third Reich, in both western and eastern Europe. There were 23 main concentration camps, with approximately 1300 sub-camps of different sizes.[34] Apart from the concentration camps, the Nazi camp system also included thousands of camps for forced Jewish and foreign labourers, camps for prisoners of war, transit camps, collection camps and 'educative work camps', designed to 'cure' unproductive and idle workers.[35] In Poland, the Nazis established the extermination camps at Chelmno, Belzec, Sobibor, Treblinka, Majdanek and Auschwitz, in order to implement the 'Final Solution'.[36] Chelmno, Belzec, Sobibor and Treblinka were death factories, whose sole function was the destruction of the Jews. Majdanek and Auschwitz were dual-purpose camps – they were simultaneously concentration camps and extermination camps.

LEGAL AND PRISON SYSTEM

While the SS-SD-police complex and concentration camp system under Himmler functioned as an autonomous apparatus of repression, it is important to note that the traditional legal system and prison system continued to operate at the same time. Nikolaus Wachsmann has noted that the Nazis' continuation of the legal system it inherited was a way of keeping the support of many Germans who championed the appearance and maintenance of law and order in their society. Although Hitler and other Nazi leaders held the legal system in low esteem, considering it to be too bureaucratic and slow, the legal apparatus continued throughout the Nazi era and played an integral part in Nazi terror. Wachsmann argues that 'had the Nazi regime relied solely on the police and concentration camps, it would have destroyed the semblance of the rule of law vital for its popular support. Instead, the continued operation of the legal bureaucracy helped to mask the terrorist nature of the Nazi regime.'[37] The legal system with its prisons and penitentiaries not only furnished the Nazi regime with a veneer of legality but also played a real part in both the criminalisation of political dissent and the politicisation of common crime. Judges, prosecutors and prison officials all played a significant role in the implementation of terror in Nazi Germany. Many of them continued in their service from the Weimar era and were not ardent Nazis, but this did not preclude their eagerness to punish Communists, Jews or social outsiders. Hence, they remained in their roles after 1933 and played an important part in the Nazi terror apparatus. The national-conservative Franz Gürtner, for example, continued in his role as Minister of Justice from the Weimar era. The majority of judges and prosecutors broadly supported the new Nazi regime. During the period of *Gleichschaltung*, legal officials dissolved their professional organisations and joined the Association of National Socialist German Jurists.

Demands for the harsher treatment of prisoners and for special policies towards 'incorrigible' criminals that had been raised during the Depression years provided an important legacy for the Nazi legal and prison systems. The legal authorities quickly accepted the will of the *Führer* and became accustomed to 'bending the law' as the wishes of the political leadership took precedence over legal principles. Special courts were established on 21 March 1933 aimed at executing 'summary justice' or 'swift justice'. They cracked down on the political enemies of the regime. Cases of treason and high treason were dealt with by the *Volksgerichtshof* (People's Court), which was set up in April 1934. Otto-Georg Thierack presided over the court between 1936 and 1942, followed by Roland Freisler. The People's Court proved to be an effective weapon against resistance. It tried approximately 3000 people, mainly German nationals, between 1934 and 1939.[38] Most of these were convicted for their political opposition, particularly communism, and received harsh penitentiary sentences of six years on average.

While some historians have suggested that the Third Reich comprised a dual state, with the legal system and the police apparatus existing as two separate entities with opposing agendas, Wachsmann suggests that this concept obscures the high level of co-operation between them.[39] Rather, he argues that they were 'separate yet enmeshed agencies of repression that served the same regime'.[40] Despite conflicts between the two agencies and differences in their approaches, they pursued a broadly similar objective, namely the incarceration or removal of those sectors of the population that were excluded from the 'national community', including Jews, Gypsies, political opponents of the regime, Jehovah's Witnesses, homosexuals, 'asocials' and 'dangerous habitual criminals'.

A new Law against Dangerous Habitual Criminals was passed on 24

November 1933. This law introduced significantly harsher punishments for repeat offenders, including the castration of certain categories of criminals. Furthermore, it gave the courts wide-ranging new powers of indefinite detention. Judges could place 'dangerous habitual criminals' in indefinite security confinement if they deemed it 'in the interests of public safety' to do so. Security confinement usually followed a custodial sentence in a prison or penitentiary. Hence, 'dangerous habitual criminals' were punished twice by the courts – first in prison, then in security confinement. The security confinement institutions were run by the legal system, not by the police or the SS. At first, special wards of existing penal institutions were used for security confinement, but in December 1936, Gürtner restructured the system due to the increasing number of prisoners. Three penal institutions, Gräfentonna, Rendsburg and Werl, were used exclusively for security confinement. By January 1939, there were 4326 inmates in security confinement. The overwhelming majority of them were sentenced for fraud or theft, while only a small percentage had been sentenced for violent or sexual crimes.[41]

It is only recently that the role of Hitler's prisons has been examined. Historians have been mainly concerned with investigating the role of the concentration camps, yet prisons, prison camps and penitentiaries held more inmates than the concentration camps, particularly during the pre-war years. For example, in 1936, the concentration camps held 5,000 inmates, while the prisons and penitentiaries held 120,000 inmates. Hence, prisons played a significant role in Nazi terror. Hunger, overcrowding and serious epidemics were all features of the German prisons and conditions within them deteriorated during the course of the Nazi era.

Legal terror was stepped up as the war progressed. One indication of the extent of the radicalisation of the justice system during the war was the increased use of the death penalty. In 1939, there were three offences punishable by death; by 1945, there were at least 46.[42] In August 1942, Thierack became the Minister of Justice and constantly called for stricter punishments. The number of death penalties soared and the number of Germans accused of serious political crimes also escalated during the last years of the war. In January 1943, as popular morale waned, the People's Court was authorised to punish the offence of 'undermining the war effort'. Making 'defeatist comments' accounted for the prosecution of the largest group of offenders of German nationality. The judges became increasingly severe towards the end of the war. In 1944 alone, the People's Court sentenced 2,097 people to death.[43] In addition to this, military courts handed out the death penalty with increasing frequency throughout the wartime period. As Wachsmann has pointed out: 'In the last year of war, around half of the convicted defendants were sentenced to death, often for no more than a single unguarded remark.'[44] The remainder received a penitentiary sentence of at least five years.

On 15 February 1945, Thierack announced the establishment of civilian drumhead courts, on Hitler's orders.[45] These courts, chaired by a judge and two assessors – a Nazi party official and an officer from the army, the police or the *Waffen-SS* – were authorised to sentence to death anyone who avoided 'duties to the community'. Martin Bormann described these courts as 'a weapon for the annihilation of all parasites of the people'.[46] In addition, during the last months of the war, the mass execution of thousands of prisoners was carried out across the land.

Coercion, terror and surveillance formed an integral part of the functioning of the Nazi dictatorship, underpinning the regime's endeavours to manufacture popular consensus. While the first six months of Nazi rule were characterised by widespread violence, after that the Nazi terror apparatus was not directed against the majority of the German population, despite the reputation of the omniscient Gestapo. Most of its efforts were targeted at political opponents, Jews, Gypsies, Jehovah's Witnesses, homosexuals, 'asocials' and 'dangerous habitual criminals'. Indeed, the Nazi regime made no secret of its use of terror and repressive policies towards such 'enemies' and 'community aliens'. It utilised both the existing legal and penal apparatus and its own enhanced SS-SD-police complex, whose power resided with Himmler, to implement these policies. From the outside, there was a blurring of the distinctions between the two systems, as both pursued the broadly similar aim of incarcerating or removing those sectors of the population that were excluded from the 'national community'. The concentration camps lay at the heart of the Nazi system of terror and were its hallmark.

NOTES

1 On this, see P. Merkl, *Political Violence under the Swastika: 581 Early Nazis* (Princeton, 1975); P. Merkl, *The Making of a Stormtrooper* (Princeton, 1980); R. Bessel, *Political Violence and the Rise of Nazism* (London, 1984).

2 N. Gregor, 'Nazism – a Political Religion? Rethinking the Voluntarist Turn', in N. Gregor (ed.), *Nazism, War and Genocide* (Exeter, 2005), p. 19.

3 R. Evans, *The Third Reich in Power* (London, 2006), p. 113.

4 Ibid., p. 21.

5 On the SA, see C. Fischer, *Stormtroopers: A Social, Economic and Ideological Analysis, 1919–1935* (London, 1983); P. Longerich, *Die braunen Bataillone. Geschichte der SA* (Munich, 1989).

6 R. Evans, *The Coming of the Third Reich* (London, 2004), pp. 380–1.

7 J. Caplan, 'Political Detention and the Origin of the Concentration Camps in Nazi Germany, 1933–1935/6', in Gregor (ed.), *Nazism, War and Genocide*, p. 28.

8 See G. Browder, *Foundations of the Nazi Police State: The Formation of the Sipo and SD* (Lexington, 1990).

9 P. Ayçoberry, *The Social History of the Third Reich, 1933–1945* (New York, 1999), p. 62.

10 On Himmler, see P. Padfield, *Himmler: Reichsführer-SS* (London, 1991).

11 On the RSHA, see M. Wildt, *Generation des Unbedingten. Das Führungskorps des Reichssicherheitshauptamtes* (Hamburg, 2002).

12 R. Gellately, *Backing Hitler: Consent and Coercion in Nazi Germany* (Oxford, 2001).

13 On the police and society, see P. Wagner, *Volksgemeinschaft ohne Verbrecher. Konzeption und Praxis der Kriminalpolizei der Weimarer Republik und des Nationalsozialismus* (Hamburg, 1996). See also P. Wagner, *Hitlers Kriminalisten. Die deutsche Kriminalpolizei und der Nationalsozialismus* (Munich, 2002).

14 Gellately, *Backing Hitler*, p. 50.

15 Ibid., p. 3.

16 K.-M. Mallmann and G. Paul, 'Omniscient, Omnipotent, Omnipresent? Gestapo, society and resistance', in D. Crew (ed.), *Nazism and German Society* (London, 1994), pp. 166–96. See also G. Paul and K.-M. Mallmann (eds), *Die Gestapo. Mythos und Realität* (Darmstadt, 1995).

17 R. Gellately, *The Gestapo and German Society: Enforcing Racial Policy, 1933–1945* (Oxford, 1990), p. 254.

18 Ayçoberry, *The Social History of the Third Reich, 1933–1945*, p. 31.

19 Gellately, *The Gestapo and German Society*, p. 258.

20 Ibid., p. 75.

21 Gellately, *Backing Hitler*, p. 193.

22 Ibid., p. 194.

23 Gellately, *The Gestapo and German Society*, p. 257.

24 V. Joshi, *Gender and Power in the Third Reich: Female Denouncers and the Gestapo, 1933–1945* (London, 2003), p. 197. See also V. Joshi, 'The Private Became Public: Wives as Denouncers in the Third Reich', *Journal of Contemporary History*, Vol. 37, No. 3 (2002), pp. 419–35.

25 On the development of the historiography on the concentration camps, see N. Wachsmann, 'Looking into the Abyss: Historians and the Nazi Concentration Camps', *European History Quarterly*, Vol. 36, No. 2 (2006), pp. 247–78.

26 E. Kogon, *The Theory and Practice of Hell* (London, 1950), p. 30.

27 Ibid., p. 32.

28 M. Burleigh and W. Wippermann, *The Racial State: Germany 1933–1945* (Cambridge, 1991), p. 62.

29 W. Sofsky, *The Order of Terror: The Concentration Camp* (Princeton, 1997), p. 82.

30 Ibid., p. 84.

31 See J. Schulte, *Zwangsarbeit und Vernichtung. Das Wirtschaftsimperium der SS* (Paderborn, 2001); M. Allen, *The Business of Genocide: the SS, Slave Labour, and the Concentration Camps* (Chapel Hill and London, 2002).

32 On this, see Gellately, *Backing Hitler*, pp. 213–17.

33 Ibid., p. 68.

34 Sofsky, *The Order of Terror*, p. 12.

35 See K. Orth, *Das System der nationalsozialistichen Konzentrationslager. Eine politische Organisationsgeschichte* (Hamburg, 1999) and U. Herbert, *Die nationalsozialistiche Konzentrationslager. Entwicklung und Struktur* (Göttingen, 1998).

36 On Auschwitz, see S. Steinbacher, *'Musterstadt' Auschwitz. Germanisierungspolitik und Judenmord in Ostoberschlesien* (Munich, 2000) and S. Steinbacher, *Auschwitz. A History* (London, 2005). On the Operation Reinhard death camps, see Y. Arad, *Belzec, Sobibor and Treblinka: The Operation Reinhard Death Camps* (Bloomington, 1999).

37 N. Wachsmann, *Hitler's Prisons: Legal Terror in Nazi Germany* (New Haven and London, 2004), p. 373.

38 Ibid., p. 117.

39 The concept of the 'dual state' was first proposed by Ernst Fraenkel. He drew a distinction between the 'normative state', centred around formal institutions and bound by the rule of law, and the 'prerogative state', whose authority was derived directly from Hitler. E. Fraenkel, *The Dual State: Law and Justice in National Socialism* (New York, 1941).

40 Wachsmann, *Hitler's Prisons*, p. 380.

41 Ibid., pp. 132–3.

42 Gellately, *Backing Hitler*, p. 86.

43 Ibid.
44 Wachsmann, *Hitler's Prisons*, p. 222.
45 Gellately, *Backing Hitler*, p. 230.
46 Wachsmann, *Hitler's Prisons*, p. 323.

3

EDUCATION

Adolf Hitler School pupils. © Ullstein-bild/akg-images

Education in Nazi Germany was fundamental to the shaping and forging of identity, self-perception and the perception of 'others'. This was closely linked with the issue of inclusion in or exclusion from the 'national community'. Education for the *Volk* produced a new national awareness.[1] Individuals were regarded as part of the total organism of the *Volk*. They functioned as members of the 'national community' and as guarantors of its strength and future. National Socialist education consciously donned an irrational character, based more on the power of suggestion than the power of reason. It conceived everyday life as a perpetual struggle for the national cause and against the 'enemies of the state' – especially Jews and Bolsheviks, but also other groups considered to be 'alien' or 'inferior'. The process of shaping the minds of the future generation was crucial to the success of the Nazi regime. This chapter explores the impact of the Nazi 'seizure of power' on education.[2] It considers Hitler's views on education and the role of the National Socialist Teachers' League. It examines education policy and changes to the curriculum under Nazism. It provides a short analysis of the Nazi elite schools as part of the regime's quest to train a 'new aristocracy' for the Third Reich. Lastly, it considers the impact of the Nazi regime on German universities.

The Nazi regime aimed at a 'total' education of youth that corresponded to Hitler's fundamental ideas on education. In *Mein Kampf*, Hitler had stated that education and training had to give German youth the conviction of absolute superiority to others. Above all, in the Nazi state: 'No boy and no girl must leave school without having been led to an ultimate realisation of the necessity and essence of blood purity.'[3] Hitler had strong opinions about the role of the state in education and was keen to remove the function of socialisation from the family and to place it instead within the realms of the schools and youth groups. He was also contemptuous of intellectual endeavour. Self-confidence and national pride were to be inculcated in German youth, instead of 'scholastic slime'. Hitler thus placed great emphasis upon the importance of physical training. The purpose of Nazi education was to fulfil 'the aims and plans of the *Führer*'.[4] Schools became a tool of politics under National Socialism.

Jewish and 'unreliable' teachers were purged from the profession within a few months of the Nazi 'seizure of power'. Hanna Bergas, a Jewish teacher, recalled her great pain at losing her job and her profession in April 1933: 'When I arrived at the school building … the principal asked me to come to his room … When we were seated, he said, in a serious, embarrassed tone of voice, he had orders to ask me not to go into my classroom. I was not permitted to teach anymore at a German school … In the afternoon … colleagues, pupils, their mothers came, some in a sad mood, others angry with their country, lovely bouquets of flowers, large and small in their arms. In the evening, the little house was full of fragrance and colours, like for a funeral, I thought; and indeed, this was the funeral of my time teaching at a German public school.'[5]

The *NS-Lehrerbund* (NSLB) or National Socialist Teachers' League had been established in 1929. The majority of its members were radicalised young teachers in their twenties and thirties who were estranged from the profession's associational life and ethos, although the Nazis also recruited older teachers. Marjorie Lamberti notes that 'enthusiasm for National Socialism among the students training for the profession in the early 1930s was especially striking'.[6] The NSLB capitalised on tensions between the generations and targeted these young teachers. It promised to raise their morale and their self-image. Membership grew from 5000 in April 1932 to 11,000 in January 1933.[7] The NSLB played an important role in the regime's initial process of *Gleichschaltung* (streamlining) to homogenise the teaching profession. Those who flocked to join the NSLB after the Nazi takeover of power were mainly opportunists, motivated by career advancement or the fear of losing their posts. By 1937, the NSLB comprised 320,000 teachers (97 per cent of all teachers). Similarly to other Nazi organisations, it grew through a mixture of opportunism and careerism on the part of individuals and propaganda and intimidation on the part of the state. The NSLB, led first by Hans Schemm and then by Fritz Waechtler, had two main functions. The first was to provide reports on the political reliability of teachers for appointments and promotions. The second was to ensure the ideological indoctrination of teachers. The organisation intended to create 'the new German educator in the spirit of

National Socialism'. It ran courses for teachers and set up special teacher training camps. By 1939, two-thirds of the teaching profession had attended these camps, whose fundamental objective was to imbue the participants with the Nazi *Weltanschauung* (worldview). The courses of instruction included compulsory physical training for those teachers under the age of 50. The camps were also intended to create a sense of unity and uniformity among teachers and to remove barriers between them, such as status. In addition, the NSLB held conferences and channelled official guidelines on education to teachers throughout the 1930s. The NSLB played a significant role in the Third Reich, as the regime required ideologically informed teachers in order to educate German children with its values.

In many ways, the Nazi regime built upon existing foundations in education policy, often adding a more radical slant or direction to policy. While the Ministry of Education stood at the centre of policy-making, it is important to understand that the primacy of Bernhard Rust's position as Minister of Education was not unchallenged by other individuals and agencies. As in other areas of Nazi policy-making, with no clear policy guidelines from Hitler, different individuals tried to take the initiative. This made it difficult for Rust to maintain control over education policy. He encountered intervention and challenges to his authority from other Nazi leaders, especially Baldur von Schirach, Martin Bormann, Robert Ley, Alfred Rosenberg, Philipp Bouhler, Heinrich Himmler and Josef Goebbels.

The major changes to the education system initiated by the Nazi government included the reorganisation of the secondary school system and the introduction of separate education for girls and boys through a reform of 20 March 1937. Boys were able to take their school-leaving certificate in modern languages, science or classics, but girls had only two options, modern languages or home economics (known as the 'pudding matric'). Girls who opted for the latter were not qualified to enter university. The number of women attending universities declined during the mid-1930s, partly in response to Nazi educational imperatives, but during the war there was a substantial increase in the number of female university enrolments as young men were drafted into military service and women filled university places.[8] The proportion of female students at German universities reached 20 per cent in September 1939, rising to 30 per cent a year later and 49.5 per cent in 1943–1944.[9]

The Nazi regime abolished public confessional or denominational schools and placed restrictions on private schools, including the abolition of private preparatory schools. These policies were carried out with the claim of 'modernising' the education system and making it more efficient and effective. However, the true aim of such policies was to ensure centralised state control over education, for example to eliminate ecclesiastical influences. At first, many teachers favoured the new Nazi government, impressed by its pledges to pursue effective educational policies and to improve the status and training of elementary school teachers. But in the end, teachers became one of the most disillusioned groups, as these promises were not kept. The rhetoric of the NSLB and the regime was empty. Education policy was underpinned by the desire to disseminate Nazi ideology as widely as possible and in this context, other educational aims were subordinated.

In 1933, Rust declared that the purpose of school textbooks was to achieve 'the ideological education of young German people'. Strict censorship was imposed upon the publishers of textbooks. This was the particular responsibility of Philipp Bouhler, the director of the National Socialist Party's Censorship Office, working in conjunction with Rust. However, such was the extent and complexity of the task that for the first four years of Nazi rule, control was sporadic. Many textbooks of the Weimar era were reprinted with only slight amendments, such as the insertion of photographs of Hitler, swastika flags and Nazi slogans. By the late 1930s, as new writing and illustrations became available in greater quantities, the older textbooks were removed from circulation and replaced with new, standardised textbooks that incorporated the central tenets of Nazi ideology. These were written by authors approved by the Ministry of Education. Gradually, blacklisted works were removed and 'whitelisted' works were put in their place. However, the Nazi censorship of school textbooks and children's literature was imperfect. Numerous loopholes in the regulations prevented total control and furthermore the regime had no effective way of regulating what children were reading at home.[10]

The Nazi regime utilised school textbooks and classroom practice to spread its *Weltanschauung*. Many subjects within the school curriculum were used to expound Nazi ideology, most notably biology, geography, history, arithmetic and German. Biology acquired an enhanced importance under National Socialism. Biology lessons became vehicles for Nazi racial doctrine, emphasising subjects such as heredity and the 'selection of the fittest'. An emphasis was placed upon 'the holistic organicist approach', which served to demonstrate the significance of the laws of nature and their application to man and the state.[11] Biology classes were also used to enhance children's comprehension of Nazi population policy. A new branch of physics teaching under National Socialism, 'the physics of weapons', was designed to awaken the ability, will and technical means to bear arms. Geography teaching was expanded to include and indeed even to justify *Lebensraum* and racial expansion. Geography educators also exploited traditional and new forms of anti-Semitism in their publications. For example, the image of the eternally wandering Jew was a favourite theme. Walter Jantzen was one of the most prominent geography educators in the Third Reich. In his book *Geography in the Service of National Political Education* (1936), he integrated Nazi ideology into the geography curriculum, particularly racial concerns about Jews, Blacks and Gypsies, but also issues of 'living space', 'blood and soil' and the decline in the birth rate since the end of the First World War. In the geography textbook *Germany as a Whole* (1938), Konrad Olbricht and Hermann Kärgel highlighted the ideological distinctions between National Socialism and 'Jewish Bolshevism'.[12]

History lessons were utilised as an opportunity to demonstrate to pupils the greatness of Germany and to inculcate nationalism in children. History was interpreted as a struggle for existence between nations.[13] It was further used to highlight the leadership principle, emphasising the role of Germany's 'great leaders' and their 'world-historical' achievements. Hitler believed that: 'From all the innumerable great names in German history, the greatest must be picked out and introduced to the youth so persistently that they become pillars of an unshakeable national sentiment.'[14] In history textbooks such as *Nation and Leader: German History for Schools* (1943), priority was given to periods when Germany had been a dominant power in Europe and especially to the triumph of Nazism. Defence history and frontier studies were added to the history curriculum.[15] There was a flurry of activity in writing a new history curriculum in the Third Reich. Publishers, teachers, professors and school administrators became involved in this process, sometimes as a way of seeking professional advancement. While the Hitler regime was not the first to use *völkisch* ideas in history instruction, it was, according to Gregory Wegner, 'the first and only regime to fully institutionalise a racist and anti-Semitic history curriculum'.[16]

Arithmetic lessons dealt with 'national political problems'. Calculations of sums were presented in terms of bullet trajectories, aircraft, bombs and so on. Numerical problems based on state expenditure on 'hereditarily ill' and 'inferior' people also exemplified the way in which Nazi ideology pervaded the curriculum. The Nazi regime used arithmetic exercises to convey its racial and political ideas. In a typical exercise, pupils were presented with this information: 'Every day, the state spends RM. 6 on one cripple; RM. $4\frac{1}{4}$ on one mentally-ill person; RM. $5\frac{1}{2}$ on one deaf and dumb person; RM. $5\frac{3}{5}$ on one feeble-minded person; RM. $3\frac{1}{2}$ on one alcoholic; RM. $4\frac{4}{5}$ on one pupil in care; RM. $2\frac{1}{20}$ on one pupil at a special school; and RM. $\frac{9}{20}$ on one pupil at an ordinary school.' They were asked a series of questions relating to this data, such as: 'What total cost do one cripple and one feeble-minded person create, if one takes a lifespan of 45 years for each?' and 'Calculate the expenditure of the state for one pupil in a special school and one pupil in an ordinary school over eight years, and state the amount of higher cost engendered by the special school pupil.'[17] The implications of such questions are self-evident.

Lessons in German were designed to foster a 'consciousness of being German' and to encourage national pride and unity among pupils. Teachers of German language and literature were urged to emphasise the nation as 'a community of blood', 'a community of fate and struggle', 'a community of work' and 'a community of mind'. Traditional German tales and sagas were supplemented with Nazi myths, war stories and *Blut und Boden* ('Blood and Soil') literature. Indeed, as Christa Kamenetsky has pointed out, many classics were adjusted to the requirements of the National Socialist state by means of 'slanted abridgements or reinterpretations', while others that did not fit into the Nazi *Weltanschauung* were banned.[18] National Socialist heroes such as Horst Wessel found their way into school textbooks. Political socialisation in readers took the form of stories about 'helping the *Führer*' and the 'national community', for example by taking part in the regime's *Winterhilfswerk* (Winter Relief Agency) and *Eintopf* ('one-pot dish') campaigns. Such stories were designed to foster a sense of togetherness, unity and belonging to the 'national community'. Examples of the more negative side of political social-isation are found in stories depicting 'the enemies of Germany', in particular Bolsheviks, Slavs and Jews. Such negative stereotypes were used to under-line the differences between 'national comrades', who belonged to the 'national community' and 'community aliens', who did not.

In addition, a new subject, *Rassenkunde* or racial science, formed an integral part of the school curriculum under National Socialism. This was formalised in a Nazi curriculum policy directive from the Ministry of Education on 13 September 1933. Racial science gave instruction about race and heredity, using books such as *The ABC of Race*. 'Aryan' and Jewish 'racial types', often in the form of caricatures, were juxtaposed so that German children would identify with the former and reject the latter as 'enemies'. Anti-Semitic text-books and teachers' manuals were produced by a number of writers, such as Fritz Fink, whose *The Jewish Question in Instruction* (1937) integrated picto-rial distinctions between Jews and 'Aryans' for teachers' use.[19] Fink called for anti-Semitism to pervade the entire curriculum as the most effective way of getting the message across in the classroom and at all age levels. Much use was also made in schools of *Der Stürmer,* a crude anti-Semitic paper published by Julius Streicher, and various publications under its aegis, such as Elvira Bauer's *Trust no Fox on Green Heath! And no Jew on his Oath!* (1936), which depicted vulgar stereotypes of Jews. Ernst Hiemer's *The Poisonous Mushroom* (1938) employed a whole array of anti-Semitic imagery, with caricatures, graphic illustrations and vivid descriptions of Jews as hideous, hook-nosed seducers of 'Aryan' women, Christ-slayers and money-grabbing usurers. Such subject matter brought anti-Semitism very blatantly into the classroom. Jewish children were segregated from the rest of the class and required to sit together in the back row. They were often the targets of racial harassment by both teachers and fellow pupils. On 25 April 1933, the Law against the Overcrowding of German Schools and Universities placed a ceiling of 1.5 per cent as the maximum number of Jewish pupils allowed within any institu-tion.[20] On 15 November 1938, this law was amended to exclude Jewish pupils from the state school system altogether and henceforth they had no choice but to attend separate Jewish schools. They were not part of the 'national community' but regarded as having a separate and inferior identity.

Physical education took on a new significance under National Socialism. Hitler addressed the German youth in Nuremberg on 11 September 1937: 'The youth which today is growing up will be educated not as in the past for enjoyment, but for hardships and for sacrifices, and above all it will be trained to discipline the body.'[21] Hitler overtly scorned intellectualism and believed that physical education was of greater value. Physical education was allocated more slots in the school timetable, largely at the expense of religious education, and more types of physical training were offered than before, including boxing and cross-country running. In addition, pupils had to be able to demonstrate a certain level of physical fitness in order to move from primary to secondary education and from secondary to higher education. Ideal physical attributes and capabilities were also bound up with the positive identity of the 'national comrade'.

In order to achieve its aims of creating a great German nation, the Hitler regime was committed to a policy of elite education that would provide the nation with future leaders.[22] Nazi elite education was designed to shape the destiny of the best and most valuable of the nation's stock. However, elite schools were not an invention of the Nazis. On the contrary, special establishments for elite education had existed in many forms long before the Nazi era, such as boarding schools for young members of the German aristocracy set up in the seventeenth and eighteenth centuries and the military schools set up for officer cadets in late nineteenth-century Prussia. But the Nazis utilised their own version of elite schools for their own ends, for a particular function that was distinctive from previous examples. What differentiated the Nazi elite institutions was a specific understanding of 'elitism' in terms of social Darwinian principles. Hence, the most significant prerequisite of Nazi elitism was 'racial blood purity'. The creation of a new kind of elite identity was based upon race rather than class or social status. The Nazi regime established three different types of educational institutions to train the future elite of German society: the *Nationalpolitische Erziehungsanstalten* (*Napolas*), the Adolf Hitler Schools (AHS) and the *Ordensburgen*.[23] These institutions represented a microcosm of the Nazi *Weltanschauung* by fostering the leadership principle, promoting competitiveness and emphasising life as a struggle and survival of the 'fittest'. They encouraged physical prowess. They excoriated the 'enemies of the Reich' and emphasised racial purity. They glorified war and fostered militarism. They underlined the necessity for *Lebensraum* and had a function in the achievement of a 'greater German empire'.

The Napolas were designed to educate future top-ranking government and army personnel.[24] They were state-run boarding schools under the aegis of the Ministry of Education. They were not affiliated to either the Party or the Hitler Youth. The first three Napolas were established in April 1933 in Plön, Köslin and Potsdam, in former cadet school premises. In 1934, five further Napolas were set up in Berlin-Spandau, Naumberg an der Saale, Ilfeld, Stuhm and Oranienstein. In 1935, another five Napolas were established. They were housed in either renovated or newly constructed buildings that corresponded with Nazi ideals, with exacting standards of hygiene in the living, sleeping and washing areas.[25] Communal rooms were designed to strengthen the sense of spirit and value of the young men. Sports facilities and equipment were comprehensive, including a gymnastics hall, a swimming pool, a boat house and stables.

Admission to the Napolas was very strict. Entrants had to pass a double selection process, consisting of a pre-inspection and an entrance examination.[26] In order to be admitted, a prospective pupil had to be of 'Aryan' descent, a member of the Hitler Youth, physically fit, healthy and sponsored by his *Gauleiter*. A series of endurance tests checked for courage, stamina and physical ability. Once admitted, pupils had a six-month probationary period, during which time they could be expelled from the institution if they failed to meet the expectations demanded of them. The Napolas were 'total institutions', designed to give a complete National Socialist education to their pupils.[27] In addition to the usual school syllabus, there was education in National Socialist principles, as well as a great emphasis upon physical activities, including boxing, war games, shooting, rowing, sailing, riding, gliding and motorcycling. Physical education was considered to be crucial to character formation. Pupils had to undertake 'toughening-up exercises' such as grappling with Alsatian dogs. The Napola pupils spent six to eight weeks on a farm and a further six to eight weeks working in a factory or coalmine as part of their training. The pupils gained an overall education that was designed to prepare them to provide exemplary service to the state and the 'national community'.

The conception and aims of the Napolas changed during the course of the war. They became 'forts of the *Führer* for the protection and strengthening of the Reich' and they came increasingly under the direction of the SS.[28] With the military successes of the Third Reich, there developed a role for the Napolas in securing its racial and ideological goals. Between 1941 and 1944, new Napolas were established across the occupied territories to educate those young people considered to be 'racially valuable'.[29] By 1944, there were 37 Napolas. While they were scarcely able to carry out the new task assigned to them, it is significant to note how different this mission was from the original conception and *raison d'être* of the Napolas.

The Adolf Hitler Schools were established in 1937, under the aegis of Robert Ley and Baldur von Schirach, in order to train future political leaders.[30] The AHS were rival institutions to the Napolas and were conceived of as Party schools. They were designed to educate the youth who would take over and secure National Socialist power in the future by working in the offices of the Party. In total, there were 12 AHS. The AHS provided an opportunity for social advancement, as social class was not a barrier to entry. Furthermore, AHS pupils' families incurred no costs for their education. The AHS admitted pupils who had been pre-selected in the Hitler Youth, but with the additional 'sifting' process of a two-week selection camp and a 'racial examination'. Prospective pupils had to be able to demonstrate a strong character and an instinct to dominate others. The superiority of the 'Aryan' race was emphasised in textbooks provided specially for the AHS.[31] Great importance was placed upon physical education, particularly combat sports such as boxing, wrestling and fencing, as well as pre-military training.

The Ordensburgen (Castles of the Order) were set up in four locations: Crössinsee, Vogelsang, Sonthofen and Marienburg.[32] The buildings were lavish in design and immense in scale. Each school was designed to hold 1000 pupils and 500 staff. Political leaders were to be trained on a four-year programme, one year at each Castle of the Order. The students were told that they were part of a Nordic Crusading Order, similar to that of the Knights Templars. At Crössinsee, students underwent pre-military training, took part in parachute jumping and learned about German history and race. They were trained to view themselves as racially superior, as 'the aristocracy of the earth'. At Vogelsang, they were instilled with bravery and heroism.[33] At Sonthofen, they studied Hitler's *Mein Kampf* and the works of other Nazi ideologues, such as Alfred Rosenberg. Finally, at Marienburg, the students learned about Nazi foreign policy and the need for 'living space'. The four-year programme was designed to equip students for their role as leaders of the Third Reich.[34] However, in reality, the academic standard of education was not particularly high and neither the Ordensburgen nor indeed any of the other Nazi elite schools succeeded in their aspirations to train a new ruling elite.

In the realm of higher education, the Nazi government attempted to clamp down on academic freedom. Its task was made easier by the activities of radical students who had taken over representative student bodies in the majority of German universities 18 months before the Nazi 'seizure of power'. The National Socialist German Students' Association had been formed in 1926, under the leadership of a law student, Wilhelm Tempel. In 1929, Baldur von Schirach had succeeded Tempel as its leader. Schirach claimed that the National Socialist German Students' Association had three main tasks: to promote the study of National Socialist ideas, to spread Nazi ideology in the German universities and to train leaders for the NSDAP. But its true ambition was to control the whole student population.[35] The Association quickly and actively set to work printing and distributing posters and pamphlets. Other student groups and organisations were passive by comparison and responded in a way that suggested they did not realise how serious the Nazi student organisation was about propaganda and power.

Once the Nazis came to power, students campaigned against Jewish and 'unreliable' professors and disrupted their lectures. Students organised and participated in book-burning demonstrations on 10 May 1933 in university towns across Germany. This was a public act 'against the un-German spirit'. Students seized 'un-German' books, including those of Marx and Freud, from the libraries and consigned them to flames, while shouting slogans against their authors. Goebbels described the public book burning as a 'strong, great and symbolic act'. The students were clear about their ideological 'enemies' and the National Socialist German Students' Association planned the event carefully so that the actions of 10 May 1933 were co-ordinated in university towns across the country. The student body certainly recognised its role in the renovation of the scholastic community and participated with eagerness at this time, although, as Geoffrey Giles has pointed out, student apathy was a problem for the Association later on in the Nazi era.[36]

The rectors who ran the universities were checked for reliability and compliance with the dictates of the regime. Those deemed unsuitable were replaced. Jewish and 'liberal' professors were forced out of their posts. Martin Heidegger, Professor of Philosophy, was elected Rector at the University of Freiburg in April 1933. He claimed that academic freedom now meant service to the 'national community' and talked of 'conquering the world of educated men and scholars for the new national political spirit'. Academic autonomy in teaching and research was subordinated to the interests of the Nazi state. By 1934, approximately 1600 out of 5000 university teachers had been dismissed.[37] Many German academics emigrated. The sciences were particularly hard hit. The world-renowned physicist Albert Einstein was among the many scientists who left their posts at German universities to take up positions in America, Britain and elsewhere. Yet the majority of university professors remained in their posts and many were supportive of the National Socialist government. Walter Schultze, leader of the National Socialist German Association of University Lecturers, stated that its main task was 'to make the universities truly National Socialist' and that education needed 'to participate in the National Socialist regeneration of our people's spiritual unity and community'. He continued by claiming: 'The Association takes into its ranks all the forces at a university whose character and ideology attest to their unconditional loyalty and readiness to serve ...', aiming 'to give the mission of the German scholar, researcher and teacher the prestige that is expected by National Socialism in the Party and in the state and, last but not least, by the people united by National Socialism.'[38]

The Nazi education system was closely linked to the ideals of the 'national community'. It emphasised distinctions between belonging and exclusion. The Nazi regime made a number of significant alterations to the education system in order to ensure the primacy of its *Weltanschauung*. Modifications to the curriculum and the introduction of new textbooks were designed to underpin these organisational changes. Racial purity lay at the heart of these moves and Jewish teachers were removed from their posts. The universities were also purged and Jewish or 'unreliable' professors were dismissed. Elite schools formed the hallmark of Nazi changes to education, aimed at creating the future leaders of the Third Reich. The most significant prerequisite of Nazi elitism was 'racial blood purity'. In this sense, Nazi elite educational institutions were unprecedented and unparalleled, but as Koch has pointed out, none of them 'produced an elite that outlived their creators'.[39] They were a part of the wider attempt of the Nazi government at the 'total education' of German youth. Nazi 'total education' was to be achieved not only in the schools but also in the youth organisations, and it is to these that we turn in the next chapter.

NOTES

1 This argument is presented in U. Herrmann, *Die Formung des Volksgenossen: Der 'Erziehungsstaat' des Dritten Reiches* (Weinheim, 1985).

2 On education under the Nazi regime, see U. Herrmann and J. Oelkers, *Pädagogik und Nationalsozialismus* (Weinheim, 1989); R. Dithmar (ed.), *Schule und Unterrichtsfächer im*

Dritten Reich (Neuwied, 1989); R. Eilers, *Die nationalsozialistische Schulpolitik* (Cologne, 1963); K.-I. Flessau, *Schule der Diktatur. Lehrpläne und Schulbücher des Nationalsozialismus* (Munich, 1977): K.-I. Flessau *et al.* (eds), *Erziehung im Nationalsozialismus: '… und sie werden nicht mehr frei ihr ganzes Leben!'* (Cologne, 1987); G. Schwingl, *Die Pervertierung der Schule im Nationalsozialismus: Ein Beitrag zum Begriff 'Totalitäre Erziehung'* (Regensburg, 1993).

3 A. Hitler, *Mein Kampf*, translated by R. Mannheim (London, 1992), p. 389.

4 E. Mann, *School for Barbarians* (New York, 1938), p. 46.

5 Cited in M. Kaplan, *Between Dignity and Despair: Jewish Life in Nazi Germany* (New York and Oxford, 1998), p. 25.

6 M. Lamberti, 'German Schoolteachers, National Socialism and the Politics of Culture at the End of the Weimar Republic', *Central European History*, Vol. 34, No. 1 (2001), p. 63.

7 Ibid., p. 58.

8 J. Pauwels, *Women, Nazis and Universities: Female University Students in the Third Reich, 1933–1945* (Westport, 1984), p. 140.

9 J. Stephenson, *Women in Nazi Germany* (London, 2001), p. 72.

10 On children's literature, see C. Kamenetsky, *Children's Literature in Hitler's Germany: The Cultural Policy of National Socialism* (Athens, Ohio, 1984).

11 Ä. Bäumer-Schleinkofer, *Nazi Biology and Schools* (Frankfurt am Main, 1995), p. 239.

12 G. Wegner, *Anti-Semitism and Schooling under the Third Reich* (New York and London, 2002), p. 153.

13 On this, see G. Blackburn, *Education in the Third Reich: A Study of Race and History in Nazi Textbooks* (Albany, 1985).

14 Hitler, *Mein Kampf*, p. 387.

15 H.-J. Hahn, *Education and Society in Germany* (Oxford, 1998), p. 82.

16 Wegner, *Anti-Semitism and Schooling under the Third Reich*, p. 126.

17 Cited in L. Pine, 'The dissemination of Nazi ideology and family values through school textbooks', *History of Education*, Vol. 25, No. 1 (1996), p. 105.

18 Kamenetsky, *Children's Literature in Hitler's Germany*, p. 149.

19 Wegner, *Anti-Semitism and Schooling under the Third Reich*, pp. 54–5.

20 L. Pine, *Nazi Family Policy, 1933–1945* (Oxford, 1997), p. 158.

21 Cited in N. Baynes (ed.), *The Speeches of Adolf Hitler, April 1922–August 1939* (Oxford, 1942), p. 550.

22 On Nazi elite education, see H. Scholtz, *Nationalsozialistische Ausleseschulen. Internatsschulen als Herrschaftsmittel des Führerstaates* (Göttingen, 1973). See also J. Leeb (ed.), *'Wir waren Hitlers Eliteschüler': Ehemalige Zöglinge der NS-Ausleseschulen brechen ihr Schweigen* (Hamburg, 1998).

23 R. Grunberger, *A Social History of the Third Reich* (London, 1971), p. 376.

24 On the Napolas, see C. Schneider, C. Stillke and B. Leineweber, *Das Erbe der Napola. Versuch einer Generationengeschichte des Nationalsozialismus* (Hamburg, 1996), pp. 33–91.

25 H. Ueberhorst (ed.), *Elite für die Diktatur. Die Nationalpolitischen Erziehungsanstalten 1933–1945. Ein Dokumentarbericht* (Düsseldorf, 1969), p. 64.

26 H. Koch, *The Hitler Youth: Origins and Development 1922–1945* (London, 1975), p. 185.

27 Schneider, Stillke and Leineweber, *Die Erbe der Napola*, p. 48.

28 Ueberhorst (ed.), *Elite für die Diktatur*, p. 93.

29 Koch, *The Hitler Youth*, pp. 192–3.

30 On the Adolf Hitler Schools, see D. Orlow, 'Die Adolf-Hitler-Schulen', *Vierteljahrshefte für Zeitgeschichte*, Vol. 13 (1965), pp. 272–84.

31 Koch, *The Hitler Youth*, p. 197.

32 M. Burleigh and W. Wippermann, *The Racial State: Germany 1933–1945* (Cambridge, 1991), pp. 217–18.

33 On Vogelsang, see H. Arntz, *Ordensburg Vogelsang 1934–1945: Erziehung zur politischen Führung im Dritten Reich* (Euskirchen, 1986).

34 For a more detailed analysis of the Ordensburgen, see H. Scholtz, 'Die "NS-Ordensburgen"', *Vierteljahrshefte für Zeitgeschichte*, Vol. 15 (1967), pp. 269–98.

35 G. Giles, 'The Rise of the National Socialist Students' Association and the Failure of Political Education in the Third Reich', in P. Stachura (ed.), *The Shaping of the Nazi State* (London, 1978), pp. 161–2.

36 G. Giles, *Students and National Socialism in Germany* (Princeton, 1985). On students under National Socialism, see also M. Grüttner, *Studenten im Dritten Reich* (Paderborn, 1995).

37 R. Evans, *The Coming of the Third Reich* (London, 2004), p. 423.

38 Cited in G. Mosse (ed.), *Nazi Culture: Intellectual, Cultural and Social Life in the Third Reich* (London, 1966), pp. 314–15. For a detailed examination of the universities during the Nazi era, see H. Heiber, *Universität unterm Hakenkreuz: Teil 1* (Munich, 1991) and H. Heiber, *Universität unterm Hakenkreuz: Teil 2* (Munich, 1992).

39 Koch, *The Hitler Youth*, p. 203.

4

THE NAZI YOUTH GROUPS: THE HITLER YOUTH AND THE LEAGUE OF GERMAN GIRLS

A column of the 'League of German Girls' on the march in Berlin. © The Wiener Library

In the creation of the 'national community', German youth was extremely important to the National Socialists. Hitler believed that German youth was malleable enough, by and large, to be instilled with the central tenets of Nazi ideology and that it was necessary to turn German young people into committed National Socialists in order to ensure the future of the German Reich. Having swept away the values of the past and been inculcated with the Nazi *Weltanschauung*, contemporary German youth would grow up to become the embodiment of the 'national community' in the future. Ernst Krieck, a leading Nazi education theorist, described the National Socialist youth as the bearer of the principles of the German revolution, out of which would come 'a new nation, a new form of humanity and a new order of living space'.[1] The Nazi youth organisations played an important part in everyday life in the Third Reich. They were designed to weaken traditional social influences and to cement allegiance to the Nazi regime. The Hitler Youth and the League of German Girls competed with schools to influence young people and fostered intergenerational conflicts between parents and children.[2] The aims, training, ethos and norms of the Nazi youth groups demonstrated a desire to form a strong and disciplined youth.[3]

THE HITLER YOUTH

Hitler had called for the creation of a youth movement of the NSDAP as early as 1922. It was to be established within the organisation of the SA. In May 1922, the official foundation of the Youth League of the NSDAP was publicly announced.[4] The earliest National Socialist youth group was organised by Gustav Adolf Lenk, but it had a very short lifespan, surviving until the fiasco of the Munich Beer Hall Putsch in November 1923. A National Socialist youth group was resurrected in 1925 by Kurt Gruber, a law student from Saxony. He introduced a uniform and established an administrative apparatus for his organisation, the Greater German Youth Movement. At first, the organisation attracted mainly working-class youth, but gradually it evolved into the official youth group of the NSDAP and in 1926 it took on the name Hitler Youth. Following a fairly protracted power struggle between Gruber and Baldur von Schirach, who had become prominent in the National Socialist German Students' Association, Hitler appointed Schirach as head of all youth activities for the NSDAP in 1931. On 17 June 1933, Schirach was made Youth Leader of the German Reich, within the Ministry of the Interior, a position he retained until August 1940, when he was replaced by Artur Axmann.[5]

At the end of 1932, the Hitler Youth had a comparatively small membership of 107,956.[6] Some 5–6 million young Germans belonged to an assortment of youth groups.[7] Many were part of the *bündisch* or free youth movement. These young people followed in the footsteps of the earlier *Wandervögel* of the Wilhelmine period, with an ethos of independence and freedom. The *bündisch* youth groups despised the traditional mores of the older generation. They also rejected the Weimar system and everything it represented. They developed a sense of youth camaraderie through hiking, camping and singing folk songs. Other young people belonged to denominational youth groups affiliated to the Protestant or Catholic churches, to sporting groups or to youth groups attached to other political parties.

Schirach's main objective in 1933 was to build a state youth organisation and to try to consolidate all of Germany's youth into the Hitler Youth. At first, the Hitler Youth appeared attractive and exciting. It presented young boys and teenagers with the opportunity to take part in a new movement, to escape from parental control and boredom at home. It offered them a sense of purpose, belonging and unity. The Hitler Youth also gave a new opportunity for participation in youth activities to some young people, particularly in rural areas, who had not previously had access to youth movements. By the end of 1933, the Hitler Youth had more than 2 million members. While part of the explanation for this rapid growth of the movement was its attraction to youth after the Nazi 'seizure of power', a large part of the reason was the process of *Gleichschaltung* ('co-ordination') of youth by the Nazi regime. The Communist Youth Association of Germany (KJVD), the Social Democratic Socialist Working Youth (SAJ) and the German Socialist Youth Association (SAP) had been dissolved and other groups, such as the Protestant youth organisations, had merged with the Hitler Youth in December 1933. The autonomy of the Catholic youth groups was temporarily protected (until 1936) by the Concordat between Hitler and the Pope. In 1936, the Gestapo banned any remaining youth groups outside the Hitler Youth. By the end of 1936, the Hitler Youth had 5.4 million members.

On 1 December 1936, the Law on the Hitler Youth stated that: 'The future of the German nation depends upon its youth and German youth must therefore be prepared for its future duties.' It decreed that:

1. The whole of German youth within the borders of the Reich is organised in the Hitler Youth.
2. All German young people, apart from being educated at home and at school, will be educated in the Hitler Youth physically, intellectually, and morally in the spirit of National Socialism to serve the nation and the community.
3. The task of educating German youth in the Hitler Youth is being entrusted to the Reich Leader of German Youth in the NSDAP. He therefore becomes the 'Youth Leader of the German Reich'. His office shall rank as Supreme Governmental Agency with its headquarters in Berlin and he will be directly responsible to the Führer and Chancellor of the Reich.
4. All regulations necessary to execute and supplement this decree will be issued by the Führer and Reich Chancellor.[8]

This law, which made Schirach directly responsible to Hitler as 'Youth Leader of the German Reich', meant that he was no longer constrained by the authority of the Ministry of the Interior. The Hitler Youth Law was also significant because it officially and legally gave the Hitler Youth an equal status to the home and the school in educating German children. However, in spite of its first provision, membership was not yet compulsory. Nevertheless, there was much social pressure to join after 1936.

On 25 March 1939, a further Youth Ordinance decreed that: 'All young people are obliged from the age of 10 to their 19th birthday to serve in the Hitler Youth.' Boys aged 10–14 were to join the *Deutsches Jungvolk* (DJ), while boys from 14–18 were to join the Hitler Youth. German girls were to join the corresponding Nazi girls' organisations, the *Jungmädelschaft* (JM) for girls aged 10–14 and the *Bund deutscher Mädel* (BDM) for girls aged 14–18, which are examined later in the chapter. It was the responsibility of the parent or legal guardian to register the children or young people into the Hitler Youth and they could be fined or imprisoned for deliberate failure to do so. Furthermore, the decree stated that: 'Anyone who maliciously prevents or attempts to prevent any young person from serving in the Hitler Youth will be punished by fine or imprisonment.'[9] The Hitler Youth members were obliged to swear an oath of loyalty to Hitler.

By the time membership became compulsory in 1939, the Hitler Youth had lost some of its original appeal. It was becoming an instrument of authoritarianism and indoctrination. The initial enticement of the slogan 'youth leads youth' wore off and the popular hikes were replaced with harder training. There were also increasing duties, including collecting money for the Winter Relief Agency and picking berries and herbs. Land Service involved Hitler Youth members in helping with harvesting, milking cows and chopping wood. This was aimed at emphasising the 'blood and soil' doctrine and at providing experience of life in the countryside to young people from the cities. It fitted in with the Nazi view of the cities as asphalt jungles, which engendered an unwholesome lifestyle. A Hitler Youth circular dated 8 January 1940 stated: 'Land Service is a political task of National Socialism. Its purpose is to bring back boys and girls from the cities to the land, to create new recruits for the agricultural occupations and thus secure their continuous existence. The best of them should be given an opportunity to settle. The Hitler Youth is the sole executor of the Land Service.'[10] From February 1940, Hitler Youth members had to report for duty on two Sundays each month. Some young people came to see the Hitler Youth as a restriction on the freedom of their leisure time, as it took up more and more of their waking hours outside school. State control had replaced parental control. Parents, too, expressed concern about the amount of time their children were spending on Hitler Youth activities.

Yet, as Michael Kater points out, even after membership became compulsory, 'too many teenagers came and went or did not enrol at all'.[11] Some disliked the monotony of the drills and routine, others were individualistic enough to reject the norms of the organisation as a whole. Many cliques and bands of youth sprang up across the Reich.[12] The Hitler Youth *Streifendienst* had been established in July 1934 to police German youth. Its original function was to combat crime, delinquency and undisciplined behaviour within the Hitler Youth. By 1937, however, the remit of the *Streifendienst* had been extended to dealing with former Hitler Youth members who had left the organisation and members of the numerous cliques and bands of youth outside the Hitler Youth. In 1940, a new type of Youth Arrest was instigated. Young offenders could be placed in solitary confinement for a period of up to four weeks with just bread and water to sustain them. As the war progressed, rebellious youths were also placed in youth protection camps, such as Moringen, and in concentration camps.[13]

Kater has shown that the Hitler Youth 'was not always an expression of monolithic cohesiveness'.[14] Inadequate training and leadership structure gave way to much incompetence, abuse and corruption on the part of the youth leaders. Schirach and Axmann tried to limit incompetence and abuse by establishing leadership courses and sessions for Hitler Youth leaders, such as the Academy for Youth Leadership in Brunswick. But these types of problems remained and indeed were exacerbated when older leaders were conscripted for military service. By 1940, 25 per cent of all Hitler Youth leaders were at the front and by 1944, boys in their mid-teens were being commanded by boys of the same age.

During the war, Hitler Youth members served in auxiliary positions on the home front. They made door-to-door collections of paper, cloth and scrap metal for the war effort and foraged for medicinal herbs and mushrooms. They also worked as air raid wardens and firefighters. As the war progressed, their obligations increased, not just on the home front. Hitler Youth members were sent to the newly conquered Polish territories to re-educate the *Volksdeutsche* (ethnic Germans) who lived on the land there. At first, this was a voluntary service. Tens of thousands of young Germans went to the border-lands where they both taught proper German to the *Volksdeutsche* and worked in the farms and fields. By 1942, it became compulsory for Hitler Youth members to serve for a six-week period in this duty.

The Hitler Youth socialised German youth in militarisation and the ultimate aim of acquiring new *Lebensraum* in the east. They played war games, studying maps and spotting enemies. They learned how to master their terrain, as well as orientation skills in darkness. They camped in tents, sang *völkisch* songs, marched and engaged in rifle practice. Boys aged 10 to 18 were taught how to shoot as part of their pre-military training, which also consisted of sports, including boxing, strenuous hikes, marches and drills. These activities prepared them for active combat in the field once the war began. In addition to their physical training, Hitler Youth members were inculcated with a militaristic spirit during their evening sessions. Topics included great soldiers of Germany's past and the war itself. These sessions were supplemented with films and pamphlets. In addition, soldiers visited the Hitler Youth groups, telling them about their experiences at the front.

Most Hitler Youth members joined the *Wehrmacht* feeling optimistic that Germany would achieve a speedy victory and with a determination to defeat their 'inferior' enemies. They were convinced of their own superiority. Once serious setbacks and defeats occurred, however, these feelings changed to disillusionment.[15] Young soldiers were also frustrated by the duplication of their Hitler Youth drills and training when they entered the *Wehrmacht*. Physical injuries, fatalities and inadequate food provision, as well as psychological scarring, all had a damaging impact on morale. The young soldiers began to question the Nazi stereotype of the cowardly, 'subhuman' 'swamp Russian' once they encountered their Soviet counterparts. Difficulties faced by young soldiers even before Stalingrad led them to doubt their own function and to question the regime. Deserters experienced the SS's 'emergency justice' in the form of summary executions and hangings.

Between 1943 and 1945, 200,000 teenagers served as canoneers to destroy enemy planes.[16] The anti-aircraft artillery training lasted just four weeks. After that, the flak helpers (as young as 15) experienced active combat, at first in their own localities but then in destinations far from their homes. Obliged to work during the night, as well as during the day, they were both deprived of sleep, and terrified. Casualties were heavy. It was also a difficult experience for them in terms of their identity and status. These young people saw themselves as outgrowing the Hitler Youth and parental control, yet they were not accepted as 'soldiers'.[17] In the last months of the war, the Hitler Youth formed anti-tank brigades against the Soviet advance and made up units to secure strategic bridges. Hitler's youth was required to take its part in the struggle – in the face of death – until the end of the war.

THE LEAGUE OF GERMAN GIRLS (BDM)

The BDM emerged in 1930 after a number of attempts to set up a youth group for girls within the Nazi movement had failed. Prior to the Nazi 'seizure of power', the BDM was just one of many youth groups for girls in Germany. After Hitler came to power, the BDM rose to a much more significant position. This was partly the result of the process of *Gleichschaltung*, by which other girls' groups were dissolved, and partly due to the desire of girls who had never been in a youth organisation before to take part in the National Socialist movement. Both of these factors led to a substantial increase in the membership of the BDM after 1933. Many girls were attracted to the BDM because it gave them the opportunity to be more independent of their parents, go on trips and take part in group activities. Others joined because they wanted to feel important and not to be excluded from the world of adults. Entry into the BDM allowed girls to escape from their tedious home lives, where they were usually under the constant scrutiny of their parents.

Girls from middle-class families, in particular, eagerly seized upon the opportunities offered to them by the BDM. In the aftermath of the Wall Street Crash, shattered prestige and finances were strongly felt by all members of middle-class households. Indeed, some girls joined the BDM as a sign of their rebellion against the authority of their parents. The BDM gave young girls a sense of peer camaraderie, involvement in their national cause and independence from their families. Melita Maschmann has described how she wished to escape from her childish life and 'to follow a different road from the conservative one prescribed ... by family tradition'.[18] Many of her contemporaries joined the BDM for similar reasons. In this respect, there is some indication that the BDM had a modernising and liberating effect upon German girls.[19] However, in the place of parental influence came societal authority and state force.[20]

The National Socialist regime claimed that youth autonomy and the principle of self-leadership were central to the BDM. However, there is much evidence to show that the BDM did not foster true independence among either its members or its leaders. As was the case in all Nazi formations and organisations, the ethos of the BDM entailed a loss of individuality for its members. They were bound to a community of peers, and above and beyond that, to the community of the nation. The BDM, therefore, was not an aggregate of the individual personalities of its members, but rather a community into which individuality was dissolved. The community ethos, which was a central part of the character formation of the group's members, was closely tied to National Socialist ideology. The objectives of the BDM were not directed at fostering the individual development or independence of its members. Maschmann has described how: 'No one made us think for ourselves or develop the ability to make moral decisions on our own responsibility. Our motto was: The Führer orders, we follow!'[21] Hence, the BDM attempted to create devoted believers in the National Socialist system.

The first prerequisites of a BDM member were that she had to be of German origin and of sound heredity. The model German girl had to be prepared to work hard to serve the 'national community', to recognise National Socialist norms and values, and to accept them unquestioningly. She was to be physically fit, healthy, clean, dressed in an orderly manner and domestically capable. The training of girls in the BDM entailed a variety of components, including physical fitness, health, hygiene, dress codes and sexual attitudes. Physical training was very closely linked to health and to racial-biological ideas. To this extent, sport was not an end in itself but a means of training German youth in accordance with National Socialist ideals.[22] Its goal was inner discipline. Consequently, no free or spontaneous sport or dance was allowed. Instead, regulation and discipline were emphasised. Many dance and exercise routines were structured within a certain form, such as a circle, a square or simply in rows. Girls were to keep their bodies firm and healthy by means of exercise, in order to be able to reproduce for the nation in the future. Physical training included a wide variety of activities including running, swimming, ball games, gymnastics, floor exercises and formation dancing. BDM training emphasised that there could be no ideological education without physical education, for physical training was the most important and effective means in the educational programme of the Nazi youth groups. Sport was considered to be important because it strengthened the will, created camaraderie and exercised each part of the body. This reflected the clear intention of the regime to create a whole generation of healthy and fit German girls. Schirach continually emphasised the need for a 'synthesis between body and spirit' as the aim of the BDM.

Health education was considered to be especially significant for girls, as they would become the bearers of the next generation. They were bombarded with mottoes and slogans such as 'You have the duty to be healthy'. To the BDM, beauty was nothing other than the expression of physical and spiritual health, the harmony of body, soul and spirit. BDM leaders had to care for the health of their members by monitoring their nutrition, clothing, physical exercise, leisure and relaxation. Health was of paramount concern, for as natural selection showed, the sick and unfit perished. This could not be allowed to happen to the German *Volk*, for only healthy nations could survive and a successful nation needed to be 'pure' and 'fit'. Hence, the National Socialist state had to promote and strive for health and fitness in order to secure the future stock of the race. Furthermore, the BDM taught girls the importance of the measures and laws introduced by the National Socialist government to preserve and protect the hereditary health of the German *Volk*, such as the Marriage Health Law and the Law for the Prevention of Hereditarily Diseased Offspring. This highlighted to the BDM girls their personal responsibility for their health, as this was an integral part of that of the whole nation.

Therefore, they had the duty to protect their health and to refrain from associating with the 'inferior', in order to ensure that future generations would be strong and fit.

The attitude towards sexual behaviour in the BDM paralleled that in the rest of society. Essentially, sexual life had its main task in serving the preservation of the race and nation. By and large, the National Socialists' 'new morality' reduced sex to its biological function of reproduction. The aim for BDM girls was childbirth and motherhood inside marriage. Early marriage, in particular, was seen as a way of both discouraging promiscuity and encouraging large numbers of legitimate children. Marriage was considered to be a dutiful, moral obligation by the youth group leaders. The demand that sexual activity should occur only inside a monogamous marriage remained the overall belief in the BDM. Hence, the desire in the BDM was not to encourage a child 'at any price' but rather to promote very specific attitudes towards motherhood, in line with the regime's aims of 'selection' of the 'desirable' and 'elimination' of the 'undesirable'.[23] Apart from these areas, sexuality was not an issue that was discussed in the BDM. Both the BDM and HJ were essentially non-sexual in their orientation. Non-sexual camaraderie and friendship were the general expectations about behaviour with fellow members of the youth movement. However, 'there was very probably a good deal of flirting during youth group activities, especially when boys and girls were working together'.[24] Lust and desire were not acceptable, and physical training and diversion were partly designed to pre-empt or substitute them. The satisfaction of sexual urges was regarded as shameful, reprehensible and biologically and medically unnecessary. Fresh, clean, clear German air was the alternative to sexual education.[25] To this extent, sexuality was mysticised and was almost completely a taboo area.

Expectations about sexual behaviour did not always correspond to reality, as exemplified by cases of girls having sexual relationships with soldiers and SS men, and of their having illegitimate babies in order to present the *Führer* with children. The lack of explanation about sexual behaviour partly explains this phenomenon. Some girls also had relationships with 'racially inferior' men from the eastern-occupied territories. Hence, there was some conflict between the emphasis on moral purity within the BDM and the popular perception of the organisation. Common jokes included the following interpretations of the initials BDM: 'Bubi Drück Mich' ('squeeze me, laddie'), 'Bedarfsartikel Deutscher Männer' ('Requisite for German Men'), 'Brauch Deutsche Mädel' ('make use of German girls'), 'Bald Deutsche Mütter' ('German mothers to be'), 'Bund Deutscher Milchkühe' ('League of German Milk Cows').[26] Such jokes clearly reveal the popular response to the BDM, suggesting both doubts about standards of morality within the organisation and some displeasure at its emphasis on procreation.

In January 1938, a new BDM agency, the *Glaube und Schönheit* (Faith and Beauty), was formed for 17–21-year-old girls.[27] By February 1939, the organisation had 500,000 members.[28] For the purpose of training, the young women were formed into working groups for different themes or subjects including sport, gymnastics, national tradition, plays and culture, handicrafts, music, foreign news, health, and household and agricultural competence. This enabled girls to take part in activities in which they were particularly interested. Physical education was at the forefront of *Glaube und Schönheit* training, for 'a healthy and beautiful body' was considered to be the prerequisite of 'a healthy and beautiful spirit'. Beyond this, the main task of the *Glaube und Schönheit* was to form 'self-assured young women', rooted in the National Socialist spirit and capable of taking their part in the creation and maintenance of the 'national community'.

While boys' training in the HJ took on a more militant nature between 1937 and 1939, with a greater emphasis on pre-military preparation, in the BDM a development towards preparation for 'female' activities was evident in this period. As early as 1936, the first BDM 'household school' had been set up, in which girls could gain experience and training in household activities. Specific training in household management and child care was given in the BDM household schools. Here, a one-year course provided its participants with everything they would need to know as future mothers. The teaching plan at the household schools involved four main areas of work: practical teaching, which included cookery, baking, gardening and needlework; theoretical training, which consisted of lessons about nutrition, health, care for infants and for the sick; studies about the 'national community', which dealt with issues of nation, race and the national economy; and sport, which included hiking as well as activities such as singing and dancing.[29]

The *Pflichtjahr* was a one-year compulsory work placement for girls, which came into effect from 1 January 1939. The rationale behind the *Pflichtjahr* was twofold – to give girls necessary experience and training and to help mothers of *kinderreich* ('rich in children') families and farmers' wives. It was deemed especially important that those girls who had spent their whole lives in towns and cities should serve in the countryside, so that for at least a year they could do farm work and get to know about rural life. This measure was intended to create a sense of closeness to the homeland. Most of the girls doing agricultural service lived in a camp with their leader and from there went to help on individual farms, starting their work at 6 a.m. each day. Other girls stayed on a farm with the farmer's family. Those doing their *Pflichtjahr* in towns were required to help with housework, washing, cooking and shopping in the households of *kinderreich* families.

During the war, the term 'domestic training' was applied more widely, ultimately changing its meaning to a total preparation to serve in any manner required by the state. Short training courses were run, teaching girls to make 'new out of old' and to help soldiers by setting up washing and mending centres for their clothes. BDM members were faced with new duties and obligations. In the first year of the war, over 9 million girls were mobilised, especially for agricultural work.[30] Youth mobilisation involved a wide variety of activities. These included the distribution of propaganda material for the

Party, the distribution of food ration cards, the harvesting of crops, the collection of money for the War Winter Relief Agency, looking after the wounded, caring for children and gathering herbs and wild fruit.[31] BDM girls carried out agricultural work and became involved in active war service, for example working in armaments factories.

The BDM girls were also involved in *Osteinsatz*.[32] From mid-1940 onwards, in conjunction with the SS, BDM girls were sent into the eastern occupied territories to clean and prepare houses for German settlers, once the SS had removed their former inhabitants. After their initial duties in the eastern territories, which lasted approximately 4–6 weeks, many BDM girls had to remain in these territories for up to one year, in order to help the newcomers settle there, assisting in the homes and schools. The BDM girls went into the villages and sang German songs and played German games with the children, so that they could learn German, as well as showing them maps of greater Germany and teaching children the basics of how to write and read German. *Osteinsatz* became an increasingly large part of BDM activities as the war progressed.[33]

The BDM was an integral part of a blood-binding community, whose members were called upon to serve their nation and take responsibility for the future of their race under National Socialism. The BDM played a significant role in the Nazi process of socialising and training German girls. As future mothers, BDM girls were to become protectors and preservers of the German race. Yet, at the same time, there were modernising effects resulting from BDM activities in practice. These were functional and were a product of the circumstances of war and the necessity of using BDM girls in roles related to it. Measures that appeared modernising were simply pragmatic attempts on the part of the regime to prevent the collapse of the agricultural workforce and to meet the requirements of state efficiency. After 1943, 13,000 girls took part in air raid protection duties and 25,000 worked on anti-aircraft batteries by spring 1945, firing anti-aircraft cannons.[34] Some girls even received instruction in the use of machine guns and grenades.[35] This was a clear contradiction of the Nazi ideological position that girls, as future mothers, were to be protected. As the conditions of the Second World War required girls to bear arms, pragmatism overrode Nazi ideological tenets.

The Hitler Youth and League of German Girls played a significant role in Nazi society. Membership of the Nazi youth groups was representative of membership of the 'national community'. At first, membership was voluntary and young Germans joined eagerly. Later, when membership became compulsory and duties became more arduous, the popularity of the Nazi youth groups declined. The socialisation of youth into the National Socialist *Weltanschauung* and the increasing amount of time spent on youth group activities and duties led to tensions between young people and their parents. As well as intergenerational tensions, there was a feeling that Hitler Youth activities had a negative impact upon traditional education.[36] Furthermore, there was a sense that the new authority of the Hitler Youth leaders compromised the traditional authority of teachers and priests. Gerhard Rempel argues that the Hitler Youth generation 'experienced a peculiar form of socialisation ... characterised by intense regimentation and forceful indoctrination, designed to inculcate an artificially defined social heritage' and that Hitler Youth members were 'compelled to assume predetermined roles without the freedom to consider alternatives'.[37] Both Hitler Youth members and their female counterparts in the BDM were ultimately obliged to play their part in the Nazi war effort – even in the face of mortal danger – and to serve the regime until its demise in 1945.

NOTES

1 E. Krieck, *Nationalpolitische Erziehung* (Leipzig, 1941), p. 48.

2 L. Pine, *Nazi Family Policy, 1933–1945* (Oxford, 1997), p. 57.

3 On the Hitler Youth, see A. Klönne, *Hitlerjugend. Die Jugend und ihre Organization im Dritten Reich* (Hanover, 1955); A. Klönne, *Jugend im Dritten Reich. Die Hitler Jugend und ihre Gegner* (Cologne, 1984); H. Boberach, *Jugend unter Hitler* (Düsseldorf, 1982); K. Huber, *Jugend unterm Hakenkreuz* (Berlin, 1982). On the League of German Girls, see M. Klaus, *Mädchen in der Hitlerjugend. Die Erziehung zur 'deutschen Frau'* (Cologne, 1980); M. Klaus, *Mädchen im Dritten Reich. Der Bund Deutscher Mädel (BDM)* (Cologne, 1983); G. Kinz, *Der Bund Deutscher Mädel. Ein Beitrag zur außerschulischen Mädchenerziehung im Nationalsozialismus* (Frankfurt am Main, 1990); B. Jürgens, *Zur Geschichte des BDM (Bund Deutscher Mädel) von 1923 bis 1939* (Frankfurt am Main, 1994).

4 H. Koch, *The Hitler Youth: Origins and Development, 1922–1945* (London, 1975), p. 47.

5 On Schirach, see M. Wortmann, *Baldur von Schirach: Hitlers Jugendführer* (Cologne, 1982).

6 Koch, *The Hitler Youth*, p. 101.

7 See P. Stachura, *The German Youth Movement 1900–1945: An Interpretative and Documentary History* (London, 1981).

8 Cited in J. Noakes and G. Pridham (eds), *Nazism 1919–1945: A Documentary Reader*, Vol. 2 (Exeter, 1984), p. 419.

9 Cited in ibid., p. 420.

10 Cited in Koch, *The Hitler Youth*, p. 231.

11 M. Kater, *Hitler Youth* (Cambridge, Mass. and London, 2004), p. 25.

12 See Chapter 11 for more detail on this. See also E. Boesten, *Jugendwiderstand im Faschismus* (Cologne, 1983) and D. Peukert, *Die Edelweisspiraten. Protestbewegung jugendlicher Arbeiter im Dritten Reich. Eine Dokumentation* (Cologne, 1980).

13 Kater, *Hitler Youth*, p. 159.

14 Ibid., p. 15.

15 Ibid., p. 178.

16 Ibid., p. 199.

17 Ibid., pp. 206–7.

18 M. Maschmann, *Account Rendered: A Dossier on My Former Self* (London, 1964), p. 12.

19 Autobiographical accounts of girls' experiences in the *Bund Deutscher Mädel* shed a useful insight into this. See R. Finckh, *Mit uns zieht die neue Zeit* (Baden-Baden, 1979); M. Hannsmann, *Der helle Tag bricht an – Ein Kind wird Nazi* (Hamburg, 1982); G. Herr, *Inhaltsreiche Jahre – aus dem Leben einer BdM-Führerin 1930–1945* (Lausanne, 1985).

20 D. Reese, 'Emanzipation oder Vergesellschaftung: Mädchen im "Bund Deutscher Mädel"', in H. Otto and H. Sünker (eds), *Politische Formierung und soziale Erziehung im Nationalsozialismus* (Frankfurt am Main, 1991), p. 212. See also D. Reese, 'Mädchen im

Bund Deutscher Mädel', in E. Kleinau and C. Opitz (eds), *Geschichte der Mädchen- und Frauenbildung*, Vol. 2 (Frankfurt am Main, 1996), pp. 271–82.

21 Maschmann, *Account Rendered*, p. 158.

22 See G. Pfister and D. Reese, 'Gender, Body Culture, and Body Politics in National Socialism', *Sport History*, Vol. 1 (1995), pp. 91–121.

23 L. Pine, 'Creating Conformity: The Training of Girls in the *Bund Deutscher Mädel*', *European History Quarterly*, Vol. 33, No. 3 (2003), p. 375.

24 Maschmann, *Account Rendered*, p. 150.

25 Klaus, *Mädchen in der Hitlerjugend*, p. 59.

26 See H. Bleuel, *Strength through Joy: Sex and Society in Nazi Germany* (London, 1973), p. 136.

27 On the *Glaube und Schönheit* organisation, see S. Hering and K. Schilde, *Das BDM-Werk 'Glaube und Schönheit': Die Organisation junger Frauen im Nationalsozialismus* (Berlin, 2000).

28 Pine, 'Creating Conformity: The Training of Girls in the *Bund Deutscher Mädel*', p. 378.

29 Ibid., p. 379.

30 D. Reese, 'Bund Deutscher Mädel – Zur Geschichte der weiblichen deutschen Jugend im Dritten Reich', in Frauengruppe Faschismusforschung (ed.), *Mutterkreuz und Arbeitsbuch: Zur Geschichte der Frauen in der Weimarer Republik und im Nationalsozialismus* (Frankfurt am Main, 1981), p. 175.

31 Pine, 'Creating Conformity: The Training of Girls in the *Bund Deutscher Mädel*', p. 380.

32 On this, see E. Harvey, *Women and the Nazi East: Agents and Witnesses of Germanisation* (New Haven and London, 2003), especially pp. 54–7, pp. 94–5, pp. 191–202, pp. 204–9, pp. 240–51.

33 For an autobiographical account of *Osteinsatz*, see H. Fritsch, *Land mein Land: Bauerntum und Landdienst BDM-Osteinsatz Siedlungsgeschichte im Osten* (Preußisch Oldendorf, 1986).

34 M. Stibbe, *Women in the Third Reich* (London, 2003), p. 122.

35 Kater, *Hitler Youth*, p. 236.

36 D. Horn, 'The Hitler Youth and Educational Decline in the Third Reich', *History of Education Quarterly*, Vol. 16 (1976), pp. 425–47.

37 G. Rempel, *Hitler's Children: The Hitler Youth and the SS* (Chapel Hill and London, 1989), p. 262.

5

WOMEN AND THE FAMILY

A Nazi Family. © The Wiener Library

As childbearers and protectors of the future of the *Volk*, women had a particularly significant role assigned to them in the 'national community'. This
chapter begins with an examination of the position of women in Nazi
Germany, a subject that has attracted much interest among historians since
the 1970s.[1] It starts by briefly examining the position of women in the
Weimar Republic and then analyses the policies of the Nazi regime towards
women. The second part of the chapter deals with the related subject of the
family. While the running together of 'women' and 'the family' is typical in
discussions of any society, it is particularly pertinent in a discussion of Nazi
society, as the regime welded the two so closely together. The family,
extolled in National Socialist ideology and propaganda as 'the germ cell of the
nation', played a very important part in the 'national community'. However,
Nazi policy did not always accurately reflect Nazi ideology and this chapter
examines the impact of Nazi policies upon the German family.

WOMEN

In 1919, the new Weimar constitution gave women the right to vote and the
right to be elected. However, despite this important achievement for German
feminism, as well as greater access for women to white-collar jobs and the
establishment of family planning centres, the organised women's movement
did not make much progress beyond these initial steps during the Weimar

Republic. There were a number of reasons for this. First, the Weimar period was too short and at times too unstable to create wide-ranging changes in existing social and occupational structures. Second, the women's emancipation movement itself became splintered and crippled. Third, attitudes in Weimar Germany towards women were still, in many cases, illiberal and reactionary. For example, the German National People's Party (DNVP) and the Catholic Centre Party favoured traditional, polarised gender roles. Many religious and conservative groups sprang up in the aftermath of the First World War that campaigned against women's emancipation, against birth control and against abortion. Such groups included the League of Queen Louise and the Evangelical Women's Federation.[2] Other groups were concerned with the sharp decline in the nation's birth rate. The National League of Large Families promoted families with four or more children as a means of action against the Weimar trend of the 'two-child' family.

Urbanisation and modernisation during the Weimar Republic were the key trends that offered the 'new woman' a liberated lifestyle.[3] Many young women moved to the cities to work in seemingly glamorous jobs, as secretaries, shorthand typists, shop assistants and waitresses. They grew in confidence as they earned their own money, became independent of their families, cut their hair into the fashionable bob, smoked cigarettes and dressed in modern, casual styles. However, this image did not apply to the majority of women and in reality, as a whole, there was no real questioning of traditional male and female stereotypes during the Weimar Republic and gender roles were still quite rigidly defined. Hence, the position of women during the Weimar era was confused and contradictory. They had achieved enfranchisement, as well as new opportunities in the world of work and new role models with which to identify. In addition, many sexual taboos were falling by the wayside in some, though not all, circles. Yet, there was a continual struggle between the forces of modernisation and those of traditionalism, with neither side ever completely triumphing.

National Socialist ideology made no secret of being completely at odds with the objectives and achievements of women's emancipation. The National Socialists accused the women's movement of having urged women to rise against men and of advocating 'unrestrained individualism'. They argued that women in the Weimar Republic had been seduced by the depraved culture of the big cities and neglected their true maternal obligations. The Nazis' rhetoric that only an organic, *völkisch* state could allow women to be true women again clearly appealed to some women. By caring for the family, home and race, they would find their true vocation through marriage and motherhood. Hence, despite the Nazis' openly anti-feminist stance, women formed a significant part of the Nazi vote. In their search for a party that would solve Germany's economic and social problems and put an end to political instability, the number of women voting for the Nazi Party steadily increased from 1928 onwards. The NSDAP increasingly mobilised support and votes from women during the last years of the Weimar Republic. Nazi women's groups had emerged during the 1920s in areas where the NSDAP was well organised. In 1931, they were formally merged into the *NS-Frauenschaft* (Nazi Women's Group).[4]

When the Nazis took power in 1933, some non-National Socialist women's groups were dissolved while others abandoned their independence during the period of *Gleichschaltung* in order to survive at all. The majority of women's groups offered little resistance to being assimilated into the apparatus of the Nazi state, expelling their Jewish members and succumbing to Nazi leadership. These 'co-ordinated' women's groups came into the orbit of the *Deutsches Frauenwerk* (German Women's Enterprise or DFW), which was founded in 1933 under the leadership of the *NS-Frauenschaft*. However, the *Bund Deutscher Frauenvereine* (Federation of German Women's Organisations or BDF), the main independent women's association, dissolved itself in May 1933.[5] This marked the end of an independent women's movement in Germany. In the meantime, the Social Democratic and Communist women's groups did not manage to put up any effective resistance to the emergence of the National Socialists because there were too many splits within them, although they had put up posters and distributed leaflets saying 'Women! To Support National Socialism is to Betray Yourselves!' and 'They want to make you into willing breeding machines!'[6] Their warnings had been largely unheeded.

The Nazi regime attempted to create gender-specific policies in accordance with its ideological belief that women had a very different 'natural' function to men. There was certainly the intention that women should serve the nation as much as men, but in different ways. Whereas men actively participated in the political and working life of the 'big world', women were restricted to the 'small world' of the home and family. A woman's 'most glorious duty', according to Goebbels, was 'to present her people and her country with a child'.[7] One of the National Socialists' main priorities was to reverse the decline in the nation's birth rate, in order to make Germany a strong and great nation once again. Women had a very significant part accorded to them in this plan. To give birth to as many children as possible was considered to be the 'obligation' or 'duty' of the German woman. If a healthy German woman failed to fulfil this duty, she was accused of committing 'racial suicide'.

The regime introduced a whole series of measures and incentives to achieve its goal of increasing the birth rate. In June 1933, the Marriage Loan Scheme was set up to promote marriages between healthy 'Aryan' partners.[8] A loan of RM 1,000 was made to a German couple in the form of vouchers for the purchase of furniture and household equipment. The loans were given to a couple only if the wife agreed to give up her job. In addition, the loan was made only if the political affiliation and 'way of life' of the couple were acceptable. It was denied to couples if either or both partners had connections with the Communist Party or had had such connections in the past, and it was denied to prostitutes and the 'workshy'. The repayment of the loan was reduced by one-quarter for each child born and was cancelled out with the birth of the fourth child. Between August 1933 and January 1937, 700,000 marriages were assisted by marriage loans. In 1937, the prerequisite that women had to give up paid employment was revoked and this instigated a large increase in applications. In 1939, 42 per cent of all marriages were loan-assisted. However, couples granted a marriage loan had, on average, only one child.[9]

Attempts were also made to raise the status of motherhood.[10] A classic example of a symbolic tribute to mothers with large families was the Cross of Honour of the German Mother. This was awarded to prolific mothers, in bronze, silver and gold, for four, six and eight children respectively.[11] There was a slight increase in the nation's birth rate in the period 1934–1939 as compared with the years 1930–1933. But this was not necessarily attributable to Nazi incentives to promote procreation. Many couples felt more secure about getting married and having children because the economic climate had improved. Hence, the number of marriages increased, but the number of children per marriage did not. In addition, Nazi incentives and propaganda were not sufficient on their own to redress the long-term trend in low birth rates.

A new divorce law was introduced in 1938 that allowed for a divorce if a couple had lived apart for three years or more and if the marriage had effectively broken down. On the surface, this appeared quite liberal. However, the reasoning behind it lay more in benefits to the state than in benefits to private individuals. The objective was to dissolve marriages that were of no benefit to the 'national community'. The National Socialists believed that once a divorce had been granted, the two partners involved might then re-marry and provide the nation with more children. Premature infertility became a ground for divorce, as did either partner's refusal to have a child.[12]

Many other measures were taken to encourage marriages between healthy 'Aryan' partners that would result in large families and to increase the nation's birth rate. Contraceptives were banned and family planning centres were dissolved. In addition, the abortion laws were tightened up by the re-introduction of Paragraphs 219 and 220 of the Criminal Code, which made provisions for harsher punishments for abortion.[13] Eventually, in 1943, the death penalty was introduced for anyone performing an abortion to terminate a 'valuable' pregnancy, as this was considered to be an act of 'racial sabotage' during the crisis of the war.

Simultaneously, the more blatantly sinister side of Nazi population policy was taking place. Legal measures were introduced to prevent marriages between Jews and 'Aryans' (Nuremberg Laws, September 1935) and to prevent marriages between healthy 'Aryans' and those deemed 'unfit' for marriage due to physical or mental illness (Marriage Health Law, October 1935). In order to marry, it was necessary to undergo a medical examination first. On passing this, the local health authorities issued a 'certificate of fitness to marry'. The regime was very strict about the implementation of these laws, for the children from 'undesirable' marriages would be 'inferior'. Sterilisation was the principal method used by the Nazi regime to prevent people it considered 'undesirable' from having children. On 1 January 1934 the Sterilisation Law, the Law for the Prevention of Hereditarily Diseased Offspring, came into effect. It called for the compulsory sterilisation of anyone suffering from 'congenital feeble-mindedness, schizophrenia, manic depression, hereditary epilepsy, Huntington's chorea, hereditary blindness, hereditary deafness, serious physical deformities' and 'chronic alcoholism'.[14] Between January 1934 and September 1939, approximately 320,000 people (0.5 per cent of the population) were forcibly sterilised under the terms of this law.[15] The majority of them were of German ethnicity; however, they were considered to be 'hereditarily ill' or simply 'feeble-minded' by the regime and its eugenic experts. The 'feeble-minded' made up two-thirds of all those sterilised, of which about two-thirds of these were women. Sterilised women became the objects of sexual abuse, especially in the cities, where soldiers or factory workers asked their colleagues on Mondays: 'Did you not find a sterilised woman for the weekend?'[16]

Another attempt to speed up the birth of 'valuable' children was Himmler's 'Lebensborn' or 'Well of Life' organisation, established in December 1935. Its task was 'to further the number of children in SS families, protect and administer to all mothers of good blood, and care for needy mothers and children of good blood'. The 'Lebensborn' maternity homes provided ante-natal and post-natal care for the wives of SS men. They also enabled unmarried mothers to have their babies discreetly, in a comfortable environment, without the knowledge of their neighbours and relatives. In addition, they organised the adoption of the children of these single women into healthy, German families. Himmler took a personal interest in the running of the 'Lebensborn' homes, for example giving advice about nutrition for pregnant women, particularly highlighting the importance of porridge and wholemeal bread in their diet.[17] He ensured that the 'Lebensborn' homes received priority treatment during the war, in terms of obtaining adequate supplies of rationed items, particularly fresh fruit. Further to their initial *raison d'être*, the 'Lebensborn' homes were also used as centres for rearing and Germanising 'racially valuable' children who had been abducted from their homes in Poland and the Soviet Union during the war.[18]

The National Socialists' preoccupation with increasing the birth rate meant that women were discouraged from working to some extent, especially in the early years of the Third Reich. The Nazi regime continued measures introduced by Brüning in the Weimar era against 'double earners' and tried to dissuade women from working in heavy industry. However, women were not entirely removed from the workforce. Rather, they were encouraged to undertake social work, domestic work or agricultural work, areas which were more suitable for them 'biologically'. Those women who did work in factories were encouraged to do routine, monotonous assembly line jobs so that their thoughts would not be distracted from their families and familial duties. In July 1934, the Women's Section of the German Labour Front was set up under Gertrud Scholtz-Klink.[19] One of its main functions was to undertake factory social work, giving advice to female workers, settling disputes, supervising hygiene in the workplace and, of course, protecting the childbearing capacity of women.[20] Hence, there were some benefits to women workers, but these were aimed at ensuring they were physically capable of and psychologically amenable to bearing children. Day nurseries and crèches were set up in factories and large enterprises appointed social workers to deal with the personal and family concerns of female factory workers.

The overall percentage of women in work grew during the first six years of the Third Reich, from 34.4 per cent in 1933 to 36.7 per cent in 1939. Hence, despite the Nazi propaganda appeals for women to stay at home, women were increasingly taking up paid work, often outside the sphere of agriculture or domestic service. The National Socialists had no greater success in driving married women out of the workplace. By 1939, 6.2 million working women were married, which was 2 million more than in 1933.[21] However, the regime did try to curb women's achievements at work. In education, for example, female teachers were removed from management positions and the ratio between male and female teachers was set at 4:1. After 1936, women were not permitted to become judges, public prosecutors or lawyers, while female doctors found it hard to find positions in hospitals.

It was from the late 1930s that one of the major discrepancies between Nazi ideology and policy occurred. At this time, the economy was beginning to demand women to fill the jobs vacated by men who had been conscripted into the armed services. In particular, as armaments factories accelerated their production in line with government demands, labour was desperately needed. Of course, these requirements became even more urgent with the duration of the Second World War. The thrust of Nazi propaganda changed, as the mass of German women were now called upon to do their Labour Service, to fulfil their new 'duties' to the nation.[22]

The Nazi organisation of women was carried out by its two main women's formations under the leadership of Gertrud Scholtz-Klink. The *NS-Frauenschaft* was the elite formation, while the *Deutsches Frauenwerk* was the mass organisation. Women joined these groups because they provided the only opportunity for them to participate in any kind of societal or organisational life and to go out without their husbands. By 1941, the aggregate number of members in these two organisations had reached approximately 6 million. Out of a total population of 30 million women over the age of 18, that made one woman in every five a member of a Nazi women's formation. The Nazi organisation of women created a 'special female public sphere', giving women new fields of activity outside the home, albeit 'with very little influence'.[23] The women in these organisations were imbued with National Socialist ideology. The leaders of these groups had the task of persuading the 'valuable' female population of its obligation to have children and of supervising child care and household duties, as well as providing courses on housekeeping, child care and cookery.

The *Reichsmütterdienst* (National Mothers' Service), an agency of the *Deutsches Frauenwerk*, was set up in 1934 to arrange for the 'training' of mothers in special 'mother schools'.[24] These schools had three main functions: home economics, including the teaching of cooking and sewing; health care, including infant care, health and home nursing; and education in National Socialist ideology. Housewives were given cookery lessons, instructed about the nutritional value of food and given practical guidelines about running a household. They were advised on pregnancy and childbirth, the care and nourishment of young children, the moral upbringing and physical and mental development of children. However, sexuality was a taboo area and no element of sexual education was incorporated into the courses run by the *Reichsmütterdienst*. Women were simply to fulfil their biological functions as child bearers. Some 5 million women and girls had attended these courses by 1944.[25] The organisation even sent out travelling instructors to the countryside and to small towns where women did not have access to the mother schools. The Nazi regime aimed to control the large, female sector of the population and it was through this type of education and training that they hoped women would be persuaded to devote themselves to National Socialism.

Another very important element in the education of women, especially in the years immediately before and during the Second World War, was the encouragement to buy as frugally as possible and to save money and materials. Priorities of autarky, armaments production and expansion meant that food production suffered, so people were encouraged to change their habits and to make do with limited food resources and consumer goods. Those who did not were stigmatised as selfish. For example, there was considerable instruction about recycling, the use of substitute goods and cooking with limited ingredients. There were demonstrations and leaflets about how to use soya instead of meat, how to preserve fruit, how to make Christmas presents instead of buying them, how to cut up old clothes to make new garments out of them instead of throwing them away, and how to use potato water as starch for ironing and as a cleaning agent instead of shop-bought cleaning materials. Timesaving food products such as soup cubes and custard powder were objected to on the grounds that they were an unnecessary expense.[26] The same was true of unnecessary kitchen gadgets, especially electrical appliances. Despite the large membership of the Nazi women's organisations, many of the women were not convinced by this barrage of advice and propaganda, nor were they active members. The Nazi regime was not completely successful in its recruitment of women into its groups, as many women remained strongly influenced by and loyal to the churches, especially in rural areas.

The Second World War had a host of implications for women. First was the issue of the conscription of women into the war effort. Labour Service for women was introduced after much debate in January 1943, but was not enforced uniformly. As a result, many working-class and lower-middle-class women began to question the notion of the 'national community' which was supposed to transcend class boundaries, as they were urged to suffer the burdens of heavy work in munitions factories and the strains of the war effort, while many upper-class and middle-class women managed to evade their Labour Service.[27] Not surprisingly, this caused indignation and some women deliberately became pregnant to avoid their Labour Service. Overall, the mobilisation of women for war production was strikingly inefficient. By the end of 1943, only 500,000 women had been mobilised. German women benefited indirectly from the presence of some 7 million foreign workers, including almost 1.5 million women, mainly from Russia, Poland and Ukraine. These were POWs, deported civilians and 'guest workers', recruited with varying degrees of force and treated considerably more brutally if they came from the east than if they were from northern or Mediterranean countries. They were put to work mainly in agriculture and industry.

Life on the home front became increasingly difficult for women, particularly with the onset of the Allied bombing campaigns. The aerial bombardment of the big cities including Cologne, Hamburg and Dresden from 1942 onwards had catastrophic effects upon them. Due to the devastation of the cities, many women and children were evacuated to the countryside. Rationing and an inadequate supply of foodstuffs led many women to buy food on the 'black market'.[28] Urban-dwelling women made 'hamstering' trips to the countryside to exchange goods for food.[29]

Towards the very end of the war, as the Red Army advanced into Germany, Soviet soldiers carried out mass and multiple rapes. Apart from the physical and psychological traumas resulting from this, the rapes had an impact on women's marriages. Some husbands saw their wives as defiled or promiscuous.[30] While British and American soldiers did not engage in this scale of rape, it was not uncommon for German women to offer sexual favours to American soldiers in exchange for chocolate, silk stockings and cigarettes.[31]

The subject of women in Nazi Germany has generated much debate among historians. Gisela Bock has argued the case for women as 'victims' of the regime, while Claudia Koonz has described German women as 'accomplices'. Many historians writing in the 1980s argued that the Nazi regime was terrible for all women, removing their rights, eliminating them from the workforce, restricting them in higher education and essentially turning them into childbearing machines. But Ute Frevert has redressed the balance and has shown that most women had no reason to regard the Nazi period as one of degradation or repression and that their status in society had by no means deteriorated in comparison with the Weimar Republic.[32]

The Nazi regime did not exercise complete control over all its women and nor were women simply the helpless victims of the Nazi state. Indeed, many Jewish, Gypsy, 'hereditarily ill' and 'asocial' women were victims, but many women were also active participants in National Socialism. Elizabeth Harvey has recently explored the role of German women in the implementation of Nazi Germanisation policies in the east. She has shown that 'a large number of young, single, mobile and mostly middle-class women ... willingly co-operated in tasks that contributed to the consolidation of German power in the East'.[33] Further recent research has highlighted the role of women as perpetrators of Nazi crimes, including doctors and nurses involved in Nazi 'euthanasia' policy, as well as female SS guards and auxiliaries in concentration camps.[34] Gudrun Schwarz has argued that SS wives provided support for their husbands by providing 'a "normal" everyday family life'.[35] Only a small minority of women undertook any form of resistance to the Nazi regime.[36] Most German women experienced complex and sometimes ambiguous relationships with the regime.[37] Adelheid von Saldern has pointed out that 'in the everyday realities produced by German fascism, ordinary men and women became complex and contradictory combinations of victims and perpetrators' and that a search for 'pure types' is unhelpful.[38] The experiences of individual women and different groups of women under National Socialism varied so considerably that care must be taken in any discussion of 'women' not to homogenise them.

THE FAMILY

The Weimar Republic brought a variety of experiences to the German family. In the early years, German families still suffered from the impact of the First World War and its aftermath. There were problems of grief for family members who had died in battle and the burden of many men who returned home from the front crippled or psychologically damaged. The mid-1920s became years of relative stability for the German family, as people searched for a sense of peace and security after the traumas of the war.[39] The Weimar era brought about some important changes in society that affected the family. The Association for Sexual Hygiene and Life Reform and the National Union for Birth Control and Hygiene, established in 1923 and 1928 respectively, introduced new educational initiatives on sexual hygiene and birth control.[40] But such changes met an unfavourable response from German conservatives, who considered sexual promiscuity, rising divorce and abortion rates and higher numbers of working married women to signify the decline and demise of the family. In the 1920s, the birth rate dropped faster than at any other point in German history. This decline was regarded as a 'national catastrophe' in traditional and conservative circles.

The position of the family waned with the effects of the great depression engendered by the Wall Street Crash of 1929, as families faced enormous financial difficulties. In particular, the economic crisis eroded the material foundations of middle-class family life as savings were lost, and of working-class family life as mass unemployment deprived workers of their jobs and incomes.[41] This placed a considerable strain upon mothers to maintain the cohesion of their families, as well as to search for cheap provisions. Young unemployed family members left home, wandering across the country and sometimes even beyond its borders, in order to relieve the strain on the family of 'unnecessary eaters'.[42] The economic crisis of the early 1930s created many social rifts, for example between the employed and the unemployed, and between generations. Such tensions were advantageous to the NSDAP, which capitalised upon the 'crisis of the family'. Intergenerational conflict had grown as parents had lost their status and prestige through unemployment and impoverishment. Many parents were no longer able to provide their children with protection and security. Hence, when the Nazis came to power, they sought to redress both the 'crisis of the family' and the decline in the nation's birth rate. They capitalised on the conservative backlash against the changes in sexuality and family life during the Weimar years and claimed that they would restore traditional models of the family. Point 21 of the NSDAP's Programme stated: 'The state has to care for the raising of the nation's health through the protection of mother and child.'

The Minister of the Interior, Wilhelm Frick, claimed in 1934: 'The family is the primordial cell of the *Volk*, that is why the National Socialist state places it at the centre of its policy.'[43] This statement encapsulated the impression that the Nazi regime wished to portray publicly, namely, a firm and solid commitment to family life. With very few exceptions, the Nazi leadership publicly exalted the ideological status of the family throughout the Nazi era. The Nazis attacked the Weimar lifestyle, in which the extravagant enjoyment of the individual had taken precedence over collective moral and national obligations. They argued that the sense of 'duty' towards the community and nation had been lost and called for German people to show a renewed sense of obligation to the 'national community'. They further claimed that the Weimar governments had encouraged egocentricity. Bachelorhood and childless marriages had been acceptable in Weimar society. The 'two-child family' had become accepted, while large families had been scorned and derided. From 1933 onwards, there was a reversal in attitudes. There was a call for women to become valuable mothers of large families. The Nazi ideal family was termed *'kinderreich'* and comprised four or more children. In the Third Reich, parents of large families were to be proud. However, the regime was careful to promote only 'hereditarily healthy', 'racially valuable', politically reliable and socially responsible families as *'kinderreich'*. 'Racially inferior' or 'asocial' large families were pejoratively labelled *'Großfamilien'* ('big families').[44]

The family was regarded as the source of 'national renewal' through reproduction. The policies implemented by the regime in order to increase the birth rate have been considered earlier in the chapter. In addition to these, in February 1934 the Nazis set up the *Hilfswerk 'Mutter und Kind'*, a new welfare agency which was specifically directed at mothers and children.[45] This agency provided welfare and recuperation for mothers and welfare for small children, as well as establishing help and advice centres. The *Hilfswerk 'Mutter und Kind'* centres offered advice about household management, breastfeeding, nutrition and other aspects of child care, including the prevention of illness. Mothers were given material assistance, such as the provision of beds, linen and children's clothes, as well as food allowances. Welfare workers visited pregnant women to educate them and care for them during their pregnancies. They gave practical advice on child care. Moreover, welfare for mothers took the form of various recuperation measures, at spas or recuperation homes. The recuperation homes had a strong educational element to them. Along with rest, wholesome food and exercise, the women received a large dose of Nazi ideology. For example, the special role accorded to women and especially mothers in the 'national community' was the subject of considerable attention. The objective of mothers' rest care was 'to toughen up German women for their tasks in the house and family'.[46] The staff in the homes observed the mothers closely and reported on their behaviour and attitudes. According to official statistics, 40,340 women went to recuperation homes in 1934. This number increased to 77,723 in 1938.[47]

Child welfare took the form of nurseries and kindergartens, where children under the age of 6 could be looked after properly, particularly if their mothers worked. The nurseries had the following tasks assigned to them: to sponsor the physical, mental and spiritual development of the children, to educate them in National Socialism and service to the 'national community', and to instil in them a sense of care for the German nation. The number of nurseries rose from approximately 1,000 in 1935 to 15,000 in 1941.[48] In addition, special 'harvest kindergartens' were set up in rural areas from 1934 onwards, run by trained kindergarten workers. These were aimed at freeing agricultural women from their familial responsibilities during the day so that they could harvest their crops. The number of 'harvest kindergartens' increased from 600 in 1934 to 8,700 in 1941.[49] Similarly to the ordinary day nurseries, the 'harvest kindergartens' promoted the physical, mental and spiritual development of the children and educated them in National Socialism.

The *Volkswirtschaft/Hauswirtschaft* (National Economy/Domestic Economy), an agency of the *NS-Frauenschaft*, was another organisation that had an impact upon German families. Its main objectives were to discourage housewives from squandering their money and to raise the status of the family in its role as protector of the nation. In addition, the organisation aimed to bring about an awareness of the connection between the individual household and the national economy. It distributed leaflets, published a magazine, organised courses and demonstrations and established advice centres to instruct women about saving and recycling, using substitute goods and cooking with limited ingredients. It gave household and cookery tips, recipes, information on how to preserve fruit, and how to sew, mend and darn. By the end of 1938, it had established 148 advice centres in towns throughout Germany.[50] The centres displayed educational material and books and ran instructional films on topics such as 'German Grain in the Household', 'Preservation of Fruit and Vegetables' and 'The Nourishment of Babies'. Mothers of needy families who could not afford luxury goods or even some of the more basic provisions took up the courses and information provided by the *Volkswirtschaft/ Hauswirtschaft*, but families on a higher income were far less willing to change their lifestyles, in terms of food and clothing, if they could still afford to maintain them.[51]

The regime employed an existing organisation, the *Reichsbund der*

Kinderreichen (National League of Large Families), to put an end to lax sexual and marital morals and to promote the ideal large family as a model for emulation. It offered advice to *'kinderreich'* families, on issues such as rent, housing and employment. It was also involved in propaganda work. Its leader, Wilhelm Stüwe, claimed that 'the more hereditarily healthy families a nation possesses, the more certain its future is'.[52] There was some concern that the organisation had 'asocial' or 'hereditarily unfit' families among its members and in 1940, under a new leader, Robert Kaiser, the organisation was renamed the *Reichsbund Deutscher Familien, Kampfbund für erbtüchtigen Kinderreichtum* (National Association of the German Family, Combat League for Large Families of Sound Heredity). The organisation redoubled its efforts to attain a larger membership of 'valuable' *'kinderreich'* families and to expound the correct ideals for German families to emulate. The Cross of Honour of the German Mother and the Honour Books awarded to large families exemplified the symbolic significance of *'kinderreich'* families.

Yet, despite the honour and status accorded to *'kinderreich'* families, the regime was unwilling to undertake major financial expenditure to assist them. While some measures were put in place to redress the inequalities between *'kinderreich'* families and single people or couples with no children or few children, such as tax reforms and child supplements, these remained insufficient to convince people to have large families. Furthermore, the Nazi regime failed to provide adequate housing provision for *'kinderreich'* families. Propaganda and piecemeal initiatives were insufficient to change the inclination of German couples to limit the size of their families. Hence, the promotion of *'kinderreich'* families was not successful. Indeed, the proportion of married women with four or more children decreased from 25 per cent in 1933 to 21 per cent in 1939.[53] Much to the dissatisfaction of the regime, the 'two-child family' was perpetuated throughout the Third Reich.

The Nazis' aims of an increased birth rate, racial homogeneity and a regimented social life invaded the private domain of the family quite profoundly. Hence, the home was not a safe haven insulated from National Socialism. The 'public sphere' of Nazi ideology and rule invaded the 'private sphere'.[54] The 'big world' of politics and the 'small world' of the family 'became inextricably intertwined'.[55] In the end, the Nazis' recognition of the importance of the family was as a vehicle for their own aims, not as a social unit *per se*. Marriage and childbirth became racial duties instead of personal decisions, as the Nazi regime systematically reduced the functions of the family to the single task of reproduction. The family under National Socialism became an institution for breeding and rearing children, with its relationships largely emptied of their emotional content. Nazi educational and youth policies removed from the family most of its role in socialisation. The Nazi youth groups, in particular, had a detrimental impact upon traditional family life, as they exploited intergenerational antagonisms. Military and labour service, as well as pressure on Party members to work long hours, often away from home, brought about a whole host of pressures on the family unit.

The Second World War had profound implications and consequences for the German family. As fathers and sons were conscripted into the armed services, women were encouraged back into the workforce to replace them. The war created almost impossible circumstances for intimate and stable family life to be conducted. Many women who were accustomed to their husbands making decisions and dealing with family finances had to manage unaided. In rural areas, women had to cope with both their sources of livelihood and their families on their own, as farmers and male farm labourers were conscripted. In urban and industrial areas, women had to bear the strain of industrial work and maintain their families single-handed. Female relatives, neighbours and friends helped each other, providing mutual support and relief. Food rationing, bombings and the destruction of gas and water supplies were among the difficulties they experienced in daily life. Air raids disrupted life and many families were made homeless and dispossessed. Many women and children were evacuated from the cities to the countryside and families became separated in the process. Almost 4 million German men had died in battle by the end of the war and 11.7 million were prisoners of war in 1945. Hence, the ultimate legacy of the Nazi regime and of the war to German family life was disastrous.[56]

Weber-Kellermann has argued: 'In the name of restoring tradition, the Nazi state did more than any other regime to break down parental autonomy and to make the family simply a vehicle of state policy.'[57] Quite contrary to their rhetoric about the restoration of the family, the National Socialists atomised family units, allowing for intrusion and intervention in everyday life. Robert Gellately has demonstrated that 'the regime found it possible to infiltrate all kinds of social spaces, eventually overriding conventions, so as to breach the private spheres of family, personal and sexual life'.[58] The Nazi regime undermined the family in an unprecedented way. It subjected the family to intervention and control, reduced its socialisation function, attempted to remove its capacity to shelter its members emotionally and subjected it to radical ideology. Its legacy was the ultimate destruction of the private sphere, not only in physical and practical terms, but also morally and spiritually.

NOTES

1 The most significant contributions to the history of women in Nazi Germany include the following: J. Stephenson, *Women in Nazi Society* (London, 1975); J. Stephenson, *The Nazi Organisation of Women* (London, 1981); R. Bridenthal, A. Grossmann and M. Kaplan (eds), *When Biology Became Destiny: Women in Weimar and Nazi Germany* (New York, 1984); T. Mason, 'Women in Germany, 1925–1940: Family Welfare and Work. Part I', *History Workshop Journal*, No. 1 (1976), pp. 74–113; T. Mason, 'Women in Germany, 1925–1940: Family Welfare and Work. Part II (Conclusion)', *History Workshop Journal*, No. 2 (1976), pp. 5–32; D. Winkler, *Frauenarbeit im 'Dritten Reich'* (Hamburg, 1977), Frauengruppe Faschismusforschung (ed.), *Mutterkreuz und Arbeitsbuch: Zur Geschichte der Frauen in der Weimarer Republik und im Nationalsozialismus* (Frankfurt am Main, 1981); R. Thalmann, *Frauensein im Dritten Reich* (Munich, 1984); D. Klinksiek, *Die Frau im NS-Staat* (Stuttgart, 1982).

2 U. Frevert, *Women in German History: From Bourgeois Emancipation to Sexual Liberation* (Oxford, 1989), p. 209.

3 The 'new woman' was also reflected and represented in the visual arts of the era. On this, see M. Meskimmon and S. West (eds), *Visions of the Neue Frau: Women and the Visual Arts in Weimar Germany* (Aldershot, 1995).

4 J. Stephenson, *Women in Nazi Germany* (London, 2001), pp. 83–4.

5 Frevert, *Women in German History*, p. 212.

6 Ibid., p. 213.

7 Cited in Frevert, *Women in German History*, p. 208.

8 L. Pine, *Nazi Family Policy, 1933–1945* (Oxford, 1997), p. 17.

9 Stephenson, *Women in Nazi Society*, p. 47.

10 I. Weyrather, *Muttertag und Mutterkreuz: Der Kult um die 'deutsche Mutter' im Nationalsozialismus* (Frankfurt am Main, 1993).

11 Frevert, *Women in German History*, p. 233.

12 G. Czarnowski, 'The Value of Marriage for the *Volksgemeinschaft*: Policies towards women and marriage under National Socialism', in R. Bessel (ed.), *Fascist Italy and Nazi Germany: Comparisons and Contrasts* (Cambridge, 1996), p. 108. For a fuller treatment of the subject, see G. Czarnowski, *Das kontrollierte Paar. Ehe- und Sexualpolitik im Nationalsozialismus* (Wiesbaden, 1991).

13 Frevert, *Women in German History*, p. 231.

14 M. Burleigh and W. Wippermann, *The Racial State: Germany 1933–1945* (Cambridge, 1991), pp. 136–7.

15 Frevert, *Women in German History*, p. 236. For a fuller analysis, see G. Bock, *Zwangssterilisation im Nationalsozialismus. Studien zur Rassenpolitik und Frauenpolitik* (Opladen, 1986).

16 G. Bock, 'Antinatalism, maternity and paternity in National Socialist racism', in G. Bock and P. Thane (eds), *Maternity and Gender Policies: Women and the Rise of the European Welfare States 1880s 1950s* (London and New York, 1994) p. 238.

17 C. Clay and M. Leapman, *Master Race: The Lebensborn Experiment in Nazi Germany* (London, 1996), p. 65.

18 On this, see G. Lilienthal, *Der 'Lebensborn e.V.': Ein Instrument nationalsozialistischer Rassenpolitik* (Stuttgart, 1985), pp. 166–217; C. Henry and M. Hillel, *Children of the SS* (London, 1976), pp. 143–77.

19 Pine, *Nazi Family Policy*, p. 21.

20 On this, see C. Sachse, *Industrial Housewives: Women's Social Work in the Factories of Nazi Germany* (London, 1987).

21 Frevert, *Women in German History*, p. 218.

22 See S. Bajohr, 'Weiblicher Arbeitsdienst im "Dritten Reich". Ein Konflikt zwischen Ideologie und Ökonomie', *Vierteljahreshefte für Zeitgeschichte*, Vol. 28 (1980), pp. 331–57.

23 A. von Saldern, 'Victims or Perpetrators? Controversies about the role of women in the Nazi state', in D. Crew (ed.), *Nazism and German Society, 1933–1945* (London, 1994), p. 151.

24 Frevert, *Women in German History*, p. 233.

25 Stephenson, *The Nazi Organisation of Women*, p. 165.

26 J. Stephenson, 'Propaganda, Autarky and the German Housewife', in D. Welch (ed.), *Nazi Propaganda: The Power and the Limitations* (London, 1983), pp. 136–7.

27 On this, see L. Rupp, '"I Don't Call That *Volksgemeinschaft*": Women, Class and War in Nazi Germany', in C. Berkin and C. Lovett (eds), *Women, War and Revolution* (New York and London, 1980), pp. 37–53.

28 Stephenson, *Women in Nazi Germany*, p. 99.

29 M. Stibbe, *Women in the Third Reich* (London, 2003), p. 154.

30 Ibid, p. 168.

31 Stephenson, *Women in Nazi Germany*, p. 108.

32 Frevert, *Women in German History*, pp. 250–2.

33 E. Harvey, *Women and the Nazi East: Agents and Witnesses of Germanisation* (New Haven and London, 2003), p. 295.

34 On women in the SS, see G. Schwarz, 'Frauen in der SS Sippenverband und Frauenkorps', in K. Heinsohn, B. Vogel and U. Weckel (eds), *Zwischen Karriere und Verfolgung. Handlungsräume von Frauen im nationalsozialistischen Deutschland* (Frankfurt am Main, 1997), pp. 233–44. See also D. Brown, *The Camp Women: the female auxiliaries who assisted the SS in running the Nazi concentration camps* (Atglen, 2002).

35 G. Schwarz, *Eine Frau an seiner Seite: Ehefrauen in der SS-Sippengemeinschaft* (Hamburg, 1997), p. 282.

36 On this, see M. Schad, *Frauen gegen Hitler. Schicksale im Nationalsozialismus* (Munich, 2001); G. Szepansky, *Frauen leisten Widerstand, 1933–1945* (Frankfurt am Main, 1983).

37 See G. Bock, 'Ordinary Women in Nazi Germany: Perpetrators, Victims, Followers and Bystanders', in D. Ofer and L. Weitzman (eds), *Women in the Holocaust* (New Haven, 1998), pp. 85–100.

38 Saldern, 'Victims or Perpetrators?', p. 157.

39 R. Sieder, *Sozialgeschichte der Familie* (Frankfurt am Main, 1987), p. 213.

40 Frevert, *Women in German History*, p. 189.

41 Pine, *Nazi Family Policy*, p. 7.

42 Sieder, *Sozialgeschichte der Familie*, p. 225.

43 Cited in Pine, *Nazi Family Policy*, p. 8.

44 Pine, *Nazi Family Policy*, p. 88.

45 Ibid., p. 23.

46 Cited in Pine, *Nazi Family Policy*, p. 27.

47 Ibid., p. 27.

48 Ibid., p. 31.

49 Ibid., p. 31.

50 Ibid., p. 83.

51 Stephenson, *The Nazi Organisation of Women*, p. 166.

52 Cited in Pine, *Nazi Family Policy*, p. 91.

53 G. Bock, 'Antinatalism, Maternity and Paternity in National Socialist Racism', p. 245.

54 Saldern, 'Victims or Perpetrators?', p. 157.

55 V. Joshi, 'The "Private" Became "Public": Wives as Denouncers in the Third Reich', *Journal of Contemporary History*, Vol. 37, No. 3 (2002), p. 435.

56 On this, see Pine, *Nazi Family Policy*, pp. 184–7.

57 I. Weber-Kellermann, 'The German Family between Private Life and Politics', in A. Prost and G. Vincent (eds), *A History of Private Life. V: The Riddle of Identity in Modern Times* (London, 1991), p. 517.

58 R. Gellately, *The Gestapo and German Society: Enforcing Racial Policy 1933–1945* (Oxford, 1990), p. 159.

6

THE CHURCHES AND THE *WEHRMACHT*

A Protestant church adorned with swastika flags. © Ullstein-SV-Bilderdienst/akg-images

The churches and the *Wehrmacht*, while not conceptually linked, are related in important ways. First, they were both significant as major institutions within German society that had a bearing on the 'national community' and were profoundly affected by National Socialism. The concept of the institution was highly significant in Nazi society because an institution entailed its own identity. There were tensions, therefore, between institutional identities and the aims of the Nazi regime to homogenise society. Second, both of these institutions influenced the lives of millions of German people and for this reason they are essential in a book that deals with society in Nazi Germany.

Third, they have both attracted considerable controversy in terms of their responses to National Socialism and its crimes. The first part of this chapter examines the Nazi stance towards Christianity and the two major Christian churches. It moves on to consider the position of the Protestant and Catholic churches in the Third Reich and their responses to National Socialism. The second part of the chapter explores the position and role of the *Wehrmacht* in Nazi Germany. This is particularly significant because the attributes of the *Wehrmacht* as a 'fighting community' were very closely linked to those of the wider 'national community'. There was a tremendous sense of solidarity between the home front and the *Wehrmacht*, both consciously contributing to Hitler's war effort, albeit in different ways.

THE CHURCHES

Nazism and Christianity were morally antithetical and institutionally incompatible. However, at first, the Nazi leaders were ambivalent in their stance towards both Christianity as a religion and towards the churches as institutions. Point 24 of the Nazi Party Programme claimed to favour 'positive Christianity'. Yet many Nazi leaders, including Heinrich Himmler and Martin Bormann, were openly contemptuous of the Christian churches. A group of radical Nazis, led by Jakob Hauer and Ernst Graf zu Reventlow, established the German Faith Movement. This was an attempt to replace Christianity with a pagan, racial cult, which advocated 'blood and soil' ideology and adulation for the *Führer*. It called for the replacement of Christian ceremonies and holidays with pagan ones. However, the German Faith Movement was largely unsuccessful in attracting membership from the German population and remained a fringe movement.[1] Conversely, many leading Nazis believed that Christianity was profoundly connected with their National Socialist ideology.[2] In 1933, Hitler privately stated that 'neither of the denominations – Catholic or Protestant, they are both the same – has any future left'. He declared his aim to stamp out 'Christianity in Germany root and branch'.[3] However, publicly he adopted a conciliatory attitude to both churches. In a broadcast on 23 March 1933, Hitler stated that his government viewed the two Christian churches as 'the most important factors for the preservation of our national culture' and regarded 'Christianity as the unshakeable foundation of our national life and morality'.[4] Hitler was aware of the enormous influence of both the Catholic and Protestant churches within German society and took care not to alienate them before he had consolidated his power and established his mechanisms for controlling the population.

While there were early moves to 'co-ordinate' the Protestant Church and to reach an accord with the Catholic Church, it was only from 1937 onwards that Nazi policies against the churches was stepped up. Hess's address to the Party *Gauleiter* at Nuremberg on 12 September 1938 clearly indicated the overall objective and direction of Nazi policy, namely, the 'deconfessionalisation' of public life and the eventual pre-eminence of the Nazi Party over the established churches: 'The more we National Socialists avoid religious controversies, abstain from Church ceremonies, but on the other hand win the confidence of the people ... the more men will feel that they belong to National Socialism. The more National Socialism is seen as a blessing as a result of our work ... the more people will recognise that National Socialism is a God-ordained order and institution. Thus they will gradually become increasingly alienated by the Churches and their dogmas in the degree to which the latter stand in our way.'[5] Richard Evans has pointed out that 'the Nazi Party was on the way to severing all its ties with organised Christianity by the end of the 1930s'.[6] However, the final resolution of the 'church question' was shelved for pragmatic reasons until after the war.

The Protestant Church

In Protestant circles, Hitler's accession to power was largely welcomed with enthusiasm. The majority of Protestant pastors interpreted this historic moment as a positive step for the German nation. They approved of the demise of the 'godless' Weimar Republic and supported the ardent nationalism of the National Socialists. On 3 February 1933, at St Mary's Church in Berlin, Pastor Joachim Hossenfelder told his congregation that God created Hitler, 'a man of purity, piety, energy and strength of character' to 'wrest the German people from despair and to give them back their belief in life'.[7] The 'Day of Potsdam' ceremony on 21 March 1933 gave an impression of unity between the new regime and the Protestant Church. The Nazi regime quickly made attempts to 'co-ordinate' the Protestant Church, which responded by reorganising itself and adapting to the new spirit of the age.

The regime used the German Christian Movement to achieve the 'co-ordination' of the Protestant Church. The German Christian Movement was strongly nationalist and anti-Semitic in its outlook and openly embraced Nazi ideology. It condemned Marxism, pacifism, internationalism and Freemasonry. It was opposed to 'the spirit of a Christian cosmopolitanism' and instead wanted to create 'a dynamic national church' to fight 'in the forefront of the decisive battle for the existence or eclipse of our people'.[8] The German Christians believed that they had a divinely ordained *völkisch* mission.[9] In 1933, a new church constitution was formulated and Ludwig Müller was appointed as Reich Bishop.[10] In the church elections of July that year, the German Christians gained over two-thirds of all mandates and established themselves in many parishes. Manfred Gailus argues that this penetration of Nazism into the Protestant churches 'was not primarily accomplished by trickery, force, terror or usurpation on the part of the Nazi party ... but rather by a process in which Protestants enthusiastically delivered up their own institutions' and openly embraced the 'ideas of 1933'.[11] The German Christians wholeheartedly hung swastika flags in their churches to show their allegiance to the new regime. Gailus has argued that after 1933, the majority of the 28 regional churches underwent 'an extensive nazification of their faith, religiosity and church structures' and that Protestantism voluntarily adapted itself to the new regime.[12] He has shown that pastors, who played a central role in forming religious attitudes, had 'a surprising degree of freedom of choice and scope for action regarding church policy' in their individual parishes under National Socialism. Yet their congregations were largely 'penetrated by Nazi ideology and reconciled to the regime'.[13] John Conway has commented too on the extent to which large sections of the Protestant Church 'willingly collaborated with the regime' and 'lent their support to the extravagant nationalism of Hitler's rhetoric'.[14]

This suggests very little resistance to Nazism on the part of the Protestant Church and invalidates the interpretation of a heroic 'church struggle' against the Nazi regime. By and large, the Protestant Church initially welcomed National Socialism and adapted to the regime. Throughout the Nazi era, the Protestant Church continuously avoided public confrontations in the hope of maintaining its institutional autonomy from Nazi control.[15] However, moves towards 'co-ordination' of the Protestant Church with the Nazi state did meet with antipathy from a number of Protestant pastors. Pastor Martin Niemöller organised the Pastors' Emergency League at Dahlem on 11 September 1933. Niemöller established the *Bekennende Kirche* (Confessing Church) in response to the Nazis' attempts to 'co-ordinate' the evangelical church. The Confessing Church rejected Nazism and claimed to represent the true Protestant Church in Germany at the Barmen Synod in May 1934.[16] It adopted a declaration based upon principles inspired by its leading theologian, Karl Barth. Conway argues that the warning voices first heard at the Barmen Synod went 'largely unheeded'.[17] In July 1935, a new Ministry of Church Affairs was established under Hans Kerrl, who set up a Reich Church Committee in order to unify the Protestant Church in line with National Socialist requirements once and for all.[18] By 1937 this attempt had failed and from this time onwards, Nazi treatment of the churches became increasingly harsh.

Only a few exceptional congregations, such as that of Dahlem in Berlin, consistently fought against Nazi attempts to reshape the church. In 1937, its pastor, Niemöller, was arrested. In 1938, he was put into Sachsenhausen concentration camp and was subsequently moved to Dachau in 1941, where he remained until 1945. By the end of 1937, 700 other Protestant pastors had also been imprisoned. However, recent research on the Confessing Church has contended that even the struggle of the Confessing Church was primarily a struggle of the 'true' evangelical church against the unscriptural theological initiatives of the German Christians rather than against the state. Conway has noted that even the members of the Confessing Church, taken as a whole, 'never displayed any willingness to become the focus of any political resistance movement'.[19] Dietrich Bonhoeffer (1906–1945) was the only leading Protestant pastor who was actively engaged in the resistance movement against National Socialism, helping to build up contacts abroad for resistance. In his attempt to overthrow National Socialism, Bonhoeffer was isolated, even in the ranks of the Confessing Church.[20] He was arrested in 1943 and executed at Flossenbürg in April 1945.

The Catholic Church

Unlike the Protestant Church, the Catholic Church was officially opposed to the NSDAP, on the grounds of its 'false teachings' and its 'hostile attitude to fundamental doctrines and claims of the Catholic Church'. The meeting of the German bishops at Fulda in August 1932 concluded that if the NSDAP came to power in Germany, 'the prospects for the church interests of the Catholics would be gloomy indeed'.[21] Hitler's conciliatory broadcast of 23 March 1933, which aimed to reassure the churches about the nature of his regime and to persuade them that their rights would not be restricted, stated specifically that he regarded friendly relations with the Vatican as a matter of the greatest importance. In response to this, the Roman Catholic bishops retracted their previous policy of outright rejection of National Socialism.

The Catholic Church was concerned to safeguard its position under the new regime, having previously experienced open hostility towards its existence during the Bismarckian era. On 20 July 1933, the Nazi government signed a Concordat with the Vatican. Article 1 stated: 'The German Reich guarantees freedom of belief and of public worship to the Catholic faith. It recognises the right of the Catholic Church – within the limits of the law of the land – to order and administer its own affairs and to make laws and regulations binding upon its members in matters within its competence.'[22] Under the terms of the Concordat, the Catholic Church was to stay out of all political activities. In return for this, the regime guaranteed the religious freedom of the Catholic Church and its educational establishments and youth groups. However, the Nazi regime quickly reneged on its word and as the years passed, its guarantees proved illusory. Catholic confessional schools were closed down and Catholic youth groups were banned. Catholic priests were harassed and arrested, often being charged with alleged pederasty.[23] Restrictions were placed upon church processions and feast days in the church calendar were abolished. Monasteries were dissolved and their assets were confiscated.[24] By 1939, the position and influence of the Catholic Church in Germany had been severely curtailed.

The very existence of the Concordat had compromised the opportunity for any true moral resistance to the Hitler regime among Catholics. In addition, the cardinals had changed their tune. For example, Cardinal Bertram of Breslau, although he had condemned Nazism in print in 1931, later lent his moral authority to the Nazi regime. He sent birthday telegrams to Hitler in 1939 and 1940, and in May 1945 he even led a requiem mass for Hitler after his suicide. Conway has described Cardinal Bertram's consistent policy of accommodation with the Nazi regime as 'a fatal flaw' and suggested that 'at no time were German Catholics ever taught to recognise the demonic nature of the Nazi regime'.[25] Hence, there was no overall alienation of the Catholics from the Nazi regime and many Catholics misguidedly believed that specific policies directed against their faith occurred without the knowledge or approval of the *Führer*.

Nevertheless, there were tensions between particular Catholic communities and the National Socialist regime, arising from strong identification with the Catholic Church in communities that represented a sub-culture that was distinctive from the 'national community'. In particular, two 'crucifix struggles' – the first in Oldenburg in 1936 and the second in Bavaria in 1941 – highlight this point. The Oldenburg crucifix struggle of November 1936 demonstrates the nature of the relationship between a particular Catholic community and the Nazi state. This was a very pious Catholic community in a predominantly rural area in north Germany. On 4 November 1936, Julius Pauly, who headed the administration of schools and churches in the Oldenburg government, issued a decree that banned crucifixes, as well as other denominational symbols, in school buildings, on the grounds that they were public buildings and religious affiliations were not to be displayed in them.[26] A wave of protest followed, including addresses by Catholic clergymen, letters, petitions and deputations on the part of local people to retain the crucifixes in their schools. As a result, the Nazi *Gauleiter*, Carl Röver, proclaimed the annulment of Pauly's earlier decree at a public meeting on 25 November 1936. Jeremy Noakes has described this outcome as 'a dramatic victory for the Catholics of Oldenburg'.[27] Despite the humiliation for the local Nazi authorities caused by this reversal of policy, it appears that the prevention of widespread popular discontent was more pressing to the Nazi regime than the issue of denominational symbols hanging in schools.

On 23 April 1941, Adolf Wagner, Minister for Education in Bavaria, issued a 'crucifix decree', in which he called for the removal of all crucifixes and Christian pictures from schools. This provoked a 'crucifix struggle' in Bavaria in the ensuing months.[28] On 28 August 1941, Wagner was obliged to revoke his 'crucifix decree', although the chaos surrounding the initial decree and its annulment lasted for several months as both decrees were applied without any uniformity. Hence, in some villages, crucifixes had not been removed at all, while in others they had been removed and then reinstated. However, in the end, the opposition to the removal of the crucifixes was successful. The Bavarian crucifix struggle demonstrates the salience of pre-existing regional and religious identities in the Third Reich and the response of the regime to them. The Nazi regime was more concerned with losing the goodwill of the population in this area during the war, and the impact of this on popular morale and the war effort, than with the particular issue of the removal of crucifixes from schools.

Yet despite these incidents, Conway has suggested that the readiness of the Catholic leaders in Germany 'to support the authoritarian, nationalist and anti-Semitic goals of the Nazi regime demonstrated how unprepared they were, institutionally and theologically, to mobilise their following in any campaign beyond the defence of the immediate interests of their own community'.[29] They were anxious to emphasise areas of agreement with the regime and to minimise those of disagreement. Tensions escalated only in those spheres of Nazi policy-making that directly interfered with their own religious practices. Indeed, the crucifix affairs both showed that the moves against Nazi policy were largely instigated at grassroots level rather than from clergy directives. However, Ian Kershaw has demonstrated how individual parish priests with strong local influence could make it difficult for the Nazi regime to penetrate tightly-knit Catholic communities, particularly in rural areas. One such example was the village of Leidersbach in Lower Franconia, where the power of the young local priest could not be diminished by the attempts of NSDAP representatives to eclipse it.[30]

Spicer has argued further that 'the very existence of the Catholic Church and the perpetuation of its inner and outer ecclesiastical life in Germany constituted a formidable pattern of resistance against the Nazi state'.[31] He argues that by directly or indirectly encouraging their parishioners 'to examine the state critically', Catholic clergymen provided them with a worldview that was different to National Socialism and that 'such clerical acts of *Resistenz* provided an alternative space for Catholics to challenge the all-pervasive momentum of Nazism and its fatal ideology'.[32] Individual priests organised opposition to Nazi anti-clerical policies among their parishioners. Many hundreds of Catholic clergymen were incarcerated in concentration camps for their opposition. Four hundred Catholic priests were imprisoned in the Priests' Block at Dachau alone for their opposition to Nazism. Bishop Clemens Graf von Galen (1878–1946), who spoke out openly against the 'euthanasia' programme in 1941, was perhaps the most noted Catholic bishop to oppose Nazi policy. However, even his opposition was selective. While he spoke out in sermons in the summer of 1941 against the seizure of ecclesiastical property and the Nazi 'euthanasia' campaign, he did not speak out against the increasingly radical Nazi anti-Semitic policies. Beth Griech-Polelle has concluded that Galen's life under National Socialism was more complex than the popular image of the 'churchman-resister' and was indicative of 'the fluid nature of selective opposition and accommodation in Nazi Germany'.[33]

But let us now turn to the response of the Vatican itself to the Nazis' attack on the Catholic Church in Germany. Pope Pius XI, recognising the futility of his earlier Concordat with the Nazi regime, published his encyclical 'With Burning Concern' in March 1937. This acknowledged the breakdown of the Concordat and the incompatibility of Roman Catholicism with National Socialism. It began with the statement: 'With burning concern and mounting consternation we have been observing for some time now the cross carried by the church in Germany and the increasingly difficult situation of those men and women who have kept the faith and remained true to her in word and deed.'[34] Pius XI noted how the Catholic Church upheld its end of the Concordat, but how 'the other side ... in the end more or less openly' violated it. The encyclical, which also condemned Nazi racism, was read out from almost every Catholic pulpit in Germany on 21 March 1937. It showed a hardening in the stance taken by Pius XI towards the Third Reich, but this line was not continued by his successor, Eugenio Pacelli, who became Pope Pius XII in 1939.

Pius XII has been presented by a number of leading experts, including Saul Friedländer, Guenther Lewy and John Morley, as a Pope who failed to follow the dictates of conscience. He favoured Nazism as an ideology that was diametrically opposed to atheistic Bolshevism, which he regarded as the greater evil. He failed to provide any effective response to the Holocaust. Only in his Christmas message in 1942 did he make any allusion to it, but even this was phrased in the vague terms that 'hundreds of thousands of people, through no fault of their own and solely because of their nation or race, have been condemned to death'. The Vatican demonstrated very little moral leadership or conviction in its response to the fate of the Jews during the Second World War.[35]

The responses of both Christian churches in Germany to National Socialism were determined by their nationalist and anti-Bolshevik sentiments. Their traditional conservatism and desire to uphold their own positions and safeguard their institutions further influenced their reactions. These attitudes either paralysed the churches in terms of their making any challenges to National Socialism or led them to reluctantly accept it. Robert Wistrich describes the 'shameful record' of the Christian churches in their dealings with National Socialism and argues that the leaders of both the Catholic and Protestant churches were 'at best disastrously naïve' and 'at worst ... complicit to a degree in its crimes'.[36] The Christian churches failed to recognise the fundamental hostility of the Nazi regime to their position. Their leaders believed that private appeals and protests would be more effective in influencing the regime than voicing public challenges to it. In public statements, the representatives of both Christian churches attempted to avoid saying too much about the Nazi regime and its policies. Theological and doctrinal anti-Semitism also led to an overall reluctance on the part of the churches to challenge Nazi anti-Semitic policies. There was no clear response to the Nazi policies towards the Jews and the other groups persecuted by the regime. The prevailing example set by the churches as institutions filtered down to their congregations, giving them an excuse for inaction. Individual acts of courage formed only a small part of the history of the relationship between the Christian churches and the National Socialist state. Victoria Barnett has concluded that 'ultimately, the Churches' lapses during the Nazi era were lapses of vision and determination'.[37] Their desire to protect their own interests and their institutional independence lay at the centre of these failures. This prevented them from developing the morally adequate response to the Nazi regime and its atrocities that might be expected of these institutions.

THE *WEHRMACHT*

The term *Wehrmacht* refers to the German armed forces between 1935 and 1945. In flagrant disregard of the Treaty of Versailles, which prohibited conscription and limited the German standing army to 100,000 soldiers, Hitler reintroduced compulsory military service in March 1935. The *Wehrmacht* grew rapidly to 36 divisions with 555,000 soldiers. Military planning in 1935 and 1936 'envisaged a quantitative and qualitative transformation in the German armed forces', in order to prepare for war.[38] The *Wehrmacht* quickly grew into a powerful and well-equipped army.[39] In September 1939, Germany mobilised an army of 2,750,000 men in 103 divisions, including six armoured divisions and four motorised infantry divisions.[40] In addition, the *Wehrmacht* had changed from an elite military cadre into a veritable 'people's army'. It was the institution in which 20 million German men experienced and fought the Second World War. Thirteen million of these soldiers fought or served 'in the east' at some point in their careers.

The soldiers of the *Wehrmacht* were ideologically committed to National Socialism and to Hitler, even though they distanced themselves from the Party apparatus. Yet the army was not a 'haven' from the regime. Instead, it was very much an institution in which the Nazi political soldier was moulded. From August 1934, all German soldiers were called upon to swear a new oath of loyalty to the *Führer*. Their allegiance to the state was thus transferred into a personal loyalty to Hitler. Furthermore, the men who became the *Wehrmacht*'s most famous generals were very closely associated with and tied to the Nazi regime. Indeed, they owed personal allegiance to Hitler, for it was Hitler who allowed them to realise their ambitions for the creation of a large conscript army able to engage in a modern war of expansion. Hitler's generals then were not detached from the regime but were 'important elements in the integration of the *Wehrmacht* into the Third Reich'.[41]

The *Wehrmacht* did not stand as a separate entity from the regime but formed an integral part of it. Furthermore, the German armed forces reflected civilian society to a larger extent than in the past. Manfred Messerschmidt has shown that Hitler's measures went further than the contractual *Burgfriede* of the First World War, arguing that 'they guaranteed a permanent state of affairs in which the identity of the *Volksgemeinschaft* with the *Wehrgemeinschaft* appeared to be vouchsafed even in peace-time'.[42] Omer Bartov further argues that 'the *Wehrmacht* was the army of the people, and the willing tool of the regime, more than any of its predecessors'.[43] The *Wehrmacht* succeeded in creating highly disciplined and motivated soldiers out of its recruits, whatever their social class. Its recruits, as Hitler's soldiers, became part of a *Kampfgemeinschaft* ('fighting community'), a construct through which the Nazi regime mobilised the whole nation for its war of expansion, conquest and destruction. The *Wehrmacht* convinced the majority of its men that they were fighting a justified and necessary war against racial and political enemies. Their veneration of Hitler and their readiness to embrace the racist goals of his regime turned these young recruits into 'tenacious, increasingly brutalised and fanaticised soldiers'.[44] While the majority of the army was system supportive, there were strands of resistance within the army hierarchy. This subject is treated within Chapter 11 on dissenters and resisters.

While the *Wehrmacht* was a huge fighting force, it was also significant for what it represented as an institution. In the immediate post-war period, and indeed for a number of decades thereafter, those who belonged to the *Wehrmacht* were portrayed as the 'good' German soldiers, untainted by Nazi ideology and uninvolved in the barbaric crimes of the Nazi regime. The SS, an organisation that was numerically much smaller and ideologically much more committed to the concept of 'Aryan' racial superiority, was held responsible for perpetrating genocide. In this depiction, the professional soldiers of the *Wehrmacht* were exculpated from responsibility for the atrocities of the Nazi regime. This view of the *Wehrmacht* was expressed by its veterans in post-war publications, such as the memoirs of its former generals. It was also the official line taken by the government of the new West German state. Clearly, the view of the professional *Wehrmacht* soldier uninvolved in the crimes of the Nazi regime suited both domestic and international circumstances after the war.

Indeed, this concept of the 'purity of arms' of the *Wehrmacht* remained unchallenged in popular opinion for many decades. While it was comforting for the German public to accept this popular myth and therefore to avoid having to come to terms with the truth about the war in the east in particular, new historical research in the 1990s has presented a very different picture of the *Wehrmacht*. It has not only investigated much more carefully and minutely the extent of the barbarity of the war in the east but also overturned the previously accepted popular image of the untarnished *Wehrmacht* that was not implicated in the destruction and extermination in the east. The controversial *Crimes of the Wehrmacht* exhibition, which opened in Hamburg in 1995 and was moved on tour across Germany in 1997, played a significant part in widening knowledge and discussion of this subject among the German public. For historians, the involvement of the *Wehrmacht* in crimes against humanity 'in the east' had been long established, but for the German public, largely unaware of the scholarly literature on the subject, the revelations of the exhibition were shocking.

The groundbreaking work of German scholars, including Jürgen Förster, Wilhelm Deist, Bernhard Kroener and Rolf-Dieter Müller, who were sceptical about the accounts of former German veterans and generals and willing to overturn the myths upon which West German society was based, has created huge historiographical strides, building upon earlier studies of the *Wehrmacht* published in the 1960s, 1970s and 1980s.[45] These scholars have explored more closely the relationship of the *Wehrmacht* with the Nazi regime. Their work has greatly expanded our understanding of the *Wehrmacht* and its connections with the policies of the Nazi regime. It has invalidated the idea of the *Wehrmacht*'s professional and ideological detachment from the regime. Since the mid-1990s, our understanding of the role of the *Wehrmacht* in the Third Reich has changed considerably.[46]

Historians including Omer Bartov have shown that the *Wehrmacht* was ideologically influenced by National Socialism from a very early date and that it remained a major instrument in the implementation of Nazi policy until the end of the war. The *Wehrmacht* High Command subjected its troops to a substantial amount of ideological training, disregarded conventional rules of warfare and participated in the planning and execution of territorial conquest. The rank and file *Wehrmacht* soldiers became involved in widespread crimes against both enemy soldiers and civilian populations. In this regard, they acted on orders from their commanding officers, on their own initiative and sometimes even against orders. Bartov has written extensively on the 'barbarisation of warfare' on the eastern front.[47] He has demonstrated that from the perspective of both the military High Command and the rank and file soldiers, the campaign in the east was conducted as a war of destruction and annihilation. The *Wehrmacht* was involved not only in the killing of POWs and partisans but also in the implementation of the 'Final Solution'. Christian Streit has shown the collaboration of the *Wehrmacht* in the genocidal policies of the Nazi regime through its close co-operation with and provision of military assistance to the *SS-Einsatzgruppen*.[48] Its soldiers were directly involved in massacres across the Nazi-occupied territories in the east, including the liquidation of almost two-thirds of the Soviet POWs taken by Germany. Hannes Heer has also demonstrated the process by which *Wehrmacht* units became directly involved in genocide.[49] The war of annihilation was fought against entire populations, not against their armies or war industries alone. Furthermore, the Jews within these populations were specifically targeted for death.

Michael Geyer has argued that in this war of extermination, 'the war of the *Wehrmacht* was deliberate and self-generated', and most significantly, that 'since the *Wehrmacht* was a genuine people's army, this war of utter destruction and enslavement of civilian populations was the war that the German people fought'.[50] The *Wehrmacht*, rather than being a totally discrete and separate institution, came increasingly to reflect German civilian society, as Bartov has pointed out.[51] Its soldiers had been through a National Socialist education and socialisation in the schools, youth groups and Labour Service of the Nazi regime. The educational work of the *Wehrmacht* was based upon the Nazi *Weltanschauung*. Its educational theorists such as Friedrich Altrichter believed that a soldier's education had to be related to the 'racial foundations' on which the community of the nation was constructed.[52] The soldiers of the *Wehrmacht* regarded their enemies as 'subhuman'. They had a clear sense of the importance of their mission and of their own superiority to the populations that lived 'in the east'.

The *Blitzkrieg* successes in Poland and western Europe had led to an assumption of the invincibility of the *Wehrmacht*, based upon its efficiency and technical superiority. But the failure of the Russian campaign soon called this into question. The combat units sustained tremendous losses. Once belief in technological superiority had faltered, a 'fanaticisation' of the troops took its place to maintain their resilience. The *Wehrmacht* soldiers accepted Hitler's call for a total spiritual and ideological commitment to a war against the 'enemies' of National Socialism. The *Wehrmacht* compensated for the loss of its military superiority by means of an intensified political indoctrination of its troops. The corollary of this was an increasing brutalisation of its soldiers. While there were excesses on the western front, they were not nearly of the scale and magnitude of those on the eastern front, which was a totally different arena.

In the Soviet campaign, launched on 22 June 1941, the combat troops of the *Wehrmacht* carried out the orders of the regime and its High Command with willingness and often even with enthusiasm. This began with the *Kommissarbefehl* (Commissar Order), which called for the immediate execution of all Red Army political officers captured by front-line *Wehrmacht* units. The paring down of military law meant that *Wehrmacht* soldiers were not tried for offences committed against enemy soldiers or civilians as long as they did not flout combat discipline. Commanders called upon their soldiers to take harsh punitive action against Jews, communists, partisans or those assisting them. For example, General Walter von Reichenau, Commander of the Sixth Army, on 10 October 1941 attempted to instil into his troops a greater understanding of the need to destroy their enemy with the following appeal: 'The essential goal of the campaign against the Jewish-Bolshevik system is the complete destruction of its power instruments and the eradication of the Asiatic influence on the European cultural sphere. Thereby the troops too have tasks, which go beyond the conventional unilateral soldierly tradition. In the East, the soldier is not only a fighter according to the rules of warfare, but also a carrier of an inexorable racial conception and the avenger of all the bestialities which have been committed against the German and related races.'[53] General Erich von Manstein, Commander of the Eleventh Army, issued a similar order on 20 November 1941. Colonel-General Hermann Hoth, Commander of the Seventeenth Army, told his troops on 25 November 1941 that 'spiritually unbridgeable conceptions' were at war. 'This battle can only end with the destruction of one or the other; a compromise is out of the question.' He tried to deter his troops from showing 'compassion and weakness' towards the enemy population and urged them to comprehend 'the necessity of the harsh measures against racially foreign elements'.[54]

The cohesion of the *Wehrmacht* through the social system of 'primary groups', that is the close personal ties between soldiers that were regarded as the backbone of the army, could not have sustained itself on the Eastern Front. The combat units could not have survived for more than a few weeks at a time in the battle conditions there. Instead, the harsh disciplinary system of the *Wehrmacht* kept its units together in the face of heavy casualties. However, breakdown among combat units did occur at moments when fear of the enemy surpassed fear of disciplining from military superiors. At least 20,000 soldiers were executed for offences such as cowardice, self-inflicted wounding and desertion. But there were no serious mutinies in the *Wehrmacht*. Overall, its soldiers complied with the harsh discipline imposed upon them and did not break down, for they were instilled with the larger fear of the consequences of a Soviet victory, which steeled them with greater determination against their enemy. However, their obedience was closely tied to their own behaviour towards enemy soldiers and civilians, on whom they vented the consequences of their emotions. *Wehrmacht* soldiers were not punished for disregarding orders against plundering and indiscriminate shooting. Bartov argues that this perversion of the nature and meaning of discipline, which had a significant impact upon the behaviour of the troops, led to 'a widespread brutalisation of combat units'.[55] This was a simultaneous process of brutalisation both within the ranks of the *Wehrmacht* (through its extremely harsh disciplinary system) and towards its enemies (through its legalisation of crimes towards its enemies and its toleration of disciplinary offences by its troops towards its enemies).

The brutality of the occupation policies of the Nazi regime and the role of the *Wehrmacht* in its war of annihilation were exacerbated by the anti-partisan campaign in Soviet territory. Hannes Heer has argued that the anti-partisan campaign stripped German soldiers of all civilised norms, replacing them with an 'extermination mentality' directed against the enemy population as a whole.[56] Ben Shepherd's recent case studies on particular *Ostheer* units have resulted in his explanation of the anti-partisan campaign in 'nuanced, differentiated terms', suggesting that motivation and conduct were 'multi-faceted in origin and varied in form'.[57] Shepherd's comparative analysis of the experiences of the 221st Security Division and the 201st Security Division has led him to conclude that anti-partisan warfare developed differently in different cases and to advocate the placing of such divisions on a 'continuum of brutality' rather than seeking to lump all units together in a mass of uniform brutality. He argues that particular circumstances propelled the 201st Security Division into greater brutality and coercion than the 221st Security Division.[58] Such circumstances included factors such as the presence and impact of SS *Einsatzgruppen* or *Ordnungspolizei* units.[59] For example, he shows that 'for the 201st Security Division … more manpower for large-scale operations, substantial assistance from the SD and possibly institutional rivalry with the SS … reinforced the ability and probably also the inclination to terrorise more and cultivate less'.[60] Hence, he argues for a more differentiated approach in which some units can be seen to have pursued more conciliatory policies than others, although he clearly states that this should not detract attention from the overall context of the racial war of extermination.[61]

Richard Bessel argues that 'the *Wehrmacht* had surrendered itself to Hitler and Nazi ideology, had willingly engaged in a war of racial extermination and had abandoned moral responsibility and military rationality'.[62] It implemented Nazi policy in its brutal treatment of enemy soldiers and civilians. Its soldiers executed anyone suspected of partisan activity and destroyed thousands of villages, killing their inhabitants in a policy of collective punishment. As the war continued, the *Wehrmacht* adopted a 'scorched earth' policy wherever it was forced to retreat by the Soviet counter-offensive, devastating vast tracts of land and annihilating civilian populations.

An analysis of the conduct of soldiers at the front enhances our perspective on the social history of the Third Reich, for the 'national community' and its military counterpart the 'fighting community' were conceptually bound together, particularly because of the close and reciprocal relationship between German society and its soldiers during the Nazi era. This relationship was cemented by the great sense of solidarity expressed between and shared by the home front and the fighting front. The consequences of this ethos for the enemies of Nazism both at home and abroad were revealed during the war. In particular, as Messerschmidt has argued, 'the idea of the vital needs of the German *Volksgemeinschaft* provided the *Wehrmacht* with something like a "clear conscience" in its brutal conduct of the war in the East'.[63]

NOTES

1 R. Steigmann-Gall, *The Holy Reich: Nazi Conceptions of Christianity, 1919–1945* (Cambridge, 2003), pp. 87–91.
2 Ibid., p. 266.
3 Cited in H. Rauschning, *Hitler Speaks* (London, 1939), pp. 57–8.
4 Cited in P. Matheson (ed.), *The Third Reich and the Christian Churches* (Edinburgh, 1981), p. 9.
5 Cited in Matheson (ed.), *The Third Reich and the Christian Churches*, p. 75.
6 R. Evans, *The Third Reich in Power* (London, 2006), p. 253.
7 Cited in M. Gailus, 'Overwhelmed by their own Fascination with the "Ideas of 1933": Berlin's Protestant Social Milieu in the Third Reich', *German History*, Vol. 20, No. 4 (2002), p. 469.
8 Cited in Matheson (ed.), *The Third Reich and the Christian Churches*, pp. 5–6.
9 On the German Christians, see especially D. Bergen, *The Twisted Cross: The German Christians in the Third Reich* (Chapel Hill, 1995). See also R. Erikson, *Theologians under Hitler* (New Haven, 1985).
10 On Ludwig Müller, see T. Schneider, *Reichsbischof Ludwig Müller: Eine Untersuchung zu Leben, Werk und Persönlichkeit* (Göttingen, 1993).
11 Gailus, 'Overwhelmed by their own Fascination', p. 468.
12 Ibid., p. 462.
13 Ibid., p. 463.
14 J. Conway, 'Interpreting the German Church Struggles, 1933–1990', *German History*, Vol. 16, No. 3 (1998), p. 381.
15 For a fuller analysis, see K. Meier, *Kreuz und Hakenkreuz. Die evangelische Kirche im Dritten Reich* (Munich, 1992).
16 On this, see S. Baranowski, *The Confessing Church, Conservative Elites and the Nazi State* (Lewiston, 1986), pp. 45–64.
17 J. Conway, *The Nazi Persecution of the Churches* (London, 1968), p. 332.
18 On this, see E. Helmreich, *The German Churches under Hitler* (Detroit, 1979), pp. 189–205.
19 Conway, 'Interpreting the German Church Struggles, 1933–1990', p. 381.
20 This point is clearly made in E. Bethge, *Dietrich Bonhoeffer: Man of Vision, Man of Courage* (New York, 1970). On Bonhoeffer, see also R. Mengus, 'Dietrich Bonhoeffer and the Decision to Resist', in M. Geyer and J. Boyer (eds), *Resistance against the Third Reich 1933–1990* (Chicago, 1994), pp. 201–13.
21 Cited in Matheson (ed.), *The Third Reich and the Christian Churches*, p. 7.
22 Cited in ibid., p. 30.
23 See Helmreich, *The German Churches under Hitler*, pp. 275–301.
24 On this, see E. Harrison, 'The Nazi Dissolution of the Monasteries: A Case Study', *English Historical Review*, Vol. 109 (1994), pp. 323–55.
25 Conway, 'Interpreting the German Church Struggles, 1933–1990', p. 386.
26 J. Noakes, 'The Oldenburg Crucifix Struggle of November 1936: A Case Study of Opposition in the Third Reich, in P. Stachura (ed.), *The Shaping of the Nazi State* (London, 1978), p. 218.
27 Ibid., p. 225.
28 On this struggle, see I. Kershaw, *Popular Opinion and Political Dissent in the Third Reich: Bavaria 1933–1945* (Oxford, 1984), pp. 340–57.
29 Conway, 'Interpreting the German Church Struggles, 1933–1990', p. 386.
30 Kershaw, *Popular Opinion and Political Dissent in the Third Reich*, pp. 198–200.
31 K. Spicer, *Resisting the Third Reich: The Catholic Clergy in Hitler's Berlin* (DeKalb, 2004), p. 185.

32 Ibid., p. 184.

33 B. Griech-Polelle, 'Image of a Churchman-Resister: Bishop von Galen, the Euthanasia Project and the Sermons of Summer 1941', *Journal of Contemporary History*, Vol. 36, No. 1 (2001), p. 57.

34 Cited in Matheson (ed.), *The Third Reich and the Christian Churches*, p. 68.

35 The large literature on this includes D. Goldhagen, *A Moral Reckoning: The Role of the Catholic Church in the Holocaust and its Unfulfilled Duty of Repair* (London, 2002); J. Cornwell, *Hitler's Pope: The Secret History of Pius XII* (London, 1999); M. Phayer, *The Catholic Church and the Holocaust, 1930–1965* (Bloomington, 2000); and P. Godman, *Hitler and the Vatican* (New York, 2004). On the Catholic Church, see also G. Lewy, *The Catholic Church and Nazi Germany* (New York, 2000) and G. Denzler, *Widerstand oder Anpassung? Katholische Kirche und Drittes Reich* (Munich, 1984).

36 R. Wistrich, 'The Pope, the Church, and the Jews', *Commentary* (April 1999), p. 25.

37 V. Barnett, 'The Role of the Churches: Compliance and Confrontation', *Dimensions*, Vol. 14, No. 1 (May 2000), p. 12.

38 R. Bessel, *Nazism and War* (London, 2004), p. 49.

39 On the army before the outbreak of the Second World War, see K.-J. Müller, *Armee und Drittes Reich 1933–1939. Darstellung und Dokumentation* (Paderborn, 1987).

40 On rearmament, see W. Deist, *The Wehrmacht and German Rearmament* (London, 1981).

41 O. Bartov, 'Soldiers, Nazis and War in the Third Reich', in C. Leitz (ed.), *The Third Reich* (Oxford, 1999) p. 145.

42 M. Messerschmidt, 'The *Wehrmacht* and the *Volksgemeinschaft*', *Journal of Contemporary History*, Vol. 18 (1983), p. 725.

43 Bartov, 'Soldiers, Nazis and War in the Third Reich', p. 149.

44 O. Bartov, 'The Missing Years: German Workers, German Soldiers', in D. Crew (ed.), *Nazism and German Society* (London, 1994), p. 46.

45 Earlier studies include M. Messerschmidt, *Die Wehrmacht im NS-Staat* (Hamburg, 1969); K.-J. Müller, *Das Heer und Hitler* (Stuttgart, 1969); H. Krausnick and H.-H. Wilhelm, *Die Truppe des Weltanschauungskrieges* (Stuttgart, 1981). See also T. Schulte, *The German Army and Nazi Policies in Occupied Russia* (Oxford, 1989); R.-D. Müller and G. Ueberschär (eds), *Hitler's War in the East 1941–1945* (Oxford, 1997). On more recent historiographical developments, see O. Bartov, 'German Soldiers and the Holocaust: Historiography, Research and Implications', *History and Memory*, Vol. 9, Nos. 1/2 (1997), especially pp. 165–71.

46 See R.-D. Müller and H.-E. Volkmann (eds), *Die Wehrmacht. Mythos und Realität* (Munich, 1999); H. Heer and K. Naumann (eds), *Vernichtungskrieg. Verbrechen der Wehrmacht 1941 bis 1944* (Hamburg, 1995); C. Gerlach, *Kalkulierte Mörde. Die deutsche Wirtschafts- und Vernichtungspolitik im Weissrussland 1941–1944* (Hamburg, 1999); R.-D. Müller, *Hitlers Ostkrieg und die deutsche Siedlungspolitik. Die Zusammenarbeit von Wehrmacht, Wirtschaft und SS* (Frankfurt am Main, 1991); K. Pohl, *Wehrmacht und Vernichtungspolitik. Militär im nationalsozialistischen System* (Göttingen, 1999).

47 See especially O. Bartov, *The Eastern Front, 1941–1945: German Troops and the Barbarisation of Warfare* (London, 1985).

48 C. Streit, *Keine Kameraden. Die Wehrmacht und die sowjetischen Kriegsgefangenen 1941–1945* (Stuttgart, 1978).

49 See Bartov, 'German Soldiers and the Holocaust: Historiography, Research and Implications', p. 173.

50 M. Geyer, *The German Army and Genocide* (New York, 1999), pp. 7–8.

51 O. Bartov, 'Soldiers, Nazis and War in the Third Reich', p. 133.

52 Messerschmidt, 'The *Wehrmacht* and the *Volksgemeinschaft*', p. 727.

53 Cited in O. Bartov, *Hitler's Army: Soldiers, Nazis, and War in the Third Reich* (Oxford, 1991), p. 129.

54 Cited in ibid., pp. 130–1.

55 Ibid., p. 58.

56 H. Heer, 'Die Logik des Vernichtungskrieges', in H. Heer and K. Naumann (eds), *Vernichtungskrieg* (Hamburg, 1995), pp. 104–38.

57 B. Shepherd, 'The Continuum of Brutality: *Wehrmacht* Security Divisions in Central Russia, 1942', *German History*, Vol. 21, No. 1 (2003), pp. 50 and 51.

58 Ibid., pp. 59–79.

59 Ibid., pp. 58–9. On the role of the *Ordnungspolizei* in Nazi extermination policy in the east, see C. Browning, *Ordinary Men: Reserve Police Battalion 101 and the Final Solution in Poland* (New York, 1992). The same police battalion is also the subject of D. Goldhagen, *Hitler's Willing Executioners* (New York, 1996).

60 Shepherd, 'The Continuum of Brutality', p. 80.

61 On this, see also B. Shepherd, '*Wehrmacht* Security Regiments in the Soviet Partisan War, 1943', *European History Quarterly*, Vol. 33, No. 4 (2003), pp. 493–529.

62 Bessel, *Nazism and War*, p. 118.

63 Messerschmidt, 'The *Wehrmacht* and the *Volksgemeinschaft*', p. 735.

PART TWO

OUTSIDE THE 'NATIONAL COMMUNITY'

7

THE JEWS

Sign at a village entrance in Nazi Germany 1935 saying 'The Jews are uninvited guests'. © The Wiener Library

Before examining the experiences of the Jews under National Socialism, it is useful for contextual purposes to consider briefly their position during the Weimar era.[1] Despite the occasional surfacing of anti-Semitism, Jews largely felt 'at home' in Germany during the Weimar Republic.[2] But although the liberal egalitarianism of the Weimar Republic meant that Jews could participate in public life, and although there was an influx of Jewish influence into both high and popular culture, these developments did not necessarily signify their social acceptance. The position of Jews in the Weimar Republic was paradoxical and ambiguous. Furthermore, most German Jews underestimated the significance of the Nazi movement. At first, many did not take the NSDAP seriously or believe that Hitler would become Chancellor. They were baffled and shocked when the Nazis gained power, as few had taken this possibility seriously or considered its consequences. They believed that they had coped with anti-Semitism before and would cope again. They did not comprehend the magnitude and nature of Nazi anti-Semitism.

When Hitler came to power there were 499,682 Jews living in Germany.[3] This constituted a tiny minority of 0.77 per cent of the overall population. The Jews were excluded from the 'national community' and victimised by the Nazi regime from its very earliest days in power. Nazi anti-Semitism differed from earlier forms of anti-Semitism. Traditional anti-Semitism, a phe-

101

nomenon that had existed in Europe over many centuries, was largely religious in character. It opposed Jews because they rejected Christianity. Traditional anti-Semitism held that if a Jew converted to Christianity, then he could be saved. A new brand of anti-Semitism emerged during the second half of the nineteenth century, influenced by Social Darwinism and racial theories, which was much more radical and uncompromising than traditional anti-Semitism. This was based upon the definition of the Jews as a 'race'. Hence, there could be no salvation through conversion to Christianity. Hitler was highly influenced by racial anti-Semitism, a phenomenon that had grown in influence in Germany in the years following the First World War and formed the basis of the Nazis' racial ideology. There can be no doubt about the centrality of anti-Semitism to Hitler's *Weltanschauung*. He consistently depicted the Jewish race as the eternal enemy of the 'Aryan' race. In *Mein Kampf* (1924), Hitler had stated: 'The personification of the devil as the symbol of all evil assumes the living shape of the Jew.' Once in power Hitler's intense personal hatred of the Jews became central to state policy. As Nazi policy was based upon racial anti-Semitism, all Jews – whether or not they practised their religion – were subjected to persecution by the regime.

Saul Friedländer has emphasised the need for greater synthesis of the history of the victims with the actions of the perpetrators, stating: 'It is all too often forgotten that Nazi attitudes and policies cannot be fully assessed without knowledge of the lives and indeed the feelings of the Jewish men, women and children themselves.'[4] Testimonies and memoirs are important sources in this respect and although they must be used and interpreted with care in order to avoid possible problems associated with their use as sources, they provide a richness of narrative unobtainable from other types of evidence.[5] The examples used in this chapter illuminate the events and reconnect them with personal experiences. They are intended as illustrations, not as overall representations, as each experience was different. No single story can paint the whole picture. Each narrative forms part of a fragmented mosaic and is important for that very reason. Personal experiences within the overall context of Nazi policy varied enormously according to a variety of circumstances including age, class, location, gender and religious orientation.

Policies designed to persecute Germany's Jews and to segregate them from the rest of society began with the National Boycott of Jewish Businesses on 1 April 1933, which set the stage for their economic harassment.[6] The boycott was instigated by Party radicals, in particular members of the SA, who were euphoric after the Nazi Party's 'seizure of power'. Posters and placards were put up outside Jewish shops and businesses, saying 'Germans defend yourselves! Do not buy from Jews!' SA men placed themselves in front of Jewish shops to deter customers. The boycott was intended to become a permanent feature of life in the Third Reich, but because many Germans ignored the SA men and the posters and continued to buy from Jewish shops, it was abandoned after a day.[7] Still, Inge Deutschkron recounts how from the day of the boycott, 'our home did not seem the same secure place as before'.[8] Edwin

Landau describes his emotions on the day of the boycott: 'I was ashamed that I had once belonged to this people. I was ashamed about the trust I had given so many who now revealed themselves as my enemies ... This was my leave-taking from everything German, my inner separation from what had been my fatherland.'[9] Many Jews shared this sense of betrayal by their fatherland. It is estimated that between 300 and 400 Jews committed suicide in response to the boycott.[10] Yet many others regarded the boycott as an example of excessive behaviour on the part of the SA and hoped that the regime's anti-Semitism would not last.

However, the first legal measure against the Jews was implemented within a week of the boycott. On 7 April 1933, Clause 3 of the Law for the Restoration of the Professional Civil Service called for the 'retirement' of Jewish officials from their positions. By May 1933, all 'non-Aryan' public sector employees were dismissed from their jobs. After this, the range of professions and occupations from which Jews were excluded gradually widened. These legal measures were accompanied by informal social ostracism. Jews were encouraged to give up their membership of clubs and organisations, while Germans began to sever their friendships and professional ties with Jews. Marion Kaplan has described this as 'a gradual yet dramatic process that led Jews toward "social death"'.[11]

Anti-Semitic legislation and social ostracism at first baffled Germany's Jews who were very attached to their homeland. Germany had formed their cultural tradition, education and language. For example, Grete Rosenzweig describes how 'we had always considered ourselves German citizens in the first place, Jews by religion'. German Jews had willingly fought in the First World War alongside their fellow countrymen. Ernest Steifel describes how 'many Jews were more German than Germans and very patriotic'.[12] Hence, faced with the choice of emigration or adapting to the new situation, many Jews stayed in Germany, not realising that 1933 had signalled 'the end of emancipation' for them. There was a general willingness to believe that the Nazi regime would cease or moderate its excesses and that the situation would not deteriorate.

The Nuremberg Laws of 15 September 1935 were comprised of two edicts designed to segregate Jews from the rest of society and to exclude them from the 'national community'. The Reich Citizenship Law denied Jews their equal civil rights, redefining them as 'subjects' instead of 'citizens'. The Law for the Protection of German Blood and Honour prohibited marriages and sexual relationships between Jews and 'Aryans'.[13] The significance of the Nuremberg Laws was their creation of a legal separation between the Jews and the rest of German society. When they were passed, many Jews saw the Nuremberg Laws as a definitive clarification of their social and legal position. They regarded the Nuremberg Laws positively, believing that if they lived within the parameters defined by them, the violence and illegal persecution would cease. This may explain why the numbers of Jews seeking to emigrate temporarily dropped after the Nuremberg Laws were passed. But the

Nuremberg Laws, in reality, brought about a grave deterioration in the situation of most Jews and had a considerable impact upon how Jews came to be regarded by their 'Aryan' compatriots. Claire Dratch (née Bacharach) recounts how her life changed after the enactment of the Nuremberg Laws: 'Friends no longer wanted to walk down the street with me. They no longer wished to sit next to me on the train, eventually they did not wish to be seen with me at all … I was the same Claire Bacharach – but I was Jewish. I was no longer invited to my Christian friends' birthday parties or holiday celebrations … I had become a non-person.'[14]

Between 1936 and 1937, the pace of anti-Semitic legislation appeared to decelerate and no major initiatives were taken with regard to the 'Jewish question'. For example, during the 1936 Berlin Olympic Games, anti-Semitic posters were temporarily taken down, so as not to draw foreign visitors' and commentators' attention to the anti-Semitic nature of the regime. Yet still new decrees were passed that marginalised Jews both from the economy and from society. The Jews were systematically and deliberately pauperised in a process known as the 'Aryanisation of the economy', which excluded Jews from employment and forced them to sell or close down their businesses.[15] Many former professionals, white-collar workers and businessmen were forced into poverty by the end of 1937. They tried to eke out an existence by hawking and peddling. Others became unemployed, still others ultimately undertook forced manual labour in work camps for construction or mining. A host of other measures were employed and laws passed to isolate and humiliate the Jews and to physically separate them from the rest of the population. For example, in July 1938, streets named after Jews were renamed and park benches were designated 'for Aryans only'.[16] In the same month, the approximately 3,000 Jewish doctors still practising their profession were prohibited from doing so. Only 709 were allowed to maintain their practices, but were designated as 'medical practitioners' to Jewish patients only. In September 1938, only 172 lawyers were allowed to continue in their profession and they were similarly designated as 'legal counsel' to Jewish clients only. By November 1938, Jews were prohibited from going to the theatre, concerts and exhibitions. They were also excluded from certain restaurants. With each successive anti-Semitic measure, contacts between Jews and 'Aryans' were minimised, formalised or banned, leading to a spatial separation of the Jews from the 'national community'.

The development of legal anti-Semitism was popularly acknowledged in Germany. Many people accepted the need to repress Jewish influence in Germany and therefore condoned the anti-Semitic measures of the Nazi regime. While some had attempted to maintain ties with their Jewish friends and neighbours at first, the impact of several years of anti-Semitic policies and anti-Semitic propaganda brought about a separation of Jews and 'Aryans'. Throughout the early years of the Third Reich, Jewish people were sometimes given a false sense of security by the kind words of a German neighbour or friend. Lisa Brauer recounts that 'there were days when we were overwhelmed by desperation, but an understanding word from an Aryan neighbour, a kind enquiry from a Gentile acquaintance gave us always new hope and confidence'.[17] By 1938, professional and personal ties were torn apart and social life was disrupted. Many Jews deliberately eschewed their former 'Aryan' friends, colleagues and acquaintances, both in order to avoid disappointment and discrimination and in some cases so as not to endanger them. Many Jewish people did not want to jeopardise their non-Jewish acquaintances. This almost forced avoidance of association added to their social alienation. Indeed, the more endangered the Jewish community became, the tenser its relations with 'Aryans' became. Mistrust and precaution replaced the good understanding of the past.

Nazi anti-Semitic policy shifted gear on the night of 9–10 November 1938, when Goebbels unleashed a pogrom known as *'Reichskristallnacht'* ('The Night of the Broken Glass').[18] Goebbels used the murder of Ernst vom Rath, a German official in Paris, by a young Polish Jew, Hershel Grynspan, as a pretext for the pogrom. Some 7,000 Jewish businesses were destroyed, almost every synagogue in the country was burned down, 26,000 Jewish men were sent to concentration camps and 91 people were killed during the course of the pogrom. Fire brigades were instructed not to extinguish fires in Jewish properties. *'Reichskristallnacht'* represented a decisive turning point in Nazi anti-Semitic policy. It was an unprecedented, widespread and violent act of persecution that took place in full view of the German public. Goebbels claimed that the pogrom was a 'spontaneous popular response' on the part of the German nation to the murder of vom Rath. But it was, in reality, a centrally planned and orchestrated action.

The reactions of the German people were mixed. Some rejected it on grounds of Christian compassion; others were appalled at the violation of law and order that the pogrom represented.[19] Testimonies show instances of kindness on the part of Christian neighbours. But while few people actively engaged in the plundering and wanton destruction carried out by the Party activists and SA squads, most were also either unwilling or unable to do anything to oppose the violence. In addition, with very few exceptions, the representatives of both the Protestant and Roman Catholic churches remained silent.[20] While the popular reaction against the Jews had not been as extreme as the regime would have wished, the pogrom did increase the sense that the Jewish question needed 'solving' in popular opinion. After a short time, however, the pogrom itself receded from popular consciousness and the German people continued to get on with their lives.

But after *'Reichskristallnacht'*, with the violent shattering of their homes, businesses and synagogues, the German Jews could not get back to their lives. They could no longer ignore or accommodate Nazi anti-Semitism, hoping that it would cease. With each earlier measure, Germany's Jews had reacted by adapting to their worsening situation. But *'Reichskristallnacht'* changed this response. Emigration became a priority, even to those Jews who had previously opposed the idea.[21] After the pogrom, an 'atonement payment' of 1 billion Reichsmarks was imposed upon the Jews. This was a great humiliation and degradation for the Jews who were held responsible for the damage. Following '*Reichskristallnacht*', Hermann Goering held a meeting on 12 November 1938, at which he told top government and Party officials that the 'Jewish question' had to be settled: 'now, once and for all, co-ordinated and solved in one way or another'. In the aftermath of this meeting, the 'solution to the Jewish question' was placed in the hands of the SS. Jews were now to be totally excluded from the economy in accordance with the Decree for the Exclusion of Jews from German Economic Life.[22] On 15 November, the Ministry of Education banned all Jewish children from state schools. On 3 December, German Jews had their driving licences revoked.[23] By the beginning of 1939, it was becoming clear that policy was aimed at the compulsory emigration of Jews, in order to make the German Reich '*judenfrei*' (free of Jews). To this end, Goering ordered Heydrich to establish a centre for Jewish emigration. However, Jews who left Germany were obliged to pay a hefty 'flight tax'.

In his 30 January 1939 Reichstag speech, Hitler declared the Jews as the enemies of National Socialism and argued that if they did not break away from their parasitic lives, they risked 'a crisis of unimaginable proportions'. He made a prophecy that 'if the international Jewish financiers in and outside Europe should succeed in plunging the nations once more into a world war, then the result will not be the Bolshevising of the earth, and thus a victory of Jewry, but the annihilation of the Jewish race in Europe'.[24] By this time, Jews had been forced into Jewish quarters in the cities, into Jewish houses, where many families lived together in cramped conditions. Ghettoisation had begun. From January 1939, Jews were assigned obligatory first names (Sara for females and Israel for males) and their passports were stamped with a red J. A decree of 21 February 1939 called for Jews to hand over all gold, platinum, silver and jewels, with the exception of their wedding rings, to the public purchasing offices within two weeks. Once the war broke out, the situation of Germany's Jews deteriorated rapidly as they were deprived of whatever rights and dignity they had left.[25] On 1 September 1939, a curfew was imposed upon the Jews, banning them from the streets between 9 p.m. and 5 a.m. in the summer and between 8 p.m. and 6 a.m. in the winter. On 29 September 1939, German Jews were required to hand over their radios.

During the period 1933–1939, the German people were fully aware of the repression and persecution of their Jewish fellow citizens. They largely accepted legal anti-Semitism, as well as anti-Semitic measures that were carried out without too much ado. The Jews did not belong to the 'national community'. Many Germans disapproved of more public exhibitions of violence, however, and were shocked by the events of '*Reichskristallnacht*'. Yet the subsequent measures taken to remove the Jews from Germany's social and economic life met almost no protest or resistance. The movement of Jews to the big cities, where they were more anonymous, and the increased emigration had reduced contact between Jews and non-Jews to a minimum. Once the war began, particularly with a ban on listening to foreign radio stations, it became harder for the Germans to ascertain the policies being carried out by the Nazi government in their name. They became preoccupied with the war and its effects on their own lives and paid little attention to the 'Jewish question'.

The speedy conquest of Poland (with its 1.7 million Jews) led to a transformation of the 'Jewish question'.[26] Emigration was no longer a realistic policy aim. By June 1940, Heydrich stated that the 'overall problem' could not be solved by emigration. 'Territorial solutions' such as the Nisko Project and the Madagascar Plan were proposed. It was hoped that in such remote locations, the Jews would be eradicated, but these plans were never realised. The Nazis established ghettoes in Poland, as a temporary arrangement, but these engendered a host of administrative problems. At first, the ghettoes were used to concentrate the Jewish population into forced areas within the larger cities, such as Warsaw and Łódź. As conditions in the ghettoes worsened, Nazi policy became increasingly radicalised. Wolfgang Benz has described the function of the ghettoes between 1940 and 1943: 'They were the waiting rooms of destruction, the antechambers of hell, the stations on the way to the camps to which human beings were deported for the express purpose of being murdered.'[27]

With the German invasion of the Soviet Union, Operation Barbarossa (22 June 1941), the 'solution to the Jewish question', entered yet another phase. This was the work of special units of the SS, the *SS-Einsatzgruppen*.[28] The *SS-Einsatzgruppen* followed in the wake of the *Wehrmacht* as it penetrated Soviet territory, waging an unprecedented campaign of murder against the Jewish populations. Heydrich's *Kommissarbefehl* of 2 July 1941, ordering that communist officials, Jews in Party and state employment and other radical elements were to be executed, sufficed to give the go-ahead to the *SS-Einsatzgruppen* to kill all Jews they encountered, including women and children. Mass shootings of Jews occurred throughout the Soviet territories occupied by the Nazis – in eastern Poland, Latvia, Estonia, Lithuania, Byelorussia, Ukraine and the Crimea. It is estimated that more than 1.3 million Jews were shot to death by the *SS-Einsatzgruppen* within the first 18 months of Germany's invasion of the Soviet Union. The actions of the *SS-Einsatzgruppen* marked a sharp radicalisation in Nazi anti-Semitic policy.

In the meantime, on 31 July 1941, Goering ordered Heydrich to make 'all necessary preparations with regard to organisational, technical and material matters for bringing about a complete solution of the Jewish question within the German sphere of influence in Europe'.[29] From 1 September 1941, the German Jews were forced to wear the Yellow Star, to mark them out, once and for all, from the rest of the German population. This visible distinction signified their total exclusion from the 'national community'. On 23 October 1941, Himmler ordered that no more Jews were allowed to emigrate from anywhere inside Germany or Nazi-occupied Europe. This was an important signal, as Jewish emigration had been a previous goal of the Nazi regime.

From the late summer, throughout the autumn and winter of 1941, a number of experiments and 'local initiatives' were taken to kill Jews. In December 1941, the first gassings were carried out at Chelmno. Hence, centralised administrative control over killing Jews was achieved only retrospectively, after localised killings had begun. This was the function of the Wannsee Conference on 20 January 1942.[30] While the Wannsee Conference was not the place at which the decision for mass murder was taken, Mark Roseman has shown that it was a powerfully symbolic event: 'Here was the distinguished ambience of an elegant villa, in a cultivated suburb, in one of Europe's most sophisticated capitals. Here were fifteen educated, civilised bureaucrats, from an educated, civilised society, observing all due decorum. And here was genocide, going through, on the nod.'[31]

German Jews were deported to death camps in Poland where they shared the fate of the rest of European Jewry in the Nazis' systematic extermination process, the 'Final Solution'.[32] The deportation of the German Jews had begun in October 1941, but it was systematised from March 1942 onwards. German Jews received a summons to present themselves for 'evacuation' at designated collection points. They were given an 'evacuation number' and their property was confiscated by the state. The deportations took place with the help of Jewish administrative bodies, as well as local and municipal authorities. The circumstances of the deportations left little doubt that the fate of the Jews was to be one of hardship and misery. Many Jews committed suicide when they were called for transportation. In addition, the deportations were not carried out secretly, but in full public view. The Jews of Heidelberg, for instance, were assembled in the market square at midday and sent on the transports from there. Most Germans accepted the deportation measures; some had misgivings about the physical violence that accompanied them or objected to the deportation of old people, women and children. But there was no serious objection or intervention on behalf of the Jews. The deportations were accepted as legitimate, because they were undertaken by government authorities, and necessary, because the Jews did not belong to the 'national community'. Most people accepted the official justification for the 'resettlement' of the Jews in the east to create more living space for the 'Aryan' population. While a few people were sympathetic to the Jews, the overall response to the deportations was public passivity. This popular response was the outcome of a widespread moral indifference.

German Jews were deported by train from the start of November 1941 from collection points at Berlin, Hamburg, Hanover, Dortmund, Münster, Dusseldorf, Cologne, Frankfurt, Kassel, Stuttgart, Nuremberg, Munich and Breslau. In this wave of deportations, approximately 20,000 Jews from Germany, as well as a further 30,000 Jews from Austria, Bohemia and Moravia, were transported to Riga or Minsk and from there to the extermination camps. From March 1942, a further 55,000 Jews from these areas, among them 17,000 from Germany, were deported to the east to meet the same fate. A further 40,000 German Jews were transported to Theresienstadt from

2 June 1942. Many thousands died at Theresienstadt, many thousands more were deported again from there to the death camps. One year later, in June 1943, Germany was announced '*judenfrei*'.

However, it is estimated that between 10,000 and 12,000 German Jews went into hiding during the war. They were known as 'U-boats'. Some hid before they were called for deportation, others after they had received their orders. They removed the Yellow Star from their clothes and attempted to pass as 'Aryans'. Some managed to obtain identity papers, others went into hiding without papers. Gabriel Ritter recalls that at the end of February 1943: 'We were looking out of the window … and saw how the Jews were being taken from the rear house. My mother … tore off our stars. We got dressed quickly and really catch-as-catch-can: I remember that my mother put on the wrong skirt with the wrong jacket.'[33] With just the clothes they were wearing and a little money, they approached various non-Jewish acquaintances. They hid with one acquaintance for three days and then with another non-Jewish family for over a year. For the German Jews attempting to survive underground, daily life became a struggle to obtain food and shelter. Those who were blonde and 'looked German' could sometimes pass as 'Aryans'. Many had to change locations many times in order to avoid arousing suspicion. For example, Inge Deutschkron hid with her mother in at least 12 different places over a 27-month period 'underground'. Some Jews told the people who hid them that they were Jewish, others concealed their identity. As Kaplan notes: 'Between hiders and hidden, much was assumed and left unsaid – and hiders who knew often feigned ignorance.'[34] People who provided support or shelter to the Jews faced serious punishment if they were discovered. During the Allied bombing campaigns, Jews pretended to be 'Aryans', claiming that their homes and identification papers had been destroyed. The 'U-boats' lived in constant fear of detection or denunciation, as well as usually poor, cramped and often unsanitary conditions. After the war, between 3000 and 5000 Jews emerged from hiding in Germany. The rest had been denounced, sometimes by 'Jewish catchers', and arrested by the Gestapo, or died from hunger, exposure or bombings.

Public concern for the Jews diminished in Germany during the war. While there had been some public indignation, even if largely passive, in response to the '*Reichskristallnacht*' pogrom of November 1938, there was very little reaction to the mass murder of Jews during the war. This was partly because the atrocities of the *SS-Einsatzgruppen* took place in Soviet territory and the extermination camps – Chelmno, Belzec, Sobibor, Treblinka, Auschwitz and Majdanek – were constructed in Poland, outside the immediate sphere of experience of the German population. The geographic location of racial anti-Semitic policies had moved outside the frame of reference of the German people. Rumours filtered back into German society from foreign radio broadcasts or soldiers on leave, but most people chose not to believe them. They preferred to accept the idea that the Jews had been resettled and located 'in the east' for labour purposes. Those who heard of the massacres in Poland and did believe the news thought they were excesses perpetrated by individual leaders rather than state-sanctioned policy. Official phraseology sought to hide the real activities of the death camps in Poland, but rumours about the death camps did get back to Germany. Some historians have argued that it was impossible to put the whole story together, while others have maintained that despite the official secrecy surrounding the 'Final Solution', every German who wanted to know about it could find out and that there was enough information filtering back to Germany for them to have an idea of what was being perpetrated in their name.[35]

In addition, the German people were so absorbed by their own immediate, day-to-day concerns, in particular the bombing raids, fear for their relatives at the front, and rationing, that they were 'anaesthetised ... to the sufferings of the Jews', a segment of the population already displaced from the 'national community'.[36] Kershaw further argues that there was 'much deliberate or subliminal exclusion of the treatment of the Jews from popular consciousness – a more or less studied lack of interest or cultivated disinterest, going hand in hand with an accentuated "retreat into the private sphere" and increased self-centredness in difficult and worrying wartime conditions'.[37] Hence, from 1943 onwards, the persecution of the Jews largely disappeared from public consciousness.

For the Jewish part of the German population (and for those Jewish populations who came under the rule of Nazi Germany throughout Europe during the war) the Hitler regime had spelled out untold and unprecedented tragedy. Not only were Germany's Jews excluded from the 'national community', they were systematically pauperised and castigated throughout the pre-war years. Once the war began, their position grew worse and worse. They were forced to wear the Yellow Star in order to be marked out once and for all from the rest of the population and to make them more easily identifiable for later deportation. Those who had not managed to emigrate to areas outside the boundaries of Nazi-occupied Europe faced the fate of the rest of European Jewry in the Nazis' 'Final Solution', the genocide of the Jews, in the death camps established in Poland for this express purpose.

NOTES

1 On the position and experiences of Jews during the Weimar era, see D. Niewyk, *The Jews in Weimar Germany* (London, 1980); D. Walter, *Antisemitische Kriminalität und Gewalt. Judenfeindschaft in der Weimarer Republik* (Bonn, 1999); A. Paucker (ed.), *Die Juden im nationalsozialistischen Deutschland. The Jews in Nazi Germany, 1933–1945* (Tübingen, 1986), pp. 31–93.

2 P. Gay, 'In Deutschland zu Hause ... Die Juden der Weimarer Zeit', in Paucker (ed.), *Die Juden im nationalsozialistichen Deutschland*, p. 33.

3 G. Ginzel, *Jüdischer Alltag in Deutschland, 1933–1945* (Dusseldorf, 1984), p. 214. This number did not include the baptised or those who considered themselves Christian because only one parent or grandparent was Jewish and who led their lives as Christians.

4 S. Friedländer, *Nazi Germany and the Jews: The Years of Persecution, 1933–1939* (London, 1997), p. 2.

5   L. Pine, 'German Jews and Nazi Family Policy', *Holocaust Educational Trust Research Papers*, Vol. 1, No. 6 (1999–2000), p. 1.

6   A. Barkai, *From Boycott to Annihilation: The Economic Struggle of German Jews, 1933–1943* (London, 1989), p. 22.

7   On the responses of the German population to the boycott, see U. Büttner, 'Die deutsche Bevölkerung und die Judenverfolgung 1933–1945', in U. Büttner (ed.), *Die Deutschen und die Judenverfolgung im Dritten Reich* (Hamburg, 1992), pp. 72–3.

8   I. Deutschkron, *Berlin Jews Underground* (Berlin, 1990), p. 1.

9   Cited in M. Richarz (ed.), *Jewish Life in Germany: Memoirs from Three Centuries* (Bloomington, 1991), p. 311.

10 K. Kwiet, 'The Ultimate Refuge: Suicide in the Jewish Community under the Nazis', *Leo Baeck Year Book*, Vol. 29 (1984), p. 147.

11 M. Kaplan, *Between Dignity and Despair. Jewish Life in Nazi Germany* (Oxford, 1998), p. 5.

12 Cited in Pine, 'German Jews and Nazi Family Policy', p. 4.

13 See H. Graml, *Antisemitism in the Third Reich* (Oxford, 1992), p. 119.

14 Cited in L. Pine, *Nazi Family Policy, 1933–1945* (Oxford, 1997), p. 151.

15 On this, see H. Genschel, *Die Verdrängung der Juden aus der Wirtschaft im Dritten Reich* (Göttingen, 1966); Barkai, *From Boycott to Annihilation*; F. Bajohr, *'Aryanisation' in Hamburg: The Economic Exclusion of Jews and the Confiscation of their Property in Nazi Germany* (New York and Oxford, 2002).

16 M. Burleigh and W. Wippermann, *The Racial State: Germany 1933–1945* (Cambridge, 1991), p. 87.

17 Cited in Pine, 'German Jews and Nazi Family Policy', p. 10.

18 On the pogrom, see W. Benz, 'Der Novemberpogrom 1938', in W. Benz (ed.), *Die Juden in Deutschland 1933–1945. Leben unter nationalsozialistischer Herrschaft* (Munich, 1989), pp. 499–544; W. Pehle (ed.), *November 1938. From 'Reichskristallnacht' to Genocide* (New York and Oxford, 1991); D. Obst, *'Reichskristallnacht'. Ursachen und Verlauf des antisemitischen Pogroms vom November 1938* (Frankfurt am Main, 1991); K. Pätzold and I. Runge, *Pogromnacht 1938* (Berlin, 1988); R. Thalmann and E. Feinermann, *Die Kristallnacht* (Frankfurt am Main, 1987).

19 On the responses of the German population, see D. Bankier, *The Germans and the Final Solution. Public Opinion under Nazism* (Oxford, 1992), pp. 84–8. See also I. Kershaw, *Popular Opinion and Political Dissent in the Third Reich: Bavaria, 1933–1945* (Oxford, 1984), pp. 268–71.

20 On the response of the Confessing Church, see W. Gerlach, *And the Witnesses were Silent: The Confessing Church and the Persecution of the Jews* (Lincoln, Neb., 2000).

21 K. Kwiet, 'To Leave or Not to Leave: German Jews at the Crossroads', in Pehle (ed.), *November 1938*, pp. 139–53.

22 Burleigh and Wippermann, *The Racial State*, p. 93.

23 Graml, *Antisemitism in the Third Reich*, p. 144.

24 Cited in Burleigh and Wippermann, *The Racial State*, p. 99.

25 On this, see M. Kaplan, 'Jewish Daily Life in Wartime Germany', in D. Bankier (ed.), *Probing the Depths of German Antisemitism: German Society and the Persecution of the Jews, 1933–1941* (New York, 2000), pp. 395–412.

26 P. Longerich, *Politik der Vernichtung. Eine Gesamtdarstellung der nationalsozialistischen Judenverfolgung* (Munich, 1998), p. 252.

27 W. Benz, *The Holocaust: A Short History* (London, 2000), p. 60.

28 On this, see I. Kershaw, *The Nazi Dictatorship: Problems and Perspectives of Interpretation* (London, 2000), pp. 113–20.

29 Cited in Burleigh and Wippermann, *The Racial State*, p. 102.

30 On this, see P. Longerich, *Die Wannsee-Konferenz vom 20. Januar 1942. Planung und Beginn des Genozids an den europäischen Juden* (Berlin, 1998).

31 M. Roseman, *The Villa, the Lake, the Meeting: Wannsee and the Final Solution* (London, 2003), pp. 87–8.

32 There is a vast literature on the 'Final Solution' and its origins. On the 'Final Solution', see C. Browning, *The Origins of the Final Solution: The Evolution of Nazi Jewish Policy, September 1939–March 1942* (Lincoln, Neb., 2004); U. Herbert, *National Socialist Extermination Policies: Contemporary German Perspectives and Controversies* (New York, 2000); O. Bartov, *The Holocaust: Origins, Implementation, Aftermath* (London, 2000); C. Browning, *The Path to Genocide: Essays on Launching the Final Solution* (Cambridge, 1992); G. Aly, *'Final Solution': Nazi Population Policy and the Murder of the European Jews* (London, 1999); C. Gerlach, *Kalkulierte Morde. Die deutsche Wirtschafts- und Vernichtungspolitik im Weissrussland 1941–1945* (Hamburg, 1999).

33 Cited in Kaplan, *Between Dignity and Despair*, p. 202.

34 Kaplan, *Between Dignity and Despair*, p. 208.

35 See E. Johnson and K. Reuband, *What We Knew: Terror, Mass Murder and Everyday Life in Nazi Germany* (London, 2005), especially pp. 385–98.

36 D. Peukert, *Inside Nazi Germany: Conformity, Opposition and Racism in Everyday Life* (London, 1987), p. 60.

37 I. Kershaw, *The Hitler Myth: Image and Reality in the Third Reich* (Oxford, 1989), p. 249.

8

THE GYPSIES

Racial purity tests (measurements) on a Gypsy woman by Eva Justin who worked with Professor Ritter. Photo (1938). © akg-images

The Gypsies (Sinti and Roma) remained forgotten victims of National Socialism for many decades. It was only in 1985, 40 years after the end of the Second World War and the collapse of Nazism, that the German President, Richard von Weiszäcker, officially acknowledged the Sinti and Roma as victims of the Nazi era. Simon Wiesenthal asked in 1989: '… Who speaks of the tragedy of the Gypsies, who knows that over a million Gypsies without a doubt perished in the extermination camps? And the Nazis would have gassed six million if the Gypsies had been as numerous.'[1] The Nazi perpetration of the genocide of the European Gypsy population was not widely recognised until the 1980s.[2]

Hitler himself had very little interest in the Gypsies. They were not the subject of his speeches and tirades in the way that the Jews were. This indication that the Gypsies were not a high priority for the Nazi regime has had important implications for the historiography of the Gypsies under National Socialism. In the early post-war period, the Nazi persecution and murder of the Gypsies was scarcely mentioned. The few publications that touched upon the subject were the survivor autobiographies and memoirs of Jews and former political prisoners, which made passing references to the Nazi persecution and murder of the Gypsies. Gypsy survivors either could not tell their own stories or did not want to. The experience of the Gypsies in the Third

Reich was not the subject of scholarly interest until much later. Donald Kenrick and Grattan Puxon published the first overall study of the Nazi persecution of Gypsies, *The Destiny of Europe's Gypsies*, in 1972.[3] This was followed by research in the 1980s and 1990s, which began to document the history of the Gypsies in the Nazi era much more fully. There have been interviews with Gypsy survivors, allowing those who were unable to write to have their stories told, or those who were unwilling to tell their stories at first the opportunity to tell them after the passage of some time. In recent years, some Gypsy survivors have published their autobiographical accounts. These developments have allowed historians to consider not only the Nazi policy-making process but also the dreadful consequences for the victims of the policy. This chapter deals largely with the actions of the perpetrators, but the experience of the victims is also presented in order to provide a more balanced analysis of the subject.

The Gypsies were excluded from the 'national community' both on account of their itinerant lifestyle and their 'racial inferiority'. In order to put this into context, it is useful to consider the experiences of the Gypsies before the Nazi era. Like the Jews, the Gypsies had been subjected to discrimination and persecution over many centuries. The Gypsies had originated in northern India and migrated across Asia westwards into Europe between the fifth and eleventh centuries. By the time they arrived in Europe most of the land was already under ownership, which made it hard for the newcomers to establish permanent settlements. They moved across the countryside living off the land. They were viewed with suspicion on account of their dark skin and nomadic lifestyle. The Persian poet, Firdausi, had written in the tenth century: 'No washing ever whitens the black Gypsy.'[4] Discrimination, scapegoating and oppression marked the history of the Gypsies throughout the following centuries.

The Gypsies were accused of cannibalism, of spreading dirt and disease, and of being spies, sorcerers, swindlers, thieves, beggars and tricksters. Throughout the medieval and early modern period, various attempts were made to expel the Gypsies or to assimilate them. The churches and trade guilds had an unfavourable attitude towards the Gypsies, but some noblemen invited Gypsy musicians and entertainers into their homes and sometimes protected them from repressive laws, offering them refuge on their estates. In western Europe, the Sinti were eventually tolerated as migratory workers and partially integrated into the host lands, but the wandering Roma eluded assimilation, despite various prohibitions against nomadism, Gypsy clothing, music and language. Gypsies were subjected to torture and punishment by the authorities, as well as 'gypsy hunts', a popular sport in a number of European lands, including Germany and Holland.[5] Myths about the Gypsies portrayed them at best as 'noble savages' but more often as 'brutes'. There were contradictions between these Gypsy myths and the way of life and culture of the Sinti and Roma, yet suspicion and dislike of the Gypsies persisted into the modern era (and indeed continues to this day).

German Gypsy policy-making in the late nineteenth century and early twentieth century was permeated by Gypsy myths and stereotypes and sought to introduce measures to combat the *Zigeunerplage* ('Gypsy Plague'). These measures provided a foundation for subsequent Nazi Gypsy policy. In Bavaria, the security police had kept a central register on Gypsies since 1899. After 1911, these records included fingerprints. On 16 July 1926, Bavaria introduced a Law for the Combating of Gypsies, Travellers and the Workshy. It stated: 'Gypsies and persons who roam about in the manner of Gypsies may only itinerate with wagons and caravans if they have permission from the police authorities.' This permission was granted for a maximum of one calendar year only and was revocable at any time. It had to be presented on demand to the police. The law further stated: 'Gypsies and travellers may not roam about or camp in bands. The association of several single persons or several families, and the association of single persons with a family to which they do not belong, is to be regarded as constituting a band. A group of persons living together like a family is also to be regarded as a band.'[6] Gypsies were allowed to park their wagons and caravans only on open-air sites designated by the local police authorities and only for a specified period of time. Furthermore, the law ruled that Gypsies could be sent to workhouses for up to two years if they could not prove to be in regular paid employment.

Once the Nazis came to power, the persecution of the Gypsies was centralised and policies against them became increasingly radicalised. The Sinti and Roma, approximately 35,000 in number, made up only 0.05 per cent of the German population in 1933.[7] They were stereotyped as marginal, inferior, criminal and unproductive. Such stereotypes provided the justification for their social exclusion in the Third Reich. The Gypsies were already marginalised, but the Nazi regime intensified their persecution. A number of new Nazi decrees had an early impact upon Germany's Gypsies. Gypsies were forcibly sterilised under the 1933 Law for the Prevention of Hereditarily Diseased Offspring and castrated under the 1933 Law against Dangerous Habitual Criminals. The 1933 Denaturalisation Law and 1934 Expulsion Law forced stateless and foreign Sinti and Roma to leave Germany. Early measures also included the arrest and detainment of Gypsies in concentration camps.

Sybil Milton has described how a 'decentralised patchwork of parallel local decrees provided the prototype for the synchronisation and radicalisation of measures against Roma and Sinti throughout the Reich after 1935'.[8] In 1936, the 'Reich Central Office for Combating the Gypsy Nuisance' was set up. It took over the 19,000 files on Gypsies from the Bavarian security police and began to classify and register Gypsies in order to make it easier for the police to persecute them in a systematic manner. Although Gypsies were not specifically mentioned in the Nuremberg Laws of September 1935, they were considered to be 'racially alien' and therefore they were not allowed to marry or have sexual relations with 'Aryans'.

In 1936, Robert Ritter, a specialist in 'criminal biology', was appointed director of a new research unit on Gypsies, the Racial Hygiene and Population Biology Research Centre. Ritter's team included the anthropologists Adolf Würth, Gerhard Stein and Sophie Ehrhardt. Eva Justin, another of Ritter's researchers, received her doctorate in anthropology in 1943 for a dissertation on the subject of Gypsy children. Ritter's investigators went around the cities and countryside collecting material on Gypsies. As well as looking at official police files and municipal records, they photographed and interviewed Gypsies and took head measurements and blood samples. Those Gypsies who failed to co-operate were threatened with arrest and internment in a concentration camp.

Ritter argued that because they had come from India, the Gypsies had originally been 'Aryans'. He claimed that they had interbred with other races over the generations and over the course of their travels into and across Europe, so that the racial characteristics of the majority of the Gypsies in Germany predisposed them to a criminal or 'asocial' lifestyle. Ritter believed that 90 per cent of Germany's Gypsies were 'part-Gypsy'. While he was prepared to allow the 'pure Gypsies' to pursue their lifestyle (although separately from the rest of the population), he called for the sterilisation and resettlement of the 'part-Gypsies', believing that they posed a genetic threat to the German 'national community'. Gerhard Stein claimed in 1936 that 'part-Gypsy bastards are generally dangerous hereditary criminals'.[9] Ritter's research unit soon became part of Himmler's SS complex. On 16 July 1937, Himmler called for its findings to be evaluated by the Reich Central Office for Combating the Gypsy Nuisance.

On 8 December 1938, Himmler's circular on the 'Struggle against the Gypsy Nuisance' called for 'the racial affinity' of all Gypsies to be established and distinctions to be made 'between pure and part-Gypsies in the final solution of the Gypsy question'.[10] He further called for the registration with the police of all 'Gypsies' and 'vagrants living a Gypsy-like existence'. He stated: 'The treatment of the Gypsy question is part of the National Socialist task of national regeneration … the aim of measures taken by the State to defend the homogeneity of the German nation must be the physical separation of Gypsydom from the German nation, the prevention of miscegenation, and finally the regulation of the way of life of pure and part-Gypsies.'[11] This was another attempt to separate the Gypsies from the rest of the 'national community'. The Gypsies were to be issued with new identity cards: brown cards for 'pure Gypsies' and brown cards with a blue stripe for 'part-Gypsies'.[12]

Throughout the 1930s, in addition to central state persecution, the Gypsies were subject to moves on the part of individuals and local authorities to remove them and place them in ad hoc camps. The first of these separate Gypsy camps was set up on the outskirts of Cologne. Plans for the establishment of a Gypsy camp at Cologne had begun in May 1934. The Sinti and Roma were removed from their caravan plots and placed in a camp at Cologne-Bickendorf. An SS man occupied the guard hut at the entrance. From this point he could see the entire camp, with the caravans arranged in two rows. A wire fence surrounded the camp. The Gypsies had to report to the guard on leaving and entering the camp. Drastic and severe measures including police intimidation were employed to keep order. The Cologne Chief of Police noted: 'There is no fixed list of rules, they arise naturally.' Non-Gypsies were not allowed entry and the Gypsies were completely isolated from the local population. Frank Sparing shows that 'internment on the edge of town ensured that there was no longer any question of Gypsies who had been driven out returning to the town proper'.[13]

Following the Cologne model, municipal Gypsy camps were set up on the outskirts of a number of other German cities, including Berlin, Dusseldorf, Essen and Frankfurt. These were established on the initiatives of local authorities or police forces, with no formal legal foundation. Their objective was to concentrate the entire Gypsy population of a town or region in a single camp. The Gypsies were then restricted in their movements, monitored and subjected to other constraints. These camps initially corralled the itinerant Roma, who corresponded most closely to the Gypsy stereotype, and later interned those Gypsies that were more integrated into German society, when all Gypsies were registered on racial grounds.

Sparing has argued that: 'In contrast to measures undertaken during the Weimar Republic, which strove to sedentarise and assimilate the Gypsy population, this policy of concentration and isolation in separate internment camps represented a fundamental break with the past.'[14] Widespread anti-Gypsy sentiment and stereotypes were built upon and became central to National Socialist policy. As there was no central state initiative for the Gypsy camps, the arrangements and the living conditions inside them varied greatly from town to town. Yet they did come to serve the larger aims of Nazi policy. The camps became reservoirs of forced labour and were the starting point for recording and classification by racial scientists. Furthermore, as Milton argues, after 1939 these camps evolved 'from municipal internment camps into assembly centres for systematic deportation to concentration camps, ghettos, and killing centres'.[15]

Shortly before the 1936 Olympics, the Berlin authorities illegally rounded up 600 Gypsies and dumped them on wasteland in Marzahn, a suburb northeast of Berlin. The authorities justified this action on the grounds that they did not want the clean image of Berlin, the host city, to be sullied by the Gypsies. Marzahn was subsequently ring-fenced and permanently guarded. The inmates received inadequate facilities, poor food and little medical attention. By 1939, the local authority was concerned about the possible spread of scarlet fever, diphtheria and tuberculosis from the Marzahn camp to the population beyond its perimeters and called for the physical restructuring and reclassification of Marzahn as a concentration camp, but this did not occur. Marzahn was a 'family' compound, where the internees were assembled and concentrated. Milton suggests that it also served 'as a transit depot for later deportations'. She further argues that Marzahn provided an example of the interagency co-operation between the police and public health officials, 'essential for subsequent developments resulting in the deportation and mass murder of German Gypsies'.

The German population's longstanding distrust and dislike of the Gypsies made it easier for the Nazi regime to implement its policies against them. The population was at worst hostile to and at best ambivalent towards the Gypsies. The majority of the population took little interest in their plight. Many were pleased that as undesirables, the Gypsies were kept away from them. They viewed their persecution as a justified struggle against an anti-social and criminal element that did not fit into the 'national community'. There was particular animosity and mistrust towards the Gypsies because of their perceived refusal to accept the norms of mainstream society. This appre-hension was mutual – the German population mistrusted the Gypsies and the Gypsies mistrusted the German population. There was virtually no empathy or compassion among the German population towards Gypsy victims of Nazi policy.

In some ways, the response of the Gypsies to the Nazi persecution resem-bled that of the Jews. They had lived with oppression and discrimination for centuries, yet some considered Germany to be their home. Katja H., a German Sinti, recalls: 'Like the Jews, we had homes there, businesses. We Sinti were upstanding Germans; we didn't think anything could happen to us. We were reared in Germany; it was our home. We thought of ourselves as Germans.'[16] However, many lived within the confines of their own culture groups and remained detached from mainstream society. As education was not consid-ered of prime significance to the Roma, and as they moved about so much that they did not receive much schooling, most could not have read the decrees issued against them even if they had known about them. Alt and Folts point out that their illiteracy, together with their general suspicion of mainstream society, 'effectively separated them from normal channels of communica-tion'.[17] While the Gypsies, like the Jews, had been used to persecution and harassment, they too were not prepared for the unprecedented scale of a state policy of systematic genocide, nor did they anticipate it.

Himmler's perception and classification of the Gypsies as an alien and infe-rior race in December 1938 provided 'a powerful new catalyst for increased anti-Gypsy agitation'.[18] In September 1939, the removal of Germany's Gypsies to Poland was proposed. In October 1939, Heydrich issued an order prohibiting all Gypsies and 'part-Gypsies' not already in camps from chang-ing their registered domiciles. Lewy points out that the escalation of anti-Gypsy measures after the outbreak of war was 'due to concerns about the alleged tendency of Gypsies to engage in espionage as well as pressure from local officials and the population at large to get rid of the Gypsy nuisance'.[19] In May 1940, 2,500 German Gypsies were rounded up: 1,000 from Hamburg and Bremen, 1,000 from Cologne, Dusseldorf and Hanover, 500 from Stuttgart and Frankfurt. Their property and possessions were confiscated and they were deported to Poland. The vast majority of the deported Gypsies were forced into compulsory labour under SS control or into ghettoes in Poland.[20] Wanda G., a German Sinti Gypsy, recalled the experience of her deportation: 'We were unloaded from the transport … We were beaten with whips … We had to lie on the floor. We had no blankets, nothing. We were not allowed to take anything on the transport ... We got no water. My mother gave us urine to drink.'[21]

Plans to send all Germany's Sinti and Roma to the General Government region of Poland were not realised. The initial expulsion of 2,500 German Gypsies in May 1940 was not followed by other deportations. The major obstacles were the jam created by the forced movement of over 300,000 Poles into the General Government, as well as the objections by the General Governor, Hans Frank. There are also indications that Himmler was more concerned with other issues by the summer of 1940. A memorandum from Frank's office, dated 3 August 1940, stated that Himmler 'has ordered that the evacuation of Gypsies and part-Gypsies into the General Government is to be suspended until the general solution of the Jewish question'.[22] Further deportations of German Gypsies, therefore, did not follow at this time. Instead, Germany's Gypsies had limitations placed upon their mobility and were subjected to an array of other restrictive and discriminatory measures. Many were forcibly sterilised, assigned to compulsory labour and dismissed from the armed services. More than ever, they were excluded from the 'national community' and treated as both social outcasts and racial aliens between 1940 and 1942.

In the meantime, Nazi annihilation actions took on a genocidal character in the east. After Operation Barbarossa, the invasion of the Soviet Union on 22 June 1941, the Gypsies became the victims of mass shootings by the *SS-Einsatzgruppen*. This marked the start of the systematic annihilation of the Gypsies. They were killed on the grounds that they were 'racially inferior' or 'partisans', 'spies' and 'agents' for the enemies of National Socialism (for example, they were accused of being Judeo-Bolshevik informers). Michael Zimmermann points out that a greater number of Gypsies were shot to death by the German Security Police and Order Police in the Soviet Union than were killed in the concentration camps and death camps.[23] In the autumn of 1941 in German-occupied Serbia, the *Wehrmacht* took numerous male Gypsies as 'hostages' and shot them to death in retaliation for the death of German soldiers and civilians.

In October 1942, Germany's remaining 'pure Gypsies' experienced a reprieve, initiated by Himmler, which incorporated some of Ritter's earlier ideas about 'pure Gypsies' being allowed to continue their lifestyle but under careful guidelines that kept them separate from the German population. On 13 October 1942, a new regulation stated Himmler's intention that: 'Racially pure Gypsies be allowed a certain freedom of movement, so that they can itinerate in a fixed area, live according to their customs and mores, and follow an appropriate traditional occupation. The Reichsführer-SS [Himmler] assumes at the same time that the Gypsies encompassed by this order will conduct themselves irreproachably and not give rise to any complaints. Part-Gypsies, who from the point of view of the Gypsies are good part-Gypsies, shall be returned to specific racially pure Sinti Gypsy clans. If they apply for membership in a racially pure clan and the latter has no objections they shall be assigned the same status as racially pure Gypsies. The treatment of the remaining part-Gypsies and of the Rom-Gypsies is not affected by this intended new regulation.'[24] It is difficult to be sure of Himmler's reasons for this. He may have intended further racial research into the pure Gypsies, possibly later to include them in the stock of German blood if investigations confirmed their 'Aryan' roots. He certainly promoted and facilitated the research of Georg Wagner on Gypsies right up until 1945. In a letter of 3 December 1942, Martin Bormann, head of the Party Chancellery, complained to Himmler about the special arrangements for the racially pure Gypsies, suggesting that it would be unpopular with Hitler, as well as the lower ranks of the Party leadership and the population, to grant special privileges to any segment of the Gypsy population. Despite ongoing objections and criticisms, Himmler's protection of Germany's 'pure Gypsies' continued and they were permitted to remain in Germany, albeit separated from the rest of the population.[25]

However, Himmler issued an order on 16 December 1942 that brought a new radicalisation to Nazi Gypsy policy. The rest of Germany's Gypsies were to be sent to Auschwitz. The procedures for this followed in an order of the RSHA, dated 29 January 1943. Zimmermann has pointed out that 'records in several cities show that the exception-provisions for "racially pure" Sinti and for "socially adapted gypsy half-castes" were not completely adhered to' and that the local criminal police frequently regarded the Auschwitz decree as 'an opportunity to make the area "gypsy free"'.[26] On 26 February 1943, the first transport of German Gypsies arrived at the 'Gypsy camp' at Auschwitz-Birkenau ('BIIe'). The Sinti and Roma were deported to Auschwitz in families because the Nazi institutions involved with the persecution of Gypsies knew about their close family ties and decided that they needed to take this into account, according to Zimmermann, in order to 'keep the friction and resultant bureaucratic problems associated with the deportation and internment as small as possible'.[27]

Elisabeth Guttenberger, deported from Stuttgart in March 1943, recalls her arrival in Auschwitz: 'The first impression that we had of Auschwitz was terrible … It was awful. The people sat motionless in these bunks and just stared at us. I thought, I'm dreaming, I am in hell.'[28] Pollo R. describes his entry to Auschwitz: 'Longingly I looked at the gate which barred my way out of the compound filled with screaming humanity. Near me on several trucks were hundreds of nude men, women and children. Although they had not been on my transport, like me they were Gypsies, only they were from Silesia. I could hear and understand their prayers in Romany. They implored God (but in vain) to spare at least their children's lives. I was only fourteen at the time, and now realise that I had no real understanding of the situation that I was witnessing. But instinctively I knew that something unimaginable was going to happen. We were told to line up quickly. Those that lagged behind were hit with batons. One SS guard barked at us as he pointed to the chimney stacks which seemed to reach for the sky like long, threatening fingers, "This will be your way out of Auschwitz!".[29]

Unusually, BIIe was arranged as a family camp. (This was not the case in other Nazi camps where Gypsy families, like those of other prisoners, were torn apart.) This allowed for a modicum of support and morale, as surviving family members lived in close proximity. The Gypsies in the family camp attempted to maintain their language, customs and music, within the realms of what was possible. The camp consisted of 32 poorly constructed barracks, located in a swampy area. At first it was not separated from the rest of the camp, but in July 1943 it was surrounded with an electric fence to separate it from other areas of Birkenau. Conditions in the Gypsy camp were appalling. Rudolf Hoess, the Commandant of Auschwitz, acknowledged in his autobiography that 'if there had been any intention of keeping the Gypsies there for the duration of the war, the place lacked every kind of pre-condition to make this possible'. There were major outbreaks of typhus, smallpox and other diseases. A disease called noma rotted the skin and left large holes in the cheeks of the Gypsy children. There was almost no medical treatment available. The Sinti and Roma at BIIe died in thousands from disease, exposure and starvation.

Furthermore, the Gypsies at Auschwitz were subjected to medical experimentation. Josef Mengele undertook experiments on Gypsy twins for Otmar von Verschuer, the Director of the Kaiser Wilhelm Institute for Anthropology in Berlin. Mengele conducted one project on 'eye colour' and another on 'specific protein bodies'. The victims of the medical experiments were subsequently gassed, shot or killed by lethal injection. From April 1944, those Gypsies capable of working or still required for medical experiments were relocated to Buchenwald, Ravensbrück and Flossenbürg. They left behind 2,897 people – the women and children, the aged and those unable to work. In August 1944, the camp was liquidated and those left behind were gassed to death and cremated in a single action known as *Zigeunernacht* ('Gypsy night'). Filip Müller, assigned to the task of burning corpses, was a witness to *Zigeunernacht*: 'Towards midnight, the changing room was full of people. The disorder grew from minute to minute. From all sides there were desperate cries, wailing and cursing accusations to be heard. Chanting got loud. "We are German citizens. We have committed no crime." ... As they made their last journey many wept in despair ... For some time we could still hear despairing screams and cries from the gas chambers until the deadly gas had carried out its work and brought the last voice to suffocation.'[30] In October 1944, 218 Gypsy women and 800 Gypsy children were transported back to Auschwitz from Buchenwald and killed in Crematorium V. In all, 20,078 Gypsies were killed at Auschwitz – 32 were shot after trying to escape, 6,432 were gassed and 13,614 died as a result of the conditions in the camp.[31]

As well as Auschwitz, the Gypsies were interned in many other Nazi camps. Daily existence in the camps and chances for survival depended upon a number of factors: the particular camp they were in, the need for their forced labour, the character and caprices of their captors, luck and their own survival skills. Day-to-day existence was a continual struggle for survival – against hunger, cold, beatings, compulsory physical labour, dirt and disease. The daily struggle for sustenance is pre-eminent among survivor recollections. The prisoners received wholly inadequate rations of food that was often, in any case, inedible. They tried to obtain food for themselves or their loved ones using any possible method – including, for those assigned to work in kitchen areas, stealing and smuggling leftover scraps. Asta F. worked extra shifts in the Ravensbrück kitchen. She recalls: 'The food we were provided with was nothing – soup without any base, just water with whatever was available thrown in. Some lard or grease, cabbage and potatoes, if we could get them. But not enough of anything solid or nourishing to chew on. But we had salt and it was hot. There was usually some kind of bread, many times hard as a rock, many times covered with blue spots of mould, but we dipped in. We survived.'[32]

Forced labour on the meagre rations meant that many prisoners could not survive. The prisoners fought against the threat of disease. Many died of smallpox, dysentery, scarlet fever, spotted fever, typhoid and tuberculosis in the concentration camps. They were worked to death through hard labour. Others died during the protracted roll calls where they had to stand for many hours in freezing temperatures. In addition to these daily trials, the Gypsy prisoners were beaten and tortured. Alt and Folts show that 'repeated brutality by the guards and Kapos severely complicated life for the Gypsies'.[33] Eugen Kogon recalled the fate of a Gypsy inmate at Buchenwald who attempted to escape in 1938: 'Commandant Koch had him placed in a wooden box, one side covered by chicken wire. The box was only large enough to permit the prisoner to crouch. Koch then had large nails driven through the boards, piercing the victim's flesh at the slightest movement. The Gypsy was exhibited to the whole camp in this cage. He was kept in the roll call area for two days and three nights without food. His dreadful screams had long lost any semblance of humanity. On the morning of the third day he was finally relieved of his suffering by an injection of poison.'[34]

SS doctors carried out lethal medical experiments on the Gypsies at Dachau, Natzweiler, Sachsenhausen, Buchenwald and Ravensbrück. At Dachau, Gypsy inmates were used in experiments to establish how much salt water a person could drink before dying. At Ravensbrück, many Gypsy women were subjected to barbarous experiments on sterilisation without anaesthetics. At Buchenwald, Gypsy prisoners were subjected to typhus fever, cold shock and other experiments.

It is difficult to be precise about the total number of Gypsies who were murdered by the Nazis. This is partly because of the haphazard methods used to capture and kill the Gypsies and because Gypsy prisoners were not a high priority to the Nazis. Few accurate records were kept of their deaths. König has argued: 'The count of half a million Sinti and Roma murdered between 1939 and 1945 is too low to be tenable; for example in the Soviet Union many of the Romani dead were listed under non-specific labels such as "remaining to be liquidated", "hangers-on" and "partisans" … The final number of the dead Sinti and Roma may never be determined. We do not know precisely how many were brought into the concentration camps; not every concentration camp produced statistical material.'[35] Furthermore, many of the massacres of Gypsies in eastern and southern Europe, which occurred at numerous sites, were not recorded as they took place in fields and forests. In addition, most Gypsy families were killed in their entirety, leaving no survivors to detail the number of dead. Estimates of the number of Gypsies who perished in the Gypsy genocide vary from 250,000 to over 1 million.

NOTES

1 Cited in B. Alt and S. Folts, *Weeping Violins: The Gypsy Tragedy In Europe* (Kirksville, 1996), p. 1.
2 A number of significant works in both German and English have appeared since the 1980s including M. Zimmermann, *Verfolgt, Vertrieben, Vernichtet. Die Nationalsozialistische Vernichtungspolitik gegen Sinti und Roma* (Essen, 1989); M. Zimmermann, *Rassenutopie und Genozid. Die nationalsozialistische 'Lösung der Zigeunerfrage'* (Hamburg, 1996); G. Lewy, *The Nazi Persecution of the Gypsies* (Oxford, 2000). The literature is summed up in I. Hancock, 'Romanies and the Holocaust', in D. Stone (ed.), *The Historiography of the Holocaust* (Basingstoke, 2004), pp. 383–96.
3 D. Kenrick and G. Puxon, *The Destiny of Europe's Gypsies* (London, 1972).
4 D. Kenrick and G. Puxon, *Gypsies under the Swastika* (Hatfield, 1995), p. 10.
5 I. Hancock, *The Pariah Syndrome: An Account of Gypsy Slavery and Persecution* (Ann Arbor, 1987), pp. 58–9.
6 Cited in M. Burleigh and W. Wippermann, *The Racial State: Germany 1933–1945* (Cambridge, 1991), pp. 114–15.
7 S. Milton, '"Gypsies" as Social Outsiders in Nazi Germany', in R. Gellately and N. Stoltzfus (eds), *Social Outsiders in Nazi Germany* (Princeton, 2001), p. 212.
8 Ibid., p. 214.
9 Cited in Milton, '"Gypsies" as Social Outsiders in Nazi Germany', p. 219.
10 Cited in Burleigh and Wippermann, *The Racial State*, p. 120.
11 Ibid., p. 121.
12 G. Lewy, 'Himmler and the "Racially Pure Gypsies"', *Journal of Contemporary History*, Vol. 34, No. 2 (1999), p. 201.
13 K. Fings, H. Heuss and F. Sparing, *From 'Race Science' to the Camps: The Gypsies during the Second World War* (Hatfield, 1997), p. 55.
14 Ibid., p. 40.
15 Milton, '"Gypsies" as Social Outsiders in Nazi Germany', p. 220.
16 Cited in Alt and Folts, *Weeping Violins*, p. 25.
17 Alt and Folts, *Weeping Violins*, p. 24.
18 Lewy, 'Himmler and the "Racially Pure Gypsies"', p. 201.
19 Ibid., p. 202.
20 M. Zimmermann, 'From Discrimination to the "Family Camp" at Auschwitz', in W. Benz and B. Distel (eds), *Dachau Review 2. History of Nazi Concentration Camps: Studies, Reports, Documents* (Dachau, 1990), p. 98.
21 Cited in Alt and Folts, *Weeping Violins*, p. 1.
22 Cited in Lewy, *The Nazi Persecution of the Gypsies*, p. 77.
23 Zimmermann, *Rassenutopie und Genozid*, p. 234.

24 Cited in Lewy, 'Himmler and the "Racially Pure Gypsies"', p. 205.
25 Lewy, 'Himmler and the "Racially Pure Gypsies"', p. 214.
26 Zimmermann, 'From Discrimination to the "Family Camp" at Auschwitz', p. 106.
27 Ibid., p. 108.
28 Cited in Fings *et al*, *From 'Race Science' to the Camps*, p. 96.
29 Cited in Alt and Folts, *Weeping Violins*, p. 55.
30 Cited in Fings *et al*, *From 'Race Science' to the Camps*, pp. 108–9.
31 Zimmermann, 'From Discrimination to the "Family Camp" at Auschwitz', pp. 109–10.
32 Cited in Alt and Folts, *Weeping Violins*, p. 49.
33 Alt and Folts, *Weeping Violins*, p. 52.
34 Cited in Lewy, *The Nazi Persecution of the Gypsies*, p. 174.
35 Cited in Hancock, 'Romanies and the Holocaust', p. 391.

9

THE 'ASOCIAL' AND THE DISABLED

Nazi school text book juxtaposing an image of disabled people with an image of 'hereditarily healthy' Germans. © The Wiener Library

This chapter deals with a further two sectors of the population that were excluded from the 'national community' – the 'asocial' and the disabled. The Nazis' desire to create a perfect and pure 'national community' meant the exclusion not only of the Jews and Gypsies, who were considered to be 'racially alien', but also of an extremely diverse group of people, largely of German ethnicity, who were categorised as 'asocial' or 'socially unfit', as well as the mentally ill and physically disabled, who were stigmatised as 'hereditarily ill', 'unproductive' and ultimately 'unworthy of life'. These groups of victims of Nazi policy did not receive much scholarly attention until the 1980s. The historiography has developed since then to explore both Nazi policies and their impact upon these excluded groups.[1]

THE 'ASOCIAL'

The term 'asocial' was employed to categorise marginal groups of the German population that deviated from the norms of National Socialist society. The regime portrayed 'asocials' as 'the dregs of society', whose inferiority was marked by 'weakness of character', 'lack of restraint', 'loose morals', 'disinterest in contemporary events', 'idleness' and 'poverty of mind'. The term 'asocial' was applied in an elastic manner to include the following groups:

'vagabonds', 'persons of no fixed abode', 'prostitutes', 'alcoholics', 'unmarried mothers', 'large, inferior families', 'criminals', 'idlers', 'good for nothings', 'wastrels', 'grumblers' and 'grousers', as well as anyone else who did not, could not or would not fit into the 'national community'. Hence, the 'asocial' was the anti-type to the ideal 'national comrade'.[2] The reactions of the social majority to deviant behaviour gave legitimisation to Nazi policies against 'asocials'.

'Asociality' was an extremely wide-ranging category of discrimination, in regard to which (often self-appointed) 'experts' wielded their power to define who was 'asocial', based upon their own social, biological, racial and eugenic interpretations. Wolfgang Knorr, an 'expert' in the Racial Political Office of the NSDAP, defined 'asocials' as people 'who are conspicuous, not by occasional crime, but by their general inability to be useful in the life of the national community'. Otto Finger, a prominent researcher in the field of racial hygiene, termed as 'asocial' people who failed to satisfy or who contradicted 'the requirements of the leading social order'.[3] Such experts created card indexes and carried out research on 'asocials'. For example, studies of *Großfamilien* (large 'asocial' families) revealed that 'inferior' hereditary factors became stronger and stronger throughout several generations of an 'asocial clan'. Such 'undesirable' families were considered to be a burden for public welfare and became excluded from welfare benefits, as well as tributes such as the Cross of Honour of the German Mother and the Book of Honour of the German Family.

The Nazis believed that 'asocial' behaviour was inherited and, therefore, that it was necessary to prevent 'asocial' people from reproducing. The Nazi regime imposed a number of measures upon 'asocials', including compulsory sterilisation, under the terms of the Law for the Prevention of Hereditarily Diseased Offspring, which was passed on 14 July 1933. This law was applied in the main to people suffering from 'hereditary diseases', as we shall see in the next part of this chapter, but it was also applied to people who deviated from the 'healthy instincts of the nation' in terms of social or sexual behaviour. Many 'asocials' were sterilised for being 'socially feeble-minded', even though they were not affected by any of the 'hereditary diseases' specified by the law and even though they could pass 'intelligence tests'.

'Asocials' were not only conceptually excluded but also physically removed from the 'national community'. In an organised swoop, known as 'Beggars Week', 18–25 September 1933, 100,000 vagrants and tramps were rounded up and taken into 'protective custody'.[4] Most of them were subsequently released because the existing prisons had no room for them. But vagrants became subjected to more and more restrictions. From 1934, the laws dealing with vagrants and beggars were made much harsher. Vagrants were registered and their movements were recorded. 'Orderly wanderers' had to carry a Vagrants' Registration Book to record their stays in approved overnight shelters. From 1 January 1934 'disorderly wanderers' who did not possess a Vagrants' Registration Book could be assigned to forced labour schemes or imprisoned.[5] As a result, most tramps obtained the Registration Books in order to avoid arrest, but conditions of issue were increasingly restricted as the years progressed. The German public was discouraged from giving money to 'work-shy' beggars and encouraged to donate money instead to the state-sponsored charity organisations.

Local and municipal welfare and labour offices often took the lead in the persecution of 'asocials', prompting the police to take action against them. They wanted to get rid of the problems posed by these sub-proletarian groups, in much the same way as municipal authorities took initiatives in anti-Gypsy measures. In addition, most people were at best indifferent to the fate of 'asocials' and at worst pleased that these elements were being removed. Hence, it was not only central state policy but also popular antagonism and localised moves that combined to exclude 'asocials' from the 'national community'. Welfare authorities wanted to off-load costs and ordinary householders wished to be rid of nuisance neighbours. One such initiative was a slum clearance scheme in Hamburg, in 1934–1935, in which whole areas of the city populated with 'criminals', 'prostitutes' and other 'asocials' were demolished. The Hamburg authorities destroyed the 'hereditary' properties of 'asocials' in order to eliminate the high incidence of crime and deviance within these vicinities.

Attempts in the mid-1930s to deal with the 'asocial question' through 're-education' also stemmed from the initiatives of local welfare authorities. Otto Wetzel, the Mayor of Heidelberg, favoured the concept of a 'closed asocial colony', in which 'asocial' families could be socially engineered, through the imposition of strict control and surveillance, into 'valuable' members of the 'national community'.[6] Advocates of 'asocial colonies' believed that they were a useful and effective way of dealing with the 'asocial problem'. Family units could be maintained in cheap, clean and durable housing, separated from the rest of a city's inhabitants, with constant surveillance and 'educational influence'. Some Nazi 'criminal-biological experts' believed that not only hereditary factors but also the milieu in which a child grew up had some bearing on its behaviour. They maintained that children who grew up in atrocious tenement housing or who led a wandering lifestyle were reared as thieves, beggars or vagrants and that their 'tendency towards asociality' because of their biological make-up was exacerbated by an 'asocial environment'.

An 'asocial colony', Hashude, was established in Bremen in 1936, on the initiative of SS member Hans Haltermann, Senator for Employment, Technology and Welfare, as a 'completely new kind of way' to deal with the 'asocial problem'. It was a testing ground for the 'fitness' of 'asocials', to establish whether or not they could be engineered into 'valuable' individuals. If they demonstrated improvement, they could become integrated into the 'national community'. But if they failed to improve, they would be regarded as 'dangerous to the nation' and treated accordingly. Hashude consisted of 84 family houses, an administration building, a bathing area and a children's home.

There were two rows of houses, meeting to form an L-shape. The administration building, complete with observation cabin, lay at this meeting point. The gate of the administration building was the only point of entry and exit for the estate. Panoptic control subjected the families to the possibility of constant surveillance.

The criteria for admission included 'unwillingness to work', 'refusal to work', 'lack of thrift', 'lack of restraint', 'drinking', 'peddling', 'begging', as well as 'disturbing community life' and 'neglect of children'. The following two examples demonstrate the type of reasons for which families were interned.[7] In May 1936, the welfare authorities proposed that the family of Friederike N. should be admitted to Hashude. On 9 May 1936 his wife wrote to Haltermann to request that the family should not be forced to go there. She included the information that her husband had been a member of the SA since November 1933 and that all her children were members of the Nazi youth groups. However, Haltermann's enquiries into the history of the family led him to the conclusion that it was necessary for them to be sent to Hashude. The main reason for this was that Friederike N. 'had not paid one penny in rent' for an entire year. He was described as a completely 'wilful debtor' and 'asocial renter'. In addition, the concepts of 'order and cleanliness' were 'unknown' to Friederike N.

In October 1938, Heinrich H. wrote to the Mayor of Bremen from Hashude, appealing for the release of his family, which had already been there for two years. He claimed that he should never have been sent there in the first place because he had never neglected his family, spent his wages on alcohol or been a member of a Marxist party – which had been the reasons given for his admission. He claimed to have been in employment permanently since 1933, working 'from early in the morning until late at night ... as a decent family father should'. Because of his internment in Hashude, his colleagues at work treated him 'like a convict' and noticeably ignored him. Both he and his wife, as 'decent national comrades', felt demeaned at being treated as 'second rate'. However, reports about Heinrich H. contradicted his statements. Gestapo records showed that he had been a member of the German Communist Party. In addition, he had rarely worked and had taken on his current job only to avoid being sent to Hashude. At one former place of employment he was guilty of 'purely Marxist wheelings and dealings'. As a whole, Heinrich H. was considered to be 'completely asocial, dangerous to the community, an alcoholic and a rabble-rouser'. His application for his family's release was refused. Families were released only once the authorities were convinced that they no longer represented a threat to the 'national community'.

Hashude was closed in July 1940, largely because of the shortage of housing in Bremen, but despite its short-lived existence, its founders claimed that the colony had had a 'very durable' influence on countless families.[8] However, the prevailing opinion in Nazi Germany was that 'asociality' was hereditary and it was argued that scarce funds would be better spent on providing welfare schemes for the 'healthy' and 'valuable' sectors of the 'national community'. The radical solution of housing 'asocials' in barracks of a very primitive nature continued to be regarded as advantageous after the Hashude experiment had been abandoned. Here, it was believed, the gradual eradication of 'asocials' would occur as a result of their auto-destruction and mutual decimation. Even before Hashude was closed down, Himmler was advocating much more radical 'solutions' to the 'asocial' question.

By 1937, Himmler was determined to put responsibility for the 'asocial question' into the hands of the SS and he accelerated the persecution of 'asocials'. In December 1937, he decreed that people who 'will not adapt themselves to the natural discipline of a National Socialist state, for example, beggars, tramps, (Gypsies), whores, alcoholics with contagious diseases, particularly sexually transmitted diseases' could be taken into 'preventive custody'.[9] This also applied to the 'work-shy', a category comprising those 'against whom it can be proved that on two occasions they have turned down jobs offered to them without reasonable grounds, or who, having taken on a job, have given it up again after a short while without a valid reason'. These categories of people, as well as those who, although not criminal, behaved in a way that gave 'offence to the community' or refused to participate in the 'national community', were to be arrested and sent to concentration camps. In March 1938, eager to mobilise the reserve army of labour among the vagrant population, Himmler passed a decree that instructed labour exchanges 'to register the inmates of doss-houses, itinerant workers' centres and other vagrants' welfare institutions for labour mobilisation and if necessary to apply police compulsion to vagrants unwilling to work'.[10]

Himmler and Heydrich ordered two major waves of arrests in 1938, known as the 'National Campaign against the Work-shy'. This was a ruthless measure against the 'sub-proletarian' strata of society, whose victims were unable to defend themselves against brutal discrimination. As the Gestapo did not have many files on the 'work-shy', labour exchanges, state and Nazi welfare offices provided information about prospective detainees. The first wave of arrests took place between 21 and 30 April 1938. It is estimated that 2,000 people were arrested and sent to Buchenwald concentration camp in this action. Between 13 and 18 June 1938, the second spate of arrests resulted in the internment of at least a further 8,000 'asocials' across the country, including some men who were not 'work-shy' but gainfully employed.[11] Heydrich had called for 200 arrests per criminal police division, but many regional divisions zealously exceeded his requirements. In Hamburg alone there were 700 arrests.[12] Unlike the swoop in 1933, when most of those taken into custody were released within days or weeks, all those caught in 1938 were sent immediately to concentration camps, at Buchenwald, Sachsenhausen, Flossenbürg and Neuengamme. Marked out by their black triangles, these 'asocials' undertook forced labour in the economic enterprises of the SS. The 'work-shy' were to be disciplined through strenuous physical labour. Out of the concept of forced labour as discipline or 'education', a programme of 'annihilation through work' grew into a horrifying reality.

After the outbreak of war in September 1939, Vagrants' Registration Books were no longer issued and vagrancy became illegal.[13] The regime continued to round up vagrants throughout the wartime period. Attempts to pass a formal law against 'asocials' or 'community aliens' were never realised. A first draft was formulated in 1940 and the Nazi regime hoped to put it into effect as quickly as possible. However, disunity and wrangles over areas of competence between the different agencies and individuals involved caused considerable delay. The final draft of February 1944 was eventually due to be passed in 1945, but the loss of the war and the collapse of the Hitler government prevented this. However, the regime continued to discriminate against, persecute and even 'eliminate' 'asocials' throughout the wartime period by means of a series of ongoing, *ad hoc* initiatives, implemented widely and thoroughly without the need for any formal legislation.

Nazi discrimination against 'asocials' spanned a whole gamut of measures, from the symbolic, such as the exclusion of mothers of 'asocial' families from the Cross of Honour of the German Mother, through the material, such as the exclusion from welfare benefits, to the biological, such as compulsory sterilisation, to internment in concentration camps and forced labour, which sometimes resulted in death. The social and racial policies of the Nazi regime proposed the 'elimination' of 'asocials'. The penetrating biological argument that 'asociality' was hereditary provided sufficient justification for 'asocials' to be forcibly sterilised, arrested, interned in concentration camps and ultimately annihilated.

THE DISABLED

The National Socialist government and the racial scientists embarked upon the implementation of a policy of exclusion aimed at improving the racial stock of the German population.[14] It was a policy of selection and eradication of 'inferior' members of society, in this case the 'hereditarily ill' and the disabled. Eugenic solutions were proposed and implemented in order to achieve the objective of safeguarding the nation's 'genetic heritage' from the threat of degeneration.[15] Henry Friedlander has noted that Nazi policies such as registration, institutionalisation, compulsory sterilisation and marriage prohibition, as well as state propaganda advocating racial hygiene, 'stigmatised and isolated the disabled as excluded outsiders to the national community'.[16]

The Sterilisation Law, the Law for the Prevention of Hereditarily Diseased Offspring was passed on 14 July 1933. It was modelled upon a voluntary sterilisation law proposed in Prussia the previous year, but instead of voluntary sterilisation, the Nazi law called for the compulsory sterilisation of any person suffering from a hereditary illness.[17] It stated: 'Anyone who has a hereditary illness can be sterilised by a surgical operation if medical science indicates that his offspring will suffer from serious hereditary physical or mental defects.' It encompassed the following conditions: congenital feeble-mindedness, schizophrenia, manic depression, hereditary epilepsy, St Vitus's Dance (Huntington's chorea), hereditary blindness, hereditary deafness, severe physical deformities and chronic alcoholism. The Sterilisation Law came into effect on 1 January 1934. Department IV of the Ministry of the Interior was responsible for the overall administration of the sterilisation process. Arthur Gütt, a strong advocate of racial hygiene, directed the department. The Nazi government augmented a separate court system in order to implement the sterilisation law. These Hereditary Health Courts were each made up of two doctors and a judge. Higher Hereditary Health Courts dealt with appeals.

The Nazi 'euthanasia' campaign emerged as the culmination of a long-standing debate on the issue of individuals deemed as 'unworthy' of living. The question of whether individuals who represented 'life unworthy of life' should be maintained within the nation had been raised in a contentious tract, *Permission for the Destruction of Life Unworthy of Life*, written by the legal scholar Karl Binding and the psychiatrist Alfred Hoche in 1920. Binding and Hoche emphasised the burden of 'unproductive persons' upon the community, their relatives and the state and argued the case for 'involuntary euthanasia'. In the Weimar Republic, a tension arose between those who believed there was no 'cure' for mental illness, raising the issue of a more radical outcome for mental patients, and those who favoured more liberal and progressive policies, such as an expansion of outpatient and community care. Both types of approach were concerned with cutting costs. While the movement towards community care and occupational therapy led to some optimism within the psychiatric profession, the discharge of numerous asylum patients into the community also had negative corollaries. The psychiatrists came across previously unknown ranges of abnormality and this in turn prompted more radical solutions to their problems, in particular eugenic solutions. For example, the issue of sterilisation was raised, in order to prevent 'degenerate' individuals from reproduction. In addition, those patients who were not capable of occupational therapy came to be regarded by some psychiatrists and eugenicists as 'unproductive' or 'incurable'. Even before the Nazi takeover of power, some psychiatrists were already considering the killing of such patients to remove the 'burden' that they represented and to 'save' resources.

Under the Nazi regime, asylums became 'freak shows', with thousands of Nazi organisation members taken on tours through the asylums to be shown the 'unworthiness' and 'lack of productivity' of the inmates. Between 1933 and 1939, more than 21,000 people toured the Eglfing-Haar asylum.[18] Furthermore, the Nazi regime endeavoured to create resentment towards mental patients, stigmatising them as a 'burden'. A number of propaganda films were produced to stigmatise the 'hereditarily ill' and the mentally ill, including *Sins of the Father* (1935) and *All Life is a Struggle* (1937). Such propaganda starkly contrasted the healthy and valuable 'national comrade' with the 'sick' and 'unproductive' asylum patients. Even arithmetic questions in school textbooks were used to emphasise to pupils the cost involved in maintaining 'ballast existences'. The Nazi press advocated the killing of mental patients. Conditions in the asylums deteriorated rapidly as the regime closed down specialist facilities, removed patients from private and religious sector care and packed patients into cheaper state-run institutions in order to centralise control and to save resources. The Nazi government did not want to spend money on those individuals it considered to be 'incurable' and the question of eliminating the 'burden' continued to be raised. In a discussion on the subject with Dr Gerhard Wagner, the Reich Physicians' Leader, Hitler said that the question of 'euthanasia' would be taken up 'in the event of war' as 'such a problem would be more easily solved in war-time'.[19] Indeed, Stephan Kühl has argued that once war broke out, influential eugenicists such as Otmar von Verschuer, Eugen Fischer, Fritz Lenz and Ernst Rüdin 'saw the necessity not only for an economic and military mobilisation, but especially for a biological one … The killing programme was the symbiosis of an economic, military and race hygienic mobilisation at the "home front"'.[20]

The 'euthanasia' programme had its immediate origins in a request from the parents of a handicapped child, Knauer, who lived in Leipzig, to Hitler, for the 'mercy killing' of their child in the winter of 1938–1939. Hitler sent his physician, Karl Brandt, to Leipzig to authorise the death. This case set a precedent and thereafter Karl Brandt and Philipp Bouhler, the head of the Chancellery of the *Führer*, one of the 'old fighters' of the NSDAP, were authorised to deal with similar petitions in the same way. Plans were then undertaken to establish the children's 'euthanasia' programme.[21] The National Committee for the Scientific Registration of Serious Hereditary and Congenital Diseases was established, comprising officials from the Chancellery of the *Führer*, the Ministry of the Interior and a number of specially selected doctors. Burleigh and Wippermann describe this committee as a 'clearing house' for reports on babies and children sent in by doctors from across the country.[22] These reports were sent to a panel of three paediatricians, Hans Heinze, Werner Catel and Ernst Wentzler. The panel decided the outcome of each individual case, whether the child was to live or die. They marked the forms with a 'plus sign' for death and a 'minus sign' for survival. The children marked out for death were taken to special clinics where they were killed by starvation or lethal injection. The 'children's euthanasia' programme claimed the lives of at least 5,200 children, including adolescents, but Michael Burleigh estimates that the total number of victims may have been as many as 6,000.[23]

Philipp Bouhler and his deputy Viktor Brack masterminded the adult 'euthanasia' programme. In order to stop the campaign being traced back to the Chancellery of the *Führer*, the headquarters of the killing programme was at Tiergartenstraße 4 in Berlin and the address provided the codename 'Aktion T4'. The T4 departments also used different letterheads for their work, denoting different organisations (which were, in effect, phantom organisations), such as the National Working Party for Nursing and Convalescent Homes, the Community Patients' Transport Service (abbreviated to Gekrat) and the Charitable Foundation for Institutional Care.

In October 1939, Hitler signed an authorisation for the killing of disabled patients, which had been prepared by the Chancellery of the *Führer*. Typed on Hitler's personal stationery, the document was predated to 1 September 1939, the day the war began. It was not an order, nor did it have any legal basis at all. However, it was used to persuade doctors and civil servants to participate in the programme. On the grounds that Hitler had authorised the killings, those involved were told they would not be liable for prosecution. The authorisation, in the form of a single sentence, read: 'Reich Leader Bouhler and Dr Brandt are charged with the responsibility of enlarging the competence of certain doctors, designated by name, so that patients who, on the basis of human judgement, are considered incurable can be granted mercy death after a discerning diagnosis.'

Following a successful experiment at Brandenburg at the end of 1939, in which eight disabled men were murdered with carbon monoxide, the T4 technicians decided upon the use of poison gas as the killing method. Extermination centres were set up and doctors were instructed in the gassing procedure. Six killing centres were established at Brandenburg, Bernburg, Grafeneck, Hadamar, Schloss Hartheim and Sonnenstein.[24] Each killing centre was equipped with a gas chamber and a crematorium.

Bouhler and Brack organised the registration, selection, transfer and murder of 70,000 victims. Questionnaire forms were sent out to clinics, hospitals and asylums across the land for every patient, to be completed by their doctors. Once the forms were returned, they were processed and sent in batches of 150 to expert assessors, to decide upon the fate of each patient. The assessors made their decisions on the basis of the questionnaires alone, without ever seeing the patients or their medical records. 'Lack of productivity' was among the criteria that meant selection for death. The assessors marked the forms with a red 'plus sign' for patients to be killed and a blue 'minus sign' for those who were to survive.

The forms marked with red plus signs were sent to the Gekrat ('Community Patients' Transport Service'). Gekrat compiled lists of names and sent them to the asylums, together with instructions about the patients' possessions and on the restraint or sedation of patients who put up any resistance to being transferred. The Gekrat used postal vans to take the selected asylum patients to the killing centres. The routine arrival of vans that never brought patients back soon caused disquiet and terror among the asylum populations. The patients' relatives received standard letters to notify them of the transfer. Approximately a week later, they received a letter to notify them of the patients' death. The death certificates usually stated that the cause of death was one of a range of diseases without visible symptoms and with a quick onset. Errors occurred, for example, when the cause of death was given as appendicitis in cases of patients who had previously had their appendix removed and the 'euthanasia' campaign soon became an open secret.

On their arrival at the extermination centres, the doctors quickly examined the patients, who were then photographed naked and taken to gas chambers, disguised as shower rooms. Once the doors were locked, the doctors turned on the gas, which entered the chambers through pipes. Within the space of one to two hours the victims were gassed to death. The 'stokers' removed the corpses. Gold teeth were extracted and in some cases organs were removed for scientific research. Then the stokers cremated the corpses. This was an assembly line mass murder, which rapidly 'disinfected' the victims. Dr Hans Bodo Gorgaß, who had been chosen for 'an extraordinarily honourable task' by the Chancellery of the *Führer*, began work as a gassing doctor at Hadamar in June 1941. He stated: 'My job was merely the carrying out of the killing.' Dr Georg Renno, a gassing doctor at Hartheim, stated that 'turning the tap on was no big deal'.[25]

By 1 September 1941, the adult 'euthanasia' campaign had claimed 70,273 lives. But by this time the T4 operation had become an open secret and there was public protest. Patients boarding the Gekrat buses shouted out incriminations such as 'Yes, we shall die, but that Hitler will go to hell!' Despite the secrecy surrounding the proceedings, including the use of remote locations for the extermination centres, the sending out of letters of condolence and fraudulent death certificates to families of the victims, the truth about the 'euthanasia' campaign emerged. Relatives' anger triggered protests from the churches and the judiciary. In his sermon of 3 August 1941, the Bishop of Münster, Cardinal Clemens August Count von Galen, stated: 'If you establish and apply the principle that you can kill "unproductive" fellow human beings then woe betide us all when we become old and frail! ... If it is once accepted that people have the right to kill "unproductive" fellow humans – and even if it only initially affects the poor defenceless mentally ill – then as a matter of principle murder is permitted for all unproductive people, in other words for the incurably sick, the people who have become invalids through labour and war, for us all when we become old, frail and therefore unproductive.'[26] A number of other clergymen followed his example in denouncing the 'euthanasia' campaign and were sent to concentration camps.

Hitler officially called a halt to the 'euthanasia' campaign on 24 August 1941. It remains unclear whether the programme was stopped because the target number of murders had been achieved or in response to public concerns, but in any case, unofficial 'euthanasia' killings in asylums continued, either by starvation, lethal injections or pills. Asylums were encouraged to kill their own patients and three new extermination centres were opened at Meseritz-Obrawalde, Eichberg and Kaufbeuren. The T4 personnel and technical equipment were relocated to the three 'Aktion Reinhard' death camps in Poland – Belzec, Sobibor and Treblinka – for the extermination of the Jews.[27] T4 also provided the camp commandants: Christian Wirth, Commandant of Belzec, Franz Stangl, Commandant of Sobibor and Treblinka, and Franz Reichleitner, Commandant of Sobibor had all been T4 operatives at Hartheim.

Michael Burleigh argues that the 'euthanasia' programme was 'a carefully planned and covertly executed operation with precisely defined objectives'.[28] Its practitioners believed that they were carrying out a necessary task.[29]

Mental patients were killed in order to save resources or to make room for ethnic German repatriates or wartime casualties. The perpetrators often claimed that they were acting in the best interests of society or of the patients' families. While some parents may have wanted to remove the burden of handicapped children – either so that they could give more attention to their other healthy children or because they wanted to eliminate any blemish such offspring had on their family's value – the 'euthanasia' murders had a tragic impact upon countless families. One woman recalled that her father had been ordered to take her brother (who suffered from epileptic fits) to the psychiatric institution in Andernach: 'I can remember clearly that we visited my brother there. My brother loved me very much and always saved up all his presents for me. My father promised my brother again and again that he would be allowed to come home. He spoke to the doctors and was always fobbed off by them.' The boy was taken to Hadamar where he was killed. 'My entire childhood was overshadowed by this murder, my parents never laughed again. Right up until he lay on his death bed, my father reproached himself most terribly for having consented to having my brother even examined ... The pain was never lessened.'[30]

While the 'euthanasia' programme was directed largely at the German (and Austrian) disabled, it is important to note that the murder of disabled Jews was carried out within this action. In 1941, the T4 killing centres also took in 'sick' inmates from concentration camps. T4 doctors visited the camps to examine prisoners pre-selected by the SS. Between April 1941 and April 1943, in a campaign code named 'Aktion 14f13', an estimated 30,000 concentration camp inmates were transferred to the T4 extermination centres and killed.[31] In addition, the Nazi regime exported its policy of the murder of the disabled to both Poland and the Soviet Union.[32] In most cases, the doctors involved in the medical crimes and murders of the Nazi era were allowed to continue with their lives and professions with almost no interference after the war.[33]

The moral climate of the Third Reich gave way to a hardening of attitudes against the unproductive and the weak. The 'asocial' or 'socially unfit' were marginalised by the state and by German society. The government took increasingly harsh measures against them throughout the duration of the Third Reich. The mentally ill and physically disabled were victimised as well. They were ultimately deemed 'unworthy of life' by the Nazi state, its eugenic experts and 'euthanasia' practitioners. Burleigh argues that 'Nazi Germany was unique in attempting to exterminate the chronically mentally ill and physically disabled in the interests of economy and racial fitness'.[34] The practitioners of the killing believed or claimed that they were carrying out a necessary task for the benefit of the *Volk*.

NOTES

1 On the 'asocial', see especially K. Scherer, *'Asoziale' im Dritten Reich. Die vergessenen Verfolgten* (Münster, 1990); A. Ebbinghaus, H. Kaupen-Haas and K. H. Roth (eds),

Heilen und Vernichten im Mustergau Hamburg. Bevölkerungs- und Gesundheitspolitik im Dritten Reich (Hamburg, 1984); W. Ayass, *'Asoziale' im Nationalsozialismus* (Stuttgart, 1995). On the disabled, see especially E. Klee, *'Euthanasie' im NS-Staat. Die 'Vernichtung lebensunwerten Lebens'* (Frankfurt am Main, 1983); G. Aly (ed.), *Aktion T-4 1939–1945. Die 'Euthanasie'-Zentrale in der Tiergartenstrasse 4* (Berlin, 1989); G. Bock, *Zwangssterilisation im Nationalsozialismus. Studien zur Rassenpolitik und Frauenpolitik* (Opladen, 1986); N. Frei (ed.), *Medizin und Gesundheitspolitik in der NS-Zeit* (Munich, 1991); M. Burleigh, *Death and Deliverance: 'Euthanasia' in Germany 1900–1945* (Cambridge, 1994); R. Lifton, *The Nazi Doctors: Medical Killing and the Psychology of Genocide* (London, 1986).

2 J. Noakes, 'Social Outcasts in the Third Reich', in R. Bessel (ed.), *Life in the Third Reich* (Oxford, 1987), p. 94.

3 Cited in L. Pine, *Nazi Family Policy, 1933–1945* (Oxford, 1997), p. 120.

4 W. Ayass, 'Vagrants and Beggars in Hitler's Reich', in R. Evans (ed.), *The German Underworld: Deviants and Outcasts in German History* (London, 1988), p. 213.

5 Ibid., pp. 219–20.

6 L. Pine, 'Hashude: The Imprisonment of 'Asocial' Families in the Third Reich', *German History*, Vol. 13, No. 2 (1995), p. 185.

7 On what follows, see Pine, *Nazi Family Policy*, pp. 137–8.

8 Pine, 'Hashude: The Imprisonment of 'Asocial' Families in the Third Reich', p. 145.

9 Cited in M. Burleigh and W. Wippermann, *The Racial State: Germany 1933–1945* (Cambridge, 1991), p. 173.

10 Cited in Ayass, 'Vagrants and Beggars in Hitler's Reich', p. 229.

11 R. Gellately, *Backing Hitler: Consent and Coercion in Nazi Germany* (Oxford, 2001), p. 98.

12 Burleigh and Wippermann, *The Racial State*, p. 174.

13 Ayass, 'Vagrants and Beggars in Hitler's Reich', p. 221.

14 On this, see R. Proctor, *Racial Hygiene: Medicine under the Nazis* (Cambridge, Mass., 1988); M. Kater, *Doctors under Hitler* (Chapel Hill, 1989); B. Müller-Hill, *Murderous Science: Elimination by Scientific Selection of Jews, Gypsies and Others: Germany, 1933–1945* (Oxford, 1988).

15 On the specific experiences of deaf people, see H. Biesold, W. Sayers and H. Friedlander, *Crying Hands: Eugenics and Deaf People in Nazi Germany* (Washington DC, 1999) and D. Ryan and J. Schuchman, *Deaf People in Hitler's Europe* (Washington DC, 2002).

16 H. Friedlander, 'The Exclusion and Murder of the Disabled', in R. Gellately and N. Stoltzfus (eds), *Social Outsiders in Nazi Germany* (Oxford, 2001), p. 150.

17 On the background to this law, see J. Noakes, 'Nazism and Eugenics: The Background to the Nazi Sterilisation Law of 14 July 1933', in R. Bullen *et al.* (eds), *Ideas into Politics* (London, 1984), pp. 75–94.

18 M. Burleigh, 'Saving Money, Spending Lives: Psychiatry, Society and the "Euthanasia" Programme', in M. Burleigh (ed.), *Confronting the Nazi Past: New Debates on Modern German History* (London, 1996), p. 100.

19 Cited in Burleigh and Wippermann, *The Racial State*, p. 142.

20 S. Kühl, 'The Relationship between Eugenics and the so-called "Euthanasia Action" in Nazi Germany: A Eugenically Motivated Peace Policy and the Killing of the Mentally Handicapped during the Second World War', in M. Szöllösi-Janze (ed.), *Science in the Third Reich* (Oxford, 2001), pp. 203–4.

21 U. Schmidt, 'Reassessing the Beginning of the "Euthanasia" Programme', *German History*, Vol. 17, No. 4 (1999), pp. 543–50.

22 Burleigh and Wippermann, *The Racial State*, p. 142.

23 Burleigh, 'Saving Money, Spending Lives: Psychiatry, Society and the "Euthanasia" Programme', p. 106.

24 Ibid., p. 107.

25 Cited in E. Klee, '"Turning the tap on was no big deal" – The gassing doctors during the Nazi period and afterwards', in W. Benz and B. Distel (eds), *Dachau Review 2. History of Nazi Concentration Camps: Studies, Reports, Documents* (Dachau, 1990), p. 47 and p. 55.

26 Cited in Burleigh and Wippermann, *The Racial State*, p. 152.

27 Ibid., p. 166.

28 Burleigh, *Death and Deliverance*, p. 4.

29 See H. Friedlander, 'The T4 Killers: Berlin, Lublin, San Saba', in M. Berenbaum and A. Peck (eds), *The Holocaust and History* (Bloomington, 1999), pp. 243–52 on the motivations of T4 practitioners.

30 Cited in Klee, '"Turning the tap on was no big deal" – The gassing doctors during the Nazi period and afterwards', p. 62.

31 Burleigh and Wippermann, *The Racial State*, p. 163.

32 See Friedlander, 'The Exclusion and Murder of the Disabled', p. 157.

33 On this, see Klee, '"Turning the tap on was no big deal" – The gassing doctors during the Nazi period and afterwards', pp. 52–66 and Burleigh, *Death and Deliverance*, pp. 269–98.

34 Burleigh, *Death and Deliverance*, p. 7.

10

SEXUAL OUTSIDERS

German woman accused of having had intimate relations with a Polish man. Her hair was shaved off in public view at Altenburg market square. The sign around her neck reads, 'I have been removed from the national community.'
© Thüringisches Staatsarchiv Altenburg

Apart from groups who were excluded from the 'national community' on grounds of race, 'asociality', mental illness or physical disability, other groups were excluded on grounds of their sexual behaviour. Homosexuals and lesbians were sexual outsiders because they deviated from Nazi sexual norms. Prostitutes were regarded as sexual outsiders in the Third Reich because they contradicted the Nazi ideal image of womanhood. In addition, Germans who engaged in sexual relationships with foreigners were castigated by the regime and regarded as betraying the 'national community'. This chapter considers Nazi policies towards these groups of sexual outsiders.

HOMOSEXUALS AND LESBIANS

Homosexuals have been regarded as 'forgotten victims' of the Nazi regime. Almost nothing was written about the fate of homosexuals under National Socialism for many decades after 1945. In addition, prejudice against homosexuals has continued and the legal position of homosexuals both in the German Democratic Republic and the Federal Republic of Germany remained unchanged from that of the Nazi era until 1968 and 1969 respectively. For these reasons, it was only in the 1970s that the taboo status of the subject was broken and only in the last two decades that the subject has been more adequately researched by historians and other scholars.[1] In addition, many homosexual victims were reluctant to relate their experiences, so that even today there are very few autobiographical accounts.[2] The Nazi position towards female homosexuality was not investigated until the 1990s.[3]

With the founding of the German Empire in 1871, male homosexuality was declared illegal. Paragraph 175 of the Criminal Code stated: 'Lewd and lascivious acts against the order of nature committed between males or between human beings and animals shall be punished by imprisonment.' Hence, 'indecent activity' between males became a crime punishable by imprisonment, but there were relatively few convictions in the decades before the Nazis came to power and even calls for a repeal of Paragraph 175. The campaign for homosexual rights was led by the reformer Magnus Hirschfeld (1868–1935), who set up the Scientific Humanitarian Committee in 1897 and the Institute for Sexual Science in Berlin in 1919, with the aim of amending the law.[4] Hirschfeld considered homosexuality to be innate, a 'sexual deviation in nature'. It was therefore not pathological or criminal, not immoral or sinful. Claudia Schoppmann has argued that 'Hirschfeld's theories contributed to the development of a positive self-image among homosexuals'.[5] There was no change to the law, but homosexual meeting places and publications grew in number during the Weimar era. A network of bars, cafés, bathhouses and other meeting places grew in the large cities, including Berlin, Munich and Hamburg. In 1932, Berlin alone had 300 bars and cafés that were mainly or exclusively patronised by homosexuals or lesbians.[6] But the level of freedom that homosexuals had managed to attain during the 1920s did not go unchallenged and criticism of both homosexuality and lesbianism was extant in Weimar society, among some circles. Schoppmann has argued that: 'Neither the Nazis' coming to power nor the end of the war represented any fundamental ideological break in attitudes towards homosexuality. What was specific to the Nazis was their way of implementing this ideology in practice.'[7]

Homosexuals were persecuted by the Nazi regime on grounds of their 'deviant' sexual behaviour. At first, random raids on homosexual meeting places occurred and arrests were made. Homosexual men, like political opponents, were taken into 'protective detention', purportedly to be shielded from the indignation of society, into 'wild camps' in the early months of the regime. In May 1933, Hirschfeld's Institute for Sexual Science was destroyed.[8] But the centrally organised and systematic persecution of homosexuals began only in the aftermath of the Röhm affair in June 1934. Hitler was concerned about the growing threat represented by the SA and the Night of the Long Knives was partially an opportunity to eliminate Ernst Röhm, both as leader of this organisation and as an open homosexual. The purge was justified as the putting down of an alleged conspiracy, the restoration of law and order and the cleansing of society from sexual 'deviants'.[9]

In 1935, the Nazis amended the Criminal Code. In addition to Paragraph 175, Paragraph 175a stated that: 'Confinement in a penitentiary not to exceed ten years and, under extenuating circumstances, imprisonment for not less than three months shall be imposed: (1) Upon a male who, with force or with threat of imminent danger to life and limb, compels another male to commit lewd and lascivious acts with him or compels the other party to submit to abuse for lewd and lascivious acts; (2) Upon a male who, by abuse of a relationship of dependence upon him, in consequence of service, employment, or subordination, induces another male to commit lewd and lascivious acts with him or to submit to being abused for such acts; (3) Upon a male who being over 21 years of age induces another male under 21 years of age to commit lewd and lascivious acts with him or to submit to being abused for such acts; (4) Upon a male who professionally engages in lewd and lascivious acts with other men, or submits to such abuse by other men, or offers himself for lewd and lascivious acts with other men.'[10] Paragraph 175b stated that: 'Lewd and lascivious acts contrary to nature between human beings and animals shall be punished by imprisonment; loss of civil rights may also be imposed.'[11] Penalties for homosexual acts were made harsher. Furthermore, the changes made to the statute book made any erotic activity between males punishable, not only sexual intercourse as had been the case previously. Under the new penal code, prosecutions for homosexual activity increased markedly and some of those convicted under Paragraph 175 were not homosexuals at all. The regime falsely accused both political opponents and Catholic clergymen of homosexual activity in order to convict them.[12]

In October 1936, the Reich Central Office for the Combating of Homosexuality and Abortion was established, headed by Josef Meisinger. This office was assigned the task of registering homosexuals and by 1940 stored personal details of 41,000 men convicted or suspected of homosexuality.[13] Special card indexes were compiled on 'rent boys' and 'corrupters of youth', who were regarded as 'incorrigible' and 'especially dangerous'. The number of prosecutions increased during this time and the period between 1936 and 1939 marked the high point in terms of the numbers of homosexuals convicted. The number of convictions rose steeply from 948 in 1934 to 5,320 in 1936, 8,271 in 1937 and 8,562 in 1938.[14]

On 18 February 1937, Himmler told SS leaders that the existence of 'two million homosexuals ... has upset the sexual balance-sheet of Germany'.[15] He argued that 'all things which take place in the sexual sphere are not the private affair of the individual, but signify the life and death of the nation'. He subsequently addressed senior police officers on the campaign against homosexuals: 'Homosexual men are enemies of the state and are to be treated accordingly. It is a question of purifying the body of the German nation and the maintenance and strengthening of the power of the German nation.'[16]

The police raided homosexual bars and meeting places and enlisted the help of porters, barbers and public bath attendants to inform on homosexuals. The Nazis disliked the alleged tendency of homosexuals to form cliques within organisations to promote their own interests.[17] Hence, the registers and lists allowed the police to swoop on buildings and remove whole groups of homosexual men, for example, from particular factories or department stores. In July 1940, Himmler ordered that 'all homosexuals who have seduced more than one partner are to be taken into police preventive custody following their release from prison'.[18] Hence, the tendency to place homosexuals into concentration camps as a means of 'preventive detention' or 'protective detention', which had begun as early as 1933, was accelerated. It was claimed that 'encouragement to perform regular work' would help to 'cure' homosexual men of their 'unnatural inclination'.[19] Another instrument of repression was castration, whose aim was the 'eradication' of homosexuality or the 're-education' of homosexual men.

It is estimated that between 10,000 and 15,000 homosexual men ended up in concentration camps. There, marked out by their 'pink triangles', they were subjected to much abuse and harassment, both from guards and fellow inmates. They were a small minority, 'utterly disunited, usually apolitical, and … particularly vulnerable to abuse'.[20] Their situation was exacerbated by the way in which the concentration camps functioned to incite different groups of inmates against each other, and because they could not exercise group solidarity among themselves to keep up their morale. While other categories of prisoners co-operated among themselves, the homosexual prisoners came from such different backgrounds that collective cohesion among them was difficult to achieve. Lautmann has stated that 'no group solidarity developed' inside the camps among homosexual prisoners.[21] Plant has even argued that the homosexual prisoners displayed the 'reverse pattern' of tightly bonded groups.[22] In addition, homosexual prisoners were isolated because other prisoners suspected them of harbouring sexual motives if they offered assistance. Plant has argued that 'both Nazi overseers and their prisoners took it for granted that the men with the pink triangles were somehow biologically programmed to seek nothing but sexual satisfaction'.[23] Hence, other prisoner categories were not interested in co-operating with homosexual prisoners.

On the whole, the SS guards regarded the homosexual prisoners as despicable deviants and humiliated them as a matter of course. A small number of homosexual SS guards and Kapos protected young homosexual prisoners ('dolly boys'), giving them extra food rations and easier work assignments in exchange for sexual favours. This angered other prisoners and increasingly isolated those homosexual prisoners. Homosexual prisoners were further dejected because in most cases their families were unwilling to stand by them. In many cases, close relatives were ashamed of a family member convicted under Paragraph 175. In other cases, relatives, friends and even former lovers hesitated to contact homosexual prisoners, fearing the repercussions. Some homosexuals in the camps also purposely avoided contacting friends and relatives outside for the same reason. Hence, 'the homosexual prisoners were virtually cut off from the world outside'.[24] Lautmann has examined the chances of survival for homosexuals in the Nazi concentration camps and has suggested that survival depended upon adaptation to camp life. He argues that four out of five homosexual inmates who spent one year or less in a concentration camp died, while of those who spent two years or more, three out of four survived.[25]

Witness accounts from members of other prisoner groups have concurred that the homosexual prisoners were treated in a particularly brutal manner in the concentration camps. Eugen Kogon, who was imprisoned at Buchenwald for six years as a political prisoner, wrote: 'The fate of homosexuals in the concentration camps can only be described as ghastly. They were often segregated in special barracks and work details. Such segregation offered ample opportunity to unscrupulous elements in positions of power to engage in extortion and maltreatment.'[26] Many of the homosexual prisoners were assigned special labour details in stone quarries and cement works, where they were often worked to death. Lautmann has concluded that the percentage of homosexuals ordered to quarries and camps such as Dora-Mittelbau was larger than that of any other group.[27] Schnabel's study of Dachau noted that 'the prisoners with the pink triangle never lived long. They were exterminated by the SS quickly and systematically'.[28]

Furthermore, homosexual prisoners were subjected to medical experimentation. While this was also true of other groups of prisoners, one particular project was directed specifically and solely at homosexual prisoners. In 1944, Himmler personally sponsored a Danish SS doctor, Carl Vaernet, to undertake hormone implants at Buchenwald concentration camp. Himmler wanted to determine whether it would be possible to 'normalise abnormal sexual desires' by implanting an artificial hormonal gland into homosexual men. Vaernet selected five prisoners in July 1944 and a further ten in December 1944.[29] He surgically implanted in them a testosterone capsule. Vaernet's report on one patient stated that after the implant 'his entire erotic mental universe has altered'.[30] Vaernet claimed that a high dosage of testosterone could eliminate homosexuality. Despite his claims, Vaernet's experiments and their results were invalid and at least two of his patients did not survive the operation. This type of experimentation exemplified the Nazi regime's desire to rationalise its persecution of 'undesirable' groups scientifically.

In contrast to their strong revulsion of homosexual men, Nazi ideologues were largely indifferent to lesbians and most jurists were disinterested in extending Paragraph 175 to apply to them. There were four main reasons for this. First, homosexual men were excluded from the reproductive process, but this did not apply to the same degree to lesbian women. Second, homosexual activity was considered to be less widespread and more unobtrusive in women and hence less likely to set a corrupting example. Third, intimate forms of friendship between women made lesbianism much more difficult to detect. Fourth, women played a comparatively smaller role in public life.[31] Although this was the prevailing opinion, there were commentators who argued for the inclusion of women in Paragraph 175, such as Ehrhard Eberhard, who regarded female homosexuality as 'a serious moral threat' and had called for the inclusion of lesbians in Paragraph 175 during the 1920s.[32] Rudolf Klare, a young lawyer, demanded the unrestricted criminalisation of lesbianism in 1937, arguing that it jeopardised population policy imperatives, as lesbians 'seduced' heterosexual women and kept them from their 'natural obligations' to bear children.[33] But, as Schoppmann argues, 'with the destruction of the women's movement, forcing it into conformity, and the subordination of Nazi women's organisations to male leadership, the Nazis saw less need to criminalise lesbians'.[34] The predominating view was that seduced women were not permanently withdrawn from heterosexual relationships or from reproduction. And so, lesbianism *per se* was not criminalised.

The Nazis did, however, destroy the beginnings of a collective lesbian lifestyle and identity, which had been developing over the previous two decades.[35] Lesbian meeting places, such as the Dorian Gray, one of the oldest women's bars in Berlin, and lesbian magazines, such as *Frauenliebe*, established in 1926 (renamed *Garçonne* in 1930), that had flourished during the Weimar years, were destroyed. This led, as Schoppmann has shown, to the 'dispersal of lesbian women and their withdrawal into private circles of friends'.[36]

There were isolated cases in which police authorities or other organisations, such as the Racial Policy Office of the NSDAP, collected information on lesbians.[37] But as a result of inadequate source material, the extent to which data were gathered on lesbians is unknown. The reactions of lesbians to life under National Socialism were varied. Some women, such as Margarete Kittel, attached great importance to 'inconspicuousness in public'. Other lesbian women entered into fictitious marriages out of fear of persecution.[38] Many lesbians got married in order to escape social pressure and in some cases to avoid losing their jobs.[39] Jewish lesbians or communist lesbians were persecuted on grounds of their 'race' or political convictions, not on account of their lesbianism. Most lesbians were spared the fate of concentration camps if they were not endangered for other reasons and if they were prepared to outwardly conform to the regime. Many adapted their appearance and choice of clothes in order to fit into a 'feminine' image of womanhood.

Schoppmann has argued that there was 'no systematic persecution of lesbians comparable to that of male homosexuals'.[40] Her portraits of lesbians in Nazi Germany demonstrate 'what it could have meant to live as a lesbian during the Third Reich'.[41] Jewish or Communist lesbians were victims of the regime, but this did not apply to all lesbians. Some were bystanders; a few, such as the writer Grete von Urbanitzky, actively collaborated with the regime; some became involved in the resistance to National Socialism. The most typical reaction, however, was to try not to attract attention and to remain as inconspicuous as possible.

PROSTITUTES

Prostitutes were regarded as sexual outsiders in the Third Reich. Hitler viewed prostitution as 'a disgrace to humanity' and argued that 'a fight against prostitution' was necessary in order to combat syphilis. He regarded 'the sickening of the body' by syphilis as 'the consequence of a sickening of the moral, social, and racial instincts'.[42] Official concerns about sex, race and health, coupled with Hitler's views on prostitution as a sign of degeneration in society, led to a crackdown on prostitutes as sexual outsiders. Prostitutes were considered to be the main source of venereal diseases. In this way, they were stigmatised as a danger to the health of the nation.

During the Weimar Republic, the 1927 Law for Combating Venereal Diseases had abolished state-regulated prostitution and created some improvements in the civil and legal status of prostitutes. The law, which decriminalised prostitution in general but banned regulated brothels, engendered significant achievements from the perspective of prostitutes' rights. It limited the capacity of the police to impose special controls on prostitutes. They were no longer prohibited from plying their trade, nor were they restricted to particular streets or houses. There was some opposition to the 1927 law, particularly in religious and conservative circles. The NSDAP appealed to these concerns about 'immorality' and presented itself as a party that defended sexual propriety. Its official newspaper, the *Völkischer Beobachter*, seized the opportunity to attack the law, claiming that it would increase venereal disease by giving prostitution a status of respectability. The Nazis claimed that the decriminalisation of prostitution, brought about by the campaigns of Jews and Social Democrats, undermined both the moral foundations of the family and the health of the nation.

After the 'seizure of power', the Nazis continued to present themselves as defenders of conventional sexual morality. The police, health and welfare authorities worked in co-operation to deal with the threat posed by prostitution. Prostitutes were marginalised, branded 'asocial' and subjected to increasingly strict control. Julia Roos has emphasised the differences between the Weimar and Nazi eras in their policies towards prostitution. She shows how 'Nazi policies aimed to reverse key Weimar achievements – most importantly, the abolition of state-regulated prostitution'.[43] Annette Timm has described the ambivalent position taken by the Nazi regime towards prostitutes: 'They were both radically criminalized and officially sanctioned.'[44] She has demonstrated that Nazi policy towards prostitutes moved through three distinct phases. The first was an official crackdown on prostitution and marginalisation of prostitutes; the second was a growing toleration or acceptance of prostitution in practice; the third, during the war years, was an active promotion of state-regulated prostitution, both to boost the morale of German soldiers and to provide incentives for industrial workers.

At first, the Nazi regime called for harsh punishments for those who deviated from its sexual norms. With its emphasis upon the family and the 'health of the nation', sexual promiscuity was not an accepted mode of behaviour for women. The purpose of sexual activity was reproduction – within marriage – and the regime aimed to promote this. Prostitutes represented an improper, erotic type of femininity that wholly contradicted the Nazi ideal type. Between 1933 and 1935, the Nazi regime campaigned and legislated against prostitution. Following the Law for the Protection of the People and State of 28 February 1933, thousands of prostitutes were rounded up and sent to workhouses and camps. In May 1933, the legislation to control venereal disease was tightened up with the revision of Section 361 of the Criminal Code. Public solicitations became outlawed once again. The new provisions called for the punishment of any individual 'who publicly and conspicuously or in a manner likely to annoy the public incites immoral acts or offers immoral services'.[45] Prostitutes were both legally and socially marginalised. Their marginalisation was used to justify unprecedented state control over prostitution. The attempt to remove prostitution from public view was especially evident in controls on prostitutes during the 1936 Olympics.[46]

By 1936, the Military Supreme Command was calling for the establishment of military brothels. Despite objections on the grounds of the spread of venereal disease, the second phase of Nazi policy towards prostitution was a limited acceptance and even an involvement in its organisation. The Nazi state accepted the need for state-sanctioned, state-run brothels. Prostitutes came to be considered as necessary, but still as social outsiders. In a speech to SS commanders on 18 February 1937, Himmler defended the use of prostitution as a way of combating homosexuality: 'One can organise the question of female prostitution … in a way that is acceptable … One cannot prevent the entire youth from drifting toward homosexuality if at the same time one blocks all the alternatives.'[47] The role of prostitutes as necessary outlets for male sexual energies soon became institutionalised. The Ministry of the Interior claimed that state brothels were hygienic and served the important function of rewarding soldiers.[48]

Simultaneously, the regime clamped down on the work of individual prostitutes in bars and on the streets. The police patrolled the streets, as well as the bars and clubs frequented by prostitutes. In Berlin, for example, the Main Health Office called for the surveillance of a particular list of bars, including Pompeji, Atlantis, Orient, Roxi, Dschungel, Jocky, Eden and Oase. Hence, during the mid to late 1930s, the Nazi regime cleaned up the streets of prostitution, removed prostitutes from public vision and excluded prostitutes from society, but at the same time it began to use state-run brothels to serve the purpose of allowing men to have their sexual needs met in private.

Roos argues that during the war 'Nazi prostitution policy truly came into its own and most clearly revealed its unique features'.[49] The third and most radical phase of Nazi policy towards prostitution began with a secret directive from the Ministry of the Interior, on 9 September 1939, which ordered the 'reconstruction of brothels and barrack-like concentration of prostitutes'. The directive was intended to provide prostitutes to German soldiers. Prostitutes were registered and made to work in brothels. They were not allowed to ply their trade in public areas. They were not allowed to manufacture, own or distribute instruments that could be used for sadistic or masochistic purposes. Those who refused to comply with these measures were arrested and sent to concentration camps for being 'asocial'. Unlicensed street walkers were brutally suppressed. The Nazi regime openly promoted a great expansion of police-controlled brothels by the end of

1939, although changes in the law to allow for this were made only in November 1940.

Furthermore, brothels were set up for civilian workers during the war. By 1942, 28 brothels operated in Berlin, under the surveillance of the Kripo. State officials maintained that men ran less risk of contracting venereal disease by using state-run brothels. Roos shows that 'in wartime Nazi Germany, the regulated brothel became a thriving state institution under the special care and protection of the police'.[50] Even cities that opposed the setting up of brothels, such as Würzburg, were obliged to have them. Hence, the establishment of supervised brothels was made compulsory for all cities and standard regulations were issued for them. The construction of both civilian and military brothels run by the state restricted prostitutes from working outside these establishments. Those who tried to do so were arrested and placed in 'protective custody'. Not only were they damaging to the health of the nation, but their behaviour did not conform to societal norms. Overt displays of female sexuality, promiscuity or 'creating a strongly erotic impression' were regarded as signs of 'asocial' behaviour. They blatantly contradicted the idealisation of motherhood and family that was such a significant component of Nazi ideology.

However, the shift in policy towards prostitution showed that the pragmatic requirements of the regime took precedence over its ideological imperatives. Ideologically and rhetorically the Nazi regime disapproved of prostitutes because they deviated from Nazi sexual norms and because of fears about the spread of venereal disease. In practice, however, the Nazi state sought to allow prostitution, in a controlled and regulated form, in order to provide soldiers and workers an outlet for their sexual needs. But sexual gratification in itself was not the goal; it was channelled for the purposes of the state. The provision of prostitutes was aimed at increasing industrial productivity and military might.

Hitler ordered the establishment of separate brothels for foreign workers in December 1940, in order to maintain the 'purity of German blood'. The first of these was opened at the Hermann Göring Works in Linz. It served as a model for brothels for foreign workers in other cities. These brothels were clearly aimed at preventing unwelcome sexual contact between German women and foreign workers. The police recruited and supervised the foreign prostitutes who worked in these brothels. German men were not allowed to visit brothels staffed with foreign girls and the latter were not permitted to work in the houses that provided for German men. Hence, distinctions were made even in wartime prostitution policy between those who belonged to the 'national community' and those who did not.

In March 1942, Himmler ordered the establishment of brothels in the concentration camps in order to provide incentives for 'industrious' male inmates. Brothel visits were to be rewards for productivity among concentration camp prisoners. The first concentration camp brothel was set up at Mauthausen in the summer of 1942. In March 1943, Himmler criticised the lack of a brothel facility at Buchenwald. He spoke of the need to take advantage of prostitution as 'an incentive for higher performance'. By the summer of 1944, brothels had been opened in eight major concentration camps, including Buchenwald, Dachau and Sachsenhausen. Prostitutes and other women were forced to work in them. Sex was reduced to a base function. One woman who was compelled to work in the brothel at Buchenwald recalled: 'It was nothing personal, one felt like a robot. They did not take notice of us; we were the lowest of the low. We were only good for this. No conversation or small talk, not even the weather was on the agenda. Everything was so mechanical and indifferent … They finished their business and left.'[51] In Nazi prostitution policy 'female sexuality was functionalised to serve the needs of the nation'.[52] But beneath the apparent contradictions in Nazi rhetoric and policy, there was a consistency of purpose: to achieve the aims of the Nazi state.[53]

GERMANS IN SEXUAL RELATIONSHIPS WITH FOREIGNERS

During the war, the Nazi regime became increasingly concerned about sexual relationships between Germans, particularly German females, and foreign labourers and prisoners of war. In January 1942, an SD report noted: 'The conscription of many millions of men into military service, the lack of a universal prohibition against sexual relations for foreigners, and the incorporation of additional foreign workers, all have increased the threat of the infiltration of the blood of the German *Volk*.'[54] The Nazi regime, despite its need for millions of foreign labourers in German agriculture and industry, wanted to prevent sexual relationships between Germans and foreign workers and to maintain the racial purity of the *Volk*. To this end, a complex series of directives and regulations was issued about the various types of foreigners in the Third Reich.

The Racial Political Office of the NSDAP expressed concern about relationships between Germans and foreigners: 'There are many German women and girls who, unmindful of their duty to the *Volk*, are not ashamed to strike up a friendship or even intimate relations with these men of an alien *Volk*.'[55] The regime was especially concerned about the impact of such liaisons between married women and foreign men, and the impact of such relationships upon the husbands of these women, who were at the front. Such relationships posed an additional danger to the stability of their families. Furthermore, this kind of sexual hedonism contradicted the Nazi ideal of sexual relationships between 'racially pure' couples in order to serve the 'national community' in legitimate reproduction.

The first decree concerning contact between Germans and prisoners of war was issued in November 1939. A series of other laws and measures followed to restrict contacts between Germans and prisoners of war. German women discovered in romantic relationships with Polish prisoners of war had their heads shaven and were publicly paraded. It was hoped that such public punishments would have a deterrent effect, but this was not necessarily the case.

Sympathetic responses sometimes ensued and in October 1941, Hitler stopped these public punishments. But the Gestapo and the courts continued to subject women accused of engaging in forbidden relationships to humiliating interrogations and trials. Sentences for forbidden contacts were variable and inconsistent. In 1943, the SD called for a uniform sentence of three years' imprisonment, but sentencing continued to depend upon a number of factors, including the court's assessment of a woman's character and age, and whether or not sexual intercourse had occurred. Married women, especially if they had children, typically received harsher sentences than single women. War wives who engaged in sexual relationships with foreigners were considered to be disgracing both their husbands and the 'national community'.[56] While French prisoners of war who engaged in sexual relationships with German women received prison sentences of between three and six years, Polish or Soviet prisoners of war and forced labourers who did so were either put into concentration camps or hanged.[57] Hence a racial ranking applied in these circumstances too – the Poles and Russians, regarded as 'subhuman', were at the bottom of this hierarchy.

Despite the severe penalties, the Nazi regime did not succeed in its aim to stamp out relationships between Germans and foreigners during the war. Jill Stephenson has highlighted the complex triangular relationships that developed between the Nazi regime, German women and foreign workers in rural Württemberg.[58] She has shown that co-operation with regulations about foreign workers by people who lived in this region was 'only partially forthcoming'.[59] In the absence of German men who were at the front, German farms often depended almost entirely on their foreign workers. Sexual relations between German women and foreign workers 'occurred more frequently in Catholic areas of southern Germany, undoubtedly because of the closer relationships which developed with Catholic Poles, in particular'.[60] Interestingly, a sexual double standard was applied to the German party involved in a relationship with a foreigner. A German man engaged in such a relationship was only half-heartedly punished, but 'the "sexual surrender" of a German woman to a foreign worker, or worse yet, to a foreign soldier was a humiliation for the entire *Volk*' and she was punished much more severely.[61]

The Hitler regime was unwilling to tolerate any outward deviation from the sexual standards it set for German society and sexual outsiders usually met with both state and popular disapprobation. There were several groups of people who were excluded from the 'national community' on account of their sexual behaviour. Nazi policies towards homosexual men, which began with random raids on homosexual meeting places, became increasingly harsh. The penal code was amended and many thousands of homosexual men were arrested and ended up in Nazi concentration camps. There were no corresponding measures taken against lesbians, who were clearly not regarded as so much of a threat to the German nation. Lesbianism was not criminalised and most lesbians, even though their social environment was destroyed, were not endangered if they were willing to outwardly conform to the dictates of the Nazi regime. Prostitutes, who clearly deviated from the Nazi ideal of womanhood, were castigated as sexual outsiders and treated accordingly. They were legally and socially marginalised. Sexual promiscuity was considered to be 'asocial' and streetwalking was suppressed. However, the Nazi government simultaneously sanctioned and ran state brothels. These brothels gave workers and soldiers an outlet for their sexual needs as an incentive to increase industrial productivity and military might. Finally, Germans who engaged in sexual relationships with foreigners – particularly married women and particularly if the foreigners were from 'the east' – were castigated by the Nazi regime. However, despite numerous decrees and even public humiliation measures, the Nazi government did not succeed in eradicating such relationships.

NOTES

1 The most significant works include: B. Jellonnek, *Homosexuelle unter dem Hakenkreuz. Die Verfolgung von Homosexuellen im Dritten Reich* (Paderborn, 1990); R. Plant, *The Pink Triangle: The Nazi War against Homosexuals* (New York, 1986); H.-G. Stümke, *Homosexuelle in Deutschland. Eine politische Geschichte* (Munich, 1989); H.-G. Stümke and R. Finkler, *Rosa Winkel, Rosa Listen. Homosexuelle und 'Gesundes Volksempfinden' von Auschwitz bis heute* (Reinbek, 1981); G. Grau, *Hidden Holocaust? Gay and Lesbian Persecution in Germany, 1933–1945* (London, 1995); J. Müller and A. Sternweiler, *Homosexuelle Männer im KZ Sachsenhausen* (Berlin, 2000); B. Jellonnek and R. Lautmann, *Nationalsozialistischer Terror gegen Homosexuelle: verdrängt und ungesühnt* (Paderborn, 2002); T. Bastian, *Homosexuelle im Dritten Reich. Geschichte einer Verfolgung* (Munich, 2000); H. Diercks, *Verfolgung Homosexueller im Nationalsozialismus* (Bremen, 1999); F. Rector, *The Nazi Extermination of Homosexuals* (New York, 1981).

2 H. Heger, *The Men with the Pink Triangle* (London, 1980); P. Seel, *I, Pierre Seel, Deported Homosexual: A Memoir of Nazi Terror* (New York, 1995); L. van Dijk, *Ein erfülltes Leben – trotzdem: Erinnerungen Homosexueller 1933–1945* (Hamburg, 1992).

3 C. Schoppmann, *Nationalsozialistische Sexualpolitik und weibliche Homosexualität* (Pfannenweiler, 1997) was the first serious study on lesbianism in the Third Reich. See also C. Schoppmann, *Verbotene Verhältnisse. Frauenliebe 1938–1945* (Berlin, 1999).

4 See J. Steakley, *The Homosexual Emancipation Movement in Germany* (New York, 1975).

5 C. Schoppmann, *Days of Masquerade: Life Stories of Lesbians during the Third Reich* (New York, 1996), p. 4.

6 W. Johansson and W. Percy, 'Homosexuals in Nazi Germany', *Simon Wiesenthal Center Annual*, Vol. 7 (1990), p. 229.

7 Schoppmann, *Days of Masquerade*, p. 10.

8 On this, see G. Grau (ed.), *Hidden Holocaust? Gay and Lesbian Persecution in Germany 1933–1945* (London, 1995), pp. 31–3.

9 M. Burleigh and W. Wippermann, *The Racial State: Germany 1933–1945* (Cambridge, 1991), p. 188.

10 Cited in Johansson and Percy, 'Homosexuals in Nazi Germany', p. 235.

11 Cited in ibid., p. 236.

12 Ibid., p. 237.

13 Grau (ed.), *Hidden Holocaust?*, p. 104.

14 H.-G. Stümke, 'From the "People's Consciousness of Right and Wrong" to "The Healthy Instincts of the Nation": The Persecution of Homosexuals in Nazi Germany',

in M. Burleigh (ed.), *Confronting the Nazi Past: New Debates in Modern German History* (London, 1996), p. 160.

15 Burleigh and Wippermann, *The Racial State*, p. 192.

16 Stümke, 'From the "People's Consciousness of Right and Wrong" to "The Healthy Instincts of the Nation": The Persecution of Homosexuals in Nazi Germany', p. 159.

17 W. Johansson and W. Percy, 'Homosexuals in Nazi Germany', pp. 230–1.

18 Stümke, 'From the "People's Consciousness of Right and Wrong" to "The Healthy Instincts of the Nation": The Persecution of Homosexuals in Nazi Germany', p. 162.

19 Grau, *Hidden Holocaust?*, p. 264.

20 Plant, *The Pink Triangle*, p. 169.

21 R. Lautmann, 'Gay Prisoners in Concentration Camps Compared with Jehovah's Witnesses and Political Prisoners', in M. Berenbaum (ed.), *A Mosaic of Victims: Non-Jews Persecuted and Murdered by the Nazis* (London, 1990), p. 203.

22 Plant, *The Pink Triangle*, p. 179.

23 Ibid., p. 166.

24 Ibid., p. 180.

25 R. Lautmann, 'The Pink Triangle: The Persecution of the Homosexual Male in Nazi Germany', *Journal of Homosexuality*, Vol. 6 (1980–81), p. 157.

26 E. Kogon, *The Theory and Practice of Hell: The German Concentration Camps and the System Behind Them* (New York, 1968), p. 44.

27 R. Lautmann (ed.), *Gesellschaft und Homosexualität* (Frankfurt, 1977), p. 350.

28 R. Schnabel, *Die Frommen in der Hölle* (Frankfurt, 1967), p. 53.

29 Grau (ed.), *Hidden Holocaust?*, p. 281.

30 Cited in Burleigh and Wippermann, *The Racial State*, p. 196.

31 Johansson and Percy, 'Homosexuals in Nazi Germany', pp. 236–7.

32 E. Eberhard, *Die Frauenbewegung und ihre erotischen Grundlagen* (Vienna and Leipzig, 1924), p. 559.

33 C. Schoppmann, 'National Socialist Policies towards Female Homosexuality', in L. Abrams and E. Harvey (eds), *Gender Relations in German History: Power, Agency and Experience from the Sixteenth to the Twentieth Century* (London, 1996), p. 183.

34 Schoppmann, *Days of Masquerade*, p. 13.

35 Schoppmann, 'National Socialist Policies towards Female Homosexuality', p. 179.

36 C. Schoppmann, 'The Position of Lesbian Women in the Nazi Period', in Grau (ed.), *Hidden Holocaust?*, p. 13.

37 Schoppmann, *Days of Masquerade*, p. 20.

38 Ibid., p. 96.

39 Schoppmann, 'National Socialist Policies towards Female Homosexuality', p. 180.

40 Schoppmann, 'The Position of Lesbian Women in the Nazi Period', p. 15.

41 Schoppmann, *Days of Masquerade*, p. 24.

42 A. Hitler, *Mein Kampf*, translated by R. Mannheim (London, 1992), p. 228 and p. 233.

43 J. Roos, 'Backlash against Prostitutes' Rights: Origins and Dynamics of Nazi Prostitution Policies', in D. Herzog (ed.), *Sexuality and Fascism* (New York and Oxford, 2005), p. 69.

44 A. Timm, 'The Ambivalent Outsider: Prostitution, Promiscuity, and VD Control in Nazi Berlin', in R. Gellately and N. Stoltzfus, *Social Outsiders in Nazi Germany* (Oxford, 2001), p. 192.

45 Cited in ibid., p. 194.

46 See A. Timm, 'Sex with a Purpose: Prostitution, Venereal Disease, and Militarised Masculinity in the Third Reich', in D. Herzog (ed.), *Sexuality and German Fascism* (New York and Oxford, 2005), p. 228 and pp. 236–7.

47 Cited in Roos, 'Backlash against Prostitutes' Rights', p. 90.

48 On this, see C. Paul, *Zwangsprostitution: Staatlich errichtete Bordelle im Nationalsozialismus* (Berlin, 1994).

49 Roos, 'Backlash against Prostitute's Rights', p. 69.

50 Ibid., p. 91.

51 Cited in ibid., p. 94.

52 Timm, 'Sex with a Purpose', p. 246.

53 Ibid., pp. 254–5.

54 Cited in B. Kundrus, 'Forbidden Company: Romantic Relationships between Germans and Foreigners, 1939 to 1945', in Herzog (ed.), *Sexuality and German Fascism*, p. 203.

55 Cited in ibid., p. 206.

56 See V. Joshi, *Gender and Power in the Third Reich: Female Denouncers and the Gestapo, 1933–1945* (London, 2003), pp. 148–60.

57 Kundrus, 'Forbidden Company', pp. 213–15.

58 J. Stephenson, 'Triangle: Foreign Workers, German Civilians and the Nazi Regime. War and Society in Württemberg, 1939–1945', *German Studies Review*, Vol. 15 (1992), pp. 339–59.

59 J. Stephenson, 'Germans, Slavs and the Burden of Work', in N. Gregor (ed.), *Nazism, War and Genocide* (Exeter, 2005), p. 101.

60 Ibid., p. 104.

61 Kundrus, 'Forbidden Company', p. 221.

11

DISSENTERS AND RESISTERS

Hans Scholl, a student of medicine and member of the 'Weisse Rose'
(White Rose) resistance group. He was executed on 22nd February 1943
aged 24. © akg-images

By definition and by choice, those groups and individuals who resisted the
Nazi regime or dissented from its ideology and policies were outside the
'national community'. This chapter considers those groups or individuals
who either failed to conform to National Socialism or who rejected it. After a
brief discussion about the nature of resistance and non-conformity, it begins
with an analysis of the fate of the Jehovah's Witnesses. The behaviour and
attitude of dissenting youth in Nazi Germany is the focus of the next part of
this chapter. This encompasses a range of groups from those who dissented

purely on grounds of youthful rebellion or because they disliked the restrictions imposed upon them by the Hitler Youth, to those who acted on moral imperatives to try to resist the actions of the Nazi government. The Rosenstrasse Protest is also mentioned – the exceptional instance of non-Jewish women who protested against the rounding up and deportation of their Jewish husbands in Berlin in February 1943. These German women too, for being in mixed marriages and for remaining true to their husbands, stood outside the 'national community'. Socialist and communist resistance is considered, as well as resistance on the part of the aristocratic conservative elites. All these groups or individuals were, or came to be if they did not start out that way, outside the 'national community'.

The subject of resistance has engendered a variety of historical interpretations and a large historiographical debate.[1] Without rehearsing the whole debate here, it is nevertheless useful to draw out a few pertinent points from it. One of the most contested issues is how to define resistance. The traditional and narrowest definition of resistance (*Widerstand*) included only organised attempts to work against the Nazi regime with the deliberate aim of undermining or destroying it. This definition of resistance is best exemplified by the bomb plot of 20 July 1944. However, research into the 'history of everyday life' in the 1970s and 1980s, notably the 'Bavaria Project', engendered a much broader definition of resistance, encompassing all forms of limited or partial rejection of Nazi rule.[2]

Furthermore, Martin Broszat added a new and much contested concept of *Resistenz* into the debate. This term allowed for a broader view of resistance than organised actions based on a purely outright moral rejection of the regime. It allowed for a partial opposition (for example, refusal to use the Hitler greeting) yet at the same time a partial acceptance of the regime to be included within the framework of resistance. Historians including Walter Hofer and Marlis Steinert rejected the concept of *Resistenz* as too broad. The danger of a definition that is too wide is that it ultimately becomes meaningless. Richard Evans has recently rejected the 'tendency to expand the concept of resistance until it covers anything short of positive enthusiasm for the regime'.[3] Yet, the benefits of a definition that is not confined to 'heroes', as Ian Kershaw has noted, is that it opens up the question of resistance to the level and the behaviour of ordinary people.[4]

Detlev Peukert distinguished between four types of dissident behaviour in the Third Reich: non-conformist behaviour, refusal, protest and resistance. Non-conformist behaviour was made up of separate individual acts against the norms of the state, but did not call into question the Nazi system as a whole. Such acts took place in the private sphere. Refusal was one stage more general and more pointedly directed against the regime. This included acts undertaken in opposition to orders, such as parents not enrolling their children into the Nazi youth groups. Protest was one stage closer to rejection of the regime and more public, but still comprised actions directed to a specific issue, such as priests sermonising against the 'euthanasia' programme.

Resistance included only those forms of behaviour that were rejections of the regime as a whole and sought to overthrow it.[5]

Kershaw concurs that a definition of 'resistance' should be restricted to one in which 'the rejection of Nazism is fundamental'. He suggests its use to describe 'active participation in organised attempts to work against the regime with the conscious aim of undermining it or planning for the moment of its demise'.[6] He argues that opposition encompassed many forms of action with limited or partial aims, not directed against the Nazi system as a whole, and sometimes arising from groups or individuals that were broadly sympathetic to the regime and its ideology. Dissent was the (often spontaneous) expression of attitudes that were critical of the regime, but without any necessary intention of action. Kershaw suggests that these categories can be viewed as 'concentric circles blurring into each other: a wide "soft pulp" of "dissent"; a narrower, though still wide band of "opposition"; and at the core, a small circle of fundamental "resistance"'.[7] He argues then that 'while political dissent and opposition to specific measures of the Nazi regime were indeed widespread, "resistance" in its fundamental sense lacked a popular base of support'.[8] The majority of Germans who fitted into the 'national community' did not resist the Nazi regime and conformed to its requirements.

JEHOVAH'S WITNESSES

In a state that did not tolerate any type of non-conformity, Jehovah's Witnesses came under attack during the Nazi era. The Jehovah's Witness movement had been founded in the United States at the end of the nineteenth century. Its members originally called themselves Bible Students, but they adopted the name Jehovah's Witnesses in 1931. There were 25,000 Jehovah's Witnesses living in Germany at the time of the Nazi 'seizure of power'. This made them a fractional minority of the population. Even so, the National Socialists regarded them as a serious threat to the *Volk* and the state. The Jehovah's Witnesses stood outside society and were publicly perceived as such. Detlef Garbe has described them as 'forgotten victims' of the Nazi regime, as very little was written about their history under National Socialism before the 1990s.[9]

In April 1933, Jehovah's Witnesses were banned by decree in several German states.[10] Despite repression, they organised a large meeting in Berlin in June 1933 at which they drafted a statement protesting about the persecution they faced. As well as presenting the statement to the authorities, they distributed 2 million copies to the public. This action met with a rapid and severe response from the police. All Jehovah's Witnesses' offices and businesses were searched and materials considered hostile to the state were confiscated. On 24 July 1933, the Nazis banned the Jehovah's Witnesses movement entirely.[11] Its members lost many of their rights and were brought before the courts for refusing to give the Hitler salute or to salute the Nazi flag, and for continuing to meet and proselytise. Yet as King has demonstrated, the Jehovah's Witnesses 'not only continued to meet, but also to preach and distribute literature'.[12] After the first arrests in 1933, the

Jehovah's Witnesses developed structures adapted to the conditions of illegality. They maintained contacts with each other and contacts abroad, produced their magazine *The Watchtower* underground and smuggled correspondence. In April 1935, a law was passed that denied Jehovah's Witnesses the right to work in public service, which led to numerous dismissals. Furthermore, many Jehovah's Witnesses lost their children for refusing to give the Hitler salute or participate in Nazi activities. Their children were sent away for 're-education'.[13]

The Nazis, who were affronted by their non-conformity and their lack of allegiance to the state, in particular their refusal to bear arms, considered the Jehovah's Witnesses as 'absolutely dangerous enemies of the state' and prosecuted thousands of them in Special Courts. In June 1936, a special unit was created within the Gestapo to deal with the Jehovah's Witnesses. Mass arrests occurred in August and September 1936. Although many of its leaders were imprisoned, the movement succeeded in continuing its underground work. By mid-1937, at least 17 Jehovah's Witnesses had died during the course of Gestapo interrogations or imprisonment. But the Jehovah's Witnesses responded to the repression by redoubling their efforts to circulate their literature. They placed tens of thousands of handbills in household letterboxes, under doormats or on park benches, proclaiming the 'persecution of Christians' in the Third Reich. A widely distributed tract of 20 June 1937, 'Open Letter to the People of Germany who Believe in the Bible and Love Christ', gave a detailed description of the maltreatment of Jehovah's Witnesses by the Nazi regime.

A wave of arrests followed in the autumn of 1937. The Jehovah's Witnesses were sent to concentration camps where they wore purple triangles.[14] Garbe has estimated that Jehovah's Witnesses made up between 5 and 10 per cent of a concentration camp's population in the period 1937 to 1939. Once the war began, this percentage dropped and by the end of the war the Jehovah's Witnesses formed a tiny minority. Many of the Jehovah's Witnesses were able to survive with the aid of a strong network of practical and emotional support established by their co-religionists. They worked out collective strategies for survival, but they refused to co-operate with other groups of prisoners or to take part in any resistance attempts led by political prisoners in the camps. Unlike many of the other victims, the Jehovah's Witnesses knew and understood why they were imprisoned in the concentration camps (because they renounced the state and were conscientious objectors to military service). Indeed, the majority remained in the camps by choice. They had only to sign a document renouncing the Jehovah's Witnesses movement in order to be freed: 'I, the undersigned … born on … herewith make the following declaration: 1. I have come to know that the International Association of Jehovah's Witnesses professes a false doctrine and pursues subversive goals under the cloak of religious activities. 2. I, therefore, left the organisation entirely and made myself absolutely free from the teachings of this group. 3. I affirm herein never again to participate in the activities of the International Association of Jehovah's Witnesses. I will immediately renounce any person attempting to win me over with the false doctrine of Jehovah's Witnesses or reveal his own membership in this group. I will immediately remit to the police all publications which come to me from this organisation. 4. In future, I wish to observe the laws of the State and to defend my homeland in the event of war, weapon in hand, and join in every way the community of the people. 5. I have been informed that I will at once be taken into protective custody if I should again act against the declaration given today.'[15] However, very few signed the declaration.

King has argued that 'inside or out, they lived in Jehovah's world, and thus the separation from family and friends was not as drastic as it was for the others'.[16] Their religious convictions offered them some emotional and psychological protection. Despite the torture and murder of many of their number, their faith remained unshakeable. This made it harder for the regime to break their resistance. The Jehovah's Witnesses upheld their beliefs with a force that the Nazis neither comprehended nor anticipated. The use of force and terror by the SS strengthened the resolve of the Jehovah's Witnesses rather than weakening it as it was designed to do. Erna Ludolph, a German Jehovah's Witness who survived the Nazi regime, stated: 'We never prayed to be set free. We prayed for strength to endure. Everything else was unimportant. What mattered was standing up for Jehovah's name.'[17] However, M. James Penton has recently pointed out that although they suffered terribly under National Socialism, the Jehovah's Witnesses 'were not candidates for destruction'.[18] The Nazi regime did not want to eradicate them.

By 1942, the situation of the Jehovah's Witnesses began to improve. It became clear that they would not renounce their faith no matter how much terror they were subjected to, nor would they try to escape or engage in resistance activities with other groups of prisoners, for religious reasons, so the SS began to use them for trusted jobs. The Jehovah's Witnesses worked with diligence and reliability, as long as their religious principles were not compromised, and they gained a reputation among the SS as trustworthy prisoners. They were employed outside the camp walls (farming, loading and unloading) and as personal staff to the SS and their families, working as secretaries, barbers and cooks. The comparatively good conditions led to a renewal of secret meetings and services. The Jehovah's Witnesses managed to smuggle their literature into the camps, for example hidden in packages of 'Elberfeld Gingerbread'.[19] They even attempted to proselytise. In the hellish conditions of the Nazi camps, prisoners from other categories joined the Jehovah's Witnesses, particularly Soviet prisoners.

The Jehovah's Witnesses took the conscious decision to oppose the Nazi regime on the grounds of their religious convictions. They refused to compromise with the Nazi state and were convinced of the correctness of their beliefs and actions, even in the face of death. Letters sent to family members before their execution demonstrated the conviction, determination and courage of these individuals. Franz Reiter wrote to his mother on 5 January 1940: 'I am strongly convinced in my belief that I am acting correctly ... I could still change my mind, but with God this would be disloyalty. All of us here wish to be faithful to God, to his honour … I will be executed tomorrow morning. I have my strength from God.'[20] Garbe has estimated the number of deaths of German Jehovah's Witnesses under National Socialism at 1,200. Approximately 250 of these were death sentences imposed for conscientious objection to military service.

YOUTH DISSENT AND RESISTANCE

Dissenting youth included those who belonged to the Hitler Youth but did not turn up regularly to its meetings, those who had left the Hitler Youth, bored or disillusioned with its requirements, or those who had never enrolled in the Nazi youth movement in the first place. In Munich, the *Blasen* (Bubbles) were made up of anti-authoritarian workers and apprentices. They resisted the limits placed upon their personal freedom by the Hitler Youth. They remained aloof from the official youth group and engaged in theft, sabotage and other transgressions of the law. Similar cliques existed in other cities. In Hamburg, working-class gangs such as the Jumbo Band wore distinctive clothing and attacked the Hitler Youth. Other dissident youth groups sprang up that had ideological affinities to the outlawed communists and socialists, such as the *Meuten* (Packs) in Leipzig, which had approximately 1,500 members.[21] They were blue-collar workers and apprentices who met at local cinemas and bars. They went on hikes, listened to Radio Moscow, dressed in unconventional clothes and wore red handkerchiefs. Moreover, they engaged in open confrontations with the Hitler Youth.

The Edelweiss Pirates sprang up spontaneously in many German cities.[22] These young people were typically aged between 14 and 18. In Cologne, the Navajos, in Dusseldorf, the Kittelbach Pirates and in other cities in the Rhineland and Ruhr, other groups of Edelweiss Pirates all attracted the animosity of the Hitler Youth because of their non-conformity. They represented a challenge to the authority of the Hitler Youth and sought conflicts with its members and patrols. The Edelweiss Pirates included girls among their number and their sexuality was open. The Hitler Youth and the Nazi government frowned upon this. The Edelweiss Pirates congregated in gangs at local parks, bars, squares or street corners. At weekends, they hiked and camped in the countryside, where they chatted, sang traditional youth songs or adapted the words to reflect their experiences. During holidays, they undertook longer journeys to assert their independence from both their parents and the regime.[23]

Another type of dissenting youth, from a middle- and upper-middle-class background, was the Swing Youth. The Swing Youth listened to jazz and swing music in private or at carefully selected nightclubs and cafés. They dressed distinctively and ostentatiously, wore their hair long and imitated American or British attitudes and styles. The Swing Youth originated in Hamburg, but groups established themselves in other cities including Frankfurt and Berlin. They attracted the attention of the authorities, both for their open sexuality and for their rejection of National Socialist cultural norms.

The Hitler Youth and the Gestapo regarded all these groups as a challenge to their authority and the regime clamped down upon them more and more as the war years progressed. On 9 March 1940, Himmler issued a police ordinance for the 'protection of youth'. This was aimed at repressing cliques and gangs. It prohibited young people from meeting in bars or on the streets after dark. Many young people who failed to comply with this restriction were arrested and placed in youth custody camps, such as Moringen. On 25 October 1944, Himmler issued an ordinance for the 'combating of youth cliques': 'In the last few years, and recently in increased numbers, gatherings of youths (cliques) have formed in all parts of the Reich ... Cliques are groupings of juveniles outside the Hitler Youth, who lead a separate way of life, whose principles are irreconcilable with the National Socialist worldview. Collectively, they reject or are indifferent to their duties towards the national community, or towards the Hitler Youth, and in particular evince a lack of will to conform with the dictates of wartime.'[24] In November 1944, the leaders of the Edelweiss Pirates were publicly executed in Cologne.

The White Rose movement was a resistance group that appeared in Munich during 1942 and 1943, centred round Hans and Sophie Scholl.[25] Together with fellow students Alexander Schmorell, Christoph Probst, Willi Graf and Professor of Philosophy at Munich University Kurt Huber, Hans and Sophie Scholl wrote and circulated a series of leaflets that openly told of the murder of Jews in Poland and called for popular mobilisation against Hitler. Between the summer of 1942 and February 1943, the White Rose distributed a series of six pamphlets at night in a number of German cities, including Cologne, Essen, Stuttgart, Frankfurt and Nuremberg, as well as Munich. The first leaflet urged Germans to resist the regime. The second leaflet told of 300,000 Jews already killed in Poland. The third asked Germans to sabotage the war industry. Christiane Moll has argued that 'their will to topple the system and their ingenuity drove them to ever more reckless campaigns'.[26] On 18 February 1943, Hans and Sophie Scholl distributed their leaflets around Munich University for the last time. Having thrown between 1,500 and 1,800 leaflets down the staircase of the main entrance at Munich University, they were caught by the caretaker and arrested. Willi Graf was arrested later the same day. The remaining three members of the White Rose were arrested within the next ten days. A Special Court was set up under Roland Freisler on 22 February 1943, which sentenced Hans Scholl, Sophie Scholl and Christoph Probst to death and they were executed the same day. Schmorell and Huber were executed on 13 July 1943 and Graf on 12 October 1943. Sophie Scholl had said to a fellow prisoner on the day of her execution: 'What does our death matter if thousands will be stirred and awakened by what we have done? The students are bound to revolt.' But they did not. On the contrary, the National Socialist German Students' Association organised a demonstration of 3,000 students to show their loyalty to the regime.

Less well known than the White Rose movement, the members of the Hübener group were among the youngest Germans to resist the Nazi regime, acting independently, without the guidance of adults.[27] This group of four teenagers from Hamburg, Helmuth Hübener, Karl-Heinz Schnibbe, Rudolf Wobbe and Gerhard Düwer, took a moral stance against the Nazi dictatorship. In contrast to the majority of German Mormons who accepted the Nazi regime, Helmuth Hübener, a 16-year-old Mormon, distributed anti-Nazi leaflets with the aid of his three co-conspirators. They continued to do this for approximately six months before they were reported to the Gestapo. Arrested in February 1942, Hübener was given the death penalty for committing treason, while his three comrades received prison sentences of between four and ten years for their part in the conspiracy. Hübener was executed in October 1942.

THE ROSENSTRASSE PROTEST

In February 1943, a group of German women fought for the liberation of their Jewish husbands who were rounded up by the Gestapo from factories in Berlin. Their defiance of the Gestapo made the Rosenstrasse Protest a unique event. When the men failed to return home from work, their German wives began to worry and tried to find out what had happened to them. They sought information from the police, from the factories and from each other. They soon found out that their husbands were being held at the Jewish Community centre at Rosenstrasse. They hurried there to take food, clothing and toiletries and to obtain further information about what was happening. They soon formed a crowd and angrily demanded their husbands back. Before leaving for the night, several of them agreed to return the next morning to continue their protest. They protested for a week outside the collection centre in Rosenstrasse. On several occasions the guards threatened to shoot if they did not disperse. Each time they ran for cover, but then returned within minutes shouting, 'We want our husbands!' Their efforts meant that the process of deportation of intermarried Jews interned there was stalled. Goebbels ordered that their husbands were to be released, as Hitler was concerned about the impact of non-compliance by intermarried Germans on popular morale and on the war effort. The Rosenstrasse Rising was an extraordinary display of courage and the singular incident of mass German protest against the deportation of German Jews.[28]

SOCIALIST AND COMMUNIST RESISTANCE

Although the SPD and the KPD were both banned in 1933, their exiled leadership abroad together with party activists remaining inside Germany continued to oppose National Socialism. One socialist resistance group in Berlin, consisting of about 3,000 members in 1933, was the Red Shock Troop. It set up an eponymous newspaper to voice its opposition. The group's leaders were arrested and imprisoned in December 1933. Another very small socialist group called New Beginning also engaged in resistance activities. Despite their attempts to conduct their opposition through private discussions, its key members were arrested in 1935 and 1938.

Clandestine resistance on the part of communists involved the printing and distribution of anti-Nazi literature. Between 1933 and 1935, the KPD continued to print and distribute the *Red Flag* newspaper and produced and circulated over 1 million anti-Nazi leaflets. However, communist resisters constantly had to elude Gestapo detection, which proved very difficult. In 1935 alone, 14,000 communists were arrested for resistance activities. By the mid-1930s, the Nazi regime had managed to suppress most socialist and communist resistance, through the arrest and internment of opponents in concentration camps. By 1939, 150,000 Communists and Social Democrats had been put into concentration camps and 12,000 had been convicted for treason.

During the war, after the Nazi invasion of the Soviet Union in 1941, a number of small communist groups became active in opposing the Nazi regime.[29] The Uhrig Group, led by Robert Uhrig, had approximately 100 active members in Berlin in 1941–1942. The group called for defence of the Soviet Union and urged workers to sabotage the Nazi government. In February 1942, Uhrig and his active supporters were arrested and executed. Another group active in 1941–1942 was Home Front. It was centred on the figures Wilhelm Guddorf, John Sieg, Martin Weise and Jon Graudenz, who had all been KPD members before 1933. They produced an anti-Nazi newspaper every fortnight, which they circulated in Berlin factories, as well as distributing pamphlets that told of war crimes on the eastern front. The Gestapo arrested the leaders of the Home Front in the autumn of 1942. Another resistance group, the Red Orchestra, led by Arvid Harnack and Harro Schulze-Boysen, passed secrets of the German war effort to the Soviet government. After identification by the Gestapo, its leaders were arrested. In 19 separate trials between December 1942 and July 1943, the Nazi military court convicted 77 members of the Red Orchestra. Of these, 45 were sentenced to death and executed.[30] The Herbert Baum Group was made up of 30 Jewish communists who worked at the Siemens plant in Berlin. It produced a monthly anti-Nazi newssheet, *The Way Out*, which urged German soldiers to fight against the Hitler regime. In May 1942, the Gestapo rounded up, tortured and executed its members.

These examples of communist and socialist resistance were the work of a comparatively small number of brave groups and individuals. One significant lone resister was Georg Elser, a craftsman from Württemberg. Although he had voted for the KPD before 1933, he did not belong to any communist resistance group. Alarmed by Hitler's decision to take Germany to war, Elser planted a bomb in a Munich beerhall on 8 November 1939, at which Hitler was due to speak, with the aim of assassinating him. The bomb exploded shortly after Hitler left the building, having given his speech. Elser was arrested and imprisoned at Sachsenhausen concentration camp as a 'special prisoner'. He was subsequently moved to Dachau in 1944 and executed on 9 April 1945.[31] Apart from the resistance attempts described above, there were some groups of factory workers who became engaged in acts of sabotage. However, resistance was not resonated among the majority of German workers.

ELITE RESISTANCE

Resistance on the part of aristocratic, conservative and military figures was centred on a number of specific groups. The Kreisau Circle included Graf Helmut von Moltke, Adam von Trott du Solz, Alfred Delp and Peter Graf Yorck von Wartenburg. It took its name from von Moltke's estate in Silesia, where its members met. Von Moltke had been a firm supporter of the Weimar Republic and had disliked National Socialism from the start. Morally against the Nazi regime and its policies, the Kreisau Circle was a group of friends which had little real opportunity for resistance, but which discussed ideas and shared values.[32] Von Moltke's rejection of National Socialism brought him into contact with other elite resistance groups and he arranged for them to meet on his estate in 1942–1943. There were only three meetings at Kreisau, yet as Freya von Moltke, his wife, has described, 'these three long weekends gave us the name "Kreisau Circle"'.[33] Von Moltke was arrested in January 1944 and was subsequently executed. 'We are hanged because we thought together,' he wrote in prison before his execution.

The main group of conservative, nationalist resisters formed around the figures of Carl Goerdeler, the former Mayor of Leipzig, and General Ludwig Beck, the former army chief of staff. While the Beck-Goerdeler group shared many of Hitler's foreign policy ambitions, and indeed had formed part of the elite of the Third Reich during the early years of the Nazi regime, they came to disagree with Hitler's style and methods. The Blomberg-Fritsch crisis of 1938 was a significant turning point in this respect. Hitler forced his two top army men, War Minister Field Marshal Werner von Blomberg and Commander-in-Chief of the Army Werner von Fritsch to resign, as well as dismissing 14 generals. Claus Schenk von Stauffenberg expressed 'shock and dismay' and 'he privately criticised the generals who failed to make a stand against the treatment to which Blomberg and Fritsch had been subjected'.[34] The Beck-Goerdeler group despised the incompetence and corruption of the other Nazi leaders and functionaries. This is not to suggest that they favoured liberalism or democracy. Indeed, Hans Mommsen has observed that 'it is highly significant that among the alternatives to National Socialism offered by the German resistance, liberal and democratic visions were almost entirely absent'.[35] The Beck-Goerdeler group was comprised of traditional German conservatives, who favoured authoritarianism and nationalism but rejected the totalitarian ambitions of Nazism.

The national-conservative resistance formed part of the military and bureaucratic elite. Mommsen has described it as a resistance of servants of the state.[36] As the regime grew increasingly radical, these men became more critical, but it is important to remember that they lacked any popular basis of support for their resistance. The Beck-Goerdeler group members, including Henning von Tresckow and Claus Schenk von Stauffenberg, were motivated in their actions by their patriotism and by the poor and irrational decisions taken by Hitler and the Nazi leadership in the latter war years. Admiral Wilhelm Canaris and Major General Hans Oster from the *Abwehr* (military intelligence group of the Foreign Office) became closely linked with the Beck-Goerdeler group. In July 1944, the Beck-Goerdeler group prepared 'Operation Valkyrie', the plan to assassinate Hitler and oust the National Socialist regime. Just before 20 July 1944, Stauffenberg said: 'It is now time that something was done. But who has the courage to do something must do so in the knowledge that he will go down in German history as a traitor. If he does not do it, however, he will be a traitor to his conscience.'[37]

On 20 July 1944, Stauffenberg planted a bomb in the Briefing Room at the Wolf's Lair military headquarters, in an attempt to kill Hitler. The plot was unsuccessful and Hitler escaped the incident with only minor injuries. He subsequently addressed the nation in a radio broadcast, stating that 'a tiny clique of ambitious, unscrupulous and at the same time criminally stupid officers hatched a plot to remove me ... It is a very small clique of criminal elements, which will now be mercilessly exterminated ... We shall settle accounts in our accustomed manner as National Socialists'.[38] Within a day, the main conspirators were either killed or arrested. They became a symbol of the 'other Germany', that is, the small minority that opposed National Socialism. Mommsen has described how 'the conspirators in the July 20 movement were engaged in a symbolic restoration of politics in the sense of a freely agreed upon common life without force or oppression'.[39]

Those individuals and groups that attempted resistance and oppositional behaviour, or even non-conformist behaviour, stood conceptually outside the 'national community'. But they stood outside it by their own preference rather than by criteria applied by the Nazi regime about who fitted in and who did not. Had they chosen to conform, even just outwardly, they would have been inside the 'national community' and carried on their daily lives like the rest of the population. By their own choice and determination, this tiny minority of the German population took a moral stance against National Socialism and the crimes it committed in the name of the German people. Within a society that largely consented to the regime, these individuals and groups had the courage to make a stand against the Nazi dictatorship, for a variety of reasons. They risked their lives and many indeed lost their lives as a result of their actions.

NOTES

1   The following books provide a good coverage of the subject: P. Hoffmann, *German Resistance to Hitler* (Cambridge, Mass., 1988); P. Hoffmann, *Widerstand, Staatsstreich, Attentat* (Munich, 1985); J. Schmädeke and P. Steinbach (eds), *Der Widerstand gegen den Nationalsozialismus* (Munich, 1985); H. Graml (ed.), *Widerstand im Dritten Reich. Probleme, Ereignisse, Gestalten* (Frankfurt am Main, 1984); C. Kleßman and F. Pingl (eds), *Gegner des Nationalsozialismus* (Frankfurt am Main, 1980); M. Balfour, *Withstanding Hitler in Germany 1933–1945* (London and New York, 1988); F. Nicosia and L. Stokes, *Germans against Nazism: Nonconformity, Opposition and Resistance in the Third Reich* (Oxford, 1990); D. Large (ed.), *Contending with Hitler: Varieties of German Resistance in the Third Reich* (Cambridge, 1991); M. Housden, *Resistance and Conformity in the Third Reich* (London, 1997); F. McDonough, *Opposition and Resistance in Nazi*

Germany (Cambridge, 2001). I. Kershaw, *The Nazi Dictatorship: Problems and Perspectives of Interpretation* (London, 2000), pp. 183–217 provides a clear summary of the historiographical debate.

2 The 'Bavaria Project', instigated in 1973 by the Institute of Contemporary History in Munich, investigated 'Resistance and Persecution in Bavaria, 1933–1945'. On this, see Kershaw, *The Nazi Dictatorship*, pp. 192–4.

3 R. Evans, 'From Hitler to Bismarck: "Third Reich" and Kaiserreich in Recent Historiography: Part II', *Historical Journal*, Vol. 26 (1983), p. 1013.

4 Kershaw, *The Nazi Dictatorship*, pp. 204–5.

5 D. Peukert, *Inside Nazi Germany* (London, 1987), pp. 81–5.

6 Kershaw, *The Nazi Dictatorship*, p. 206.

7 Ibid., p. 207.

8 Ibid., p. 214.

9 The main works on the subject are: D. Garbe, *Zwischen Widerstand und Martyrium. Die Zeugen Jehovas im Dritten Reich* (Munich, 1994); H. Hesse, *'Am mutigsten waren immere wieder die Zeugen Jehovas.' Verfolgung und Widerstand der Zeugen Jehovas im Nationalsozialismus* (Bremen, 1998); M. Reynaud and S. Graffard, *The Jehovah's Witnesses and the Nazis: Persecution, Deportation, and Murder, 1933–1945* (New York, 2001). See also C. King, *The Nazi State and the New Religions* (New York, 1982) and M. Kater, 'Die Ernsten Bibelforscher im Dritten Reich', in *Vierteljahrshefte für Zeitgeschichte*, Vol. 17 (1969), pp. 181–218. For a personal narrative, see H.-W. Kusserow, *Der Lila Winkel. Die Familie Kusserow. Zeugen Jehovas unter der Nazidiktatur* (Bonn, 1998).

10 Reynaud and Graffard, *The Jehovah's Witnesses and the Nazis*, p. 6.

11 Ibid., p. 11.

12 C. King, 'Jehovah's Witnesses under Nazism', in M. Berenbaum (ed.), *A Mosaic of Victims: Non-Jews Persecuted and Murdered by the Nazis* (London, 1990), p. 191.

13 Reynaud and Graffard, *The Jehovah's Witnesses and the Nazis*, p. 56.

14 See J. Bergman, 'The Jehovah's Witnesses' experience in the Nazi concentration camps: a history of their conflicts with the Nazi State', *Journal of Church and State*, Vol. 38. No. 1 (1996), pp. 87–113.

15 Cited in Reynaud and Graffard, *The Jehovah's Witnesses and the Nazis*, pp. 38–9.

16 King, 'Jehovah's Witnesses under Nazism', p. 191.

17 Cited in J. Chu, 'God's Things and Caesar's: Jehovah's Witnesses and political neutrality, *Journal of Genocide Research*, Vol. 6, No. 3 (2004), p. 337.

18 M. James Penton, *Jehovah's Witnesses and the Third Reich: Sectarian Politics under Persecution* (Toronto, 2004), p. 237.

19 Reynaud and Graffard, *The Jehovah's Witnesses and the Nazis*, p. 173.

20 Cited in Chu, 'God's Things and Caesar's', p. 336.

21 M. Kater, *Hitler Youth* (London, 2004), p. 137.

22 See D. Peukert, *Die Edelweißpiraten. Protestbewegungen jugendlicher Arbeiter im Dritten Reich* (Cologne, 1980). See also M. von Hellfeld, *Edelweißpiraten in Köln* (Cologne, 1983).

23 Peukert, *Inside Nazi Germany*, pp. 156–7.

24 Cited in Burleigh and Wippermann, *The Racial State: Germany 1933–1945* (Cambridge, 1991), p. 238.

25 On the White Rose, see H. Siefken (ed.), *The White Rose: Student Resistance to National Socialism 1942–1943* (Nottingham, 1991) and I. Jens (ed.), *At the Heart of the White Rose: Letters and Diaries of Hans and Sophie Scholl* (New York, 1987).

26 C. Moll, 'Acts of Resistance: The White Rose in the Light of New Archival Evidence', in M. Geyer and J. Boyer (eds), *Resistance against the Third Reich 1933–1990* (Chicago, 1994), p. 200.

27 On this, see B. Holmes and A. Keele (eds), *When Truth was Treason: German Youth against Hitler* (Urbana and Chicago, 1995).

28 For a detailed examination, see N. Stoltzfus, *Resistance of the Heart: Intermarriage and the Rosenstrasse Protest in Nazi Germany* (New Brunswick, 2001).

29 On this, see A. Merson, *Communist Resistance in Nazi Germany* (London, 1985). See also D. Peukert, *Die KPD im Widerstand. Verfolgung und Untergrundarbeit an Rhein und Ruhr 1933 bis 1945* (Wuppertal, 1980).

30 S. Brysac, *Resisting Hitler: Mildred Harnack and the Red Orchestra* (Oxford, 2000), p. 383.

31 On Elser, see H. Haasis, *'Den Hitler jag' ich in die Luft': der Attentäter Georg Elser: eine Biographie* (Berlin, 1999).

32 On the Kreisau Circle, see T. Childers, 'The Kreisau Circle and the Twentieth of July', in Large (ed.), *Contending with Hitler*, pp. 99–117. See also G. van Roon, *Neuordnung im Widerstand. Der Kreisauer Kreis innerhalb der deutschen Widerstandsbewegung* (Munich, 1967).

33 F. von Moltke, *Memories of Kreisau and the German Resistance* (Lincoln, Nebraska, 2003), p. 26.

34 P. Hoffmann, *Stauffenberg: A Family History, 1905–1944* (Cambridge, 1995), p. 87.

35 H. Mommsen, 'The Political Legacy of the German Resistance', in Large (ed.) *Contending with Hitler*, p. 162.

36 See H. Mommsen, *Alternatives to Hitler: German Resistance under the Third Reich* (London, 2003), especially pp. 23–41.

37 Cited in P. Hoffmann, *German Resistance to Hitler* (Cambridge, Mass. and London, 1988), p. 135.

38 Cited in J. Noakes (ed.), *Nazism 1919–1945, vol. 4: The German Home Front in World War II* (Exeter, 1998), pp. 624–5.

39 H. Mommsen, 'The German Resistance against Hitler and the Restoration of Politics', in M. Geyer and J. Boyer (eds), *Resistance against the Third Reich 1933–1990* (Chicago, 1994), p. 166.

PART THREE

CULTURAL LIFE AND THE 'NATIONAL COMMUNITY'

12

THE RADIO AND PRESS

Nazi poster advertising the 'People's Receiver' (*Volksempfänger*). © The Wiener Library

This chapter examines the fortunes of the radio and press under National Socialism. Both Hitler and Goebbels were conscious of the power of the radio as a propaganda medium. They knew that they could reach the masses easily and directly through the radio. Radio was a modern medium that was well suited to the dissemination of Nazi ideology.[1] It was 'the ideal medium to forge a reinvented and re-imagined national community'.[2] The press too was an important channel of communication employed by the National Socialist government to express its goals for the 'national community'. The written word in the Nazi press and the spoken word in radio broadcasts complemented each other. Together, they brought Hitler's message to the German people.

THE RADIO

In his address to the controllers of German radio on 25 March 1933, Goebbels clearly stated his intention that the radio was to be placed in the service of Nazi ideology. He told his audience that 'the correct attitudes must be conveyed, but that does not mean they must be boring' and that National Socialist ideology was to be brought to the people 'in a way which is modern, up to date, interesting and appealing'.[3] Goebbels quickly reorganised the German radio industry and brought it into line with National Socialist imperatives. German radio was unified into the Reich Radio Company. All former radio stations became branches of this company. Headed by the new Director of Broadcasting, Eugen Hadamovsky, the Reich Radio Company was made responsible for the political, cultural, administrative and technical management of the German broadcasting system. Within the first six months of Nazi rule, 13 per cent of broadcasting staff were expelled from the industry. Goebbels managed to bring control of the radio within his own remit within the first year of National Socialist rule, under the direction of Department Three of the Ministry of Popular Enlightenment and Propaganda. The Reich Chamber of Radio, a sub-chamber of the Reich Chamber of Culture, was the other main agency involved in the implementation of Goebbels' plans for German radio.

The Nazi regime promoted radio ownership and listening. It commissioned manufacturers to produce two new types of cheap radios, costing 75 Reichsmarks and 35 Reichsmarks. In 1933, 1.5 million radio sets were produced. The cheaper version, the People's Receiver, could be paid for in instalments. The People's Receiver sets had a very limited reception capacity so that they were unable to receive foreign radio broadcasts. Posters advertising the new, cheap radio sets read: 'All Germany listens to the *Führer* with the People's Radio.' The emphasis on national unity was explicit. In 1933 alone, Hitler made at least 50 radio broadcasts. By 1939, 70 per cent of German households had a radio. This was three times as many as in 1932. Hence, the regime succeeded in creating a mass radio audience, with a rapid growth of radio ownership across all social classes. Radio was transformed from a small-scale form of communication into a medium of mass communication.[4] The Nazi regime encouraged communal radio listening, in factories, offices and cafés. Loudspeaker columns were erected in city squares and other public places. In this way, Nazi propagandists hoped that they could reach those people who did not possess a radio set. They believed that the popular impact of speeches and rallies broadcast on the radio would be greater in public places than in the private home environment. Communal listening to important announcements and speeches became a significant feature of societal life in the Third Reich. Radio wardens were responsible for setting up loudspeakers in town squares, offices and factories to encourage communal listening.

They played a part in popularising the radio, reporting on audience preference and passing on listeners' requests to the Reich Radio Company.

Goebbels was eager to make the best possible use out of the medium as a propaganda tool. He regarded the radio as 'the most modern and the most important instrument of mass influence'. On 15 March 1933, he declared: 'I have a vision of a new and topical radio, a radio that really takes account of the spirit of our time ... a radio that is aware of its great national responsibility.'[5] Goebbels utilised the radio as a means of creating uniformity and forging the 'national community'. Significant national events ('moments of the nation') and speeches by Hitler were broadcast across the nation in order to imbue the German population with a sense of 'national community'. Goebbels' radio propaganda campaign, for example, played a decisive role in influencing the result of the Saarland plebiscite in January 1935 – in which 91 per cent of voters chose to be returned to Germany – and Nazi propagandists were convinced of its effectiveness for all their political goals. They mobilised the radio into 'the voice of the nation' to emphasise a variety of themes. For example, the 1935 radio series 'German Nation on German Soil' aimed to give city-dwellers a sense of affinity with the German land. It was a typical 'Blood and Soil' presentation, aimed at integrating the German people with their homeland and emphasising that 'blood and soil are eternal'.[6]

Political broadcasts were undoubtedly important for the dissemination of Nazi ideology. By 1935, Hitler's speeches reached a radio audience of more than 56 million people. In 1936, Goebbels noted: 'We National Socialist propagandists have transformed the radio into the sharpest of propaganda weapons. Before we took power, the German radio was run by amateurs. What we have now made of it is a tool for ideological education and a top-class political force.'[7] But Goebbels, ever the pragmatist, was nevertheless concerned to keep the interest of the population. There was a high proportion of light entertainment programmes.[8] Between 1932 and 1937, the amount of broadcasting time allocated to music grew from 59 per cent to 69 per cent. Indeed, this trend increased during the war. By 1942, well over two-thirds of radio broadcasting was given over to light music, in order to sustain popular morale. The programmes included light operas, dance music, *völkisch* music and marches.

The Nazi regime directed much of its radio propaganda at the female sector of the population. Kate Lacey has studied radio programming aimed at influencing women's patterns of consumption in particular.[9] She identifies two main ways in which the National Socialists used the radio to 'speak' to women. First, they followed the example of broadcasting in the Weimar era and used stories, dialogues, chat shows and conversations in order to disseminate their ideology.[10] Second, they brought the voices of political leaders directly into the home. This was much more explicit. Hitler's voice entered the household (and the factory) in the nationwide broadcasts entitled 'Hour of the Nation'. As Lacey shows, 'housewives in the home were expected to "down tools" with workers in factories and public institutions to participate in the synchronised ritual of the leadership cult and national community'.[11] The range of women's programming was narrower than it had been during the Weimar Republic, focusing on motherhood and the family, the health of the nation and women's role as consumers in the domestic economy.

A large number of radio programmes, on both national and regional radio, were aimed directly at housewives. National broadcasts included programmes such as 'Preparations for the First Child', 'Healthy Mothers – Happy Mothers' and 'Gymnastics for the Housewife'. Regionally, the following programmes were featured: in Berlin, 'Economical Cooking' and 'Cooking with Potatoes'; in Breslau, 'Making the House Beautiful with a Brush and Colours'; in Frankfurt, 'Tricks in the Kitchen'; in Hamburg, 'What Shall We Cook Next Week?'; in Königsberg, 'The Housewife at the Centre of the National Economy'; in Leipzig, 'The Potato. A Food for the Nation' and 'How Can a Mother Prevent Illness in her Family?'[12] In addition, there were broadcasts for mothers and children to listen to together, such as a regular programme in Berlin entitled 'Gymnastics for Mother and Child'. Other programmes centred on the theme of German culture and family life, such as 'Children Sing *Heimat* Songs'. The 'Day of German House Music' in November 1937 was intended 'to prepare the way for the true hour celebration' of the German family.[13]

Furthermore, there were daily programmes on population policy themes, including speeches by Nazi leaders, advice for families and interviews with the fathers and mothers of *kinderreich* families. On festival days or special occasions, the number of such broadcasts increased. In particular, on Mother's Day, radio broadcasts consisted almost entirely of programmes about the family. On Mother's Day in 1936, the following programmes were typical of the broadcasts that went out: on national radio, 'Honour the Mother!', 'The Mother's Song', 'Mother and Child' and 'New Poems about Mother and Child; in Berlin, 'The Soldier's Mother' and 'Dear Son – Dear Daughter!'; in Cologne, 'For Mother's Day – a Tranquil Hour in Word and Song'; in Königsberg, 'The Story of a Mother', 'Mother with the Little Ones on Mother's Day' and 'Don't Forget Mother'; and in Leipzig, 'Mothers and Sons'.[14]

Regional radio stations sent out cookery programmes and market reports to influence the shopping habits of German women. Campaigns such as 'Fight against Wastage' and 'Proper Washing: Wash Washing Wisely' emphasised to housewives that they had a direct influence upon the nation's economy, in terms of their patterns of consumption. Patriotic consumption meant buying German goods. It also, by extension, meant avoiding Jewish shops and businesses, as the exclusion of the Jews was a central part of the creation of the 'national community'. While there was little explicit anti-Semitic propaganda in women's programming, much of the rhetoric was framed in terms of this exclusion. Goering described women as the 'trustees of the nation's wealth' and the regime used the radio to influence women in its attempt to achieve economic autarky in line with the imperatives of the Four Year Plan.[15] For example, radio programming in Hamburg in June 1939 included advice on preserving and pickling, darning stockings and the 'Fight against Wastage'. In July 1939, the same radio station was broadcasting programmes that encouraged women to buy plain goods instead of luxury items, or to forego certain commodities altogether, such as 'Breakfast tastes just as good without coffee'. Programming during the war was similarly designed to influence consumption to serve the needs of the war economy, such as conversational pieces entitled 'We Don't Throw Anything Away' or 'The Good Customer'. Lacey has argued that these campaigns, by urging women to act in the best interests of the nation, were 'overtly designed to influence and change actual behaviour, and to leave women in no doubt as to their function and status in Nazi society'.[16]

On 1 September 1939, new 'extraordinary radio measures' prohibited the German population from listening to foreign radio stations. Clearly, these measures were designed to control the access of information and to restrict what people could listen to, even in their own homes. The decree stated that 'in modern war the enemy fights not only with military weapons, but also with methods intended to influence and undermine the morale of the people. One of these methods is the radio'.[17] Although the regime hoped that responsible German citizens would not want to listen to the enemy propaganda of foreign broadcasts, the new decree made 'black listening' into a criminal offence. During the war, the duties of the radio wardens were expanded to include reporting on people who listened to foreign radio broadcasts. However, although 'black listening' was an illegal activity, it was fairly widespread. Eric Johnson and Karl-Heinz Reuband contend that listening to foreign radio stations was 'far and away the most common form of illegal activity that German citizens involved themselves in'.[18] Surveys they conducted among Germans who lived through the Nazi era show that between 40 and 50 per cent of respondents in Cologne, Krefeld, Dresden and Berlin listened illegally to foreign radio broadcasts either occasionally or regularly. Radio listening was comparatively easy to keep secret and less likely to come to the attention of the Gestapo than other illegal activities, especially if people listened quietly and did not talk to anyone about what they were doing or what they heard.

Apart from the overtly political content of some broadcasts, the radio was still intended to entertain people and particularly during the wartime period there was an increased emphasis on light entertainment.[19] During the war, a popular Sunday morning programme, 'Treasure Trove', presented high-quality music interspersed with renditions from German plays and poems. Sunday afternoons featured the 'Request Concert', broadcast from Berlin.[20] This two-and-a-half-hour programme consisted of music requested by soldiers for their loved ones, as well as requests for soldiers from their families or girlfriends. At peak listening times on Sunday evenings, listeners could choose between light music on their local radio station or classical concerts by the Berlin Philharmonic Orchestra or the Vienna Philharmonic Orchestra which were broadcast on national radio. Radio plays were also very popular.[21] These kinds of broadcasts demonstrate that the radio played a significant role in providing light entertainment and thereby maintaining public morale during the war.

THE PRESS

In the Weimar Republic, a plethora of different types of newspapers flourished. The German press was decentralised, with no national press emanating from Berlin to serve the whole country, and by 1932 there were 4,703 different newspapers.[22] Each of the large cities had a number of daily newspapers: Berlin had 20, Hamburg had 10, Cologne and Stuttgart had 8 each, Frankfurt had 6 and Leipzig had 5. The provincial towns typically had two or three daily newspapers and there was a vast array of small local or regional newspapers with modest circulations. Approximately a quarter of the German press was politically oriented, as each political party had its own press, publishing newspapers and magazines. For example, the German Communist Party published the *Rote Fahne* (*Red Flag*), the Social Democratic Party published *Vorwärts* (*Forwards*), the German Nationalist Party published *Der Tag* (*The Day*) and the National Socialist Party published the *Völkischer Beobachter* (*People's Observer*). The Catholic Centre Party produced its own newspapers and other publications. There were also the prestigious quality daily newspapers such as the liberal *Frankfurter Zeitung*. In addition, there was an array of cheap newspapers sold on the streets, known as the 'boulevard press'.[23] These sensationalist illustrated papers covered sport, entertainment, crime and scandal. They sometimes had a political slant and many of their scandal stories were aimed at undermining the Weimar Republic.

At the end of 1932, the Nazis had 59 daily newspapers with a total combined circulation of 782,121 (2.5 per cent of overall newspaper circulation). By the end of 1933, their circulation had risen to 2.4 million copies per day.[24] The *Völkischer Beobachter*, transformed from a 'combat paper' into the official government organ, particularly enjoyed a sharp rise in circulation after Hitler came to power. Much of its success was due to the requirement that all Party officials had to subscribe to it. Party members could also show their loyalty to the regime by subscribing to its official newspaper.

The regime quickly set about 'co-ordinating' the newspaper industry by placing strict controls on publishers and journalists. The Nazi Party managed to 'co-ordinate' and take control of the press with comparative ease. This was partly because of the lack of unity among the different parts of the publishing industry and because of the long-standing rift between the editors' association and the publishers' association that prevented co-operation between them. The overcrowding of the industry was another contributing factor. In addition, a sharp curtailment of press freedom had already occurred through emergency decrees implemented by the Brüning and Papen governments.

The Nazi regime was clear from the outset in its intentions for the German press: 'The National Socialist *Weltanschauung* sees in the press a means of educating the people for National Socialism. In consequence, the press is an instrument of the National Socialist state. The National Socialist *Weltanschauung* demands total acceptance and does not tolerate the propagation of other basic political ideas. On this basis a state whose foundation is the National Socialist movement recognises only the National Socialist press.'[25] This required the elimination of numerous privately owned newspapers or their takeover by the Nazi press. Max Amann, director of the Party's own publishing house, *Eher Verlag*, who was directly responsible to Hitler, was in charge of the transfer of ownership of hundreds of private newspapers to his Party press empire. This policy continued throughout the Nazi era into the wartime period.

Oron Hale has shown that apart from controlling the work of editors and journalists, the new regime 'largely despoiled the publishers of their rights and properties', as part of its plan to use the press as 'an instrument of social control and integration'.[26] *Eher Verlag* took over the ownership of most of the German press. On 30 April 1933, the Reich Association of the German Press 'co-ordinated' itself and elected Otto Dietrich, the Nazi press chief, as its chairman. It announced that henceforth all journalists had to belong to the Association and all members were to be politically reliable and racially pure. By 1935, 1,300 Jewish and 'Marxist' journalists had been excluded from the profession.[27] The German Newspaper Publishers' Association 'co-ordinated' itself with the regime on 28 June 1933. It appointed Max Amann as its chairman and purged itself of politically unreliable members, replacing them with Nazi ones. Thereafter, the German Newspaper Publishers' Association became an instrument of Party control and exploitation. During the spring and summer of 1933, all Communist and Social Democratic newspapers were destroyed. KPD and SPD properties and plants that were suitable to continue to function as presses were confiscated and taken over by the Nazi press. Otherwise, they were destroyed and their equipment and assets were seized and taken to the nearest Nazi publishing plant.[28] The majority of other political as well as Catholic imprints were either closed down or taken over by the Nazi press. Hence, through confiscation, forced mergers and distress sales, the Nazi regime instigated a wholesale transformation of the German newspaper industry. The liberal *Frankfurter Zeitung* and the *Berliner Tageblatt* continued to exist for a while longer, although they were ultimately considered unsuitable by the regime and were eventually closed down.

The Ministry of Popular Enlightenment and Propaganda regulated not only the personnel involved in press activity but also the content of the newspapers. The content of publications was controlled by the state press agency, the *Deutsches Nachrichtenbüro* (DNB), which was formed in December 1933. The DNB provided guidance for the press and pre-censored publications.[29] In addition, the Ministry of Popular Enlightenment and Propaganda held daily press conferences, which stipulated what was to be printed and completed the process of censorship. Its directives laid down the length of articles, as well as the subject matter and layout. As a result, journalistic autonomy was almost completely suppressed.[30] Press directives were so detailed that the newspapers were practically written by the Ministry of Popular Enlightenment and Propaganda. Goebbels was clear about the bold style of reporting that he wanted: 'The reader should get the impression that the writer is in reality standing behind him.'[31]

Otto Dietrich, Reich Press Chief of the NSDAP and State Secretary within Goebbels' ministry, played an important part in the Nazi regulation of the press. He was the driving force behind the Editors' Law of 4 October 1933, which set the cornerstone of Nazi press control. This law had a huge impact upon journalists, editors and publishers. Journalists were legally obliged to 'regulate their work in accordance with National Socialism as a philosophy of life and conception of government'.[32] Editors had to follow the directives and instructions given by the Ministry of Popular Enlightenment and Propaganda. Publishers were deprived of all rights to determine the contents of their newspapers. The publisher's former position of authority and influence within his press was now legally taken over by the Ministry of Popular Enlightenment and Propaganda. Any attempt by a publisher to influence his editor was a criminal offence, punishable by a fine and imprisonment or a revocation of the publisher's licence. The Editors' Law contained an 'Aryan' clause which excluded Jews or those in mixed marriages from the profession. Furthermore, it prohibited the publication of any material that 'confuses the public between individually useful aims and aims of common use' or that might 'weaken the strength of the German Reich abroad or at home, the community will of the German people, German defence, culture or the economy', as well as anything 'immoral' or 'offensive to the honour or dignity of a German'.[33] Hence, the press was heavily censored and it was the professional and legal responsibility of newspaper editors to ensure compliance with these restrictions.

The Reich Press Chamber (one of the sub-chambers of the Reich Chamber of Culture), headed by Max Amann, played a significant role in the Nazi regulation and domination of the press industry. It ensured that all editors and journalists were 'racially pure' and politically reliable. The Association of German Newspaper Publishers and the Reich Association of the German Press came under its control, as did 11 other professional and trade organisations relating to the production, sale and distribution of printed materials.[34] Hale has argued that these all became 'captive organisations through which the state and party controlled all reportorial and creative writing, all publishing, and the dissemination of printed materials throughout Germany'.[35] These steps formed a significant part of the Nazi control of the press. In 1933 and 1934, the Nazi government removed the Nazi papers from the control of regional leaders and placed them under the control and management of the *Eher Verlag*.[36]

On 24 April 1935, Amann put into place three new regulations that enabled him to control the press. The first ordinance called for the withdrawal of publishing rights from any publisher whose publications tainted the honour of the press through sensationalism or immorality. The second ordinance asserted Amann's power to close newspaper enterprises where the number of competing newspapers created unhealthy economic conditions. The third ordinance aimed to hasten the demise of private ownership in the press industry and its eclipse by the Party press empire. These ordinances, issued under the authority of the Reich Chamber of Culture, were designed to transfer the ownership of private presses and publishing houses to Party ownership and to rationalise the industry through the merger or closure of uneconomic enterprises. Amann closed down many private publishing firms and banned confessional, vocational and special interest presses. Provincial city presses were particularly hard hit, as cities such as Kassel, Darmstadt, Brunswick, Mannheim and Essen each had several daily newspapers, which Amann considered to be excessive and economically impracticable.[37] Furthermore, Amann purged the confessional presses by either closing them down or by taking them over through subsidiary companies of *Eher Verlag*, such as the Phoenix Publishing Company, which was a holding and management company for former Catholic Centre Party papers. In 1934, he negotiated through duress the takeover of Ullstein, Germany's largest private publishing house. This set the tone for the Party acquisition of many other private publishing firms. Many newspapers retained their old titles and imprint so that readers were unaware of the changeover in ownership. In a period of 18 months, between 500 and 600 newspapers disappeared, merged or were bought by *Eher Verlag*.[38] Furthermore, the number of learned journals and periodicals halved from 10,000 to 5,000 in the first five years of Nazi rule.

The *Völkischer Beobachter* spearheaded Amann's press empire. Its circulation increased from 116,000 in 1932 to 1,192,500 in 1941. Alfred Rosenberg was editor until 1938 and was then succeeded by Wilhelm Weiss, who had been head of the Reich Association of the German Press since 1934. Weiss attempted to give the *Völkischer Beobachter* more popular appeal and to improve its news service and coverage. Julius Streicher's *Der Stürmer* also saw a marked increase in its circulation, from 65,000 copies in 1934 to nearly 500,000 in 1937. This publication had a much wider readership than the number of copies it sold, as it was featured in display cases in the streets in order to bring its message to the public at large. Anti-Semitic propaganda was presented in a thoroughgoing manner in the Nazi press in order to prepare the way for anti-Semitic laws and measures. Both the *Völkischer Beobachter* and *Der Stürmer* were vehemently racist in their depictions of 'the Jew'. These newspapers emphasised other aspects of Nazi ideology, particularly anti-Bolshevism. In addition, the press made appeals for national unity, extolling the merits of the Strength through Joy and Winter Relief Agency programmes. The press reported on the amount of money donated to the regime's state-sponsored charities and emphasised the unity of the nation in this way.

In the meantime, as the power of the SS grew, so too did the influence of its weekly journal, *Das Schwarze Korps*. The SS journal first appeared in March 1935. By November 1935, its circulation was 200,000. By March 1944, its circulation was over 750,000 copies per week, making it the second largest weekly newspaper in Germany.[39] *Das Schwarze Korps* had a wide public resonance that was not restricted to SS members. It contained an abundance of racist material and anti-Bolshevik propaganda, with photographs of 'enemies' and 'criminals' designed to arouse hatred, fear and anger among its readers. As Nazi racial policy became more radical, the terms and words used to describe Jews, Gypsies and Slavs became increasingly abusive. At the same time, the journal urged the reinvigoration of the 'Aryan' race through Nazi population policy and emphasised the role of the German peasant in national renewal. *Das Schwarze Korps* encouraged healthy, valuable Germans to place the needs of the 'national community' ahead of their own preferences, for example when choosing a spouse or deciding upon the number of children to have.[40] Gunter d'Alquen, the editor, promoted anti-Semitism and the vilification of other 'enemies' and 'aliens' throughout his ten-year direction of the SS journal. *Das Schwarze Korps* was consistent in its anti-Semitism and its promotion of 'racial purity'. Furthermore, it attacked Christianity, both ridiculing clerics and gleefully reporting on sexual crimes committed by clerics, as well as other scandals. By contrast, *Das Schwarze Korps* presented favourable coverage of the SS leaders and extolled their work.

The concentration camps were widely reported in the German press to try to ensure popular compliance with the regime and the eradication of potential opposition. Press reports covered the beating and torture of political opponents. Newspaper journalists were sometimes given access to the concentration camps in order to report on the 'educative' work being done to reform Communists and other prisoners. For example, Hermann Larcher, the editor of the *Bayerischer Heimgarten*, who visited Dachau in June 1933, reported that its inmates were being 're-educated to practical, honest work' and that they worked 'cheerfully and willingly'.[41] Pictures from Dachau and other camps showed their 'healthy and productive' nature. The accompanying stories emphasised that through doing useful work, the prisoners were being educated. The camps appeared clean and orderly. By 1936, the press was featuring articles about a broader range of 'political criminality', particularly involving Jews and 'asocials'. Hence, the coercive side of Nazi policy was not hidden, but on the contrary was widely publicised in the press. The newspapers published many crime and punishment stories and publicised the preventive arrests of 'enemies' and 'aliens', as well as the concentration camps themselves. Indeed, Robert Gellately argues that 'all these matters were played up in the press'.[42]

Between 1936 and 1939, Nazi policy towards the press changed as the regime became increasingly concerned with regaining public confidence in the press, which had been steadily declining over the previous years. This was partly the result of the mergers and closures, which had resulted in the permanent loss of some newspaper readers. Many people, when left without the paper of their choice, opted to buy no newspaper at all. The regime urged the publication of newspapers with popular appeal so that more households would subscribe to them. Goebbels launched a national advertising campaign at the end of 1936 to try to revamp the deflated newspaper market. Posters and placards displayed slogans such as: 'Who Reads Newspapers gets Ahead Faster!' and 'Without Newspapers one Lives on the Moon'.[43] In addition, Goebbels banned all public criticism of the press in order to try to reverse the crisis of confidence in the nation's newspapers. The campaign culminated in 'German Press Day', which was held in Berlin in December 1936. While this attempt to restore the reputation of the press did result in an increase in newspaper sales, it did not completely make up for losses in the preceding years. There was also an increase in newsstand sales, particularly at the time of the 1936 Berlin Olympic Games. However, millions of Germans had stopped reading the newspapers because they were too uniform or dull in content. This trend continued until the outbreak of war in September 1939. The Reich Press Chamber appealed to the industry to produce more original and interesting newspapers, but both publishers and editors remained unsure and feared reprisals if they moved away from the uniformity that had been imposed upon them. Although Goebbels admitted that the work of the daily journalist was 'quite unsatisfying', he did not lend his support to mooted revisions of the Editors' Law and the restrictions on the autonomy of the press remained in place.

Between 1936 and 1939, Amann's press empire continued to expand with further acquisitions of privately owned papers. The Anschluß provided the opportunity to establish the Vienna edition of the *Völkischer Beobachter* and the Austrian press was quickly brought into line with that of Germany. By 1939, *Eher Verlag* owned two-thirds of the German press.[44] Amann's position as owner of such a vast press empire gave him great power in relation to the press. Personal rivalry and friction developed within this realm as Goebbels tried to maintain his supremacy. The position of Dietrich, as Reich Press Chief, reporting directly to Hitler, added to Goebbels' frustration. Tensions in press control escalated during the wartime period.[45] The difficulties between Goebbels and Dietrich, in particular, are revealed in Goebbels' view that Dietrich was 'a stupid amateur' who had 'not the slightest idea about how to influence the masses'.[46] Goebbels was disgruntled by Dietrich's proximity to Hitler and detested his 'intriguing with the *Führer*'.[47]

Once the war began, newspaper sales increased substantially as the population craved information. In response to the rising interest of the German public in news during the war, Goebbels launched the weekly newspaper *Das Reich* in 1940. It employed talented writers who addressed current issues and by 1943 its circulation was 1.5 million. It was the largest selling weekly newspaper. However, wartime conditions and emergency measures, from the rationing of newsprint paper and manpower shortages to the destruction of printing plants during the Allied bombing raids, took their toll on the publishing industry. In May 1941, the Reich Press Chamber closed down 500 newspapers. In 1943, a further radical curtailment of the press was implemented with the suspension of approximately 950 newspapers.[48] The internationally renowned *Frankfurter Zeitung* was the most notable of those culled in this round of closures. Further suspensions and consolidations occurred in the severe conditions of the following year and by October 1944, Amann controlled at least 80 per cent of the German press.[49]

The radio and press were important channels of communication, which the Nazi regime controlled and harnessed for its propaganda purposes. Radio was transformed into a medium of mass communication under National Socialism. It was utilised both to disseminate Nazi ideology and to maintain popular morale during the war. Goebbels tried continually to ensure that radio audiences were not bored with a constant bombardment of propaganda. However, he was not always successful in maintaining the balance between propaganda and popular entertainment in practice. The overriding objective of the press in the Third Reich was to disseminate National Socialist ideology to the German population. In order to achieve a 'National Socialist press', not only were journalists and editors subject to the scrutiny and control of the Ministry of Propaganda and Popular Enlightenment, but also publishers and owners had to conform to Nazi principles. Both the radio and press suffered from the loss of their autonomy under the National Socialist dictatorship. Their output as determined by the Ministry of Popular Enlightenment and Propaganda confined their listeners and readers respectively to a narrow fare of entertainment and news.

NOTES

1 On radio in Nazi Germany, see A. Diller, *Rundfunk im Dritten Reich* (Munich, 1980); N. Drechsler, *Die Funktion der Musik im deutschen Rundfunk, 1933–1945* (Pfaffenweiler, 1988); I. Marssolek and A. von Saldern (eds), *Zuhören und Gehörtwerden, I: Radio im Nationalsozialismus. Zwischen Lenkung und Ablenkung* (Tübingen, 1998); F. Cebulla, *Rundfunk und ländliche Gesellschaft 1924–1945* (Göttingen, 2004).

2 K. Lacey, 'Driving the message home: Nazi propaganda in the private sphere', in L. Abrams and E. Harvey (eds), *Gender Relations in German History: Power, Agency and Experience from the Sixteenth to the Twentieth Century* (London, 1996), p. 193.

3 Cited in D. Welch, *The Third Reich: Politics and Propaganda* (London, 1993), pp. 148–9.

4 U. Schmidt, 'Der Volksempfänger: Tabernakel moderner Massenkultur', in I. Marsollek and A. von Saldern (eds), *Radiozeit: Herrschaft, Alltag, Gesellschaft (1924–1960)* (Potsdam, 1999), pp. 136–59.

5 Cited in Welch, *The Third Reich*, p. 30.

6 Cited in R. Grunberger, *A Social History of the Third Reich* (London, 1971), p. 509.

7 Cited in H. Bergmeier and R. Lotz, *Hitler's Airwaves* (New Haven and London, 1997), pp. 7–8.

8 On radio drama, see R. Döhl, *Das Hörspiel zur NS-Zeit* (Darmstadt, 1992) and W. Wessels, *Hörspiele im Dritten Reich. Zur Institutionen-, Theorie- und Literaturgeschichte* (Bonn, 1985).

9 K. Lacey, *Feminine Frequencies: gender, German radio and the public sphere, 1923–1945* (Ann Arbor, 1996).

10 On this, see K. Lacey, 'From *Plauderei* to propaganda: on women's radio in Germany 1924–35', *Media, Culture and Society*, Vol. 16 (1994), pp. 589–607.

11 Lacey, 'Driving the message home', p. 195.

12 L. Pine, *Nazi Family Policy, 1933–1945* (Oxford, 1997), p. 80.

13 Ibid., p. 80.

14 Ibid., p. 103.

15 Lacey, 'Driving the message home', pp. 198–9.

16 Ibid., p. 201.

17 Cited in R. Gellately, *Backing Hitler* (Oxford, 2001), p. 184.

18 E. Johnson and K. Reuband, *What We Knew: Terror, Mass Murder and Everyday Life in Nazi Germany* (London, 2005), p. 358.

19 C. Zimmermann, 'From Propaganda to Modernization: Media Policy and Media Audiences under National Socialism', *German History*, Vol. 24 (2006), pp. 439–40.

20 On this, see H.-J. Koch, *Das Wunschkonzert im NS-Rundfunk* (Cologne, 2003).

21 G. Hay, 'Rundfunk und Hörspiel als "Führungsmittel" des Nationalsozialismus', in H. Denkler and K. Prümm (eds), *Die deutsche Literatur im Dritten Reich: Themen, Traditionen, Wirkungen* (Stuttgart, 1976), pp. 366–81.

22 O. Hale, *The Captive Press in the Third Reich* (Princeton, 1964), p. 3.

23 R. Evans, *The Coming of the Third Reich* (London, 2004), p. 120.

24 Welch, *The Third Reich*, p. 36.

25 Cited in Hale, *The Captive Press*, pp. 154–5.

26 Ibid., p. 14.

27 Ibid., p. 83.

28 Ibid., p. 68.

29 See A. Uzulis, *Nachrichtenagenturen im Nationalsozialismus. Propagandainstrumente und Mittel der Presselenkung* (Frankfurt am Main, 1996).

30 See N. Frei and J. Schmitz, *Journalismus im Dritten Reich* (Munich, 1989).

31 Cited in Grunberger, *A Social History of the Third Reich*, p. 494.

32 Cited in Hale, *The Captive Press*, p. 86.

33 Cited in Welch, *The Third Reich*, p. 157.

34 Hale, *The Captive Press*, p. 91.

35 Cited in ibid., p. 91.

36 Ibid., p. 94.

37 On this, see N. Frei, *Nationalsozialistische Eroberung der Provinzpresse* (Stuttgart, 1980).

38 Hale, *The Captive Press*, p. 151.

39 W. Combs, *The Voice of the SS: A History of the SS Journal 'Das Schwarze Korps'* (New York, 1986), p. 58.

40 Ibid., p. 118.

41 Cited in Gellately, *Backing Hitler*, p. 53.

42 Ibid., p. 7.

43 Hale, *The Captive Press*, p. 234.

44 Ibid., p. 267.

45 See D. Kohlmann-Viand, *NS-Pressepolitik im Zweiten Weltkrieg* (Munich, 1991).

46 J. Goebbels, *The Goebbels Diaries 1939–1941*, translated and edited by F. Taylor (London, 1982), p. 337.

47 Ibid., p. 292.

48 Hale, *The Captive Press*, p. 287.

49 Ibid., p. 307.

13

THE CINEMA AND THEATRE

The 'UFA-Palast' cinema in Berlin at the opening of Leni Riefenstahl's 'Triumph of the Will' 1935. © The Wiener Library

This chapter explores the impact of National Socialism upon the German cinema and theatre. The Weimar Republic had been a period of much innovation and experimentation, and the cinema and the theatre had both flourished. Under National Socialism, both of these forms of entertainment took on a more politicised stance, although this was not necessarily evident at a superficial level. This chapter examines the way in which the Nazi regime dominated the film industry and analyses the main leitmotivs of its feature films. The cinema reflected the Nazi ideals for German society and clearly showed the distinctions between valuable 'national comrades' and the 'enemies' of the regime. Robert Reimer has described the cinema under National Socialism as one 'that both reflected and influenced the dreams and lives of citizens during the Third Reich'.[1] The theatre under National Socialism was also different from that of the Weimar Republic. The Nazi regime sponsored certain types of theatrical productions while it prohibited others, in line with its imperative to eliminate 'cultural Bolshevism'.

THE CINEMA

Once the Nazis came to power, Goebbels ensured that the Nazis came to dominate the film industry. Through the Reich Film Chamber, established on 14 July 1933, its membership was controlled, its content was scrutinised by means of censorship and pre-censorship, and the industry itself was monopolised through nationalisation. There was a great exodus of film talent from Germany. Film directors including Josef von Sternberg, Fritz Lang, Erich Pommer and G.W. Pabst left the country. Many actors and actresses also departed, including Peter Lorre, Conrad Veidt and Marlene Dietrich. One of the main purposes of Goebbels' monopolisation of the film industry was to create a more active popular participation in the National Socialists' 'New Order'. He recognised the importance of film as a way of manipulating the population. Indeed, he stated to the Reich Film Chamber on 9 February 1934: 'Film is one of the most modern and far reaching media that there is for influencing the masses.' Yet Goebbels was astute enough to realise that a monolithic cinema would be counterproductive. His policy advocated a mixture of entertainment and propaganda. In this respect, he differed from Hitler, who wanted to exploit film entirely for propaganda purposes, or the 'lie direct'.[2]

The film industry was subjected to a process of censorship and control.[3] The Reich Cinema Law of 16 February 1934 introduced a system of *Prädikate* (distinction marks).[4] This was part of an endeavour by the Ministry of Popular Enlightenment and Propaganda to encourage the production of suitable films. David Welch has described the *Prädikate* system as 'a form of negative taxation'.[5] The award of the highest distinction mark, 'politically and artistically especially valuable', meant complete exemption from entertainment tax, while the lower distinction marks reduced the amount of tax in proportion to their value. This measure was designed both to promote the making of 'valuable' films and to guide cinema audiences. Another significant change was that the Nazi regime brought the cinema to a much wider public than before by making films available in small villages, which did not have cinemas of their own, through its Regional Film Services. By 1935, the Regional Film Services had organised 121,345 film showings, attended by 21 million people.[6] This allowed people in rural areas to participate in an aspect of leisure and cultural life that had been inaccessible to them previously and thereby gave the regime a wider impact through its use of the film medium.

Between 1933 and 1945, 1,097 feature films were produced. In line with Goebbels' view, only about one-sixth of these had a directly political content.[7] Yet this did not mean that the rest of the feature films were devoid of propaganda. As Siegfried Kracauer has argued, 'all Nazi films were more or less propaganda films – even the mere entertainment pictures which seem to be remote from politics'.[8] Indeed, at a superficial level, much of the German cinema under Nazism did appear to facilitate *Wirklichkeitsflucht* (escapism). However, in reality, the screen was heavily ideologised, as the political films had a disproportionate amount of money and publicity spent on them. In particular, the Nazi cinema produced feature films on several central themes in order to disseminate Nazi propaganda: glorification of the NSDAP and its martyrs; the leadership principle; blood and soil; anti-Bolshevism; anti-Semitism; hostility towards the British; militarism and war. In this way, the regime used feature films as a way of underpinning its goals for society. Feature films reflected Nazi beliefs about who fitted into society and who did not, and emphasised to the German cinema-going public who were the 'enemies' – both internal and external – of the 'national community'.

In 1933, three films were produced that openly glorified the Nazi Party and its martyrs, despite Goebbels' view that their propaganda content was too overt. The significance of these films lay in their presentation and idealisation of Nazi archetypes. In these films, the screen was exploited purely for the expression of Nazi ideology. *SA-Mann Brand*, *Hitlerjunge Quex* and *Hans Westmar* exalted self-sacrifice for the fatherland, idealised the Nazi Party and extolled its martyrs. Together, these three films, produced when Hitler was consolidating his regime, made an important political statement about National Socialism. Glorifying the attributes of heroic death, portraying the mystical significance of Nazi symbols and idealising the 'Aryan' stereotype, these films were overt propaganda films that aimed to attract the masses, especially the youth, to National Socialism. Their appeal to the youth contributed to their success. Jay Baird has described *Hitlerjunge Quex* as 'at once a propaganda and aesthetic success'.[9]

The most outstanding example of a film on the leadership theme was Leni Riefenstahl's *Triumph des Willens* (1935). This film documented the 1934 Party Rally at Nuremberg and was commissioned by Hitler himself. It was Riefenstahl's second Party Rally film, in which she perfected 'ideas worked out through trial-and-error a year before', in her *Sieg des Glaubens*, the official film of the Nazi Party Rally of 1933.[10] In *Triumph des Willens*, the *Führer* embodied the nation and guided its destiny. More than any other film produced in the Third Reich, *Triumph des Willens* reflected the ability of Nazi propaganda to manipulate the emotions of the German masses. The ritual of mass gatherings was a crucial part of the projection of the leadership theme. Only Hitler was shown in isolation, while the individuality of the people was submerged in mass scenes. *Triumph des Willens* celebrated the leadership principle, together with an overall display of the vitality and strength of the German people, and its youth in particular. Leadership, loyalty, unity and strength were the central themes of the film. Goebbels described *Triumph des Willens* as 'the great cinematic vision of the Führer'.[11]

After *Triumph des Willens*, no other film about Hitler would match its power and so none was commissioned. But there were a number of variations on the leadership theme in Nazi film. The most notable example was Veit Harlan's *Der Herrscher* (1937). Starring Emil Jannings as Matthias Clausen, the head of an industrial empire, this film allegorised the relationship between the ruler and the people. Moreover, a number of extravagant historical films were produced that projected the leadership principle. *Bismarck* (1940), *Friedrich Schiller* (1940) and *Paracelsus* (1943) exemplified such dramatisations. Frederick the Great was the subject of historical parallel, for example, in the film *Der Grosse König* (1942). Films that depicted the great men of Germany's past encouraged audiences to compare them with Hitler. Hence, the filmmakers of the Third Reich manipulated historical parallels to project National Socialist ideas and principles.

A number of feature films dealing with different aspects of the 'blood and soil' theme were produced, including *Schimmelreiter* (1934), *Ein Volksfeind* (1937) and *Opfergang* (1944). Peasant values and the sacredness of the German soil were emphasised. In *Ewiger Wald* (1936), the changing relationship between a people and its forest was the central theme, but it was also used to encourage patriotism and an acceptance of the policy of *Lebensraum* in the audience. It emphasised the mythical importance of the forest and the bond between the German people and its soil. Furthermore, the screen was used to create stereotypes in the portrayal of enemies and to persuade the German populace to accept Nazi policies against them. The feature film *Ich Klage an* (1941) brought the issue of 'euthanasia' of the incurably ill to the attention of the cinema-going public. It aimed to create a climate of opinion that accepted the Nazi 'euthanasia' campaign.[12]

Anti-Bolshevik films, such as *Friesennot* (1935), juxtaposed German with Russian, the superior 'Aryan' with the 'subhuman' Slav. The stereotypes were reinforced in terms of both behaviour and physical appearance. The vices of the Russians were contrasted with the virtues of the Germans. The Russians were portrayed as unattractive, unshaven and drunken. In the final scene, the rape of a German maiden by a 'subhuman' Bolshevik was presented. Between 1939 and 1941, the period of the Nazi–Soviet pact, anti-Bolshevik films were not produced. However, after Hitler's decision to invade the Soviet Union, Bolshevism became the enemy again and new anti-Bolshevik films were made, such as *GPU* (1942).

Nazi filmmakers employed the screen as a vehicle for anti-Semitic propaganda. Jews were stereotyped in film by repellent physical features and were characterised as an insidious threat to the 'national community'. In 1940, three major anti-Semitic films were screened as part of a wider propaganda campaign to justify the increasingly harsh and discriminatory treatment of the Jews by the regime and to prepare the population for more radical anti-Semitic policies. *Die Rothschilds* showed the rise to power and wealth of the Rothschild family and the emergence of the 'Jewish–British plutocracy'. It revealed the 'historical fact' that Jewish financiers had profited from the death of German soldiers. The Jews were portrayed as a racial and economic threat. Veit Harlan's *Jud Süss* showed the inherent rootlessness of 'the Jew' and his ability to assimilate himself into any society. Süss, the elegant and fashionable lawyer, personified 'the Jew in disguise'. The rest of the Jews in the film were portrayed as dirty, hooknosed and physically repellent. They represented 'authentic Jewry'. In contrast, 'Aryan' archetypes were depicted, for example Dorothea, the classic German maiden played by Kristina Söderbaum.[13] This film, which created popular antipathy towards the Jews under the guise of entertainment, was a huge box office success.[14]

By contrast, Fritz Hippler's *Der ewige Jude* was one of the most virulent propaganda films ever made. A large part of its effectiveness lay in its pretence of documentary objectivity. It claimed to be a documentary film about world Jewry. The substance and message of the film reflected Hippler's own belief that 'in the cinema ... the spectator must know whom he should hate and whom he should love'.[15] The main tenet of the film was that 'the Jew' had cunningly assimilated himself into European society. The film showed pictures of Jews with beards and traditional garb. Each shot faded into one of the same man 'disguised' in European clothing. Hence, the Jews were represented as an almost invisible threat to the nation. Moreover, they were associated with vermin to emphasise to the audience that they were 'disease-bearers' and 'subhuman'. The film covered the entire gamut of Nazi allegations against the Jews, culminating in a slaughterhouse scene, an example of anti-Semitic propaganda at its crudest and most blatant level. This scene was immediately followed by shots of Hitler's Reichstag speech of 30 January 1939, in which he prophesied that the war would bring about 'the annihilation of the Jewish race in Europe'. A sequence of blond 'Aryan' stereotypes ended the film, a vision of the future without the Jews. *Der ewige Jude* was acclaimed by Party fanatics, but it did not enjoy the same popular success as *Jud Süss*. While *Jud Süss* was a well-acted drama that appealed to cinemagoers, *Der ewige Jude* was a hate-filled pseudo-documentary, which was tedious, odious and unpopular.[16]

During the war, film was used to disseminate anti-British propaganda. Goebbels attacked the British as 'Jews among the Aryan Race' and attacked the British plutocracy and ruling elite. For example, *Die Rothschilds* (1940) showed the British plutocracy to be dependent upon Jewish financial support. Between 1940 and 1943, Britain was portrayed increasingly as a brutal oppressor of small nations. Kimmich's *Der Fuchs von Glenarvon* (1940) and *Mein Leben für Irland* (1941) depicted the Irish struggle for independence from Britain. Films attacking British imperialist conduct in Africa included Selpin's *Carl Peters* (1941) and Kimmich's *Germanin* (1943). But Steinhoff's *Ohm Krüger* (1941) was the most impressive anti-British propaganda film of the Third Reich. It portrayed Krüger, played by Emil Jannings, as an honest, courageous family man engaged in a heroic battle against the British in the Boer War. Reinterpreting the events of the Boer War and showing the decadence of the British system, *Ohm Krüger* played upon prevalent anti-British sentiments. The production cost more than 5.5 million Reichsmarks, an indication of the degree of significance attached to the film by Goebbels. Krüger's closing words were: 'England subjugated our small nation by the cruellest means ... Great and powerful nations will rise against the English tyranny. They will crush England and then the way will be open to a better world.'[17] The message for the 1941 German audience was clear and the film deepened anti-British feeling.

Militarism and war featured heavily in Nazi propaganda films. Goebbels encouraged the portrayal of an aggressive militarist spirit. In order to justify the war, the screen extolled the invincibility of German military might and romanticised its heroes. In wartime Germany, propaganda had to instil in the people an absolute obedience, a willingness to die and an unshakeable belief in victory. The *Zeitfilm* genre was particularly suited to this type of emotional appeal. The genre was most associated with Karl Ritter, who described it as follows: 'The *Zeitfilm* is about tanks, aircraft and the troops at the front. It must bear the characteristics of contemporary Germany, it must be heroic, as our fate at this time demands.'[18]

Feature-length documentaries, aiming to educate the masses about the magnitude of Hitler's *Blitzkrieg* successes, figured prominently in Goebbels' wartime film schedule. *Feldzug in Polen* (1940) portrayed the part played by the *Wehrmacht* in the Polish campaign and *Feuertaufe* (1940) depicted the destruction of Poland by the *Luftwaffe*. Such films aimed to convey the devastating power of the German armed forces and to reinforce the German population with a sense of military self-confidence. They celebrated the image of the German soldier as a brave 'Aryan' willing to die for *Führer* and fatherland. Kracauer noted: 'Wherever isolated German soldier faces are picked out in the campaign films, their function is to denote the face of the Third Reich.'[19] By presenting a distorted and romanticised vision of warfare, such films encouraged an aggressive military spirit. *Feuertaufe* exemplified how careful Nazi filmmakers were to evade reality – in particular, war was depicted without human suffering – although always trying to convey the impression of objectivity. In the campaign films, reality was subordinated to propaganda aims.

Although from 1942 onwards Goebbels called for the production of escapist entertainment films, he did commission an extremely expensive prestige film, *Kolberg* (1945). Loosely based on events at Kolberg in the Franco-Prussian War of 1806–1807, the purpose of this film was to show that a united people could overcome any enemy. The film showed the resistance to Napoleon's army by the fortress town Kolberg. In reality, the Kolbergers were eventually defeated by the French, but it was a measure of how far Nazi propaganda had become entrenched in a make-believe world that historical fact was disregarded. The expense of *Kolberg* (8.5 million Reichsmarks), together with Goebbels' withdrawal of, according to the director Veit Harlan, 187,000 soldiers and 4,000 sailors from active service to complete the film on time, when Soviet soldiers were crossing the East Prussian border, showed both the importance that Goebbels attached to this film and the extent to which his propaganda had lost touch with military reality.[20] *Kolberg* brought together themes of heroic leadership, nationalism, obedience and sacrifice. With its falsification of a historical parallel, the message of the film was for the German people to be strong and to hold out, to be obedient and prepared for sacrifice.[21]

Hence, Nazi propaganda films embraced a whole host of themes. The leadership principle, glorification of the Nazi Party and its martyrs, self-sacrifice for the nation, hatred of enemies, especially Jews, exaltation of war and militarism were among the most prominent. These subjects manifested themselves repeatedly in the feature films of the Third Reich. The subtle use of composition and camera angles aroused collective enthusiasm or hatred, both in feature films and in documentaries. Film was employed by the regime 'as a major weapon of Nazi long-term ideological indoctrination'.[22]

Goebbels made a deliberate decision in 1942 to increase the output of purely entertainment films for relaxation and escapism at the time of 'total war'.[23] The cinema of the Third Reich was utilised by the regime for its ideological imperatives and agenda. The complex relationship between entertainment, escapism and propaganda in the Third Reich was particularly evident in the context of film. As Eric Rentschler has pointed out, 'feature films in the Third Reich were principally the function of a genre cinema, which in turn was part of an elaborate mass culture'.[24] Although only a small proportion of films were overtly propaganda films, ideology was often masked as entertainment. The cinema co-existed with other presentations of everyday culture in Nazi Germany with the same ends. During the war, the cinema was extremely popular, with large and enthusiastic audiences. Comedies were particularly appealing.[25] Much of the entertainment was very fanciful, allowing viewers to escape from politics and the realities of the war. Rentschler has argued, however, that Nazi escapism 'offered only the illusion of escape from the Nazi *status quo*'.[26]

THE THEATRE

During the Weimar Republic there had been a considerable manifestation of innovation in theatrical production, particularly in the areas of design and direction.[27] The German theatre changed substantially under National Socialism, with its condemnation of 'undesirable' plays, its promotion of desirable works and its careful selection of theatrical pieces and monitoring of their production.[28] The Nazis aimed to eradicate all that was 'un-German' from the German theatre and sought to cleanse the theatre of Judeo-Bolshevik influences. The 'national community' was to be presented with acceptable performances of true German culture, not to be lambasted with communist views or degrading experimental productions. As in other areas of social, cultural and professional life, there was a purge of 'racial aliens' from their jobs. Jews were excluded from the Reich Theatre Chamber, following a decree of 1 November 1933. The *Jüdischer Kulturbund* became the only legal organisation for Jews working in the theatre and its members were allowed to play only to Jewish audiences.[29] There was a great departure of theatrical talent from Germany. John London estimates that 4,000 people connected with the theatre fled from the new regime.[30] This number included many actors and actresses, such as Fritz Kortner and Elisabeth Bergner, as well as playwrights and directors. In their place, remaining German actors and directors, as well as playwrights, became the beneficiaries of the new regime, which promoted their work with enticements and incentives, such as prizes, titles and honours. Indeed, the number of theatres increased markedly during the Nazi era – from 200 in the 1932–1933 season to 358 in the 1942–1943 season.[31] In addition to the permanent theatres, there were 182 performing troupes that travelled around the country. The number of people working in the theatre grew from 36,441 in the 1934–1935 season to 38,400 in the 1939–1940 season. During the last theatrical season of the Third Reich, approximately 45,000 people were working in the theatre. The number of theatregoers also increased markedly from 520,000 in 1932 to 1.6 million in 1936 and continued to grow until 1943.[32]

The Reich Theatre Chamber aimed at ideological conformity and the exclusion of undesirable plays from the German theatre. The first president of the Theatre Chamber, Otto Laubinger, claimed that 'the theatre of the new state must be a people's theatre'. After his death in 1935, his position was taken over by Rainer Schlösser until 1938. His conception of a German 'blood brotherhood' gave the theatre a role in underpinning racial distinctions. Ludwig Körner took over as President of the Theatre Chamber until 1942 and Paul Hartmann was the last President of the Theatre Chamber between 1942 and 1945.

Within the space of a year, Goebbels established the prerequisites for control of the German theatres. Moreover, he quickly removed the competition of Nazi rivals to his pre-eminence in this realm, particularly Hermann Goering, who controlled the Prussian State Theatres, and Alfred Rosenberg, who headed the Combat League for German Culture. In May 1934, the Ministry of Popular Enlightenment and Propaganda gained control over the private theatre companies, which had comprised 20 per cent of German theatre companies, and made them subject to the same policies as the state theatres. This allowed Goebbels to appoint theatre managers and artistic directors and to ban the performance of 'undesirable' plays. Goebbels' Ministry maintained rigid control of the theatres. Rainer Schlösser had been appointed as *Reichsdramaturg* in August 1933 and the Theatre Act of May 1934 confirmed his role as chief censor. He was responsible for ensuring the promotion of National Socialist cultural principles in the German theatre. The Theatre Section of the Ministry of Popular Enlightenment and Propaganda dealt with all issues relating to personnel, theatre budgets and programme policy, in conjunction with the Reich Theatre Chamber. It oversaw the hiring of managers and artistic directors and the support of theatrical employees. It supervised the entire production in the areas of drama, opera and operetta. It managed the funds for the theatres, promoted theatre culture, assisted travelling theatres and oversaw the preparation and staging of special performances. Furthermore, the Theatre Section supervised the execution of the Theatre Law and dealt with theatre matters abroad, as well as foreign artists within Germany.

The Theatre Section swiftly brought the theatre repertory into line with the political requirements of the regime. The works of specific 'unsuitable' and Jewish playwrights were banned straightaway. The works of 'degenerate' German writers of the Weimar Republic were also proscribed. Even late nineteenth-century naturalistic dramas were rejected. All prospective theatre programmes had to be sent to the Theatre Section for approval in advance of each season. The censors examined the lists and made recommendations about changes to the programmes or the artistic direction of prospective performances. The theatres fell into line with the new regulations and did not attempt to include work by banned authors in their programmes. Nor did they fail to heed the recommendations of the censors.

Censorship was imposed not only on 'undesirable' works but also on works by acceptable writers who 'due to internal or external political considerations were no longer deemed to be appropriate for presentation'.[33] One key example of this was *The Endless Road* by Sigmund Graff and Carl Ernst Hintze, a 'front play', which had won the Dietrich Eckart Prize in 1933 but was banned two years later. On 8 December 1937, Goebbels issued a decree banning any references – positive or negative – in theatres to politics, the state, the police and the army. Even Schiller's much-performed *Wilhelm Tell*, one of Hitler's favourite plays, was banned from the stage in 1941 because some of the ideas contained in it contradicted Nazi plans for the 'New Order' in Europe.[34]

The most prominent example of the Nazi concept of a 'theatre for the people' was the introduction of the *Thingspiele*. These were large-scale, open-air displays of Nazi pageantry to mass audiences and were regarded as the ultimate dramatic expression of National Socialism.[35] Between 1933 and 1936, the *Thing* plays were a fundamental component of Nazi theatre. They used mass choruses and marching bands as a way of fostering a sense of 'national community' among both the participants and the audiences. A massive building campaign was initiated in order to construct the outdoor stages (*Thingplätze*) for these spectacles all over Germany. Five stages were ready by the end of 1934.[36] Eleven more *Thingplätze* were constructed in the following year. The premiere of Kurt Heynicke's *Der Weg ins Reich* (The Road to the Reich, 1935) drew an audience of more than 20,000 people to the Heidelberg *Thingplatz* in 1935.[37] At its opening, Goebbels described the Heidelberg *Thingplatz* as 'National Socialism in stone' and stated that it gave 'a living, tangible and monumental expression' to the Nazi *Weltanschauung*.[38]

The structure, plots and themes of the *Thing* plays were very similar. Most of them portrayed the corruption and decadence of the Weimar Republic and emphasised the unemployment and poverty that were rife in Germany before Hitler came to save the nation from this bleak situation. For example, the character of the War Cripple in Richard Euringer's *German Passion* (1933) spoke of Jews, democrats, pacifists and Marxists (who were responsible for the 'contamination' of the German nation during the Weimar era) 'getting into milk and flour'.[39] The leadership principle was another prevalent theme. In addition, the *Thing* plays portrayed a union of all social classes for the national cause. This renewed sense of national responsibility was represented by a zeal for hard work to save Germany. For example, at the end of Erich Müller-Schnick's *Soldiers of the Soil*, a vast array of German workers marched on to the stage singing: 'Our German land needs deeds, Enough words have been spoken. Germany, you most beautiful of lands, It is to you we dedicate the work of our hands! We serve you with the spade, Because we are soldiers, work soldiers.'[40] There was a clear association here with militarism, which was another prominent theme of the *Thingspiele*.

The mass audiences listened to large, emotive choruses of *völkisch* and 'blood and soil' themes. They were invited to identify with the stage action. Individuals were submerged into the evocation of the spirit of the 'national community'. This was partly evoked by the layout of the *Thingplätze*, in which there was no clear physical separation between the actors and the audience. The stages often merged with the first row of the audience. Marching bands walked through the audiences and actors were sometimes positioned among the spectators. The new drama was a sign that theatre was not a preserve of entertainment for the moneyed classes but an experience for every member of the 'national community'. The Nazi press celebrated the cultic theatre: 'The aim of our festivities is the creation and consolidation of the *Volksgemeinschaft*. One of our most important tasks is to integrate the celebrants into the celebratory action and to turn them into the immediate protagonists of the festivity. The confessional force of our festivities can be significantly enhanced by making the *Volksgemeinschaft* confess themselves, at significant climaxes, to the represented ideals and principles.'[41]

The Nazis utilised the symbolic language of drama and theatre to turn their ideology into a living force. Rituals were used to disseminate the Nazi *Weltanschauung* and to create a sense of belief in it. Günter Berghaus argues that 'the rituals and their underlying mythology were created, designed, and organised with specific psychological functions in mind'.[42] The Nazis aimed to create a willing and binding acceptance for their ideology in the audience. They employed rituals as a form of political manipulation. However, by 1936, the *Thing* plays had lost their importance to the regime. While financial and technical difficulties formed part of the reason for their demise, their repetitive themes had become too familiar by 1936 and audiences had lost interest in them. The Hitler regime was well established by this time and the *Thingspiele* had outlived their usefulness. In May 1936, Goebbels prohibited the use of 'declamatory choruses'. As these choruses were such an essential element of the *Thingspiele*, this ban served to bring an end to the genre. The regime subsequently attempted to encourage mass attendance at traditional theatres as a pursuit that was no longer restricted to the middle classes but accessible to all 'racially valuable' Germans.

The Reich Theatre Festival Week became a prominent annual event from 1934 to 1939, forming part of the regime's attempts to bring people to the theatre. The first Theatre Week took place in Dresden from 27 May to 3 June 1934. It opened with Wagner's *Tristan and Isolde* at the State Opera House, with both Hitler and Goebbels as honoured guests. The second Theatre Festival Week took place in Hamburg from 16 to 23 June 1935. The Reich Theatre Festival Weeks continued until 1939 inclusive, but they were abandoned in the wartime period as they were too costly to stage. In addition, the Nazi regime was particularly concerned to bring young people to the theatre. Rainer Schlösser believed that 'the success or failure of our efforts to win over the youth for the theatre is tantamount to the life or death of our theatre culture'.[43] Reich Theatre Days of the German Youth were organised in Bochum in 1937 and in Hamburg in 1938, and Hitler Youth Theatre Weeks took place in different towns, including Weimar and Erfurt.

The Strength through Joy (KdF) organisation subsidised theatre outings for workers and through its regimentation of leisure created large audiences by purchasing blocks of tickets for its members. In Berlin alone, KdF ticket holders occupied more than half of the theatre seats.[44] In addition, the KdF established new 'People's Theatres' in the big cities. It organised touring theatrical troupes and mobile theatres in order to bring German culture to the countryside and small towns. The 'New Order' theatre was made accessible to all members of the 'national community'.

The Nazi regime politicised the stage effectively and succeeded in combining theatre with propaganda. At first, dramas of Nazi heroes, such as Horst Wessel and Herbert Norkus, were presented. Hanns Johst's *Schlageter* was a typical example of such a play. It was based on the story of Albert Schlageter, who had been executed after attacking the French occupation troops in the Ruhr in 1923. Schlageter became a National Socialist hero. Johst's play premiered on 20 April 1933 at the Staatliches Schauspielhaus in Berlin, with Albert Bassermann, Emmy Sonnemann and Lothar Müthel playing the main roles. Its nationalist sentiments against the Treaty of Versailles made Johst popular with the new regime. Johst despised the Weimar system and yearned for the 'rebirth of a spiritual community', to be realised in the theatre of the Nazi era. He became one of the main architects of Nazi performance aesthetics. Eberhard Wolfgang Möller was another significant Nazi playwright. His anti-Weimar sentiments pervaded his plays, which condemned the Jewish, capitalist and foreign influences that had polluted the German nation. His play *Rothschild siegt bei Waterloo* (Rothschild Wins at Waterloo, 1934), with the character of Rothschild as the Jewish villain, underpinned Nazi anti-Semitism, while his *Panamaskandal* (Panama Scandal, 1936) and *Der Untergang Karthagos* (The Fall of Carthage, 1938) served to focus hatred on the Weimar Republic and by extension to bolster the consolidation of the Nazi government.[45] The playwrights Richard Billinger, Paul Joseph Cremers and Eugen Ortner, whose works accorded with Nazi ideology, also benefited from career advancement after 1933.

Very quickly, the 'theatre of the Left' disappeared, while the 'theatre of the Right', which had begun in the early 1930s in the aftermath of the Depression, flourished. Within three years of the National Socialist rebuilding of the German theatre, a journalist noted: 'The un-German, sensationalist plays catering to the basest instincts have disappeared together with the Marxist-oriented problem plays and the agitational reportages. In addition to the tribute to the classics and the good old German entertainment play, their place has been taken by the new historical drama, the *völkisch* drama of the day ...'[46] A whole genre of nationalist, *völkisch* drama was created to serve the spirit and aims of National Socialism.

The theatre repertoire included plays that accorded with the political objectives of the National Socialist regime. Nationalism, the glorification of war and heroic death became popular subjects. Ideological concepts such as the leadership principle, sacrifice for the 'national community', 'blood and soil' and 'racial struggle' became prominent themes, although specific mention of Hitler or other Nazi leaders was prohibited. However, most theatrical productions were not overtly political in their content. Melodrama and light comedy were popular genres, although many of the new works were of poor quality.

Classics were still presented to packed theatres, particularly in Berlin, and there was still much theatrical talent. Plays by Shakespeare, Goethe and Schiller continued to be the most performed classics. The works of the German dramatist Heinrich von Kleist also regained popularity under National Socialism. The main character in his *Die Hermannsschlacht* was identified with Hitler. The play underlined the concepts of the chosen leader and the 'national community'. Christian Dietrich Grabbe, whose works portrayed a great sense of German heroism, enjoyed a renewed popularity in the Nazi era. Rainer Schlösser described Grabbe as 'the single *Volk* visionary of his time'.[47]

Historical dramas or historical 'people's plays' were popular and were heavily endorsed by the regime. German playwrights produced an array of history plays of varying quality and there was a marked increase in their production. The most favoured period covered by history plays was 1789–1914. The years 1550–1788 and the medieval period were the next most popular subjects. August Hinrichs' *Die Stedinger* (The Stedingers, 1934) and Rolf Lauckner's *Der letzte Preuße* (The Last Prussian, 1938) were typical examples of the many history plays that evoked the medieval era. Serious historical dramas interpreted and reconfigured events from the past to influence cultural life in Nazi Germany. Historical dramas that showed the struggle for national ideals were promoted. Hermann Heinz Ortner's *Isabella of Spain* and Hanns Johst's *Thomas Paine* exemplified such plays. The main propaganda aim of historical drama was to portray the fortunes of the German *Volk* through its history and the redemption of the past for the present and future of the Third Reich. Many plays of this genre focused on central characters to evoke parallels with Hitler. Others centred on 'forgotten Germans' or took their inspiration from leading figures in German history, such as Martin Luther or Frederick the Great. For example, Heinrich Ziller's *Martin Luther, oder die höllische Reise* (Martin Luther, or the Hellish Journey) was staged in 1933, during celebrations of the 450th anniversary of Luther's birth. Hans Rehberg's The Seven Years' War (*Der Siebenjährige Krieg*), which premiered at the Berlin Staatstheater in April 1938, showed the glory that Frederick the Great had brought to his country.

Furthermore, the regime encouraged the production of *völkisch* dramas, particularly peasant plays based on the 'blood and soil' theme. Among the most popular writers of such plays was August Hinrichs. There was also a proliferation of plays about the experiences of soldiers during the First World War, known as *Frontstücke* or 'front plays', such as Otto Paust's *Weg in den Morgen* (Road in the Morning, 1934). They exalted the camaraderie and heroism of front-line soldiers. The nationalist theme of *Heimkehr* (homecoming) formed a popular genre of German plays during the 1930s. Sigmund Graff's *Die Heimkehr des Matthias Bruck* (The Return of Matthias Bruck, 1933) typified this genre. It told the story of a German soldier returning home after many years at the front to find that in his absence his wife had remarried. Having confirmed his affinity with his land, the main protagonist committed suicide.

At the start of the war, Schlösser issued a circular to discourage the performance of pessimistic and depressing plays. During the war, the theatre was intended more than ever to be a form of light popular entertainment to offer opportunities for relaxation on the home front. In addition, 'soldier stages' were established to entertain the troops. During the wartime period, the KdF welcomed soldiers and armaments workers to the Bayreuth Festival as honoured guests. The KdF accommodated approximately 30,000 guests at Bayreuth in 1943, and even as late as 1944 soldiers and war workers attended the Bayreuth Festival.[48] During the war, the KdF continued its efforts to provide cheap entry to theatres – providing low-cost tickets to performances of high culture and light entertainment – as a way of maintaining popular commitment to the 'national community' and the war effort. Although many permanent theatres were destroyed in the bombings, theatrical troupes performed in improvised venues. The regime showed a determination to keep theatres open for as long as possible in the wartime conditions. However, on 20 August 1944, Goebbels finally decreed that all theatres, music halls and cabarets were to close down by 31 August that year.

In a speech at the Berlin Theater des Volkes in November 1939, Goebbels had stated that Germans were defending not only their '*Lebensraum*, daily bread and machines' against enemy powers but also 'German culture'.[49] This signalled the way for theatrical activity not only at the front but also in the occupied territories. Until 1944, German theatrical troupes travelled across Nazi-occupied Europe presenting German cultural performances, attempting to demonstrate that the Hitler regime dominated Europe culturally as well as militarily. In this sense, too, the theatre played a significant cultural–political role in serving the aims of the Nazi regime.

The Nazi regime was clear in its intention to eliminate 'cultural Bolshevism' from the German cinema and theatre. Goebbels' domination over these forms of entertainment, both through his own Ministry and through the Reich Film Chamber and Reich Theatre Chamber, brought about far-reaching changes. Both the cinema and theatre were obliged to serve the cultural and political ambitions of the regime. Depictions of the past, both as historical dramatisations and parallels and as portrayals of an idyll, were significant in film and theatre representations. The cinema and theatre worked together, along with other cultural and propaganda media, to reinforce key ideological themes and to promote the 'national community'. During the war, they were used to bolster popular morale for as long as possible, by providing escapism and popular entertainment.

NOTES

1 R. Reimer (ed.), *Cultural History through a National Socialist Lens: Essays on the Cinema of the Third Reich* (New York, 2000), p. ix. Other significant recent contributions to the growing secondary literature on film under National Socialism include: L. Schulte-Sasse, *Entertaining the Third Reich: Illusions of Wholeness in Nazi Cinema* (London, 1996); H. Hoffmann, *The Triumph of Propaganda: Film and National Socialism, 1933–1945* (Providence, 1996); S. Hake, *Popular Cinema of the Third Reich* (Austin, 2001); E. Carter, *Dietrich's Ghosts: The Sublime and the Beautiful in Third Reich Film* (London, 2004). Earlier studies include: E. Leiser, *Nazi Cinema* (New York, 1974); J. Petley, *Capital and Culture: German Cinema 1933–1945* (London, 1979); B. Phillips, *Swastika: Cinema of Oppression* (London, 1976). See also D. Weinberg, 'Approaches to the Study of Film in the Third Reich', *Journal of Contemporary History*, Vol. 19, No. 1 (1984), pp. 105–26.

2 D. Welch, *Propaganda and the German Cinema, 1933–1945* (London, 2001), p. 37. On Goebbels, see also F. Möller and V. Schlöndorf, *Der Filmminister. Goebbels und der Film im Dritten Reich* (Berlin, 1998).

3 On this, see M. Phillips, 'The Nazi Control of the German Film Industry', *Journal of European Studies*, Vol. 1 (1971), pp. 37–68.

4 On the Reich Cinema Law, see Welch, *Propaganda and the German Cinema*, pp. 13–18.

5 D. Welch, 'Educational Film Propaganda and the Nazi Youth', in D. Welch (ed.), *Nazi Propaganda: The Power and the Limitations* (London, 1983), p. 75.

6 C. Zimmermann, 'From Propaganda to Modernization: Media Policy and Media Audiences under National Socialism', *German History*, Vol. 24 (2006), p. 453. On this, see also C. Zimmermann, 'Landkino im Nationalsozialismus', *Archiv für Sozialgeschichte*, Vol. 41 (2001), pp. 231–43.

7 Welch, *Propaganda and the German Cinema*, p. 36.

8 S. Kracauer, *From Caligari to Hitler: A Psychological Study of German Film* (Princeton, 1947), p. 275.

9 J. Baird, 'From Berlin to Neubabelsberg: Nazi Film Propaganda and Hitler Youth Quex', *Journal of Contemporary History*, Vol. 18 (1983), p. 511.

10 M. Loiperdinger and D. Culbert, 'Leni Riefenstahl, the SA, and the Nazi Party Rally Films, Nuremberg 1933–1934: *Sieg des Glaubens* and *Triumph des Willens*', *Historical Journal of Film, Radio and Television*, Vol. 8, No. 1 (1988), p. 17.

11 Cited in R. Taylor, *Film Propaganda: Soviet Russia and Nazi Germany* (London, 1979), p. 188.

12 On this, see M. Burleigh and W. Wippermann, *The Racial State: Germany 1933–1945* (Cambridge, 1991), pp. 156–61. See also K. Rost, *Sterilisation und Euthanasie im Film des 'Dritten Reiches'. Nationalsozialistische Propaganda in ihrer Beziehung zu rassenhygienischen Massnahmen des NS-Staates* (Husum, 1987).

13 On the representation of women in Nazi cinema, see A. Ascheid, *Hitler's Heroines: Stardom and Womanhood in Nazi Cinema* (Philadelphia, 2003) and J. Fox, *Filming Women in the Third Reich* (Oxford, 2000).

14 On the background to the making of this film, see S. Tegel, 'Veit Harlan and the Origins of *Jud Süss*, 1938–1939: Opportunism in the Creation of Nazi anti-Semitic Film Propaganda', *Historical Journal of Film, Radio and Television*, Vol. 16, No. 4 (1996), pp. 515–31.

15 Cited in Taylor, *Film Propaganda*, p. 190.

16 On differing responses to these two films, see O. Bartov, *The 'Jew' in Cinema: From The Golem to Don't Touch my Holocaust* (Bloomington, 2005), pp. 14–15. For a fuller discussion, see D. Culbert, 'The Impact of Anti-Semitic Film Propaganda on German

Audiences: *Jew Süss* and *The Wandering Jew* (1940)', in R. Etlin (ed.), *Art, Culture, and Media under the Third Reich* (Chicago, 2002), pp. 139–57.

17 Quoted in Taylor, *Film Propaganda*, p. 214.

18 Quoted in Welch, *Propaganda and the German Cinema*, p. 161.

19 Kracauer, *From Caligari to Hitler*, p. 289.

20 Welch, *Propaganda and the German Cinema*, p. 196.

21 On *Kolberg*, see P. Paret, '*Kolberg* (1945) as Historical Film and Historical Document', *Historical Journal of Film, Radio and Television*, Vol. 14, No. 4 (1994), pp. 433–48.

22 M. Phillips, 'The German Film Industry and the New Order', in P. Stachura (ed.), *The Shaping of the Nazi State* (London, 1978), p. 258.

23 For a further overview of the wartime period, see B. Drewniak, *Der deutsche Film 1938–1945. Ein Gesamtüberblick* (Düsseldorf, 1987). On wartime newsreels, see D. Welch, 'Nazi Wartime Newsreel Propaganda', in K. Short (ed.), *Film and Radio Propaganda in World War II* (London, 1983), pp. 201–19.

24 E. Rentschler, *The Ministry of Illusion: Nazi Cinema and its Afterlife* (Cambridge, Mass., 1996), p. 215.

25 On comedies, see K. Witte, *Lachende Erben, toller Tag: Filmkomödie im Dritten Reich* (Berlin, 1995).

26 Rentschler, *The Ministry of Illusion*, p. 218.

27 On Weimar theatre, see J. Willett, *The Theatre of the Weimar Republic* (New York, 1988).

28 See B. Drewniak, *Das Theater im NS-Staat. Szenarium deutsches Zeitgeschichte, 1933–1945* (Düsseldorf, 1983); T. Eicher *et al.*, *Theater im 'Dritten Reich': Theaterpolitik, Spielstruktur, NS-Dramatik* (Seelze-Velber, 2000).

29 J. London (ed.), *Theatre under the Nazis* (Manchester, 2000), p. 33. On the *Jüdischer Kulturbund*, see R. Rovit, 'Jewish theatre: repertory and censorship in *the Jüdischer Kulturbund*, Berlin', in London (ed.), *Theatre under the Nazis*, pp. 187–221.

30 London (ed.), *Theatre under the Nazis*, p. 1.

31 B. Drewniak, 'The Foundations of Theater Policy in Nazi Germany', in G. Cuomo (ed.), *National Socialist Cultural Policy* (New York, 1995), pp. 70–1.

32 Drewniak, 'The Foundations of Theater Policy in Nazi Germany', p. 71.

33 B. Panse, 'Censorship in Nazi Germany', in G. Berghaus (ed.), *Fascism and Theatre: Comparative Studies on the Aesthetics and Politics of Performance in Europe, 1925–1945* (Oxford, 1996), p. 142.

34 Drewniak, 'The Foundations of Theater Policy in Nazi Germany', p. 82.

35 On the *Thing* movement, see R. Stommer, *Die inszenierte Volksgemeinschaft. Die 'Thing-Bewegung' im Dritten Reich* (Marburg, 1995).

36 W. Niven, 'The birth of Nazi drama? *Thing* plays', in London (ed.), *Theatre under the Nazis*, p. 56.

37 B. Zortman, 'Hitler's Theatre', in M. Balfour (ed.), *Theatre and War 1933–1945: Performance in Extremis* (New York and Oxford, 2001), p. 49.

38 Cited in Niven, 'The birth of Nazi drama? *Thing* plays', p. 56.

39 Cited in ibid., p. 64.

40 Cited in ibid., p. 65.

41 G. Berghaus, 'The Ritual Core of Fascist Theatre', in Berghaus (ed.), *Fascism and Theatre*, p. 57.

42 Ibid., p. 51.

43 Cited in Drewniak, 'The Foundations of Theater Policy in Nazi Germany', p. 73.

44 S. Baranowski, *Strength through Joy: Consumerism and Mass Tourism in the Third Reich* (Cambridge, 2004), p. 56.

45 On Möller, see R. Cadigan, 'Eberhard Wolfgang Möller: Politically Correct Playwright

of the Third Reich', in G. Gadberry (ed.), *Theatre in the Third Reich, the Prewar Years* (Westport, 1995), pp. 65–74.

46 Cited in Drewniak, 'The Foundations of Theater Policy in Nazi Germany', p. 82.

47 Cited in London (ed.), *Theatre under the Nazis*, p. 29.

48 On Bayreuth, see F. Spotts, *Bayreuth: A History of the Wagner Festival* (New Haven, 1994).

49 Cited in London (ed.), *Theatre under the Nazis*, p. 31.

14

ART AND ARCHITECTURE

Hitler visits the exhibition 'Entartete Kunst' in Munich 1937. © The Wiener Library

For many decades after the end of the Second World War, the art of the Third Reich was considered unworthy of scholarly attention. It was regarded as the cultural production of a barbaric and reactionary regime that suppressed modernity. In the history of architecture, too, there has been a tendency to view Nazi architecture as the expression of a monolithic ideology. However, recent research in the areas of both art and architecture has brought fresh insights into these subjects and a more complex view of Nazi culture has appeared in the historiography in recent years.[1] Inconsistencies existed between Nazi ideology and the execution of Nazi policy. This meant that despite Nazi rhetoric, the visual arts were not necessarily purely monolithic representations of Nazi ideology. The existence of modernist elements in Nazi aesthetics has been acknowledged and the pragmatic acceptance by Nazi leaders of artistic trends that were ideologically problematic to them has been explored. In particular, Jonathan Petropoulos has shown that the Nazi leadership devoted much time and energy to the visual arts. He argues that the Nazi leaders represented a 'union of barbarism and culture' and that their interest in the visual arts was important both officially as state policy and privately.[2]

ART

Abstract and expressionist artists such as Paul Klee, Vassily Kandinsky, Emil Nolde and Ernst Barlach had gained prestige both nationally and internationally during the Weimar Republic. They were at the forefront of advances in their field. Simultaneously, during the 1920s, the Nazi Party criticised the art and culture of the Weimar era and despised the 'alien' and 'degenerate' influences upon German culture represented by the Jews in particular.[3] From its earliest days, the Nazi movement had called for cultural purification in Germany. Once in power, the Nazis used culture and the arts to legitimise their rule (by posing as the guardians of true German culture) and to assist in the creation of the 'national community'. They purged 'alien' influences from German artistic and cultural life. They maintained that racial degeneration was the main cause of aesthetic deterioration. Alan Steinweis has argued that 'the cultural policies of the Nazi regime were inextricably intertwined with the policies of persecution and marginalisation, driven by racist ideology, that were targeted at Jews, Roma and Sinti, homosexuals and other groups'.[4] Hence, cultural purification constituted a central component in the development of the 'national community' during the Nazi dictatorship. The Reich Chamber for the Visual Arts closely controlled the work of its 42,000 members. In addition, it strictly monitored membership so that politically unreliable or 'racially inferior' artists were ineligible and therefore not allowed to continue to practise their profession. Prominent artists such as Paul Klee and Otto Dix were expelled from their positions. Many artists and painters whose work was disapproved of by the Nazi regime went into exile, although others stayed on in Germany.

The desire of the Nazi regime to purify and cleanse society was reflected in its policy towards the arts, with its simultaneous process of encouraging pure and wholesome contemporary German art and purging decadent, 'degenerate' or unwholesome art. The Nazi regime aimed to eliminate all forms of art that it regarded as 'alien' or 'degenerate'.[5] It excoriated many of the artistic innovations that had flourished during the Weimar era, such as Dadaism and Expressionism. The modern section of the National Gallery in Berlin was closed down in 1934. In 1936–1937, the Reich Chamber of Culture initiated and carried out a purge of German art in galleries and museums across the country. Adolf Ziegler, the president of the Reich Chamber for the Visual Arts, was assigned the task of selecting and collecting works of 'degenerate' German art, for the Degenerate Art Exhibition, which opened in Munich on 19 July 1937.[6] Ziegler and his commission confiscated 16,000 works of art. Among the most prominent of the artists whose works were seized were Max Beckmann, Ernst Barlach, Otto Dix, Georg Grosz, Paul Klee, Oskar Kokoschka and Emil Nolde, but in all the campaign confiscated works by 1,400 artists.[7] Works by 112 of these artists were selected for the exhibition. Ziegler, in his opening speech, described the works that had been produced by modern artists as 'monstrosities', 'the crippled products of madness, insolence, lack of ability and degeneration'.[8] The paintings were displayed in a deliberately poor manner, crammed into crowded galleries, many without frames, accompanied by pejorative captions.

The German Art Exhibition opened simultaneously in the House of German

Art in Munich. This juxtaposition was designed to demonstrate the triumph of Nazi art over degenerate art. At the opening of the House of German Art, Hitler described how the 'Dadaist sensationalists, Cubist plasterers and Futurist canvas smearers' had damaged the achievements of the arts. He stated that 'degenerate' artists created 'deformed cripples and cretins, women who inspire nothing but disgust, human beings that are more animal than human ... But in the name of the German people I mean to forbid these pitiable unfortunates, who clearly suffer from visual disorders, from attempting to force the results of their defective vision onto their fellow human beings as reality, or indeed, from serving it up as "art".'[9] Hitler spoke about laying 'the foundations for a new and genuine German art'. Robert Wistrich argues that National Socialist art, cleansed of abnormality, decomposition and ugliness, aimed at the reconstruction of 'a hierarchical, ordered society with a coherent vision of man, with a "heroic" ideal and the ability to totally reintegrate the individual into the community'.[10] The Nazi regime was keen to promote the concept of 'eternal German art' to support the vision of the thousand-year Reich. The House of German Art, designed by Paul Ludwig Troost, was intended to be more than just a showplace for paintings.[11] It was to be a temple of German art and as such was a monumental classical-style building with a marble interior and lavish decor. Hitler demanded a high-quality display of contemporary art and the exhibition was only to show 'the best and most perfect products of German art'. However, it is significant to note that there were sometimes contradictions in the Nazis' selection of acceptable works in the visual arts. For example, the sculptor Rudolf Belling (1886–1972) had one of his works displayed in the Degenerate Art Exhibition, while his bust of the boxer Max Schmeling was simultaneously on display at the first Great German Art Exhibition.[12]

The eight exhibitions held in the House of German Art in Munich between 1937 and 1944 offered what the regime considered to be a cross section of the best artistic work in Germany. There were relatively few paintings depicting specifically National Socialist themes or figures. Landscape paintings and depictions of 'womanhood' and 'manhood' dominated the exhibition. There were also portraits, still life paintings and paintings of animals. The importance of content and subject matter in Nazi art was evident too in the many thematic art exhibitions that were organised in individual towns and sent on tour across Germany. Exhibition titles included 'German Farmer – German Land' (1938), 'Man and Landscape' (1938) and 'Wife and Mother' (1941).

Genre painting frequently portrayed the faces and figures of farmers, hunters, fishermen, shepherds and woodcutters. It idealised simple peasant values and traditional rural life. The 'Blood and Soil' theme was popular in depictions of landscapes and the relationship of the German people to their land, for example Erich Erler's *Blood and Soil* and Ferdinand Spiegel's *Farm Family*. Such paintings celebrated the eternal values of country life as a source of strength for the nation. The art functioned to express what the National Socialist system wanted it to represent. Landscapes were not just landscapes in the traditional sense. The titles of the paintings showed that they had specific symbolic significance within the broad parameters of Nazi ideology, for example Hanns Bastanier's *Fruitful Land* and Werner Peiner's *German Earth*. The mother and child theme was another much exploited subject in German art of the Third Reich, for example Karl Diebitsch's *Mother*, Heinrich Eduard Linde-Walther's *Motherliness* and Wolfgang Willrich's *Guardian of the Race*. Family life provided another important subject for paintings, such as Georg Siebert's *German Family*, Richard Heymann's *In Good Hands* and Sepp Hilz's *Peasant Bride*.

There was also a great emphasis on the portrayal of women and of the female nude in particular. Such paintings aimed to show perfect and healthy physical forms, exemplified by Karl Ziegler's *Leda*, Adolf Ziegler's *Judgement of Paris*, Sepp Hilz's *Peasant Venus*, Oskar Martin-Amorbach's *Peasant Grace*, Johann Schult's *Expectation*, Carl Josef Bauer-Riedick's *Bathing Amazon* and Wilhelm Hempfing's *Youth*. In addition, there were paintings of marching columns and youth groups, battles, industrial enterprise and the new motorways. Paintings on these themes included Rudolf Otto's *Ready for Battle*, Ferdinand Staeger's *SS On Guard* and *We are the Work Soldiers*, and Jürgen Wegener's *German Youth*. Farmers, workers and soldiers symbolised the 'national community' striving for a common ideal. Franz Eichhorst's paintings *Workers*, *Farmer*, *Tank Defense*, *Street Fighting* and *Machine Gun Nest* exemplified such themes. Hence, the representations in art served as role models for the ideal society. War paintings showed readiness to fight and die for the nation as the highest virtue. Werner Peiner became one of the most prolific battle painters of the Nazi era.

There were, of course, many portraits of the *Führer*. Among the most notable was Hubert Lanzinger's 1934 portrayal of Hitler as a medieval knight, the warrior-leader carrying the swastika flag and echoing the earlier struggle of the Teutonic Order against the heathen east. Heinrich Knirr's 1937 portrait of Hitler showed the *Führer* in conventional military uniform, a dependable image. Hermann Otto Hoyer's *In the Beginning was the Word* depicted Hitler addressing a beer hall during the early days of the National Socialist movement. The title is significant with its quasi-religious symbolism and the sense of the import of Hitler's early words for the future of Germany.

The Nazi regime controlled German artistic life in a number of ways. It removed the influence of 'undesirable' artists through the imposition of bans on the right to teach, to exhibit and to paint. It supervised artists, museums and academies, published magazines, organised exhibitions, undertook cultural exchanges with other nations, expropriated the artistic property of enemies and engaged in large-scale plundering campaigns. Art was used instrumentally in the Third Reich to express the Nazi *Weltanschauung*, 'a moral force permeating the whole of German society'.[13] It was, as Peter Adam argues, 'considered one of the most important elements in building the new Reich and the new man'.[14] Nazi art policy had many aspects — to create popularly accessible art, to open up art as an arena for all classes and to lend legitimacy and respectability to the regime.

Once the 'degenerate' art had been eliminated, art enjoyed a prestigious place in Nazi society. In 1938, there were 170 competitions for painters, sculptors, graphic artists and architects, with 1.5 million Reichsmarks as prize money.[15] The official German art exhibitions in Munich were well attended. In 1939, the House of German Art attracted 400,000 visitors and the number increased each year to nearly 850,000 visitors in 1942.[16] The openings, with their impressive pageantry and ceremony, helped to reinforce the prestige and image of the regime as the guardian of culture, both at home and abroad. They were intended as a great celebration of the 'national community' and its achievements. This populist dimension underlined the intention of the Nazi regime to make art accessible to the masses for the first time in German history.

Sculpture provided the ideal visual representation of youth, beauty and masculinity. It extolled the perfection of the naked form and depicted a strong healthy race. After 1936, as Wistrich argues, 'sculpture became ever more obviously monumental, propagandist and subservient to those virtues of obedience, discipline and steely courage promoted by the regime'.[17] Monumental sculptures decorated public buildings, squares and stadiums, boasting the Nazi ideal of the healthy 'Aryan'. Josef Thorak (1889–1952) was one of the leading sculptors of the Nazi era and indeed the early favourite sculptor of Hitler. His work was exhibited at the Olympic Stadium in Berlin in 1936 and at the opening of the House of German Art in Munich in 1937. His sculptures closely represented the Nazi regime and its ideology. In return, the Nazi government was generous towards him and he became wealthy and famous for the duration of the Nazi era.[18] However, Arno Breker (1900–1991) soon supplanted Thorak as Hitler's favourite sculptor. Breker, who became the most pre-eminent sculptor of the Nazi era, created aesthetically ideal images of masculinity and strength in his massive sculptures that represented 'Aryan' supermen. By the mid-1930s, he was awarded an increasing number of official commissions and titles. In 1937, he joined the NSDAP and was named 'Official State Sculptor'.[19] Yet Petropoulos describes his transformation into official state sculptor as 'gradual and complicated', showing his progressive accommodation with the Nazi regime.[20] An ambitious individual, Breker gave up some elements of his pre-1933 style to satisfy the Nazi regime, adding monumentality to his work. In 1939, he sculpted two huge bronze figures for the inner courtyard of the Reich Chancellery. They represented *The Army* and *The Party*. Breker's sculptures depicted a new political ideal of human form, incorporating racial perfection and physical might. Breker's sculptures represented 'the new type of human being whose creation was one of the primary aims of Nazi cultural policy, unthinkingly physical, aggressive, ready for war'.[21] They were the ultimate sculptural expression of Hitler's ideology.

By contrast, it is instructive to consider the impact of National Socialism upon artists who remained in Germany despite the disapprobation of the regime. The case of Emil Nolde (1867–1956) provides an interesting example. Nolde, perhaps the most established of the German Expressionist painters, had received a great deal of critical acclaim in the Weimar Republic and had been elected to membership of the Prussian Academy of Arts in 1931. For a short period after the Nazi 'seizure of power', the policy of the new regime towards Nolde was conciliatory, as he shared its emphasis on national renewal, and he received support from some of the Nazi leadership. However, by 1937 he was placed firmly into the 'degenerate' category. Twenty-seven of Nolde's works were included in the Degenerate Art Exhibition. Having been expelled from the Prussian Academy, Nolde appealed in a letter to Goebbels, stating that his art was 'German, strong, austere and sincere'. His letter remained unanswered, however, and the attacks upon his work continued. In August 1941, an immediate 'painting ban' was placed on him. The Gestapo made a number of visits to his home over the following years to enforce the ban. Realising that the use of oils would make his disobedience too obvious, he painted more than 1,300 watercolours on scraps of paper, small enough to be concealed, which he called his 'Unpainted Pictures'. After 1945, he spent his remaining years transforming most of these into large oil paintings. His status was resurrected and his work was widely recognised with awards and honorary appointments.[22]

Käthe Kollwitz (1867–1945), German graphic artist and sculptor, is another interesting example. Kollwitz had been made a member of the Prussian Academy of Arts in 1919. One of the central themes of her work was the plight of the oppressed. In 1920, she had produced a great memorial woodcut of the KPD leader, Karl Liebknecht. Within three weeks of the Nazi 'seizure of power', Kollwitz was forced to resign from the Academy and prohibited from teaching art. Gradually, over the next few years, the Nazis removed her works from public display; her works were taken away from special exhibitions in Berlin in 1936 and 1937. Kollwitz was excluded from both the House of German Art and the Degenerate Art Exhibition in 1937. Her work was simply disregarded and the regime drove her into oblivion, in Germany at least, although her work was exhibited in America in 1937. Many of her works were among those seized by the regime in its campaign to purify German art. Nevertheless, she refused to leave the country and continued to work in silence and obscurity, mainly on small sculptures. After the war, Kollwitz's work was exhibited again and gained both critical recognition and popular acclaim.[23]

These examples demonstrate the Nazi regime's coercion of certain artists into silence and obscurity through its prohibition of their right to paint, teach or exhibit. The Hitler government simultaneously projected into fame, wealth and acclaim those artists whose work accorded to its ideals and who upheld its aims between 1933 and 1945.

As the Nazi era progressed, art policy became increasingly radicalised by the competition between ministers with their own agendas and initiatives. In particular, competition existed between Goebbels, Rust and Rosenberg, but there was also intervention from Himmler and Goering, as well as initiatives on the part of Nazi regional leaders and rulers in the occupied territories. From 1938 onwards, the Nazi authorities 'adopted a more violent and lawless cultural policy'.[24] The Nazis' radical and often illegal actions were designed to eliminate any art that conflicted with their perception of what German art should be. The disposal of modern art from state collections and the expropriation of artworks owned by Jews formed the core of this shift to a more radical policy. The purged 'degenerate' artwork was either destroyed or sold. Goebbels, Goering and Rust collaborated to liquidate numerous artworks. Furthermore, Goebbels commissioned particular art dealers to sell some of the 'degenerate' artworks abroad.[25] The sale of 'degenerate' art continued up until 1942 and brought in more than 1 million Reichsmarks of revenue, which was placed into a Special Account for Degenerate Art at the Reichsbank. Petropoulos has noted that the Nazi disposal of purged art was remarkable not only because of its excessive illegality but also because of the relative co-operation among Nazi leaders in its execution. The Nazis also became increasingly ruthless in their confiscation of artworks belonging to Jews and their plunder and expropriation of artworks during the war.

Furthermore, the Nazi leaders used art to define their status and their relationships with each other. They collected art 'to achieve legitimacy and social recognition'.[26] The traditional aristocracy regarded them as parvenus, so they collected art as a means of gaining social recognition and acceptance. In the same way that they quickly established huge estates and residences to show off their new power, they used art to express their newfound status. Moreover, art collecting enhanced the status of the Nazi leaders within the Party itself and the size of their private collections conveyed a sense of their relative power within the Nazi elite. Hitler collected 6,755 paintings, of which 5,350 were by old masters. Goering collected between 1,700 and 2,000 artworks. The sizes of the art collections of Himmler, Goebbels and Ribbentrop were indicative of their positions of power, as well as a display of their wealth. The Nazi leaders developed a tradition of gift giving in order to curry favour with Hitler or to cement their relationships with each other. Artworks were the main form of gift in this elaborate culture. Petropoulos argues that artworks emerged as a *lingua franca* for the Nazi leaders, offering them 'a particularly expressive means of communication: as tribute to the dictator, as ritualised gift-giving to help convey the appearance of group solidarity, or as representations of rank'.[27] Hence the Nazi leaders utilised art for their personal aspirations as well as to express the regime's ideological goals.

ARCHITECTURE

During the Weimar era, the success of modern architecture engendered a bitter public controversy about the political significance of architecture, a debate the National Socialists joined vociferously after 1930. National Socialism condemned 'architectural bolshevism' and rejected the modern style of the Bauhaus architects such as Walter Gropius and Ludwig Mies van der Rohe. The new Bauhaus style (which developed in other European countries as well as in Germany) represented a radical rejection of architectural traditions. Bauhaus architects believed that the First World War had brought to an end an outmoded system of values and that they had to create a wholly new style of architecture to represent the new era. They developed new structures and used new materials, with a total lack of reference to the past. Their work was a radical expression of the new political era, although it should be noted that there were other types of modern architecture that grew out of older traditions, and that the buildings designed by the Bauhaus architects represented only a minority of the total construction during the Weimar years.

Bauhaus architects, including Gropius, Mies van der Rohe and Erich Mendelsohn, received extensive publicity and acclaim but simultaneously a hostile political counter-reaction. While they designed buildings from factories to department stores, their largest commissions were large-scale mass housing projects in many major German cities in the 1920s. Thus the Bauhaus style attracted wide publicity and became associated with the public image of the Weimar Republic. By 1930, it had come to broadly symbolise the political, cultural and social characteristics of the Weimar Republic. Opposition took the form of calls for a more traditional style of architecture and a return to the true 'German' style rather than the 'bolshevik' style of the radical architects. The NSDAP, realising the political value of the controversy, opportunistically added its voice to the opposition and pledged a building programme that reflected its own ideology. Radical architecture was declared a threat to the German people. Its iconoclasm reflected wider trends that would lead to the destruction of national traditions. The new architecture was a symbol of the urbanisation and decadence of Weimar society. Nazi propaganda described the new architecture not only as a symbol of social and cultural decline but also as its cause. It argued that the Weimar governments used the new architecture as a tool to destroy German traditions. The National Socialists attacked the rootless urban architecture as the product of an era of decline. Their Party newspaper, the *Völkischer Beobachter*, launched scathing attacks on the Bauhaus architects in the early 1930s. In an article in November 1932, it claimed: 'These men reveal their character as typical nomads of the metropolis, who no longer understand blood and soil ... Now their secret is known! The new dwelling is an instrument for the destruction of the family and the race.'[28] Only the National Socialists would redress this cultural decline and restore German cultural traditions against 'bolshevik', avant-garde and foreign influences.

Once in power, the new regime shut down the Bauhaus school in Berlin on 12 April 1933 and a number of prominent Bauhaus architects lost their posts. The 'co-ordination' of municipal building administrations and building societies removed the influence of radical architects by ensuring that they no longer received commissions for their work. The reorganisation of the professional architectural organisations during the spring and summer of 1933 further deprived Bauhaus architects of their influence within their profession.[29] Hence, the prominent Bauhaus architects, Gropius, Mendelsohn, Mies van der Rohe, Martin Wagner and Ludwig Hilberseimer, were unable to work under the Nazi regime and they emigrated to Britain or America.

Hitler and other Nazi leaders spoke of the necessity for a specifically 'National Socialist architecture'. The new regime initiated a huge building programme, accompanied by a propaganda campaign to highlight the ideological significance of Nazi architecture. The official buildings of the Nazi regime were designed in a variety of styles, some of which were based upon older architectural traditions, but some of which showed the clear influence of the modern movement. This diversity reflected the differing views of the various party leaders involved in architectural policy. Barbara Lane has argued convincingly that 'the varying stylistic preferences of Nazi patrons reflect very clearly the fundamental conflicts in Nazi ideology as it affected architecture'.[30] Some leaders favoured neoclassicism, while others preferred a rustic style in line with 'blood and soil' ideology, and others still commissioned modern buildings to emphasise the 'modern' side of the Nazi regime. A huge propaganda campaign publicised the different types of Nazi architecture and their ideological purposes. Hitler's preferences were expressed in the monumental public buildings that he commissioned directly for the specific purpose of signifying the power and strength of the Party and the *Volk*.

Hitler believed not only that architecture expressed national greatness but also that it could help to create it. Architecture had a significant role in awakening the 'national consciousness', fostering a sense of the unity of the 'national community'. In addition, Hitler regarded architecture as the visible demonstration of the higher qualities of the German people and as a signifier of their right not only to exist but also to expand at the expense of 'inferior' nations. Hitler's architectural designs were vast and monumental in their scale. He utilised architecture to express National Socialist thoughts in a permanent form – 'the word in stone'. Architecture was regarded as part of the Nazi revolution and the regime used buildings 'as an act of faith'.[31] As early as 1933, Hitler's ambitions for monumental public buildings began to be realised, such as the *Braunes Haus* in Munich and the two Party buildings, the *Führer* Building and the Administrative Building of the NSDAP. The projects that he commissioned personally and supervised closely as '*Führer* buildings' (the Party buildings in Munich, the House of German Art, the new chancellery in Berlin and the buildings for the Party Congresses at Nuremberg) were built in a neoclassical style, fulfilling Hitler's desire to emulate the 'Greek spirit', which combined both beauty and function. Troost's House of German Art in Munich served as a symbol not only of the architecture of the Nazi regime but also of its cultural credentials more widely, as it housed German art and sculpture.[32] The monumentality of Albert Speer's work at Nuremberg signified national strength and fostered the spirit of the 'national community'.

Nazi architecture was concerned not with improving the infrastructure of the cities but with adding a new aesthetic dimension to them.[33] A large number of public spaces were created or altered for mass rallies, meetings and celebrations. Rather than buildings that were socially useful, the regime was concerned to erect memorials to Nazi martyrs and other monumental buildings. The two Temples of Honour in Munich, designed by Troost, to house the coffins of those Nazi martyrs who had fallen in the Munich Putsch of November 1923 each displayed eight coffins, open to the sky, as a symbol of willingness for self-sacrifice.[34] Such buildings had a higher purpose to which the needs of the people were subordinated. Much of the architecture of the Third Reich was symbolic, to express timelessness and eternity. The buildings of Troost in Munich and Speer in Nuremberg exemplified this.[35] They were laid out in massive rectilinear forms. Monumentalism and neoclassicism were the two main trends for public buildings. The structures of the buildings were grand, but the façades were not overly decorated. The grand scale of the buildings was designed to intimidate and impress, as well as to unite the people.

After Troost's death in January 1934, Speer became Hitler's principal architect. Speer's close relationship with the *Führer* developed from the end of 1933 when Hitler began to invite him increasingly often to discuss architecture in general as well as specific plans.[36] Hitler commissioned Speer to design the vast parade grounds and buildings for the Nuremberg Party Congresses. The *Zeppelinfeld* was the first and only building in this plan to be completed. It was striking, not only in its size (it had the capacity to hold 100,000 people) but also in its overall effect, with Party flags and lights. Thirty-four flag platforms edged the *Zeppelinfeld* on three sides. Speer created impressive 'light cathedrals' in the night sky using approximately 150 searchlights. At Nuremberg in September 1937, Hitler claimed: 'These works of ours shall also be eternal, that is to say, not only in the greatness of their conception, but in their clarity of plan, in the harmony of their proportions, they shall satisfy the requirements of eternity … magnificent evidence of civilisation in granite and marble, they will stand through the millennia … these buildings of ours should not be conceived for the year 1942 nor for the year 2000, but like the cathedrals of our past they shall stretch into the millennia of the future.'[37]

Hitler commissioned Speer to rebuild Berlin as a capital city befitting the Third Reich and appointed him Inspector-General for the Building of the Reich Capital. In a speech on 27 November 1937, Hitler claimed: 'It is my unalterable will and determination to provide Berlin with those streets, buildings and public squares which will make it appear for all time fit and worthy to be the capital of the German Reich.'[38] Hitler had grandiose plans to transform Berlin into the world capital 'Germania'. He envisaged an axis of massive boulevards across Berlin with a huge triumphal arch at the centre. Speer produced a model of Hitler's plans and the two spent endless hours in discussion over the model, making plans and adjustments for the construction of an eternal city.

In a recent contribution to the literature, Paul Jaskot has demonstrated the links between the SS, forced labour and Hitler's monumental building programme.[39] Jaskot looks at the operative political function of architecture in this context. He examines the involvement of SS companies in the production of building materials for Hitler's monumental projects. He demonstrates that the German Earth and Stone Works, the largest SS concern, which was established after a meeting between Hitler, Himmler and Speer, affirmed 'the connection of forced labour to state and Party architecture'.[40] The German Earth and Stone Works was set up on 29 April 1938 in order to exploit concentration camp labour for the production of bricks and the quarrying of stone. These materials were used for Hitler's prominent public buildings. The most important projects, such as Speer's new Reich Chancellery building in Berlin, were built almost entirely of granite, limestone and marble. The German Earth and Stone Works provided the materials for 'specific monumental state and Party projects'.[41] There is an interesting link here between architectural policy and the victims of National Socialism. Concentration camp inmates, excluded from the 'national community', provided the hard labour to produce bricks and stone for the buildings whose very purpose was to underline Nazi power. Another important link here is between architecture as ideology and as practical policy. Jaskot argues that the tendency to deal with the history of Nazi architecture as a separate issue from the regime's political history hinders our understanding of the relationship between the two. He describes 'a caesura between architecture and politics, between architecture as an expression of ideological and aesthetic goals and the integration of architectural policy with non-artistic state and Party objectives'.[42] His examination of the role of the SS in architecture and the monumental building economy begins to bridge this gap.

Germany's vast and innovative motorway network became the best example of the use of modern techniques and design in the Third Reich.[43] The *Autobahnen* (motorways) were another sign of Nazi success and achievement. The motorways had a large propaganda impact as well as putting people to work. They were a symbol of the power and unity of the 'national community'.[44] Fritz Todt, an engineer and early Party member, was appointed Inspector-General of the German Road System.[45] The new motorways were not merely roads, but 'technology elevated to art'.[46] Todt regarded the *Autobahnen* as 'an artistic commission', constructed in harmony with the German landscape. Troost claimed that the new bridges demonstrated 'a power binding the *Volk* together'.[47] Hence, the architects had their role to play in the achievement of the 'national community'. Paul Bonatz's concrete bridges became famous, as did his steel beam bridge over the Elbe near Dessau and his steel suspension bridge over the Rhine at Rodenkirchen.[48] They opened up the possibility of discovering other parts of the country and thus engendered a 'rediscovery of Germany'. The motorways were popularised by painters, photographers, newspapers and film-makers. The regime exploited their propaganda possibilities to the full, as the ultimate symbol of National Socialist innovation and achievement.

In reality, however, Nazi architecture had a greater remit than the highly publicised *Führer* buildings and the motorway system, and the regime championed a variety of architectural styles. A number of prominent Nazi leaders, including the ideologue Gottfried Feder and the Minister of Food and Agriculture Walter Darré, as well as the housing officials of the DAF, all favoured a rural type of architecture, rooted in 'blood and soil', in which the German people could feel their affinity with their homeland. '*Volk*' styles were encouraged for hostels and administrative buildings as well as houses, as they reflected a commitment to official Nazi 'blood and soil' ideology.[49] Robert Ley, leader of the German Labour Front, was responsible for a substantial proportion of new construction. He commissioned a large number of Party buildings, including local party offices and 'community centres'. These buildings, as well as the Ordensburgen, which he also commissioned, drew their influence from the medieval period. Although the Nazis attacked the Bauhaus, some Nazi leaders tolerated and even admired other types of modern design, which developed out of earlier styles and had roots in the past. For example, Baldur von Schirach, commissioned modern buildings that used new building materials for the Hitler Youth. A large volume of building was carried out by the armed services, especially by Goering for the Air Force. Goering commissioned some very modern designs, for instance Ernst Sagebiel's new Air Force Ministry building in Berlin.

Public housing under National Socialism had a strong ideological purpose. The Nazi government promised a new housing policy that would bring workers back to the soil, in line with 'blood and soil' ideology, but in reality the planning and style of public housing did not live up to this pledge. There were a few 'model' developments that accorded with this policy, but the majority of housing did not fit this ideal. Gottfried Feder claimed that the purpose of Nazi housing was 'the dissolution of the metropolis, in order to make our people be settled again, to give them again their roots in the soil ... The metropolis has destroyed men's feeling for their homeland ... The re-incorporation of the metropolitan populations into the rhythm of the German landscape is one of the principal tasks of the National Socialist government.'[50] The new housing policy, under the slogan 'Away from the metropolis!', was designed to strengthen the race and the 'national community'. However, this policy was not properly implemented by the regime. The majority of Nazi new housing projects continued the Weimar trend of building row housing and blocks of flats on the outskirts of the cities. The Nazis did build a number of housing developments outside cities that consisted of single-family houses with large gardens, which more closely matched Feder's claims. Some of these houses had thatched roofs or other references to *Volk* tradition, but the majority were white stucco or whitewashed brick without any adornment. The Nazi propaganda machine publicised specific examples, such as the Ramersdorf Siedlung built outside Munich in 1934, to conceal the reality that 'the dissolution of the metropolis', promised by the regime, was not occurring. Such developments served as symbols of a 'return to the soil' that was never accomplished. In addition, Nazi propaganda greatly exaggerated the amount of construction that was taking place.

'National Socialist architecture' encompassed a variety of styles – from the neoclassicism of the prominent Party buildings, to 'blood and soil' type housing developments, to modern buildings. While the official buildings were most widely publicised, these other styles of architecture were equally valid examples of Nazi architecture. The ideological significance attached to architecture by Nazi leaders, as well as the political propaganda that surrounded it, were the most distinctive features of Nazi architecture. Apart from preventing the most radical architects from continuing their work in Germany by excluding them from their professions and ensuring that they received no commissions, Nazi architecture did not confine itself to a particular style. National Socialist architecture was aimed at different aspects of creating popular consensus and the 'national community'. For this purpose, the *Thingplätze* and large-scale outdoor meeting places had a significant role. Architects played an important part in serving the 'national community' with their work. The elevation of the 'national community' over the individual was emphasised through the grandeur of large-scale public buildings – stadiums, halls and parade grounds – as community architecture. The Nuremberg Party Rally Grounds provided the best example of the Nazi desire to create a sense of 'national community' in stone.

Architecture had a significant role in extolling National Socialist ideology, both to members of the 'national community' and to the wider world. This was the purpose of the didactic, monumental style of the *Führer* buildings. They demonstrated Germany's might and represented the character and achievements of the German people. Symbols and inscriptions added a particular significance. Eagles and swastikas were the most recurrent symbols. For example, a geometric pattern of swastikas adorned the ceiling of the portico of the House of German Art. Mottoes or extracts of Hitler's speeches were carved over doorways or into walls.[51] Oak leaves and oak trees were also important symbols of the strong links of the German people with their land. The 'blood and soil' theme was interwoven with familiar sentiments and values to give it a wider popular resonance.

Wistrich has argued that it is important to understand the 'undeniable mass appeal of the Nazi culture industry'.[52] It was a significant facet of the Nazi regime, which sought popular consensus as well as using terror and propaganda, that Nazi architecture in particular was designed to reflect the power and grandeur of the Third Reich. It had a public role and a symbolic function. Indeed, Jochen Thies has argued that its final goals were extremely far-reaching, as a representation of world power for the Third Reich.[53] Together, art and architecture played an important role in Nazi Germany. Although neither was in practice an absolute representation of Nazi dogma, both were employed by the Nazi regime to endorse its power and to promote its aims for the 'national community'. Modernism was attacked as the product of international, Jewish, Bolshevik and 'alien' influences. The visual arts were a significant part of the Nazi 'spiritual revolution', aimed at articulating and representing the racial spirit of the people. To this end, officially endorsed artists, sculptors and architects whose work captured the essence of National Socialism and its aims, such as Ziegler, Thorak, Breker and Speer, were able to reap rewards, in terms of material wealth, titles and commissions, as well as status and prestige.

NOTES

1 K. Backes, *Hitler und die bildenden Künste. Kulturverständnis und Kunstpolitik im Dritten Reich* (Cologne, 1988); R. Merker, *Die bildenden Künste im Nationalsozialismus. Kulturideologie – Kulturpolitik – Kulturproduktion* (Cologne, 1983); O. Thomae, *Die Propaganda-Maschinerie. Bildende Kunst und Öffentlichkeitsarbeit im Dritten Reich* (Berlin, 1978); P. Reichel, *Der schöne Schein des Dritten Reiches. Faszination und Gewalt des Faschismus* (Frankfurt am Main, 1993); S. West, *The Visual Arts in Germany 1890–1937: Utopia and Despair* (Manchester, 2000); F. Spotts, *Hitler and the Power of Aesthetics* (London, 2002); H. Weihsmann, *Bauen unterm Hakenkreuz. Architektur des Untergangs* (Vienna, 1998); J. Thies, *Architekt der Weltherrschaft. Die 'Endziele' Hitlers* (Königstein im Taunus, 1980); J. Dülffer, J. Thies and J. Henke, *Hitlers Städte. Baupolitik im Dritten Reich. Eine Dokumentation* (Cologne, 1978). See especially B. Taylor and W. van der Will, 'Aesthetics and National Socialism', in B. Taylor and W. van der Will (eds), *The Nazification of Art: Art, Design, Music, Architecture and Film in the Third Reich* (Winchester, 1990), pp. 1–13.

2 J. Petropoulos, *Art as Politics in the Third Reich* (Chapel Hill and London, 1996), p. 5.

3 On this, see A. Steinweis, 'Weimar Culture and the Rise of National Socialism: The *Kampfbund für deutsche Kultur*', *Central European History*, Vol. 24 (1992), pp. 402–23.

4 A. Steinweis, 'The Nazi Purge of German Artistic and Cultural Life', in R. Gellately and N. Stoltzfus (eds), *Social Outsiders in Nazi Germany* (Princeton and Oxford, 2001), p. 99.

5 S. Barron (ed.), *Degenerate Art: The Fate of the Avant-Garde in Nazi Germany* (Los Angeles, 1991)

6 On this, see P.-K. Schuster (ed.), *Die 'Kunststadt' München 1937: Nationalsozialismus und 'entartete Kunst'* (Munich, 1988); K. Arndt, *Nationalsozialismus und 'Entartete Kunst': Die 'Kunststadt' München 1937* (Munich, 1988).

7 B. Hinz, *Art in the Third Reich* (New York, 1979), pp. 39–40.

8 Cited in R. Wistrich, *Weekend in Munich: Art, Propaganda and Terror in the Third Reich* (London, 1995), p. 57.

9 Cited in Hinz, *Art in the Third Reich*, p. 42.

10 Wistrich, *Weekend in Munich*, p. 61.

11 K. Arndt, 'Das "Haus der deutschen Kunst" – ein Symbol der neuen Machtverhältnisse', in Schuster (ed.), *Die 'Kunststadt' München 1937*, pp. 61–82.

12 P. Adam, *Art of the Third Reich* (New York, 1992), p. 109.

13 B. Taylor and W. van der Will, 'Aesthetics and National Socialism', in Taylor and van der Will (eds), *The Nazification of Art*, p. 4.

14 Adam, *Art of the Third Reich*, p. 9.

15 Taylor and van der Will, 'Aesthetics and National Socialism', in Taylor and van der Will (eds), *The Nazification of Art*, p. 12.

16 Wistrich, *Weekend in Munich*, p. 64.

17 Ibid., p. 79.

18 For a fuller treatment of Thorak, see J. Petropoulos, *The Faustian Bargain: The Art World in Nazi Germany* (London, 2000), pp. 262–71.

19 R. Evans, *The Third Reich in Power* (London, 2006), p. 167.

20 Petropoulos, *The Faustian Bargain*, p. 222. See also J. Petropoulos, 'From Seduction to Denial: Arno Breker's Engagement with National Socialism', in R. Etlin (ed.), *Art, Culture, and Media under the Third Reich* (Chicago, 2002), pp. 205–29.

21 Evans, *The Third Reich in Power*, p. 168.

22 On Nolde, see W. Bradley, *Emil Nolde and German Expressionist Art: A Prophet in his own Land* (Ann Arbor, 1986); R. Pois, *Emil Nolde* (Washington, D.C., 1982); P. Selz, *Emil Nolde* (New York, 1962).

23 On Kollwitz, see M. Klein and H. Klein, *Käthe Kollwitz: Life in Art* (New York, 1972); O. Nagel, *Käthe Kollwitz* (London, 1971); W. Timm, *Käthe Kollwitz* (Berlin, 1980).

24 Petropoulos, *Art as Politics in the Third Reich*, p. 51.

25 Ibid., p. 78.

26 Ibid., p. 7.

27 Ibid., p. 286.

28 Cited in B. Lane, *Architecture and Politics in Germany 1918–1945* (Cambridge, Mass., 1968), p. 163.

29 Ibid., pp. 173–4.

30 Ibid., p. 186.

31 Adam, *Art of the Third Reich*, p. 211.

32 On Troost, see K. Arndt, 'Paul Ludwig Troost als Leitfigur der nationalsozialistischen Räpresentationsarchitektur', in I. Lauterbach (ed.), *Bürokratie und Kult: Das Parteizentrum der NSDAP am Königsplatz in München: Geschichte und Rezeption* (Munich, 1995), pp. 147–56.

33 Hinz, *Art in the Third Reich*, p. 191.

34 R. Taylor, *The Word in Stone: The Role of Architecture in the National Socialist Ideology* (Berkeley, 1974), p. 192.

35 See J. Petach, 'Architektur als Weltanschauung: Die Staats- und Parteiarchitektur im Nationalsozialismus', in B. Ogan and W. Weiss (eds), *Faszination und Gewalt: Zur politischen Ästhetik des Nationalsozialismus* (Nuremberg, 1992), pp. 197–204.

36 J. Fest, *Speer: The Final Verdict* (London, 2001), p. 39.

37 Cited in Adam, *Art of the Third Reich*, p. 225.

38 Cited in Taylor, *The Word in Stone*, p. 46.

39 P. Jaskot, *The Architecture of Oppression: The SS, Forced Labour and the Nazi Monumental Building Economy* (London, 2000).

40 Ibid., p. 12.

41 Ibid., p. 29.

42 Ibid., p. 141.

43 On the *Autobahnen*, see R. Stommer (ed.), *Reichsautobahnen: Pyramiden des Dritten Reichs: Zur Ästhetik eines unbewältigten Mythos* (Marburg, 1982); E. Schütz and E. Gruber, *Mythos Autobahnen. Bau und Inszenierung der 'Strassen des Führers' 1933–1941* (Berlin, 1996).

44 J. Shand, 'The Reichsautobahnen. Symbol for the Third Reich', *Journal of Contemporary History*, Vol. 19 (1984), pp. 189–200.

45 On Todt, see F. Seidler, *Fritz Todt: Baumeister des Dritten Reiches* (Munich, 1986).

46 Adam, *Art of the Third Reich*, p. 219.

47 Cited in Taylor, *The Word in Stone*, p. 199.

48 H. Frank, 'Bridges: Paul Bonatz's Search for a Contemporary Monumental Style', in Taylor and van der Will (eds), *The Nazification of Art*, p. 154.

49 Lane, *Architecture and Politics in Germany 1918–1945*, p. 199.

50 Cited in ibid., pp. 205–6.

51 Taylor, *The Word in Stone*, p. 13.

52 R. Wistrich, *Weekend in Munich*, p. 19.

53 J. Thies, 'Hitler's European Building Programme', *Journal of Contemporary History*, Vol. 13 (1978), pp. 413–31. See also J. Thies, 'Nazi Architecture – A Blueprint for World Domination: The Last Aims of Adolf Hitler', in D. Welch (ed.), *Nazi Propaganda: The Power and the Limitations* (London, 1983), pp. 45–64.

15

MUSIC AND LITERATURE

Title page of the exhibition guide for the first Reichsmusikage (National Music Festival) in Dusseldorf 24 May 1938. © akg-images

Similarly to art and other aspects of cultural life, music in Nazi Germany is a subject that was not properly treated by historians until comparatively recently. For almost four decades after 1945, it was largely held that there was nothing to say about the music of the Third Reich except that it was reactionary. In 1994, Erik Levi challenged this view and argued that it is incorrect to view the artistic achievement in the Third Reich in isolation, as a period of intense reaction.[1] The same held true for Nazi literature, which for many decades was deemed unworthy of serious scholarly attention. Very little was written on the subject before the 1980s. The historiography of both these areas has expanded and new perspectives have been presented.[2]

MUSIC

While there were undoubtedly reactionary elements in German music in the Nazi era, Levi argues that stylistic elements that had been established in the Weimar Republic, including *Gebrauchsmusik* (utilitarian music) and *Gemein-schaftsmusik* (community music), were accommodated and adopted by the Hitler regime. The Weimar era had been an age of experimentation and toler-ance. In the field of music, some of the most influential composers of the period were drawn to Berlin, including Arnold Schoenberg and Paul Hindemith. Kurt Weill, Hanns Eisler, Ernst Toch and Ernst Krenek also forged their reputa-tions during the Weimar years. However, the Weimar Republic was not solely about progress and experimentation. Pamela Potter argues that many of the elements of backwardness and oppression held to be the hallmark of the Third Reich were already present in the Weimar Republic.[3] Three elements of con-servative cultural opinion were extant in the Weimar era. The first was a tra-ditional conservatism of the upper and upper-middle classes that aimed at preserving the status quo, but which accommodated itself with the Weimar Republic. The second was a more radical conservatism of middle-class intel-lectuals who rejected modernism and wanted to restore German culture to its spiritual origins. The third was the most extreme strand on the German right, National Socialism, which proposed to restore Germany to its former cultural glory and completely rejected foreign influences.

In 1929, Alfred Rosenberg set up the *Kampfbund für deutsche Kultur* ('Combat League for German Culture' or KfdK), a cultural association that attacked 'mod-ernism' and aimed to preserve German values. Its purpose was to 'inform the German people about the interconnection between art, race, knowledge and moral values' and to 'give wholehearted support for the genuine expression of German culture'.[4] Rosenberg attacked the prevailing musical climate and called for a ban on jazz music and any music with 'Jewish' or 'negroid' influ-ences. The membership of the KfdK grew from 600 in January 1930 to 2,100 in January 1932 and it continued to increase after the Nazi 'seizure of power'. But once Goebbels became established as Minister for Popular Enlightenment and Propaganda, Rosenberg struggled to maintain his influence. The Reich Chamber of Music (RMK), one of the seven sub-chambers of the Reich Cham-ber of Culture, challenged his organisation. There developed, as Levi points out, 'a complex relationship between Nazi music ideology … and its practical application in the Nazi state'.[5] This was largely the result of divisions over policy-making between Rosenberg and Goebbels. Rosenberg was absolutely set on ideology, while Goebbels was much more concerned with the practical ramifications of policy. Hence, music policy, like many other aspects of Nazi policy, was beset with ambiguities and inconsistencies.

The RMK was established to 'further the advance of German music', but its functions in practice were highly restrictive. It regulated the music profession and membership of the RMK became a prerequisite to work as a musician in Germany. Membership was confined to musicians who were racially 'valuable' and politically 'reliable'. Goebbels appointed Richard Strauss and Wilhelm Furtwängler respectively as the first President and Vice President of the RMK. The presence of two of Germany's leading musicians gave initial credibility to the organisation, although Furtwängler resigned in December 1934 and Strauss was obliged to resign in July 1935.[6] They were replaced with strong supporters of Nazi ideology: the conductor Peter Raabe, as President, and the composer Paul Graener, as Vice President. Yet by 1937, Goebbels was determined to have more direct control over the regulation of music by his Ministry rather than through the RMK. In 1937, he set up the State Music Censorship Reading Panel, headed by Heinz Drewes, to censor new music publications and recordings that were considered to be 'alien' to the German spirit. Goebbels called for further 'purification' of the music profession by his Ministry and by 1939 the role of the Ministry of Popular Enlightenment and Propaganda in controlling the music of the Third Reich was firmly established.

Central to the Nazis' goal of regenerating German music was the removal of Jewish influence. In 1933, only 2 per cent of the German music profession was of Jewish origin. Within a matter of months, the new regime passed legislation to deny employment to Jewish musicians in German concert halls and opera houses. Jewish musicians were barred from membership of the RMK, which effectively meant that they were excluded from their profession. Music by Jewish composers was removed from both concert programmes and radio broadcasts.[7] Some factions within the Nazi Party, in particular those loyal to Rosenberg, called for 'the wholesale expurgation of Judaic influence from the concert and operatic platform'.[8] At first, such extreme demands met with some resistance, but gradually this dissent was eroded. By 1938, the Nazis had succeeded in completely removing the name of the Jewish composer Felix Mendelssohn (1809–1847) from the lists of recording and publishing catalogues. During the war, the 'Aryanisation of musical repertoire' at last acquired the support of the Ministry of Popular Enlightenment and Propaganda.

Another key aspect of the Nazi 'purification' of German music was the desire to proscribe 'modernism'. As a result, the majority of music written between 1933 and 1945 in Germany was a reaction against the experimental pluralism of the Weimar era. But Levi argues that 'an overall survey of contemporary musical activity in the two or three years before the Nazis came to power already suggests a growing reactionary tendency, which reached its summation in the first years of the Third Reich'.[9] Exemplifications of this included the dissolution of the annual contemporary music festivals at Baden-Baden after 1930 and the abolition of the experimental Kroll Opera in Berlin in 1931. Hence, reaction was already evident before 1933. Nevertheless, by June 1933 the Nazi regime had succeeded in ousting a considerable number of 'degenerate' musicians. The composers Schoenberg, Weill, Eisler and Toch were among the most notable émigrés from Nazi Germany in their field. Yet Nazi policy was characterised by tensions, inconsistencies and contradictions. For example, Hitler positively received Werner Egk's opera *Peer Gynt*, even though it had been rejected by critics for its 'modernism'.[10]

In addition, the Nazis were against atonality, a movement that they considered to be 'subversive'. Rosenberg stated that 'the atonal movement in music is against the blood and soul of the German people', while Ziegler declared that it represented 'the extreme of decadent and artistic bolshevism'. Yet the censorship of atonal music was not uniformly applied. For example, atonal passages in Richard Strauss were tolerated, but Schoenberg was not accepted because he was Jewish as well as atonal. The Nazis also attacked the *Neue Sachlichkeit* (New Objectivity) movement of the Weimar era, especially Krenek and Weill. Yet a more ambivalent response was accorded to the music of Hindemith and Egk. The attack on 'modernism' was rather arbitrary. Levi argues that 'much of the music emanating from the Nazi period quite clearly does not reject all the stylistic features of the previous era' and that 'modernism in music survived in Nazi Germany, albeit in a modified form'.[11] Orff and Egk 'were impelled by the Nazi regime to conduct themselves as specifically modern "German" composers. Like Strauss's, their new music was officially represented at the German-hosted Olympic Games in Berlin; they took part, actively or passively, in Nazi RMK competitions'.[12] Orff received state commissions in Frankfurt and Vienna, while Egk received state commissions in Dusseldorf.

In May 1938, the Entartete Musik (Degenerate Music) exhibition opened in Dusseldorf.[13] While the Entartete Musik exhibition attracted considerably less attention than Munich's 1937 Entartete Kunst (Degenerate Art) exhibition, it nevertheless remained one of the clearest examples of musical repression during the Third Reich. The exhibition centred round a series of photographs and portraits of the contemporary composers deemed to have had the most destructive influence on German music. Schoenberg, Stravinsky and Hindemith were among the central figures included in the exhibition, as well as Jewish operetta composers Oscar Straus and Leo Fall, and some less well-known musicians. The organiser of the exhibition, Hans Severus Ziegler, opened it with the following statement: 'The Entartete Musik exhibition presents a picture of a veritable witches' Sabbath portraying the most frivolous intellectual and artistic aspects of cultural Bolshevism ... and the triumph of arrogant Jewish impudence ... Degenerate music is thus basically de-Germanised music for which the nation will not mobilise its involvement.'[14] Ziegler clearly believed German musicians were being polluted by 'degenerate' music and called for them to be able to 'breathe, live and work freely in a clean atmosphere'.

While the musical profession was purged of 'alien' and 'undesirable' influences, Michael Kater has argued that 'other musicians succeeded in the Third Reich through a combination of respectable talent and demonstrable National Socialist conviction'.[15] Hence political opportunism and career advancement were often linked during the Nazi era. Those musicians who had no talent at all and tried to use Party affiliation to advance still failed because of incompetence, but those who demonstrated some talent as well as political dedication to the regime were virtually guaranteed professional success. Kater has emphasised too that those musicians with great prestige and talent yet minimal ties to the regime could still have an impressive career, as long as they did not go out of their way to upset or oppose the regime.[16]

Contradictions were evident in the regime's attitude to jazz music. Jazz was associated with the Weimar Republic. The Nazis maligned and condemned jazz because of its American, black and Jewish associations.[17] The Nazis also disliked the principle of improvisation represented by jazz and its syncopated rhythm and individualistic nature.[18] Contemporary critics such as Hans Petsch described jazz as a 'cancerous growth that has to be removed from Germany at all costs'.[19] By 1935, the Weintraub Syncopators, one of Germany's most prominent (and mainly Jewish) jazz combos, had emigrated. In October 1935, the broadcasting authorities officially banned jazz. But despite the ban, Goebbels realised that jazz was too popular to eliminate entirely and German bands played popular swing music on the radio. This was termed 'German dance music'. 'Hot jazz' was censored. Public performances by visiting black musicians were prohibited.[20] Yet the regime allowed white musicians, such as Jack Hylton, and their bands to visit because they entered and left the country as a unit and could be easily controlled and because access to their music placated the upper-middle classes.[21] Hence, policy towards jazz music and its performance was ambivalent and inconsistent.

Goebbels even considered it to be against the interests of the war effort to ban jazz after 1939. This belief was based upon his pragmatic concern not to lose the support of the masses. Goebbels encouraged popular music that would help to bolster the morale of both the troops and the home front. Swing clubs sprang up in Hamburg, Kiel, Berlin and other large cities, frequented by young middle-class people, and a sub-culture of 'swing youth' developed in response to the regime's ambivalent stance on jazz.[22] Hence, jazz survived throughout the Nazi era, despite the anti-jazz rhetoric and ideology of the regime. Kater has shown that after 1942, circumstances for jazz became more difficult, with the recurrent bombing raids on Berlin. He argues that by the end of 1942, there was no atmosphere in Berlin or elsewhere for jazz to continue to flourish. In 1944, with Goebbels' ban on light entertainment, jazz music became restricted to illegal, obscure venues or private parties.[23] As a whole, between 1933 and 1945, despite the Nazis' condemnation of jazz music, 'not only was there … no clearly enunciated and therefore nationally binding prohibition of jazz, but there existed, throughout, a confusing mix of tolerance, acquiescence, indictment and policy reversal'.[24]

Opera in the Third Reich also displayed some ambiguities. Nazi critics in the 1920s had despaired at the state of the opera in Germany, particularly great popular successes such as Weill's *Dreigoschenoper* and Krenek's *Jonny spielt auf!*. They had criticised the iconoclastic Kroll Opera, which had opened in Berlin in 1924 and offered an avant-garde repertoire. There were also radical repertoires in Dresden, Leipzig and Frankfurt, but in the rest of the country, conservatism prevailed, exemplified by the Bavarian State Opera in Munich. Once in power, the Nazis hoped to create an operatic repertoire that would dovetail with Nazi ideology. They aimed to suppress work that they considered to be politically or artistically unacceptable, to revive older material that had been disregarded in the Weimar Republic and to establish a new repertoire that would attain both popular and official approval. Nazi critics such as Fritz Stege argued against the 'racially alien products of Slavs, Magyars and others' in operatic repertoires.[25] The Nazi opera revived the *Volksoper* of the nineteenth century, which was inspired by legends and fairy tales, and young composers were encouraged to write contemporary versions of this genre. Contemporary operas with a political message were not successful at the box office. The German public wanted light-hearted themes, particularly once the war began. Productions such as Carl Orff's *Der Mond* in Munich in 1939 and Strauss's *Capriccio* in Munich in 1942 were very popular. Hence, the opera offered an opportunity for escapism. Between 1932 and 1940, the five most popular operatic composers were Wagner, Verdi, Puccini, Mozart and Lortzing. Levi argues that 'the public taste in Germany continued to favour operas from the late nineteenth and early twentieth century. In this respect, the general status quo remained rather unaffected by the unique demands of the Nazi era'.[26]

Concert life too did not undergo a decisive break from the past. An analysis of the major German symphony orchestras gives a mixed picture. While the orchestras in Munich and Leipzig were rather conservative, those in Dresden, Berlin and Hamburg were more adventurous. The outlook was dependent on the main conductor of the orchestra. Hence, concert life did not necessarily retreat into parochialism and reaction. The Nazis did establish their own NS Reich Symphony Orchestra, which was set up by Franz Adam in 1931. Once the Nazis came to power, their orchestra was permanently established as a travelling orchestra. It performed mainly in small towns and villages, schools and factories. The NS Reich Symphony Orchestra gave almost 200 concerts per year. It accorded with Nazi cultural policy and played almost exclusively German music.[27]

Kater argues that because many musicians either gained employment or enhanced their status on the basis of their affiliation to the Party, moral considerations did not prevail. He concludes that 'one and all – musicians and singers, composers and conductors – emerged in May 1945 severely tainted, with their professional ethos violated and their music compromised'.[28] Michael Meyer highlights the politicisation of music in the Nazi era, stating that as a public servant, the musician 'was forced to participate in the construction of the cultural façade from the heights of the Philharmonic and the State Opera to the village band, from manipulated expressions of high art to political music at party functions'.[29] Meyer stresses the very 'public orientation' of the musician in the Third Reich. Yet, in the end, 'there was a mixture of aesthetic styles and forms' in the music of the Third Reich, including jazz.[30] This suggests inconsistencies between Nazi ideology and policy with regard to music. In particular, ambiguities relating to jazz and modern music demonstrate that the regime did not, in reality, create an entirely monolithic and reactionary diet of music, despite its ideological imperatives and rhetoric. It sought to establish a balance between its ideological aims and the need to keep the population entertained.

LITERATURE

As in other areas of cultural life, National Socialism was keen to remove the influence of Jewish and Bolshevik writers from German literature. The Nazi regime approved literature that was pure and wholesome, a racially based literature that would serve to underpin its political aims. In place of the 'literature of the city', which had made a great impact during the Weimar era, it called for the 'literature of the peasant'. Nazism rejected works it considered to be decadent or degenerate, as well as the writings of 'enemies' of the regime and the German 'national community'. All Jewish writers were excluded from membership of the Reich Chamber of Literature. Radical left-wing writers such as Carl von Ossietzky and Erich Mühsam were arrested within weeks of the Nazi takeover of power. Ernst Toller, a German Jewish socialist writer, lived in exile between 1933 and 1939, when he committed suicide. Thomas Mann, who had won the Nobel Prize for Literature in 1929, lived in exile in Switzerland from February 1933. Many other prominent writers, including Arnold Zweig, Alfred Döblin, Erich Maria Remarque and Lion Feuchtwanger, went into exile. Heinrich Mann, author of *Blue Angel*, was forced to give up his presidency of the Prussian Academy of Poetry, a position taken over by the writer Hanns Johst. The Academy was purged of 'racial aliens' and 'degenerate' writers. Richard Grunberger estimates that 2,500 writers left Germany either voluntarily or under pressure from the Nazi state.[31] Richard Evans argues that by the end of 1933 'there was scarcely a writer of any talent or reputation left in Germany'.[32]

Writers including Werner Beumelberg, Hans Grimm, Hans Friedrich Blunck, Agnes Miegel, Hermann Stehr, Erwin Guido Kolbenheyer, Emil Strauss and Börries von Münchhausen filled the gap left by this great exodus of German literary talent. Beumelberg wrote *Fronterlebnis* stories (stories about the war experience), such as *Gruppe Bosemüller*. The *Fronterlebnis* genre became a major category of literature under National Socialism. Grimm's most famous work was his 1,300-page novel *People Without Living Space* (1926), which underlined the Nazi argument for *Lebensraum*. Despite his extreme nationalism and belief in German superiority over other 'races', which closely accorded with Nazi ideology, Grimm remained a nationalist conservative. He did not join the NSDAP. Kolbenheyer was another advocate of German power. A Sudeten German, Kolbenheyer was fiercely nationalistic and anti-Slav. He opportunistically concurred with Nazi ideology, hoping this would help him to gain recognition for his work. Blunck, President of the Reich Chamber of Literature, wrote *völkisch* sagas, such as *Great Journey,* and advocated German racial supremacy.[33] Miegel and Strauss wrote about the land and the people. Josef Weinheber was another ultra-nationalist writer who was an early convert to National Socialism. As an Austrian, he shared Hitler's pan-German aspirations for a union between Austria and Germany. The Anschluß of 1938 was the realisation of this hope and Weinheber wrote a *Hymn to the Homecoming* of Austria. This was presented at Hitler's birthday celebration at the Burgtheater in Vienna on 20 April 1938 and it underlined Weinheber's wholehearted commitment to National Socialism. The poem ends with the lines: 'Germany, eternal and great, Germany we greet you! *Führer*, scared and strong, *Führer* we greet you! Homeland, happy and free. Homeland, we greet you!'[34]

Heimatroman or *Blut und Boden* ('blood and soil') novels were immensely popular during the Nazi era. They described a rural idyll that was attractive to the traditional sentiments of their readers. They appealed to the harmony of the 'national community'. Such literature engendered a sense of security in the German countryside, away from the evils associated with urbanisation. This type of literature, as well as being regressive, was, as Ritchie points out, 'also extremely aggressive'.[35] There was a call for the peasant, like the soldier, to defend himself and his land. For example, Hermann Löns's *The Wehrwolf*, first published in 1910, had a significant message in the Third Reich. The book described the actions taken by peasants against invading soldiers and looters in the Thirty Years War. The novel showed that the task of the peasant was greater than simply to tend the land. It was to defend the land, with blood if necessary. Löns' novel suggested the exclusion of foreigners and demonstrated the importance of an undivided community working together industriously for the benefit of the whole. Hermann Burte, author of *Wiltfeber, the Eternal German. The Story of a Man Seeking his Homeland* (1912), steeped in *völkisch* ideology, was another writer assured of success in Nazi Germany. Anti-Semitic works were promoted by the regime too. Artur Dinter's *The Sin against the Blood* (1922) became one of the most acclaimed novels of the Nazi era. It told the story of Johanna, a German maiden seduced by a Jewish officer, who when she later married a German man, Hermann, gave birth to a 'Jewish child'. Dinter's novel explains how 'racial miscegenation' ruined the German girl for good and concluded with a moral that stated: 'Now consider the damage which year in, year out, is inflicted upon the German race by Jewish youths who every year seduce thousands upon thousands of German maidens!'[36]

The National Socialist poet Dietrich Eckart wrote *Germany Awaken!* to encourage people to unite for the national cause, even before Hitler came to power. It ended: 'Awaken Germany! Storm, storm, storm, storm, storm, storm! Sound the bells from tower to tower! Ring out the young men, old men and boys, ring out the sleepers from their rooms, ring the girls down the steps, ring the mothers away from the cradles, the air must hum and scream, rage, rage in vengeance's thunder, ring out the dead from their tombs. Awaken Germany!'[37] This type of agitation poetry appealed to basic emotions and called for the unity of the whole nation. Horst Wessel's marching song was another exclamatory rhyme designed to stir up the emotions of the masses. It called for raising the flag and marching, making way for the SA who stood 'ready to fight'. Although in reality he met his death at the hands of a pimp in Berlin, Horst Wessel became a National Socialist martyr and the Nazi propaganda machine created a great and heroic legend around him.

Following on from Eckart and Wessel, other Nazi party poets included Heinrich Anacker, Gerhard Schumann and Herbert Böhne.

Gottfried Benn became an advocate of the Nazi cause. In some ways, his stance was surprising, as he had formerly been an apolitical Expressionist poet and essayist. However, he was undoubtedly in agreement with Nazi eugenic policies. He was also pleased to be elected to the Prussian Academy and as a result he quickly and opportunistically fell into line with the Nazi regime. However, by March 1938 it was decided that the spirit of his works was alien to that of National Socialist culture and he was excluded from the Reich Chamber of Literature, had a 'writing ban' imposed upon him and was despised by the regime.[38] Arnolt Bronnen, another 'betrayer' of Expressionism, became a firm devotee of National Socialism. He wrote a Nazi novel, *The Battle of the Ether*, and was a close associate of Josef Goebbels. Bronnen's political opportunism meant that he was able to pursue a reasonable writing career in the Nazi era.

Once the Jews and 'cultural bolshevists' had been removed, German writers were to produce a new literature befitting the Third Reich. In order to refute claims of barbarity, the Nazi regime went to great lengths to promote literature, by means of national book prizes and Book Weeks. National Socialism tried to prove its credentials of respectability and legitimacy by ensuring that the works of respectable writers (tolerable to Nazism) continued to be published. By 1939, the Ministry of Popular Enlightenment and Propaganda controlled the work of 2,500 publishing houses, 23,000 bookshops and 3,000 writers, and administered 50 national literary prizes.[39] However, a number of government agencies were concerned with censorship and cultural affairs, and hence policy towards literature was not always co-ordinated or consistent. Approved authors received many incentives – prizes, publicity and preferential paper allocation in wartime. Other writers could continue to publish under the patronage of one Nazi leader, even if they were out of favour with another. Werner Bergengruen, for example, was tolerated by Goebbels, although Rosenberg was suspicious of his first novel, *The Grand Tyrant and the Law*. His *In Heaven as it is on Earth*, published in 1940, sold 60,000 copies in one year before being banned. Bergengruen also printed and distributed his poems anonymously. While they did not call for active resistance, they nevertheless rejected the evils of National Socialism. In addition, the regime tolerated Reinhold Schneider, who also distributed copies of his poems illegally. His historical novel *Las Casas and Charles V* (1938) met Goebbels' requirement for 'pure' literary products and he was able to continue his career undisturbed. Both Schneider and Bergengruen, despite their illegal activities, escaped the attention of the Gestapo. Frank Thiess was another author who was tolerated by the regime, particularly by Goebbels who was aware of the necessity for 'pure' literary products and entertainment literature during the war. Thiess's *The Neapolitan Legend* (1942) was very popular.

Ernst Wiechert, a reactionary conservative writer who extolled 'blood and soil' ideals, was at first courted by the Nazi regime, as his attitudes appeared to reflect those of National Socialism. His novels included *Of Forests and Men* and *A Simple Life*. Between 1935 and 1938, however, Wiechert engaged in a number of openly defiant acts against the regime. He was arrested in 1938 and sent to Buchenwald concentration camp, although he was subsequently released. The Prussian aristocratic writer Friedrich Percyval Reck-Malleczewen, author of *Diary of a Desperate Man* (1936) and *Bockelson: History of a Mass Hysteria* (1937), clearly expressed his distaste for National Socialism in his writings. He was arrested in December 1944 and died in Dachau in February 1945. The writer Albrecht Haushofer, who was in contact with the German resistance, was arrested in December 1944 and shot dead in April 1945.

In the space between pro-Nazi writers and those who opposed the regime were the 'inner emigration' authors, who kept their distance from the regime but did not write anything flagrantly oppositional to it.[40] Inner emigration was the route followed by Christian writers such as Werner Bergengruen, Reinhold Schneider and Jochen Klepper, whose religious values kept them aloof from the regime. Even conservative writers began to distance themselves. Ernst Jünger was a conservative, nationalist writer who was favoured by the Nazi regime at first. The First World War was clearly his most formative experience and many of his novels, such as *Storm of Steel* (1920), *The Adventurous Heart* (1929) and *Total Mobilisation* (1931), revealed his preoccupation with the subject. His works inspired many supporters of Nazism and encouraged young Germans to follow in the footsteps of front-line soldiers who had paved the way for the 'national awakening'. The themes in these books drew him close to the Nazi regime, although he did not join the Party. In time, however, he moved away from National Socialism and the publication of his novel *On the Marble Cliffs* (1939) has been cited as the point of his transformation to inner emigration.[41] This story of despotism and rule by terror, with its echoes of the rise of National Socialism, could have been interpreted as 'resistance' literature, but it was not banned and nor did the author receive any penalties. While he did not call upon his readers to resist, Jünger's language was so complex that if there was any seditious message in the work, it was so well camouflaged that it could not be clearly proven. Jünger is an interesting case of an ambivalent author who has been closely associated both with National Socialism and with 'resistance' to it. Clearly, the Nazi leadership did not regard him as a threat.[42]

Authors such as Bergengruen, Jünger, Thiess and Schneider were able to continue to publish their books and enjoyed large sales. During the 1933–1945 period, the term 'inner emigration' was applied to German writers who, like the émigrés, had lost their spiritual homeland once the Nazis came to power and were isolated, although they remained in Germany. After 1945, however, it came to signify only those writers who had stayed in Germany and had engaged in resistance through writings. Otherwise, writers who remained in Germany and whose works were approved by the Nazi state could be accused, sometimes rightly, of being opportunistic and sympathetic to the regime. Hence, there is a certain amount of controversy surrounding the writers who remained in Germany when the Nazis came to power. As Ritchie points out: 'It took very close reading to notice the difference between writers of the so-called inner emigration and National Socialist followers and sympathisers, for after all they had all received the same stamp of approval from the same censors.'[43] There was not a great deal of literary difference between them. Indeed, Thomas Mann stated in May 1945 that 'any books ... printed at all in Germany between 1933 and 1945 are worse than worthless and not objects one wishes to touch. A stench of blood and shame attaches to them. They should all be pulped'.[44]

Music and literature in the Third Reich were made to conform, by and large, to the dictates of the Nazi regime. While there was some inconsistency in Nazi policy towards both music and literature, the Hitler regime was ideologically clear about the type of cultural output it considered to be suitable for presentation to the German 'national community'. Many talented musicians, composers and writers were purged from their professions on grounds of their exclusion from the 'national community' for being 'racially inferior' or politically unreliable. The remaining musicians and writers who continued their careers under Hitler have been regarded as tainted because of their association with National Socialism.

NOTES

1 E. Levi, *Music in the Third Reich* (London, 1994).

2 On music, see F. Prieberg, *Musik im NS-Staat* (Frankfurt am Main, 1989); H.-W. Heister and H.-G. Klein, *Musik und Musikpolitik im faschistishen Deutschland* (Frankfurt am Main, 1984); J. Wulf, *Musik im Dritten Reich. Eine Dokumentation* (Frankfurt am Main, 1983); M. Kater and A. Riethmüller (eds), *Music and Nazism: Art under Tyranny, 1933–1945* (Laaber, 2003). On literature, see H. Denkler and K. Prümm (eds), *Die deutsche Literatur im Dritten Reich: Themen, Traditionen, Wirkungen* (Stuttgart, 1976); U.-K. Ketelsen, *Literatur und Drittes Reich* (Cologne, 1994); J.-P. Barbian, *Literaturpolitik im 'Dritten Reich'. Institutionen, Kompetenzen, Betätigungsfelder* (Frankfurt am Main, 1993); T. Schneider, 'Bestseller im Dritten Reich. Ermittlung und Analyse der meistverkauften Romane in Deutschland 1933–1944', *Vierteljahrshefte für Zeitgeschichte*, Vol. 52 (2002), pp. 77–97.

3 P. Potter, 'The Nazi "Seizure" of the Berlin Philharmonic, or the Decline of a Bourgeois Musical Institution', in G. Cuomo (ed.), *National Socialist Cultural Policy* (New York, 1995), p. 39.

4 Cited in Levi, *Music in the Third Reich*, p. 9.

5 Ibid., p. xiii.

6 Ibid., p. 29. On the relationship between Richard Strauss and the regime, see M. Kater, *Composers of the Nazi Era: Eight Portraits* (Oxford, 2000), pp. 211–63. On Furtwängler, see F. Prieberg, *Trial of Strength: Wilhelm Furtwängler and the Third Reich* (London, 1991) and S. Shirakawa, *The Devil's Master: The Controversial Life and Career of Wilhelm Furtwängler* (Oxford, 1992).

7 On the purge of Jews from musical life, see Levi, *Music in the Third Reich*, pp. 41–9.

8 Ibid., p. 71.

9 Ibid., p. 82.

10 On the relationship between Egk and the Nazi regime, see M. Kater, *Composers of the Nazi Era: Eight Portraits* (Oxford and New York, 2000), pp. 3–30.

11 Levi, *Music in the Third Reich*, p. 123.

12 Kater, *Composers of the Nazi Era*, pp. 269–70.

13 On this, see A. Dümling, 'The Target of Racial Purity: The Degenerate Music Exhibition in Düsseldorf, 1938', in R. Etlin (ed.), *Art, Culture, and Media under the Third Reich* (Chicago, 2002), pp. 43–72.

14 Cited in Levi, *Music in the Third Reich*, p. 96.

15 M. Kater, *The Twisted Muse: Musicians and their Music in the Third Reich* (Oxford and New York, 1997), p. 27.

16 Ibid., pp. 12–13.

17 M. Kater, *Different Drummers: Jazz in the Culture of Nazi Germany* (Oxford and New York, 1992), pp. 29–30.

18 M. Kater, 'Forbidden Fruit? Jazz in the Third Reich', *American Historical Review*, Vol. 94 (1989), p. 13.

19 Cited in Levi, *Music in the Third Reich*, p. 121.

20 Kater, 'Forbidden Fruit?', p. 18.

21 Ibid., p. 23.

22 D. Peukert, *Inside Nazi Germany: Conformity, Opposition and Racism in Everyday Life* (London, 1987), p. 167 and pp. 202–3.

23 Kater, *Different Drummers*, pp. 163–5.

24 Kater, 'Forbidden Fruit?', p. 43.

25 Cited in Levi, *Music in the Third Reich*, p. 183.

26 Ibid., p. 124. For a more detailed account of opera in the Third Reich, see E. Levi, 'Opera in the Nazi Period', in J. London (ed.), *Theatre under the Nazis* (Manchester, 2000), pp. 136–86.

27 Levi, *Music in the Third Reich*, pp. 208–9.

28 Kater, *The Twisted Muse*, p. 6.

29 M. Meyer, *The Politics of Music in the Third Reich* (New York, 1991), p. 386.

30 Kater, *The Twisted Muse*, p. 6.

31 R. Grunberger, *A Social History of the Third Reich* (London, 1971), p. 431.

32 R. Evans, *The Coming of the Third Reich* (London, 2003), p. 412.

33 On Blunck, see W. Hoerle, *Hans Friedrich Blunck: Poet and Nazi Collaborator, 1888–1961* (Oxford, 2003).

34 Cited in J. Ritchie, *German Literature under National Socialism* (London, 1983), p. 25.

35 Ibid., p. 13.

36 Cited in ibid., p. 20.

37 Cited in ibid., p. 77.

38 On Benn, see G. Cuomo, 'Purging an "Art-Bolshevist": The Persecution of Gottfried Benn in the Years 1933–1938', *German Studies Review*, Vol. 9 (1986), pp. 85–105. See also J. Ritchie, *Gottfried Benn: The Unreconstructed Expressionist* (London, 1972).

39 Grunberger, *A Social History of the Third Reich*, p. 456.

40 R. Schnell, *Literarische innere Emigration: 1933–1945* (Stuttgart, 1976).

41 Ritchie, *German Literature under National Socialism*, p. 126.

42 On Jünger, see E. Neamann, *A Dubious Past: Ernst Jünger and the Politics of Literature after Nazism* (Berkeley, 1999).

43 Ritchie, *German Literature under National Socialism*, p. 113.

44 Cited in ibid., p. 115.

CONCLUSION

WHAT WAS THE IMPACT OF THE NAZI REGIME UPON SOCIETY IN GERMANY AND HOW DID IT ACHIEVE POPULAR CONSENSUS?

The Nazi regime attempted to homogenise society and to create an acceptance of its ideology and policies among the German population. It sought to shape its ideal 'national community' through a variety of methods. It employed the process of *Gleichschaltung* to streamline society and to eliminate any potential sources of resistance or dissent. It utilised an array of propaganda media and the 'Hitler myth' to forge the 'national community'. It endeavoured to break down religious, gender, regional, institutional and class barriers to societal uniformity. However, it did not fully succeed in this objective, as sectional and institutional identities were not always reconciled to the 'national community'. Furthermore, it is important to recognise the gap between the myth of the classless 'national community' and the reality of life in the Third Reich. For there was not a revolutionary transformation of society between 1933 and 1945 that eliminated class distinctions. Dick Geary has pointed to developments in post-war Germany that demonstrated this, including the rapidity with which trade unions, Social Democratic and Communist organisations reappeared after 1945.[1] The classless society claimed by National Socialism was superficial, yet the Nazi regime did impose upon German society a different type of hierarchy, in which some sectors were valuable while others were expendable. The Nazi government reordered German society to accord with its concept of perfection. This entailed the creation of types – the ideal 'national comrade' who belonged to society, and the 'inferior' and the 'unfit' who did not. In the Third Reich, a variety of measures was undertaken to socialise the majority of Germans into reliable, fit and productive members of society, and simultaneously to exclude, terrorise and even annihilate those groups that did not conform to the Nazi ideal.

How can the level of public consent in everyday life be accounted for? Some historians have argued that the nation was seduced by the irresistibility of Nazi propaganda. Others have maintained that the Nazi apparatus of surveillance and terror was so thoroughgoing that people had no choice but to consent to the regime and its policies. While such arguments contain some element of validity, Detlev Peukert's contention that 'as all-or-nothing accounts, they are distortions of the historical reality' is accurate.[2] Hence, while propaganda and control were undoubtedly highly significant features of life in the Third Reich, on their own they do not fully explain the popular consensus for the Nazi regime and its policies. We must seek our answer in an explanation of the 'fundamental needs and activities in which the population's active consent, or passive participation, took root', which enabled the 'Final Solution' to happen and to continue until 'the bitter end'.[3]

The German nation needed security, recovery and order and the Hitler government appeared to bring all these things. The mid-1930s were characterised by a large degree of popular enthusiasm for the *Führer* and loyalty to the National Socialist regime. Many Germans were caught up in the excitement of the new era, the spirit of intense nationalism and the *Führer* myth. The population largely approved of Nazi social and economic policies, as well as the regime's clampdown on its 'enemies'. The hopes and needs of large sections of the population were reflected in Nazi ideology and policies. It was this factor that created popular consent for the Nazi regime, despite tensions that may have existed between individual identities and that of the 'national community'.

Hence, while propaganda played a significant role in mobilising popular support for the regime, it was not sufficient on its own to sustain Nazism for the duration of its rule. Coercion, terror and surveillance played their part too. The Nazi terror apparatus formed an integral part of the Nazi system of rule from the beginning. This encompassed not only Himmler's SS-SD-police complex but also the traditional legal and prison systems. From the outset, the Nazi regime openly used violence and terror against those sectors of the population that it regarded as 'enemies' or 'community aliens'. Furthermore, fear and terror provided a backdrop to everyday life in the Third Reich. The concentration camps were the hallmark of the Nazi system of terror, used for the brutal suppression of 'enemies' and as a warning to 'national comrades' to conform to the requirements of the regime.

Education in Nazi Germany was central to the formation of national identity for a whole generation of young Germans. Education for the *Volk* produced a new national awareness and a sense of inclusion in the 'national community'. Young members of the German 'national community' were the guarantors of its strength and future. Education and socialisation were used to define and portray those individuals and groups of people who were excluded from the 'national community', especially Jews and Bolsheviks, but also other groups considered to be 'alien' or 'inferior'. The process of shaping the minds of the future generation was crucial to the success of the Nazi regime, which made a number of significant alterations to the education system in order to ensure the primacy of its *Weltanschauung*. Curricular changes and the introduction of new textbooks underpinned these moves. Racial purity lay at the heart of these policies and Jewish schoolteachers and university professors were removed from their posts. The Nazi government aimed at the 'total education' of German youth. This was to be achieved not only in the schools but also in the youth organisations. The Hitler Youth and the League of German Girls played a significant role in everyday life in the

Third Reich. They weakened traditional social influences and sought to cement allegiance to the Nazi regime. The aims, training and ethos of the Nazi youth groups clearly showed a desire to form a strong and disciplined youth. Members of the Hitler Youth and the League of German Girls were required to take part in the Nazi war effort and to serve the regime until its demise in 1945.

Women played a particularly important role in the 'national community'. Ideologically, they were regarded as 'mothers of the nation'. However, Nazi policy did not necessarily accord with its ideology and the Nazi regime did not exercise complete control over all its women. The experiences of individual women and different groups of women varied quite considerably under National Socialism. The Nazi regime welded women and the family closely together. The family, extolled in National Socialist ideology and propaganda as 'the germ cell of the nation', played a significant part in the 'national community'. Yet, contrary to their rhetoric about the restoration of the family, the National Socialists atomised family units and undermined the family in an unprecedented way by subjecting it to intervention and control, reducing its socialisation function and attempting to remove its capacity to shelter emotionally its members. It took until the early 1950s for the family to regain its true sense of harmony.[4]

The Protestant and Catholic churches were major institutions within German society that had a bearing upon the lives of millions of German people and were profoundly affected by National Socialism. The responses to National Socialism of both Christian churches in Germany were determined by their traditional conservatism. In addition, their desire to uphold their positions and to safeguard the autonomy of their institutions influenced their reactions. These attitudes prevented the churches from making any serious challenges to National Socialism or led them to reluctantly accept it. In public statements, the representatives of both Christian churches avoided saying much about the Nazi regime and its policies. Furthermore, theological and doctrinal anti-Semitism led to an overall reluctance on the part of the churches to challenge Nazi anti-Semitic policies. There was no clear response from the churches as institutions to the Nazi policies towards the Jews and the other groups persecuted by the regime, although a number of individual clergymen did speak out against particular Nazi policies, such as the 'euthanasia' campaign.

The position and role of the *Wehrmacht* in Nazi Germany was particularly important because the attributes of the *Wehrmacht* as a 'fighting community' were very closely linked to those of the wider 'national community'. The *Wehrmacht* implemented Nazi policy in its brutal treatment of enemy soldiers and civilians, particularly in the war on the Eastern Front. Developments in the historiography of the Nazi era over the last decade have overthrown the notion that the Germans were the innocent victims of National Socialism and the Second World War. Most notably, the work of Omer Bartov and Christian Streit *inter alia* has shown the role of the *Wehrmacht* in Nazi atrocities on the

Eastern Front and in the execution of the 'Final Solution'. No longer can the blame be placed exclusively on the SS. An analysis of the conduct of soldiers at the front enhances our understanding of the Nazi dictatorship. The 'national community' and its military counterpart the 'fighting community' were conceptually bound together, particularly because of the close and reciprocal relationship between German society and its soldiers during the Nazi era.

The National Socialist regime employed a variety of measures to create and bolster the 'national community' and public consent for its rule. These initiatives were broadly aimed at the majority of the German population – men, women, teenagers and children – who were acceptable as 'national comrades'. They included propaganda, education, socialisation and the 'co-ordination' of groups and associations. In addition, they encompassed the imposition of Nazi ideological influence upon institutions such as the family, the churches and the army in order to make them more amenable to the 'New Order'. Terror was always present as a threat, in order to ensure compliance in instances when it was not willingly given, but for the most part, terror was reserved for those sectors of the population and individuals who were outside the circle of 'national comrades'.

WHO WAS EXCLUDED FROM THE 'NATIONAL COMMUNITY'?

Exclusion from the 'national community' was based primarily on the concept of 'racial inferiority'. Nazi anti-Semitism meant that the Jews were excluded from the 'national community' and victimised by the Nazi regime from its very earliest days in power. For the Jewish part of the German population (and for those Jewish populations who came under the rule of Nazi Germany throughout Europe during the war), the Hitler regime brought untold and unprecedented tragedy. Germany's Jews were excluded from the 'national community' and were systematically pauperised and castigated throughout the pre-war years. Once the war began, their position continued to deteriorate. They were forced to wear the Yellow Star in order to be clearly distinguished from the rest of the population and to make them more easily identifiable for later deportation. Those who had not managed to emigrate to areas outside the boundaries of Nazi-occupied Europe faced the fate of the rest of European Jewry in the Nazis' 'Final Solution', the genocide of the Jews, in the death camps established at Chelmno, Belzec, Majdanek, Sobibor, Treblinka and Auschwitz in Poland for this purpose.

The Gypsies were outsiders from the 'national community' on account of both their 'racial inferiority' and their itinerant lifestyle. The Gypsies were persecuted by the Nazi regime from its earliest days in power and were ultimately subjected to their own genocide. Estimates of the total number of Gypsies who were murdered by the Nazis vary from 250,000 to over 1 million. The National Socialists' desire to create a perfect and pure 'national community' meant the exclusion not only of the Jews and Gypsies, who were considered to be 'racially alien', but also of a diverse group of people, largely of German ethnicity, who were categorised as 'asocial' or 'socially unfit', as well as the mentally ill and physically disabled, who were stigmatised as 'hereditarily ill', 'unproductive' and ultimately 'unworthy of life'. Nazi discrimination against 'asocials' spanned a wide range of measures, including compulsory sterilisation, internment in concentration camps, forced labour and death. The moral ethos of life in the Third Reich gave way to a hardening of attitudes against the weak. The Nazi 'euthanasia' programme attempted to exterminate the chronically mentally ill and physically disabled.

Apart from groups who were excluded from the 'national community' on grounds of race, 'asociality', mental illness or physical disability, other groups were excluded on grounds of their sexual behaviour. Homosexuals and lesbians were sexual outsiders because they deviated from Nazi sexual norms. Furthermore, prostitutes were regarded as sexual outsiders in Nazi Germany and were excluded from the 'national community'. In addition, Germans who engaged in sexual relationships with foreigners were castigated by the regime and regarded as betraying the 'national community'. Hence, there were several groups of people who were excluded from the 'national community' on account of their sexual behaviour. Recent research has demonstrated that not only was the majority of Germans aware of repression and discrimination against 'social outsiders' and marginal groups, but that they supported it. Long-standing popular antagonism towards particular sectors of society, such as the Gypsies and the 'asocials', found an outlet under National Socialism, when the exclusion of many groups became state policy. But the important point is that it would not have been possible to carry out such state policy without the consent – sometimes tacit, sometimes active – of the majority of the population.

By definition and by choice, those groups and individuals who resisted the Nazi regime or dissented from its ideology and policies remained outside the 'national community'. This category included the Jehovah's Witnesses, Catholic and Protestant clergymen who spoke out against the regime or its policies, and dissenting youth. Those who resisted the Nazi government on moral or political grounds stood outside the 'national community'. They included the White Rose movement led by Hans and Sophie Scholl and the women who engaged in the Rosenstrasse Protest against the rounding up and deportation of their Jewish husbands in Berlin in February 1943. These women, for being in mixed marriages and for remaining true to their husbands, stood outside the 'national community'. So, too, did Socialist and Communist resisters, as well as resisters among the aristocratic and conservative elites. All these groups or individuals were or came to be, if they did not start out that way, outside the 'national community'. Within a society that largely consented to the regime, they had the courage to make a stand against the Nazi dictatorship. They risked their lives and many indeed lost their lives as a result of their actions.

WHAT WERE THE LINKS BETWEEN CULTURAL LIFE AND THE 'NATIONAL COMMUNITY'?

The connections between culture and society are important in understanding any historical period or place. The two are 'mutually constitutive and inextricably linked'.[5] They are particularly significant in trying to comprehend Nazi society and the reaction of the German population to the Nazi regime and its policies. The links between cultural life and the 'national community' were very clear. They acted to legitimise each other, in aims and outcomes. Cultural life mirrored and underpinned the changes that took place in German society under National Socialism.

The radio was a modern medium that was well suited to the dissemination of Nazi ideology. The press was another important channel of communication employed by the National Socialist government to express its goals for the 'national community'. The written word in the Nazi press and the spoken word in radio broadcasts complemented each other. Together, they brought Hitler's message to the German population. Hence, the Nazi regime controlled and harnessed both the radio and the press for its propaganda purposes. Both were employed to disseminate Nazi ideology and to maintain popular morale during the war. In order to achieve a 'National Socialist press', not only were journalists and editors subject to the scrutiny and control of the Ministry of Popular Enlightenment and Propaganda but also publishers and owners had to conform to Nazi principles. Similar policies were applied to the broadcasting industry. The homogenisation of the press and the expansion of radio in the Third Reich enabled the Nazi regime to disseminate its ideology widely throughout the German population.

The Nazi regime had a significant impact upon the German cinema. It dominated and closely controlled the film industry. The cinema of the Third Reich reflected the Nazi ideals for German society and clearly showed the distinctions between valuable 'national comrades' and the 'enemies' of the regime. In addition, the advent of National Socialism brought about notable changes to the German theatre. The Nazi regime aimed to eliminate 'cultural Bolshevism' and so it sponsored certain types of theatrical productions while it banned others. The Nazi regime was clear in its intention to eliminate 'cultural Bolshevism' from both the cinema and the theatre. Goebbels' domination over these forms of entertainment, both through his own Ministry and through the Reich Film Chamber and Reich Theatre Chamber, brought about far-reaching changes. Both the cinema and the theatre were obliged to serve the cultural and political ambitions of the regime. They both promoted the 'national community' and during the war they were utilised to bolster popular morale for as long as possible.

Art and architecture were both employed by the Nazi regime to endorse its power and to promote its aims for the 'national community'. The art of the Third Reich represented Nazi aesthetic ideals. Clear distinctions were made between art that was acceptable, that fitted the true German culture, and art that was unacceptable, 'degenerate' and therefore banned. Nazi architecture was designed to reflect the power and grandeur of the Third Reich. It had a public role and a symbolic function, as well as extremely far-reaching goals. Music and literature, similarly to other aspects of cultural life, were made to conform, by and large, to the dictates of the Nazi regime. Again, a clear distinction was made between what was allowed and what was prohibited in the context of the 'national community'. While there was some inconsistency in Nazi policy towards both music and literature, the Hitler regime was ideologically clear about the type of cultural output it considered to be suitable for presentation to the German 'national community'. Many talented musicians, composers and writers were purged from their professions on grounds of their exclusion from the 'national community' for being 'racially inferior' or politically unreliable. The remaining musicians and writers who continued their careers under Hitler have been regarded as tainted because of their association with National Socialism, although some of them went into 'inner emigration'.

The Nazi regime sought control across all aspects of cultural life and artistic endeavour. It broadly applied the term 'degenerate' to any influences upon artistic or cultural life of which it disapproved. The German populace was made amply aware of what was acceptable and what was not. The Nazis excoriated the experimental across cultural life – atonality in music, expressionism in art, avant-garde in architecture and agitprop in theatrical productions. It utilised cultural life to control leisure, through the activities of the KdF, subsidised theatre and cinema, large-scale displays and pageants, and by bringing theatrical troupes, orchestras and mobile cinemas to small towns and rural areas. Furthermore, entertainment was used to lull the German population into a sense of acceptance and to divert the public from the negative aspects of life in the Third Reich, particularly during the war, when light-hearted musicals and frivolous entertainment films and theatrical productions were encouraged.

Cultural and social life were very closely linked during the Nazi era. Indeed, the aims of the regime for German society and for its artistic and cultural life broadly coincided. Society was to be made up of healthy, 'racially pure', fit and politically reliable 'national comrades' and presentations of German culture were to underpin and promote this goal. Jews, Bolsheviks, Gypsies, sexual outsiders, the 'unfit', dissenters and resisters were excluded from society and were excluded from cultural life too. Finally, it is important to underline the undeniably broad appeal of Nazi culture. Richard Overy has argued that 'National Socialist culture did reflect the wider values and interests of significant sections of the population'.[6] This was a very significant facet of a regime which sought popular consensus for its policies, as well as using terror and manipulation. The inner irrationalities of National Socialism and the tensions between Nazi ideology and the implementation of policy meant that the regime did not succeed entirely in achieving its goals for German society and cultural life. Nevertheless, the 'national community' broadly approved of its social and cultural policies and conformed to its requirements. The consequences of the National Socialist 'national community' were felt not only by those living through the Third Reich but also by subsequent generations of Germans who continue to experience a need to come to terms with the Nazi past.

NOTES

1 D. Geary, 'Working-Class Identities in the Third Reich', in N. Gregor (ed.), *Nazism, War and Genocide* (Exeter, 2005), especially p. 46 and p. 54.

2 D. Peukert, *Inside Nazi Germany: Conformity, Opposition and Racism in Everyday Life* (London, 1987), p. 67.

3 Ibid., p. 68.

4 L. Pine, *Nazi Family Policy, 1933–1945* (Oxford, 1997), p. 187. See also R. Moeller, 'Reconstructing the Family in Reconstruction Germany: Women and Social Policy in the Federal Republic, 1949–1955', in R. Moeller (ed.), *West Germany under Construction: Politics, Society, and Culture in the Adenauer Era* (Ann Arbor, 1997), pp. 109–33.

5 This argument is elaborated upon in the 'Editorial', *Cultural and Social History*, Vol. 1 (2004), pp. 1–5.

6 R. Overy, *The Dictators: Hitler's Germany and Stalin's Russia* (London, 2004), p. 391.

GLOSSARY

AHS (*Adolf Hitler Schule*)	Adolf Hitler Schools
BDM (*Bund Deutscher Mädel*)	League of German Girls
Blut und Boden	Blood and Soil
DAF (*Deutsche Arbeitsfront*)	German Labour Front
DFW (*Deutsches Frauenwerk*)	German Women's Enterprise
Eintopf	one-pot dish
Führer	leader
Gau	region (main territorial division of the NSDAP)
Gauleiter	regional leader
Gestapo (*Geheime Staatspolizei*)	Secret State Police
Gleichschaltung	'co-ordination' or streamlining
HJ (*Hitler Jugend*)	Hitler Youth
KdF (*Kraft durch Freude*)	Strength through Joy
kinderreich	'rich in children'
KPD	German Communist Party
Kripo	Criminal Police
Lebensborn	Well of Life
Lebensraum	'living space'
Luftwaffe	air force
Machtergreifung	'seizure of power'
Napolas	National Political Educational Institutions
NSDAP	National Socialist German Workers' Party
NS-Frauenschaft	Nazi Women's Group
NSLB (*Nationalsozialistischer Lehrerbund*)	National Socialist Teachers' League
Ordensburgen	Castles of the Order
POWs	prisoners of war
Reichskristallnacht	Night of the Broken Glass
Reichsmütterdienst	National Mothers' Service
RKK (*Reichskulturkammer*)	Reich Chamber of Culture
RSHA (*Reichssicherheitshauptamt*)	Reich Security Main Office
SA (*Sturmabteilungen*)	stormtroopers
Schönheit der Arbeit	Beauty of Labour

SD (*Sicherheitsdienst*)	Security Service
SPD	German Social Democratic Party
SS (*Schutzstaffeln*)	Nazi elite formation headed by Heinrich Himmler
Volk	nation, people
völkisch	nationalist
Völkischer Beobachter	*People's Observer*
Volksgemeinschaft	'national community' or 'people's community'
Volksgenossen	'national comrades' or 'people's comrades'
Wehrmacht	armed forces
Weltanschauung	worldview
Winterhilfswerk	Winter Relief Agency

SELECT BIBLIOGRAPHY

For ease of reference, the select bibliography includes only the main works published in English relating to each chapter. Full references to all other English and German works cited can be found in the endnotes to each chapter.

INTRODUCTION

Ayçoberry, P., *The Social History of the Third Reich, 1933–1945* (New York, 1999).

Bessel, R., 'Living with the Nazis: Some Recent Writing on the Social History of the Third Reich', *European History Quarterly*, Vol. 14 (1984), pp. 211–20.

Bessel, R. (ed.), *Life in the Third Reich* (Oxford, 1987).

Burleigh, M., *The Third Reich: A New History* (London, 2000).

Burleigh, M. and Wippermann, W., *The Racial State: Germany 1933–1945* (Cambridge, 1991).

Crew, D. (ed.), *Nazism and German Society* (London, 1994).

Dahrendorf, R., *Society and Democracy in Germany* (London, 1968).

Evans, R., *The Coming of the Third Reich* (London, 2004).

Evans, R., *The Third Reich in Power* (London, 2006).

Grunberger, R., *A Social History of the Third Reich* (London, 1971).

Herf, J., *Reactionary Modernism: Technology, Culture and Politics in Weimar and the Third Reich* (Cambridge, 1984).

Kershaw, I., *The Nazi Dictatorship: Problems and Perspectives of Interpretation* (London, 2000).

Mason, T., *Social Policy in the Third Reich: The Working Class and the 'National Community'* (Oxford, 1993).

Mason, T., *Nazism, Fascism and the Working Class: Essays by Tim Mason* (Cambridge, 1995).

Noakes, J., 'Nazism and Revolution', in N. O'Sullivan (ed.), *Revolutionary Theory and Political Reality* (London, 1983), pp. 73–100.

Peukert, D., *Inside Nazi Germany: Conformity, Opposition and Racism in Everyday Life* (London, 1987).

Schoenbaum, D., *Hitler's Social Revolution* (New York, 1967).

CHAPTER 1

Ayçoberry, P., *The Social History of the Third Reich, 1933–1945* (New York, 1999).

Baranowski, S., *Strength through Joy: Consumerism and Mass Tourism in the Third Reich* (New York, 2004).

Burleigh, M., *The Third Reich: A New History* (London, 2000).

Burleigh, M. and Wippermann, W., *The Racial State: Germany 1933–1945* (Cambridge, 1991).

Evans, R. and Geary, D. (eds), *The German Unemployed: Experiences and Consequences of Mass Unemployment from the Weimar Republic to the Third Reich* (London, 1987).

Gregor, N. (ed.), *Nazism, War and Genocide* (Exeter, 2005).

Herbert, U., '"The Real Mystery in Germany". The German Working Class During the Nazi Dictatorship', in M. Burleigh (ed.), *Confronting the Nazi Past* (London, 1996), pp. 23–36.

Herbert, U., *Hitler's Foreign Workers: Enforced Foreign Labour in Germany under the Third Reich* (Cambridge, 1997).

Kershaw, I., *The 'Hitler Myth': Image and Reality in the Third Reich* (Oxford, 1989).

Kirwan, G., 'Waiting for Retaliation – a Study in Nazi Propaganda Behaviour and German Civilian Morale', *Journal of Contemporary History*, Vol. 16, No. 3 (1981), pp. 565–83.

Kirwan, G., 'Allied Bombing and Nazi Domestic Propaganda', *European History Quarterly*, Vol. 15 (1985), pp. 341–62.

Merritt, M., 'Strength through Joy: Regimented Leisure in Nazi Germany', in O. Mitchell (ed.), *Nazism and the Common Man: Essays in German History (1929–1939)* (Washington D.C., 1981), pp. 67–90.

Noakes, J. and Pridham, G. (eds), *Nazism 1919–1945: State, Economy and Society* (Exeter, 1984).

Noakes, J., 'Nazism and High Society', in M. Burleigh (ed.), *Confronting the Nazi Past: New Debates on Modern German History* (London, 1996), pp. 51–65.

Noakes, J., 'Leaders of the People? The Nazi Party and German Society', *Journal of Contemporary History*, Vol. 39, No. 2 (2004), pp. 189–212.

Overy, R., *War and Economy in the Third Reich* (Oxford, 1994).

Peukert, D., *Inside Nazi Germany: Conformity, Opposition and Resistance in Everyday Life* (London, 1987).

Rupp, L., '"I Don't Call That *Volksgemeinschaft*": Women, Class and War in Nazi Germany', in C. Berkin and C. Lovett (eds), *Women, War and Revolution* (New York and London, 1980), pp. 37–53.

Salter, S., 'Structures of Consensus and Coercion: Workers' Morale and the Maintenance of Work Discipline, 1939–1945', in D. Welch (ed.), *Nazi Propaganda: The Power and the Limitations* (London, 1983), pp. 88–116.

Semmens, K., *Seeing Hitler's Germany: Tourism in the Third Reich* (London, 2005).

Smelser, R., *Robert Ley: Hitler's Labour Front Leader* (Oxford, 1988).

Stern, J., *Hitler. The Führer and the People* (London, 1975).

Weisbrod, B., 'The Crisis of Bourgeois Society in Interwar Germany', in R.

Bessel (ed.), *Fascist Italy and Nazi Germany. Comparisons and Contrasts* (Cambridge, 1996), pp. 23–39.

Welch, D., 'Propaganda and Indoctrination in the Third Reich: Success or Failure?', *European History Quarterly*, Vol. 17 (1987), pp. 403–22.

Welch, D., *The Third Reich: Politics and Propaganda* (London, 2002).

Welch, D., 'Nazi Propaganda and the *Volksgemeinschaft*: Constructing a People's Community', *Journal of Contemporary History*, Vol. 39, No. 2 (2004), pp. 213–38.

CHAPTER 2

Allen, M., *The Business of Genocide: the SS, Slave Labour, and the Concentration Camps* (Chapel Hill and London, 2002).

Arad, Y., *Belzec, Sobibor and Treblinka: The Operation Reinhard Death Camps* (Bloomington, 1999).

Bessel, R., *Political Violence and the Rise of Nazism* (London, 1984).

Browder, G., *Foundations of the Nazi Police State: The Formation of the Sipo and SD* (Lexington, 1990).

Burleigh, M. and Wippermann, W., *The Racial State: Germany 1933–1945* (Cambridge, 1991).

Evans, R., *The Third Reich in Power* (London, 2006).

Fischer, C., *Stormtroopers: A Social, Economic and Ideological Analysis, 1919–1935* (London, 1983).

Gellately, R., *The Gestapo and German Society: Enforcing Racial Policy, 1933–1945* (Oxford, 1990).

Gellately, R., *Backing Hitler: Consent and Coercion in Nazi Germany* (Oxford, 2001).

Gregor, N. (ed.), *Nazism, War and Genocide* (Exeter, 2005).

Joshi, V., 'The Private Became Public: Wives as Denouncers in the Third Reich', *Journal of Contemporary History*, Vol. 37, No. 3 (2002), pp. 419–35.

Joshi, V., *Gender and Power in the Third Reich: Female Denouncers and the Gestapo, 1933–1945* (London, 2003).

Kogon, E., *The Theory and Practice of Hell* (London, 1950).

Mallmann, K. and Paul, G., 'Omniscient, Omnipotent, Omnipresent? Gestapo, Society and Resistance', in D. Crew (ed.), *Nazism and German Society* (London, 1994), pp. 166–96.

Merkl, P., *Political Violence under the Swastika: 581 Early Nazis* (Princeton, 1975).

Merkl, P., *The Making of a Stormtrooper* (Princeton, 1980).

Padfield, P., *Himmler: Reichsführer-SS* (London, 1991).

Sofsky, W., *The Order of Terror: The Concentration Camp* (Princeton, 1997).

Steinbacher, S., *Auschwitz: A History* (London, 2005).

Wachsmann, N., *Hitler's Prisons: Legal Terror in Nazi Germany* (New Haven and London, 2004).

Wachsmann, N., 'Looking into the Abyss: Historians and the Nazi

Concentration Camps', *European History Quarterly*, Vol. 36, No. 2 (2006), pp. 247–78.

CHAPTER 3

Bäumer-Schleinkofer, Ä., *Nazi Biology and Schools* (Frankfurt am Main, 1995).

Blackburn, G., *Education in the Third Reich: A Study of Race and History in Nazi Textbooks* (Albany, 1985).

Giles, G., 'The Rise of the National Socialist Students' Association and the Failure of Political Education in the Third Reich', in P. Stachura (ed.), *The Shaping of the Nazi State* (London, 1978), pp. 160–85.

Giles, G., *Students and National Socialism in Germany* (Princeton, 1985).

Grunberger, R., *A Social History of the Third Reich* (London, 1971).

Hahn, H., *Education and Society in Germany* (Oxford, 1998).

Kamenetsky, C., *Children's Literature in Hitler's Germany: The Cultural Policy of National Socialism* (Athens, Ohio, 1984).

Koch, H., *The Hitler Youth: Origins and Development 1922–1945* (London, 1975).

Lamberti, M., 'German Schoolteachers, National Socialism and the Politics of Culture at the end of the Weimar Republic', *Central European History*, Vol. 34, No. 1 (2001), pp. 53–82.

Mann, E., *School for Barbarians* (New York, 1938).

Mosse, G. (ed.), *Nazi Culture: Intellectual, Cultural and Social Life in the Third Reich* (London, 1966).

Pauwels, J., *Women, Nazis and Universities: Female University Students in the Third Reich, 1933–1945* (Westport, 1984).

Pine, L., 'The dissemination of Nazi ideology and family values through school textbooks', *History of Education*, Vol. 25, No. 1 (1996), pp. 91–109

Wegner, G., *Anti-Semitism and Schooling under the Third Reich* (New York and London, 2002).

CHAPTER 4

Bleuel, H., *Strength through Joy: Sex and Society in Nazi Germany* (London, 1973).

Harvey, E., *Women and the Nazi East: Agents and Witnesses of Germanisation* (New Haven and London, 2003).

Horn, D., 'The Hitler Youth and Educational Decline in the Third Reich', *History of Education Quarterly*, Vol. 16 (1976), pp. 425–47.

Kater, M., *Hitler Youth* (Cambridge, Mass. and London, 2004).

Koch, H., *The Hitler Youth: Origins and Development, 1922–1945* (London, 1975).

Maschmann, M., *Account Rendered: A Dossier on My Former Self* (London, 1964).

Noakes, J. and Pridham, G. (eds), *Nazism 1919–1945: A Documentary Reader*, Vol. 2 (Exeter, 1984).

Pfister, G. and Reese, D., 'Gender, Body Culture, and Body Politics in National Socialism', *Sport History*, Vol. 1 (1995), pp. 91–121.

Pine, L., 'Creating Conformity: The Training of Girls in the *Bund Deutscher Mädel*', *European History Quarterly*, Vol. 33, No. 3 (2003), pp. 367–85.

Pine, L., *Nazi Family Policy, 1933–1945* (Oxford, 1997).

Rempel, G., *Hitler's Children: The Hitler Youth and the SS* (Chapel Hill and London, 1989).

Stachura, P., *The German Youth Movement 1900–1945: An Interpretative and Documentary History* (London, 1981).

CHAPTER 5

Bock, G., 'Antinatalism, maternity and paternity in National Socialist racism', in G. Bock and P. Thane (eds), *Maternity and Gender Policies: Women and the Rise of the European Welfare States 1880s–1950s* (London and New York, 1994), pp. 233–55.

Bock, G., 'Ordinary Women in Nazi Germany: Perpetrators, Victims, Followers and Bystanders', in D. Ofer and L. Weitzman (eds), *Women in the Holocaust* (New Haven, 1998), pp. 85–100.

Bridenthal, R., Grossmann, A. and Kaplan, M. (eds), *When Biology Became Destiny: Women in Weimar and Nazi Germany* (New York, 1984).

Clay, C. and Leapman, M., *Master Race: The Lebensborn Experiment in Nazi Germany* (London, 1996).

Czarnowski, G., 'The Value of Marriage for the *Volksgemeinschaft*': Policies towards women and marriage under National Socialism', in R. Bessel (ed.), *Fascist Italy and Nazi Germany: Comparisons and Contrasts* (Cambridge, 1996), pp. 94–112.

Frevert, U., *Women in German History: From Bourgeois Emancipation to Sexual Liberation* (Oxford, 1989).

Harvey, E., *Women and the Nazi East: Agents and Witnesses of Germanisation* (New Haven and London, 2003).

Mason, T., 'Women in Germany, 1925–1940: Family Welfare and Work. Part I', *History Workshop Journal*, No. 1 (1976), pp. 74–113.

Mason, T., 'Women in Germany, 1925–1940: Family Welfare and Work. Part II (Conclusion)', *History Workshop Journal*, No. 2 (1976), pp. 5–32.

Pine, L., *Nazi Family Policy, 1933–1945* (Oxford, 1997).

Rupp, L., '"I Don't Call That *Volksgemeinschaft*": Women, Class and War in Nazi Germany', in C. Berkin and C. Lovett (eds), *Women, War and Revolution* (New York and London, 1980), pp. 37–53.

Sachse, C., *Industrial Housewives: Women's Social Work in the Factories of Nazi Germany* (London, 1987).

von Saldern, A., 'Victims or Perpetrators? Controversies about the role of women in the Nazi state', in D. Crew (ed.), *Nazism and German Society, 1933–1945* (London, 1994), pp. 141–65.

Stephenson, J., *Women in Nazi Society* (London, 1975).

Stephenson, J., *The Nazi Organisation of Women* (London, 1981).

Stephenson, J., 'Propaganda, Autarky and the German Housewife', in D.

Welch (ed.), *Nazi Propaganda: The Power and the Limitations* (London, 1983), pp. 117–42.

Stephenson, J., *Women in Nazi Germany* (London, 2001).

Stibbe, M., *Women in the Third Reich* (London, 2003).

Weber-Kellermann, I., 'The German Family between Private Life and Politics', in A. Prost and G. Vincent (eds), *A History of Private Life. V: The Riddle of Identity in Modern Times* (London, 1991), pp. 503–37.

CHAPTER 6
The churches

Baranowski, S., *The Confessing Church, Conservative Elites and the Nazi State* (Lewiston, 1986).

Barnett, V., 'The Role of the Churches: Compliance and Confrontation', *Dimensions*, Vol. 14, No. 1 (May 2000), pp. 9–12.

Bergen, D., *The Twisted Cross: The German Christians in the Third Reich* (Chapel Hill, 1995).

Bethge, E., *Dietrich Bonhoeffer: Man of Vision, Man of Courage* (New York, 1970).

Conway, J., *The Nazi Persecution of the Churches* (London, 1968).

Conway, J., 'Coming to Terms with the Past: Interpreting the German Church Struggles, 1933–1990', *German History*, Vol. 16, No. 3 (1998), pp. 377–96.

Cornwell, J., *Hitler's Pope: The Secret History of Pius XII* (London, 1999).

Erikson, R., *Theologians under Hitler* (New Haven, 1985).

Gailus, M., 'Overwhelmed by their own Fascination with the "Ideas of 1933": Berlin's Protestant Social Milieu in the Third Reich', *German History*, Vol. 20, No. 4 (2002), pp. 462–93.

Godman, P., *Hitler and the Vatican* (New York, 2004).

Goldhagen, D., *A Moral Reckoning: The Role of the Catholic Church in the Holocaust and its Unfulfilled Duty of Repair* (London, 2002).

Griech-Polelle, B., 'Image of a Churchman-Resister: Bishop von Galen, the Euthanasia Project and the Sermons of Summer 1941', *Journal of Contemporary History*, Vol. 36, No. 1 (2001), pp. 41–57.

Harrison, E., 'The Nazi Dissolution of the Monasteries: A Case Study', *English Historical Review*, Vol. 109 (1994), pp. 323–55.

Helmreich, E., *The German Churches under Hitler* (Detroit, 1979).

Lewy, G., *The Catholic Church and Nazi Germany* (New York, 2000).

Matheson, P. (ed.), *The Third Reich and the Christian Churches* (Edinburgh, 1981).

Noakes, J., 'The Oldenburg Crucifix Struggle of November 1936: A Case Study of Opposition in the Third Reich', in P. Stachura (ed.), *The Shaping of the Nazi State* (London, 1978), pp. 210–33.

Phayer, M., *The Catholic Church and the Holocaust, 1930–1965* (Bloomington, 2000).

Spicer, K., *Resisting the Third Reich: The Catholic Clergy in Hitler's Berlin* (DeKalb, 2004).

Steigmann-Gall, R., *The Holy Reich: Nazi Conceptions of Christianity, 1919–1945* (Cambridge, 2003).

The *Wehrmacht*

Bartov, O., *The Eastern Front, 1941–1945: German Troops and the Barbarisation of Warfare* (London, 1985).

Bartov, O., *Hitler's Army: Soldiers, Nazis, and War in the Third Reich* (Oxford, 1991).

Bartov, O., 'The Missing Years: German Workers, German Soldiers', in D. Crew (ed.), *Nazism and German Society* (London, 1994), pp. 41–66.

Bartov, O., 'German Soldiers and the Holocaust: Historiography, Research and Implications', *History and Memory*, Vol. 9, Nos. 1/2 (1997), pp. 162–88.

Bartov, O., 'Soldiers, Nazis and War in the Third Reich', in C. Leitz (ed.), *The Third Reich* (Oxford, 1999), pp. 133–50.

Bessel, R., *Nazism and War* (London, 2004).

Deist, W., *The Wehrmacht and German Rearmament* (London, 1981).

Geyer, M., *The German Army and Genocide* (New York, 1999).

Messerschmidt, M., 'The *Wehrmacht* and the *Volksgemeinschaft*', *Journal of Contemporary History*, Vol. 18 (1983), pp. 719–44.

Shepherd, B., 'The Continuum of Brutality: *Wehrmacht* Security Divisions in Central Russia, 1942', *German History*, Vol. 21, No. 1 (2003), pp. 49–81.

Shepherd, B., '*Wehrmacht* Security Regiments in the Soviet Partisan War, 1943', *European History Quarterly*, Vol. 33, No. 4 (2003), pp. 493–529.

CHAPTER 7

Bankier, D., *The Germans and the Final Solution. Public Opinion under Nazism* (Oxford, 1992).

Bankier, D. (ed.), *Probing the Depths of German Antisemitism: German Society and the Persecution of the Jews, 1933–1941* (New York, 2000).

Barkai, A., *From Boycott to Annihilation: The Economic Struggle of German Jews, 1933–1943* (London, 1989).

Benz, W., *The Holocaust: A Short History* (London, 2000).

Browning, C., *The Path to Genocide: Essays on Launching the Final Solution* (Cambridge, 1992).

Browning, C., *The Origins of the Final Solution: The Evolution of Nazi Jewish Policy, September 1939–March 1942* (Lincoln, Neb., 2004).

Burleigh, M. and Wippermann, W., *The Racial State: Germany 1933–1945* (Cambridge, 1991).

Deutschkron, I., *Berlin Jews Underground* (Berlin, 1990).

Friedländer, S., *Nazi Germany and the Jews: The Years of Persecution, 1933–1939* (London, 1997).

Graml, H., *Antisemitism in the Third Reich* (Oxford, 1992).

Johnson, E. and Reuband, K., *What We Knew: Terror, Mass Murder and Everyday Life in Nazi Germany* (London, 2005).

Kaplan, M., *Between Dignity and Despair: Jewish Life in Nazi Germany* (Oxford, 1998).

Kershaw, I., *The Hitler Myth: Image and Reality in the Third Reich* (Oxford, 1989).

Kershaw, I., *The Nazi Dictatorship: Problems and Perspectives of Interpretation* (London, 2000), pp. 93–133.

Kwiet, K., 'The Ultimate Refuge: Suicide in the Jewish Community under the Nazis', *Leo Baeck Year Book*, Vol. 29 (1984), pp. 135–67.

Pehle, W. (ed.), *November 1938. From 'Reichskristallnacht' to Genocide* (New York and Oxford, 1991).

Peukert, D., *Inside Nazi Germany: Conformity, Opposition and Racism in Everyday Life* (London, 1987).

Pine, L., 'German Jews and Nazi Family Policy', *Holocaust Educational Trust Research Papers*, Vol. 1, No. 6 (1999–2000), pp. 1–22.

Richarz, M. (ed.), *Jewish Life in Germany: Memoirs from Three Centuries* (Bloomington, 1991).

Roseman, M. *The Villa, the Lake, the Meeting: Wannsee and the Final Solution* (London, 2003).

CHAPTER 8

Alt, B. and Folts, S., *Weeping Violins: The Gypsy Tragedy in Europe* (Kirksville, 1996).

Burleigh, M. and Wippermann, W., *The Racial State: Germany 1933–1945* (Cambridge, 1991).

Fings, K., Heuss, H. and Sparing, F., *From 'Race Science' to the Camps: The Gypsies during the Second World War* (Hatfield, 1997).

Hancock, I., *The Pariah Syndrome: An Account of Gypsy Slavery and Persecution* (Ann Arbor, 1987).

Hancock, I., 'Romanies and the Holocaust', in D. Stone (ed.), *The Historiography of the Holocaust* (Basingstoke, 2004), pp. 383–96.

Kenrick, D. and Puxon, G., *The Destiny of Europe's Gypsies* (London, 1972).

Kenrick, D. and Puxon, G., *Gypsies under the Swastika* (Hatfield, 1995).

Lewy, G., 'Himmler and the "Racially Pure Gypsies"', *Journal of Contemporary History*, Vol. 34, No. 2 (1999), pp. 201–14.

Lewy, G., *The Nazi Persecution of the Gypsies* (Oxford, 2000).

Milton, S., '"Gypsies" as Social Outsiders in Nazi Germany', in R. Gellately and N. Stoltzfus (eds), *Social Outsiders in Nazi Germany* (Princeton, 2001).

Zimmermann, M., 'From Discrimination to the "Family Camp" at Auschwitz', in W. Benz and B. Distel (eds), *Dachau Review 2. History of Nazi Concentration Camps: Studies, Reports, Documents* (Dachau, 1990), pp. 87–113.

CHAPTER 9

Ayass, W., 'Vagrants and Beggars in Hitler's Reich', in R. Evans (ed.), *The German Underworld: Deviants and Outcasts in German History* (London, 1988), pp. 210–37.

Biesold, H., Sayers, W. and Friedlander, H., *Crying Hands: Eugenics and Deaf People in Nazi Germany* (Washington D.C., 1999).

Burleigh, M., *Death and Deliverance: 'Euthanasia' in Germany 1900–1945* (Cambridge, 1994).

Burleigh, M., 'Saving Money, Spending Lives: Psychiatry, Society and the "Euthanasia" Programme', in M. Burleigh (ed.), *Confronting the Nazi Past: New Debates on Modern German History* (London, 1996), pp. 98–111.

Friedlander, H., 'The Exclusion and Murder of the Disabled', in R. Gellately and N. Stoltzfus (eds), *Social Outsiders in Nazi Germany* (Oxford, 2001), pp. 145–64.

Gellately, R., *Backing Hitler: Consent and Coercion in Nazi Germany* (Oxford, 2001).

Kater, M., *Doctors under Hitler* (Chapel Hill, 1989).

Klee, E., '"Turning the tap on was no big deal" – The gassing doctors during the Nazi period and afterwards', in W. Benz and B. Distel (eds), *Dachau Review 2. History of Nazi Concentration Camps: Studies, Reports, Documents* (Dachau, 1990), pp. 46–66.

Kühl, S., 'The Relationship between Eugenics and the so-called "Euthanasia Action" in Nazi Germany: A Eugenically Motivated Peace Policy and the Killing of the Mentally Handicapped during the Second World War', in M. Szöllösi-Janze (ed.), *Science in the Third Reich* (Oxford, 2001), pp. 185–210.

Lifton, R., *The Nazi Doctors: Medical Killing and the Psychology of Genocide* (London, 1986).

Müller-Hill, B., *Murderous Science: Elimination by Scientific Selection of Jews, Gypsies and Others: Germany, 1933–1945* (Oxford, 1988).

Noakes, J., 'Social Outcasts in the Third Reich', in R. Bessel (ed.), *Life in the Third Reich* (Oxford, 1987), pp. 83–96.

Pine, L., 'Hashude: The Imprisonment of 'Asocial' Families in the Third Reich', *German History*, Vol. 13, No. 2 (1995), pp. 182–97.

Proctor, R., *Racial Hygiene: Medicine under the Nazis* (Cambridge, Mass., 1988).

Ryan, D. and Schuchman, J., *Deaf People in Hitler's Europe* (Washington D.C., 2002).

Schmidt, U., 'Reassessing the Beginning of the "Euthanasia" Programme', *German History*, Vol. 17, No. 4 (1999), pp. 543–50.

CHAPTER 10

Berenbaum, M. (ed.), *A Mosaic of Victims: Non-Jews Persecuted and Murdered by the Nazis* (London, 1990).

Burleigh, M. and Wippermann, W., *The Racial State: Germany 1933–1945* (Cambridge, 1991).

Grau, G., *Hidden Holocaust? Gay and Lesbian Persecution in Germany, 1933–1945* (London, 1995).

Heger, H., *The Men with the Pink Triangle* (London, 1980).

Johansson, W. and Percy, W., 'Homosexuals in Nazi Germany', *Simon Wiesenthal Center Annual*, Vol. 7 (1990), pp. 225–63.

Kogon, E., *The Theory and Practice of Hell: The German Concentration Camps and the System Behind Them* (New York, 1968).

Kundrus, B., 'Forbidden Company: Romantic Relationships between Germans and Foreigners, 1939 to 1945', in D. Herzog (ed.), *Sexuality and German Fascism* (New York and Oxford, 2005), pp. 201–22.

Plant, R., *The Pink Triangle: The Nazi War against Homosexuals* (New York, 1986).

Roos, J., 'Backlash against Prostitutes' Rights: Origins and Dynamics of Nazi Prostitution Policies', in D. Herzog (ed.), *Sexuality and Fascism* (New York and Oxford, 2005), pp. 67–94.

Schoppmann, C., 'National Socialist Policies towards Female Homosexuality', in L. Abrams and E. Harvey (eds), *Gender Relations in German History: Power, Agency and Experience from the Sixteenth to the Twentieth Century* (London, 1996), pp. 177–87.

Schoppmann, C., *Days of Masquerade: Life Stories of Lesbians during the Third Reich* (New York, 1996).

Seel, P., *I, Pierre Seel, Deported Homosexual: A Memoir of Nazi Terror* (New York, 1995).

Stephenson, J., 'Triangle: Foreign Workers, German Civilians and the Nazi Regime. War and Society in Württemberg, 1939–1945', *German Studies Review*, Vol. 15 (1992), pp. 339–59.

Stümke, H.-G., 'From the "People's Consciousness of Right and Wrong" to "The Healthy Instincts of the Nation": The Persecution of Homosexuals in Nazi Germany', in M. Burleigh (ed.), *Confronting the Nazi Past: New Debates in Modern German History* (London, 1996), pp. 154–66.

Timm, A., 'The Ambivalent Outsider: Prostitution, Promiscuity, and VD Control in Nazi Berlin', in R. Gellately and N. Stoltzfus (eds), *Social Outsiders in Nazi Germany* (Oxford, 2001), pp. 192–211.

Timm, A., 'Sex with a Purpose: Prostitution, Venereal Disease, and Militarised Masculinity in the Third Reich', in D. Herzog (ed.), *Sexuality and German Fascism* (New York and Oxford, 2005), pp. 223–55.

CHAPTER 11

Balfour, M., *Withstanding Hitler in Germany 1933–1945* (London and New York, 1988).

Berenbaum, M. (ed.), *A Mosaic of Victims: Non-Jews Persecuted and Murdered by the Nazis* (London, 1990).

Bergman, J., 'The Jehovah's Witnesses' experience in the Nazi concentration camps: a history of their conflicts with the Nazi State', *Journal of Church and State*, Vol. 38, No. 1 (1996), pp. 87–113.

Brysac, S., *Resisting Hitler: Mildred Harnack and the Red Orchestra* (Oxford, 2000).

Childers, T., 'The Kreisau Circle and the Twentieth of July', in D. Large (ed.),

Contending with Hitler: Varieties of German Resistance in the Third Reich (Cambridge, 1991), pp. 99–117.

Chu, J., 'God's things and Caesar's: Jehovah's Witnesses and political neutrality', *Journal of Genocide Research*, Vol. 6, No. 3 (2004), pp. 319–42.

Geyer, M. and Boyer, J. (eds), *Resistance against the Third Reich 1933–1990* (Chicago, 1994).

Hoffmann, P., *German Resistance to Hitler* (Cambridge, Mass. and London, 1988).

Hoffmann, P., *Stauffenberg: A Family History, 1905–1944* (Cambridge, 1995).

Holmes, B. and Keele, A. (eds), *When Truth was Treason: German Youth against Hitler* (Urbana and Chicago, 1995).

Housden, M., *Resistance and Conformity in the Third Reich* (London, 1997).

Jens, I. (ed.) *At the Heart of the White Rose: Letters and Diaries of Hans and Sophie Scholl* (New York, 1987).

Kershaw, I., *The Nazi Dictatorship: Problems and Perspectives of Interpretation* (London, 2000), pp. 183–217.

King, C., *The Nazi State and the New Religions* (New York, 1982).

Large, D. (ed.), *Contending with Hitler: Varieties of German Resistance in the Third Reich* (Cambridge, 1991).

McDonough, F., *Opposition and Resistance in Nazi Germany* (Cambridge, 2001).

Merson, A., *Communist Resistance in Nazi Germany* (London, 1985).

von Moltke, F., *Memories of Kreisau and the German Resistance* (Lincoln, Neb., 2003).

Mommsen, H., *Alternatives to Hitler: German Resistance under the Third Reich* (London, 2003).

Nicosia, F. and Stokes, L., *Germans against Nazism: Nonconformity, Opposition and Resistance in the Third Reich* (Oxford, 1990).

Penton, M. James, *Jehovah's Witnesses and the Third Reich: Sectarian Politics under Persecution* (Toronto, 2004).

Reynaud, M. and Graffard, S., *The Jehovah's Witnesses and the Nazis: Persecution, Deportation, and Murder, 1933–1945* (New York, 2001).

Siefken, H. (ed.), *The White Rose: Student Resistance to National Socialism 1942–1943* (Nottingham, 1991).

Stoltzfus, N., *Resistance of the Heart: Intermarriage and the Rosenstrasse Protest in Nazi Germany* (New Brunswick, 2001).

CHAPTER 12

Bergmeier, H. and Lotz, R. *Hitler's Airwaves* (New Haven and London, 1997).

Combs, W., *The Voice of the SS: A History of the SS Journal 'Das Schwarze Korps'* (New York, 1986).

Gellately, R., *Backing Hitler* (Oxford, 2001).

Grunberger, R., *A Social History of the Third Reich* (London, 1971).

Hale, O., *The Captive Press in the Third Reich* (Princeton, 1964).

Johnson, E. and Reuband, K., *What We Knew: Terror, Mass Murder and Everyday Life in Nazi Germany* (London, 2005).

Lacey, K., 'From *Plauderei* to propaganda: on women's radio in Germany 1924–35', *Media, Culture and Society*, Vol. 16 (1994), pp. 589–607.

Lacey, K., 'Driving the message home: Nazi propaganda in the private sphere', in L. Abrams and E. Harvey (eds), *Gender Relations in German History: Power, Agency and Experience from the Sixteenth to the Twentieth Century* (London, 1996), pp. 189–210.

Lacey, K., *Feminine Frequencies: gender, German radio and the public sphere, 1923–1945* (Ann Arbor, 1996).

Welch, D., *The Third Reich: Politics and Propaganda* (London, 1993).

Zimmermann, C., 'From Propaganda to Modernization: Media Policy and Media Audiences under National Socialism', *German History*, Vol. 24 (2006), pp. 431–54.

CHAPTER 13

Ascheid, A., *Hitler's Heroines: Stardom and Womanhood in Nazi Cinema* (Philadelphia, 2003).

Baranowski, S., *Strength through Joy: Consumerism and Mass Tourism in the Third Reich* (Cambridge, 2004).

Berghaus, G., 'The Ritual Core of Fascist Theatre', in G. Berghaus (ed.), *Fascism and Theatre: Comparative Studies on the Aesthetics and Politics of Performance in Europe, 1925–1945* (Oxford, 1996), pp. 39–71.

Carter, E., *Dietrich's Ghosts: The Sublime and the Beautiful in Third Reich Film* (London, 2004).

Culbert, D., 'The Impact of Anti-Semitic Film Propaganda on German Audiences: *Jew Süss* and *The Wandering Jew* (1940)', in R. Etlin (ed.), *Art, Culture, and Media under the Third Reich* (Chicago, 2002), pp. 139–57.

Drewniak, B., 'The Foundations of Theater Policy in Nazi Germany', in G. Cuomo (ed.), *National Socialist Cultural Policy* (New York, 1995), pp. 67–94.

Fox, J., *Filming Women in the Third Reich* (Oxford, 2000).

Gadberry, G. (ed.), *Theatre in the Third Reich, the Prewar Years* (Westport, 1995).

Hake, S., *Popular Cinema of the Third Reich* (Austin, 2001).

Hoffmann, H., *The Triumph of Propaganda: Film and National Socialism, 1933–1945* (Providence, 1996).

Kracauer, S., *From Caligari to Hitler: A Psychological Study of German Film* (Princeton, 1947).

Leiser, E., *Nazi Cinema* (New York, 1974).

London, J. (ed.), *Theatre under the Nazis* (Manchester, 2000).

Niven, W., 'The birth of Nazi drama? *Thing* plays', in J. London (ed.), *Theatre under the Nazis* (Manchester, 2000), pp. 54–95.

Panse, B., 'Censorship in Nazi Germany', in G. Berghaus (ed.), *Fascism and Theatre: Comparative Studies on the Aesthetics and Politics of Performance in Europe, 1925–1945* (Oxford, 1996), pp. 140–56.

Phillips, M., 'The Nazi Control of the German Film Industry', *Journal of European Studies*, Vol. 1 (1971), pp. 37–68.

Phillips, M., 'The German Film Industry and the New Order', in P. Stachura (ed.), *The Shaping of the Nazi State* (London, 1978), pp. 257–81.

Reimer, R. (ed.), *Cultural History through a National Socialist Lens: Essays on the Cinema of the Third Reich* (New York, 2000).

Rentschler, E., *The Ministry of Illusion: Nazi Cinema and its Afterlife* (Cambridge, Mass., 1996).

Schulte-Sasse, L., *Entertaining the Third Reich: Illusions of Wholeness in Nazi Cinema* (London, 1996).

Spotts, F., *Bayreuth: A History of the Wagner Festival* (New Haven, 1994).

Taylor, R., *Film Propaganda: Soviet Russia and Nazi Germany* (London, 1979).

Weinberg, D., 'Approaches to the Study of Film in the Third Reich', *Journal of Contemporary History*, Vol. 19, No. 1 (1984), pp. 105–26.

Welch, D. (ed.), *Nazi Propaganda: The Power and the Limitations* (London, 1983).

Welch, D., *Propaganda and the German Cinema, 1933–1945* (London, 2001).

Willett, J., *The Theatre of the Weimar Republic* (New York, 1988).

Zimmermann, C., 'From Propaganda to Modernization: Media Policy and Media Audiences under National Socialism', *German History*, Vol. 24 (2006), pp. 431–54.

Zortman, B., 'Hitler's Theatre', in M. Balfour (ed.), *Theatre and War 1933–1945: Performance in Extremis* (New York and Oxford, 2001), pp. 46–52.

CHAPTER 14

Adam, P., *Art of the Third Reich* (New York, 1992).

Barron, S. (ed.), *Degenerate Art: The Fate of the Avant-Garde in Nazi Germany* (Los Angeles, 1991).

Etlin, R. (ed.), *Art, Culture, and Media under the Third Reich* (Chicago, 2002).

Fest, J., *Speer: The Final Verdict* (London, 2001).

Hinz, B., *Art in the Third Reich* (New York, 1979).

Jaskot, P., *The Architecture of Oppression: The SS, Forced Labour and the Nazi Monumental Building Economy* (London, 2000).

Lane, B., *Architecture and Politics in Germany 1918–1945* (Cambridge, Mass., 1968).

Petropoulos, J., *Art as Politics in the Third Reich* (Chapel Hill and London, 1996).

Petropoulos, J., *The Faustian Bargain: The Art World in Nazi Germany* (London, 2000).

Shand, J., 'The Reichsautobahnen. Symbol for the Third Reich', *Journal of Contemporary History*, Vol. 19 (1984), pp. 189–200.

Steinweis, A., 'Weimar Culture and the Rise of National Socialism: The *Kampfbund für deutsche Kultur*', *Central European History*, Vol. 24 (1992), pp. 402–23.

Steinweis, A., 'The Nazi Purge of German Artistic and Cultural Life', in R. Gellately and N. Stoltzfus (eds), *Social Outsiders in Nazi Germany* (Princeton and Oxford, 2001), pp. 99–116.

Taylor, B. and van der Will, W. (eds), *The Nazification of Art: Art, Design, Music, Architecture and Film in the Third Reich* (Winchester, 1990).

Taylor, R., *The Word in Stone: The Role of Architecture in the National Socialist Ideology* (Berkeley, 1974).

Thies, J., 'Hitler's European Building Programme', *Journal of Contemporary History*, Vol. 13 (1978), pp. 413–31.

Thies, J., 'Nazi Architecture – A Blueprint for World Domination: The Last Aims of Adolf Hitler', in D. Welch (ed.) *Nazi Propaganda: The Power and the Limitations* (London, 1983), pp. 45–64.

West, S., *The Visual Arts in Germany 1890–1937: Utopia and Despair* (Manchester, 2000).

Wistrich, R., *Weekend in Munich: Art, Propaganda and Terror in the Third Reich* (London, 1995).

CHAPTER 15

Cuomo, G., 'Purging an "Art-Bolshevist": The Persecution of Gottfried Benn in the Years 1933–1938', *German Studies Review*, Vol. 9 (1986), pp. 85–105.

Etlin, R. (ed.), *Art, Culture, and Media under the Third Reich* (Chicago, 2002).

Grunberger, R., *A Social History of the Third Reich* (London, 1971).

Hoerle, W., *Hans Friedrich Blunck: Poet and Nazi Collaborator, 1888–1961* (Oxford, 2003).

Kater, M., 'Forbidden Fruit? Jazz in the Third Reich', *American Historical Review*, Vol. 94 (1989), pp. 11–43.

Kater, M., *Different Drummers: Jazz in the Culture of Nazi Germany* (Oxford and New York, 1992).

Kater, M., *The Twisted Muse: Musicians and their Music in the Third Reich* (Oxford and New York, 1997).

Kater, M., *Composers of the Nazi Era: Eight Portraits* (Oxford and New York, 2000).

Kater, M. and Riethmüller, A. (eds), *Music and Nazism: Art under Tyranny, 1933–1945* (Laaber, 2003).

Levi, E., *Music in the Third Reich* (London, 1994).

Levi, E., 'Opera in the Nazi Period', in J. London (ed.), *Theatre under the Nazis* (Manchester, 2000), pp. 136–86.

Meyer, M., *The Politics of Music in the Third Reich* (New York, 1991).

Neamann, E., *A Dubious Past: Ernst Jünger and the Politics of Literature after Nazism* (Berkeley, 1999).

Peukert, D., *Inside Nazi Germany: Conformity, Opposition and Racism in Everyday Life* (London, 1987).

Potter, P., 'The Nazi "Seizure" of the Berlin Philharmonic, or the Decline of a Bourgeois Musical Institution', in G. Cuomo (ed.), *National Socialist Cultural Policy* (New York, 1995), pp. 39–66.

Prieberg, F., *Trial of Strength: Wilhelm Furtwängler and the Third Reich* (London, 1991).

Ritchie, J., *Gottfried Benn: The Unreconstructed Expressionist* (London, 1972).

Ritchie, J., *German Literature under National Socialism* (London, 1983).

Shirakawa, S., *The Devil's Master: The Controversial Life and Career of Wilhelm Furtwängler* (Oxford, 1992).

INDEX